The Cert Finance Professionals' Handbook

The Essential Guide to the Commercial Equipment Lease and Finance Industry

Eighth Edition
Second Printing

Deborah Reuben, CLFP

To all who desire to expand their understanding of
the equipment leasing and finance industry,
this book is for you.

The Certified Lease & Finance Professionals' Handbook
Written and Illustrated by Deborah Reuben, CLFP

Disclaimer
Although every effort has been made in the preparation of this book to ensure the
accuracy of the information contained therein, this book is provided "AS-IS" and the
CLFP Foundation, the publisher, the author(s), their distributors and retailers, as well
as all affiliated, related or subsidiary parties take no responsibility for any inaccuracy
and any and all damages, direct or consequential, caused, either directly or indirectly,
by the use of such information.

The CLFP Foundation has attempted to properly provide trademark information on
all companies and products mentioned in this book by use of the ™ symbol.
However, The CLFP Foundation cannot guarantee the accuracy of such information.

Bulk Copies
The CLFP Foundation offers trade discounts on purchases of five or more copies of
this book. For more information, please contact our sales offices at the address or
number below.

The CLFP Foundation
P.O. Box 146
Northbrook, IL 60065
206-535-6281

http://www.CLFPFoundation.org

Thank You to Our Partners

It is with their generous and loyal support this Edition of the CLFP Handbook could be published.

Corporate Partners

Platinum ($2,500)

AP Equipment Financing
Ascentium Capital
ECS Financial Services
Financial Pacific Leasing
First American Equip. Fin.
IDS
LTi Technology Solutions
NorthTeq, Inc.
Odessa
Orion First Financial
Tamarack Technology, Inc.
Wintrust Specialty Finance

Silver ($1,000)

Amur Equipment Finance
BMO Harris
Oakmont Capital Services

Bronze ($500)

AACFB
Arvest Equipment Finance
Ivory Consulting Corp.
Pawnee Leasing Corp.

Personal Partners

Benefactor ($250+)

Kip Amstutz, CLFP
Robert Boyer, CLFP
Donnie Bunn, CLFP
Tina Cartwright, CLFP
Andrew Clark, CLFP
Craig Colling, CLFP
Mike Coon, CLFP
Jeff Elliott, CLFP
Chris Enbom, CLFP
Bob Fisher, CLFP
Paul Fogle, CLFP
Lisa Genereux, CLFP
Nate Gibbons, CLFP
Ben Hall, CLFP
Jaimie Haver, CLFP
Jaime Kaneshina, CLFP
Marc Keepman, CLFP
Timothy Kehoe, CLFP
Joe Leonard, CLFP
Shari Lipski, CLFP
Toby McDonough, CLFP
Mic Mount, CLFP
David Normandin, CLFP
Kevin Prykull, CLFP
Reid Raykovich, CLFP
Candace Reinhart, CLFP
Chris Santy, CLFP

Pete Sawyer, CLFP
Dave Schaefer, CLFP
Amy Spragg, CLFP
Stephen Stuesser, CLFP
Don Wampler, III, CLFP

Sponsor ($100 - $249)
Derek Anniston, CLFP
Teresa Billick, CLFP
Eric Bunnell, CLFP
Tracey Elfering, CLFP
Kirstin Elmer, CLFP
Nick Fong, CLFP
John Freeman, CLFP
Nick Gibbens, CLFP
Michael Green, CLFP
Brent Hall, CLFP
Jack Harvey, CLFP
Theresa Kabot, CLFP
Mark McKissick, CLFP
Katie O'Mara, CLFP
Greg Pabich, CLFP
Shervin Rashti, CLFP
Deborah Reuben, CLFP
Colin Rosenmeyer, CLFP
Brenton Russell, CLFP
Andrea Schmid, CLFP
Tony Sedlacek, CLFP
Jen Stich, CLFP
Spencer Thomas, CLFP
Matt Vazzana, CLFP
Dave Verkinderen, CLFP
Vic Villegas, CLFP
Carl Villella, CLFP

Sponsor ($100 - $249) ct'd
Annette Watkins-Harris, CLFP
Christine Williams, CLFP
Bruce Winter, CLFP
Terry Wood, CLFP

Supporter ($50 - $99)
Paul Crnkovic, CLFP
Lori Dennis, CLFP
Suzann Fakhoury, CLFP
John Harders, CLFP
Katharine Harris, CLFP
Judi Jenks, CLFP
Nathan Kary, CLFP
Larry Kellmayer, CLFP
Jessica Kort, CLFP
Christy Kusilek, CLFP
Ray Lavin, CLFP
Dave Maslyk, CLFP
Peter McCaffrey, CLFP
Tim Miller, CLFP
Kevin Peterson, CLFP
Rhonda Rester, CLFP
Kathie Russell, CLFP
Ron Schutz, CLFP
Joe Sclafani, CLFP
Don Segura, CLFP
Kristi Serrano, CLFP
Molly Simon, CLFP
Kevin Vick, CLFP
Lisa Whitehead, CLFP
Mike Wiedemer, CLFP

LOOKING TO GROW YOUR ASSET FINANCE BUSINESS?

WE'RE HERE TO HELP

You're working hard to grow your business. You deserve an origination and portfolio management system that ensures all of your hard work and smart decisions pay off.

IDScloud is a true software-as-a-service (SaaS) platform that makes it easy and affordable for you to move to the cloud — you only pay for the features and capacity you need!

BENEFITS OF MOVING TO THE CLOUD

Uncover Powerful Analytics-Driven Insights
Pay for Only What You Use
Affordable Scalability
Fast Deployment & Easy Onboarding

READY TO LEARN MORE?

Watch a demo or check out a case study at
idsgrp.com/exploreIDScloud.

IDS | Asset Finance Technology

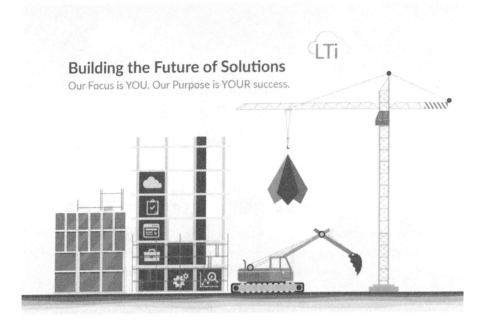

Building the Future of Solutions
Our Focus is YOU. Our Purpose is YOUR success.

ASPIRE, our comprehensive equipment lease and loan software, taps into identifying your organization's challenges and constraints and then delivers solutions to propel your organization forward.

We are in the business of solving problems. Our solutions are rooted in the knowledge of our people, which is manifested through a cutting-edge technology platform used by all types and sizes of equipment finance companies to achieve their strategic objectives.

Your ASPIRE journey begins here

ASPIRE can meet all your needs

ASPIRE in the LTiCloud

ASPIRE Customer Portal

Proud Supporter of
the CLFP Foundation

 402-493-3445 | www.LTiSolutions.com

northteq

transform your customer experience

origination   portals   crm

Acknowledgements

A book such as this is not the work of a lone author, but a labor of love influenced by many.

Thank you to all of the talented and dedicated authors and contributors to past CLFP Handbook editions, your work made it possible for me to earn my CLFP designation and created a solid starting point for creating this new book.

Thank you to the dozens of subject matter experts and reviewers who contributed to this project. From interviews to doc reviews, through revising, refining, and final editing, this content is not possible without your wisdom, depth of experience, and expertise. I am so impressed by your accomplishments, your industry knowledge and kind willingness to pitch in and help. It is a privilege to work with you.

Numerous people in and around this industry have encouraged me and advocated for me throughout my career and in a sense have indirectly contributed to this work. There are too many to name individually, so I'll merely say, "Thank you." You know who you are.

I would like to thank the following people especially:

- My husband, Corey Reuben, my love, my best friend, for his unwavering faith in me and for encouraging me to pursue dreams boldly.
- My parents, examples of strength, faith, and perseverance and my inspiration to never to give up.
- Craig Dahl. My entry into this industry began with him. When I look at my career and connect the dots going backward, I don't see how I would have ended up doing a project like this if I had not said, "yes" to his challenging question so many years ago.
- Kristian Dolan, founder of NorthTeq, Inc., a great friend and collaborator over the years. It was because of him that I learned about the CLFP program and took the exam.
- The CLFP Foundation board, for catching the vision and allowing me the privilege of working on this project.
- Reid Raykovich, Executive Director of the CLFP Foundation. It is always a joy to collaborate with her. I appreciate her red pen; it was essential to the completion of each edition.

- Mike Dickinson, my editor on this project, his thoughtful questions, careful attention to detail is a superpower. He provided the polish to make the final product shine.
- Dale Laszig, Senior Staff Writer at The Green Sheet, and friend. Early in this effort she encouraged me and gave me valuable strategic advice that helped me survive the intensity of this writing project.

Along with the CLFP Foundation, we wish to express gratitude to each of the talented and dedicated individuals who contributed to the publication of this Handbook.

Sudhir Amembal, CLFP	Bob Humber, CLFP
Joe Bonanno, Esq.	Terey Jennings, CLFP
Rob Boyer, CLFP	Chris Lerma, CLFP
Todd Buzard, CPA, CLFP	Barry Marks, Esq., CLFP
Tom Cadle, CLFP	Chris Maudlin, CLFP
Tina Cartwright, CLFP	Beth McLean, CLFP
Cathy Casseday	David Normandin, CLFP
Michael Colangelo	Raquel O'Leary, CLFP
Diana Crews, CLFP	Ralph Petta
Kristian Dolan, CLFP	Kevin Prykull, CLFP
Jeff Elliott, CLFP	Reid Raykovich, CLFP
Chris Enbom, CLFP	Mike Romanowski
Randy Ernst	John Rosenlund, CLFP
Erin Fackler	Joe Schmitz, CLFP
Jennie Fisher	Mark Skochdopole
Paul Fogle, CLFP	Marci Slagle, CLFP
Dwight Galloway	Stephanie Smith
Nancy Geary, CPA, CLFP	Bob Teichman, CLFP
Lisa Genereux, CLFP	Lia Wax, CLFP
Nick Gibbens, CLFP	Thomas Ware
Shawn Halladay, CLFP	Scott Wheeler, CLFP
David Holmgren, CLFP	John Wright

Additional past contributors whose content may also appear include:

Lisa Collins, CLFP	James G. McCommon
Stephen P. Crane, CLFP	Bruce Owens, CLFP
Steven B. Geller, CLFP	Spencer Richman, CLFP
Theresa Kabot, CLFP	David T. Schaefer, CLFP
H. Krollfeifer, Jr., CLFP	Mark Schrews
Brian Link	Chris Walker, CLFP (Deceased)
Paul Menzel, CLFP	Terrance J. Winders, CLFP
James K. Merrilees	Bruce J. Winter, CLFP

About the Author

Deborah "Deb" Reuben, CLFP, is CEO and Founder of TomorrowZone and the Beyond Convention EF Innovators UnConference, a platform inspiring fresh ideas and collaborations to shape the future of equipment finance. She inspires new thinking to explore the art of the possible through her extensive technical knowledge, equipment finance experience, and passion for challenging the status quo. Her expertise will enhance and broaden your company's products and services and create efficiencies that will produce a competitive advantage for your business.

Her broad background includes system design and development in financial services (Wells Fargo and TCF) and the software industry (HCL and Linedata Capitalstream). Specializing in industry trends and strategic direction, her approach is holistic and relatable to help clients understand potential impacts and discover new opportunities for advanced technology. Additionally, she provides experiential virtual workshops that help leaders clearly understand current state realities and future possibilities.

A member of ELFA's Board of Directors, Reuben chairs the ELFA's Technology Innovation Working Group and serves on the Monitor Editorial Board, co-founded the Disrupted+ conference series with Monitor. She authored The Certified Lease and Finance Professionals' Handbook, 6th and 7th and 8th editions. She is the recipient of both the CLFP Foundation Cindy Spurdle Award of Excellence and the ELFA Michael J. Fleming Distinguished Service Award. Monitor Magazine honored her as one of the 50 Most Powerful Women Leaders in Equipment Finance.

Learn more at:
Website: tomorrowzone.io
Twitter: dreuben
LinkedIn: www.linkedin.com/in/deborahreuben
Email: deborah@tomorrowzone.io

Preface

The Certified Lease & Finance Professional Program is presented to the commercial equipment leasing and finance industry as a service of the CLFP Foundation. The prestigious CLFP designation identifies you as a knowledgeable professional to your employer, clients and customers, as well as, your peers in the leasing industry. Participation in the CLFP program is entirely voluntary and is open to all qualifying individuals.

The CLFP Program was developed by recognized industry leaders and covers major aspects of commercial equipment leasing and financing. The designation and program were initially created by a group of individuals from the United Association of Equipment Leasing (UAEL). As it developed and expanded, the UAEL gave the program and the designation to the entire industry in 2000 and along with the National Association of Equipment Leasing Brokers (NAELB) and the Eastern Association of Equipment Lessors (EAEL), they created a stand-alone entity called the CLFP Foundation to administer certification. Today, a volunteer Board of Directors, made up of CLFPs, governs the CLFP Foundation which is comprised of CLFPs in good standing and continues to be supported by the American Association of Commercial Finance Brokers (AACFB), previously NAELB and the National Equipment Finance Association (NEFA), the new association formed in 2008 by the merger of UAEL and EAEL, as well as the Equipment Leasing and Finance Association (ELFA).

This book was originally written for leasing practitioners. It was the intention of the original authors to provide an in-depth action handbook for those already on a career path in leasing. To accomplish this task, recognized subject matter experts were contacted and asked to write chapters in their areas of expertise and share their secrets of success. This new CLFP Handbook follows this footprint and has again called on contributors who are experts within their sectors of the industry that worked with one author in order to provide a consistent voice throughout the book.

The result is a handbook that is short on theory and long on the practical aspects of participating in the commercial equipment leasing and finance industry. Although the book is comprehensive, its style is to provide information in a reader-friendly manner. Whether you're a college student, entry-level leasing associate or a seasoned veteran within the industry, this book is an invaluable resource. The handbook may also be utilized as the cornerstone of a candidate's study path toward achieving CLFP designation.

We hope you find this text useful and trust it will remain a valuable asset in your library.

CLFP Body of Knowledge Framework

The equipment finance and leasing industry is comprised of a fascinating ecosystem of participants, financial products, business models, and practices. The CLFP Handbook is meant to provide a broad overview of the industry. There are a lot of pieces to the equipment finance business; the following framework is a guide map to help you understand where to begin your learning journey.

The following diagram provides a framework for thinking about how to take in the content in this book. This handbook is designed to help you build broad knowledge of the equipment finance and leasing industry; with so much material to cover, we recommend taking it in chunks or "building blocks."

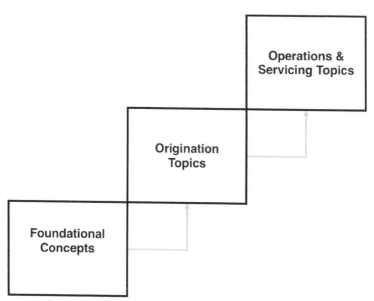

Figure 1 Body of Knowledge Building Blocks

The recommended initial building block is Foundational Concepts which describe foundational concepts that underpin the industry. Once you are familiar with the foundational concepts, the next building block is Origination Topics which describes the origination of new equipment finance and leasing transactions through each of the major transaction phases and the nuances for various origination models. The final building block is Operations & Servicing Topics which describes equipment finance and leasing company operations, portfolio management, and various aspects of asset management and servicing for customers and contracts.

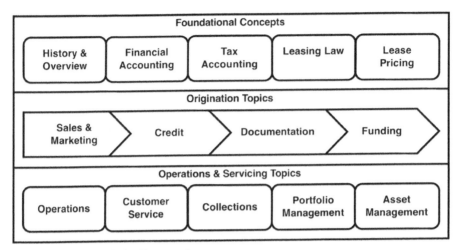

Figure 2 Body of Knowledge Framework

Although the author and the CLFP Foundation have made every effort to ensure that the information in this book was correct at press time, the author and the CLFP Foundation do not assume and hereby disclaim any liability to any party for any loss, damage, or disruption caused by errors or omissions, whether such errors or omissions result from negligence, accident, or any other cause. While names of companies have been used, they are for illustration purposes only and do not imply any sort of endorsement from the author or CLFP Foundation.

Although every effort has been made in the preparation of this book to ensure the accuracy of the information contained therein, this book is provided "AS-IS" and the CLFP Foundation, the publisher, the author(s), their distributors and retailers, as well as all affiliated, related or subsidiary parties take no responsibility for any inaccuracy and any and all damages, direct or consequential, caused, either directly or indirectly, by the use of such information.

The CLFP Foundation has attempted to properly provide trademark information on all companies and products mentioned in this book by use of the ™ symbol. However, The CLFP Foundation cannot guarantee the accuracy of such information.

CLFP Body of Knowledge Framework

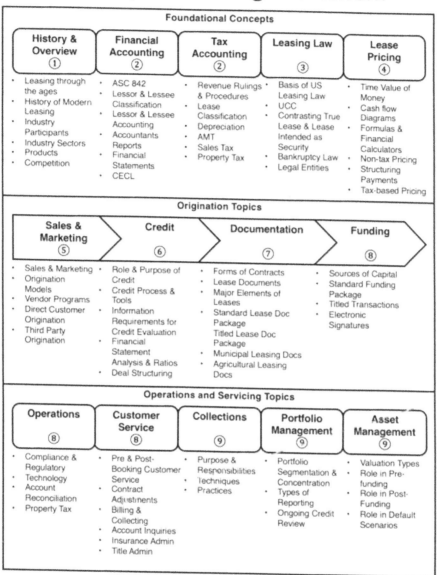

Foundational Concepts

History & Overview ①	Financial Accounting ②	Tax Accounting ②	Leasing Law ③	Lease Pricing ④
• Leasing through the ages • History of Modern Leasing • Industry Participants • Industry Sectors • Products • Competition	• ASC 842 • Lessor & Lessee Classification • Lessor & Lessee Accounting • Accountants Reports • Financial Statements • CECL	• Revenue Rulings & Procedures • Lease Classification • Depreciation • AMT • Sales Tax • Property Tax	• Basis of US Leasing Law • UCC • Contrasting True Lease & Lease Intended as Security • Bankruptcy Law • Legal Entities	• Time Value of Money • Cash flow Diagrams • Formulas & Financial Calculators • Non-tax Pricing • Structuring Payments • Tax-based Pricing

Origination Topics

Sales & Marketing ⑤	Credit ⑥	Documentation ⑦	Funding ⑧
• Sales & Marketing • Origination Models • Vendor Programs • Direct Customer Origination • Third Party Origination	• Role & Purpose of Credit • Credit Process & Tools • Information Requirements for Credit Evaluation • Financial Statement Analysis & Ratios • Deal Structuring	• Forms of Contracts • Lease Documents • Major Elements of Leases • Standard Lease Doc Package • Titled Lease Doc Package • Municipal Leasing Docs • Agricultural Leasing Docs	• Sources of Capital • Standard Funding Package • Titled Transactions • Electronic Signatures

Operations and Servicing Topics

Operations ⑧	Customer Service ⑧	Collections ⑨	Portfolio Management ⑨	Asset Management ⑨
• Compliance & Regulatory • Technology • Account Reconciliation • Property Tax	• Pre & Post-Booking Customer Service • Contract Adjustments • Billing & Collecting • Account Inquiries • Insurance Admin • Title Admin	• Purpose & Responsibilities • Techniques • Practices	• Portfolio Segmentation & Concentration • Types of Reporting • Ongoing Credit Review	• Valuation Types • Role in Pre-funding • Role in Post-Funding • Role in Default Scenarios

CLFP Handbook Chapters

① History & Overview
② Financial & Tax Accounting
③ Leasing Law
④ Lease Pricing
⑤ Sales and Marketing
⑥ Credit
⑦ Documentation
⑧ Funding & Operations
⑨ Portfolio Management

Figure 3 Body of Knowledge Framework Chapter Guide

Table of Contents

Chapter 1 - History and Overview

Learning Goals for this Chapter

- Understand at a high level, how the concept of leasing and equipment finance has evolved from ancient times to the present day.
- Recognize the triggers for the shift to the modern era of leasing and rise of vendor programs, independent, captive, and bank leasing.
- Understand the different definitions of a lease from three primary perspectives: tax, accounting, and legal.
- Understand the role in recent history of Internal Revenue Service (IRS) rulings, the creation in 1976 of the Financial Accounting Standards Board (FASB), and the role their resulting statements and opinions have played in shaping the direction of the industry.
- Know the key participants and market segments of the equipment finance industry.
- Know the various names given to equipment finance and leasing products.

Within the CLFP Body of Knowledge Framework, this chapter covers the highlighted topic.

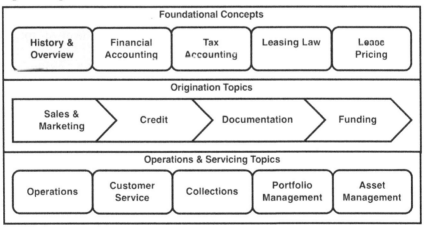

Each year, American companies acquire over $1.5 trillion of capital equipment and software (personal property), of which leasing and equipment financing account for over 50 percent. The U.S. equipment finance and leasing industry (hereafter referred to as "equipment finance") provides access to roughly $1 trillion of capital to help businesses operate efficiently, hit their growth targets and fuel a global economy. An estimated eight out of ten companies finance or lease their equipment acquisitions which include a variety of equipment such as agricultural, commercial and corporate aircraft, manufacturing machinery, construction equipment, business equipment, IT equipment and software, and more.

Sources: BEA; previous Foundation end-user surveys; Keybridge LLC. Note: The generic term "equipment finance" is used to denote public and private equipment and software acquired via lease, secured loan, or line of credit. Non-financed equipment is acquired through cash, credit card (paid in full), or another method.

Figure 4 Equipment Finance Industry Size, Billions of Dollars[1]

How did the industry evolve into what it is today? As you will see throughout this chapter, our industry has a rich history. In reviewing its history, we refer to many of the legal, accounting and IRS rulings relative to the equipment finance industry. Such references are made to highlight the myriad of ever-changing conditions and regulations under which the leasing and finance industry continues to adjust. Learning this contextual background makes it possible to discover how the industry has evolved in the past, and more confidently project where it may go in the future.

Although the industry has evolved to include other forms of financing, this chapter focuses primarily on the history of leasing.

As a CLFP and bank president stated,

> "A standout feature of our industry is knowledge of equipment lifecycle in addition to finance."

---

[1] Source: 2019 Equipment Leasing & Finance Industry Horizon Report. https://www.leasefoundation.org

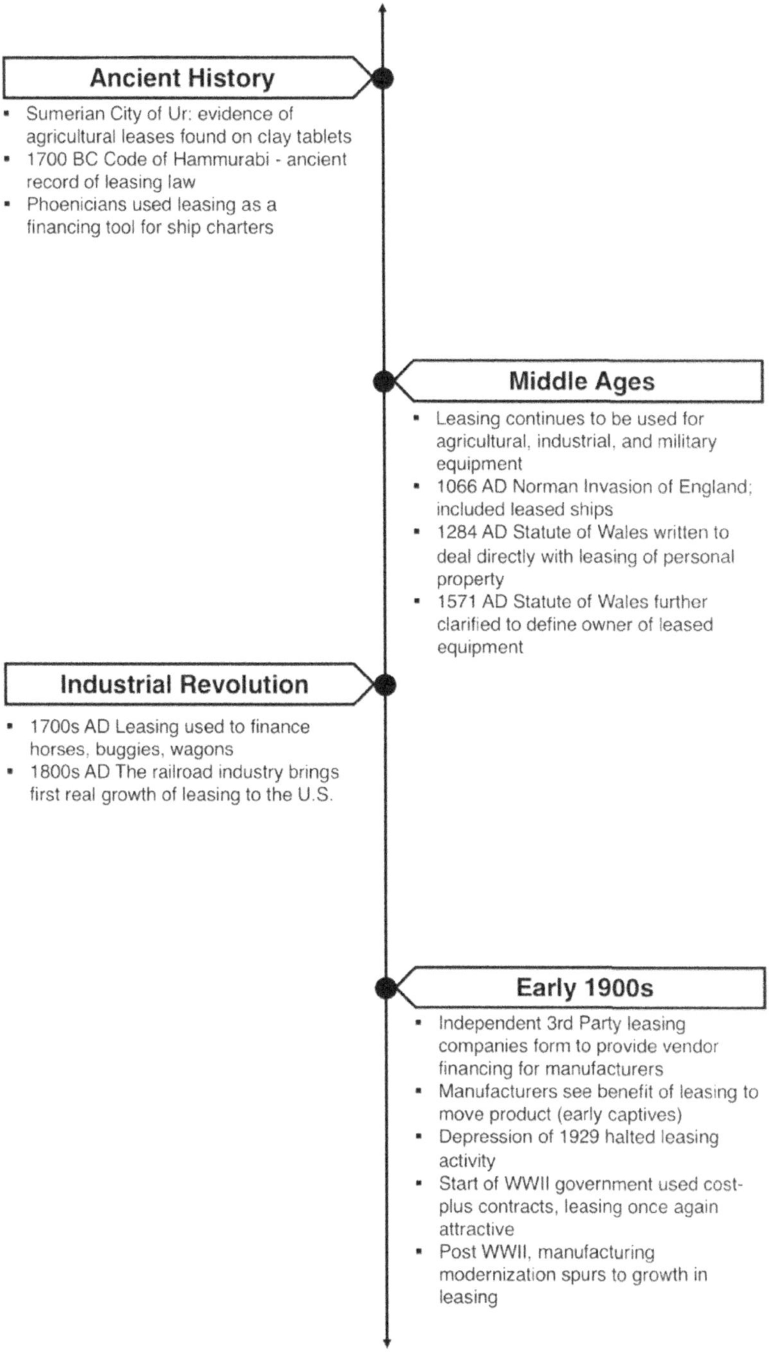

Ancient History

- Sumerian City of Ur: evidence of agricultural leases found on clay tablets
- 1700 BC Code of Hammurabi - ancient record of leasing law
- Phoenicians used leasing as a financing tool for ship charters

Middle Ages

- Leasing continues to be used for agricultural, industrial, and military equipment
- 1066 AD Norman Invasion of England; included leased ships
- 1284 AD Statute of Wales written to deal directly with leasing of personal property
- 1571 AD Statute of Wales further clarified to define owner of leased equipment

Industrial Revolution

- 1700s AD Leasing used to finance horses, buggies, wagons
- 1800s AD The railroad industry brings first real growth of leasing to the U.S.

Early 1900s

- Independent 3rd Party leasing companies form to provide vendor financing for manufacturers
- Manufacturers see benefit of leasing to move product (early captives)
- Depression of 1929 halted leasing activity
- Start of WWII government used cost-plus contracts, leasing once again attractive
- Post WWII, manufacturing modernization spurs to growth in leasing

Figure 5 Slow Evolution of Equipment Finance Through the Ages

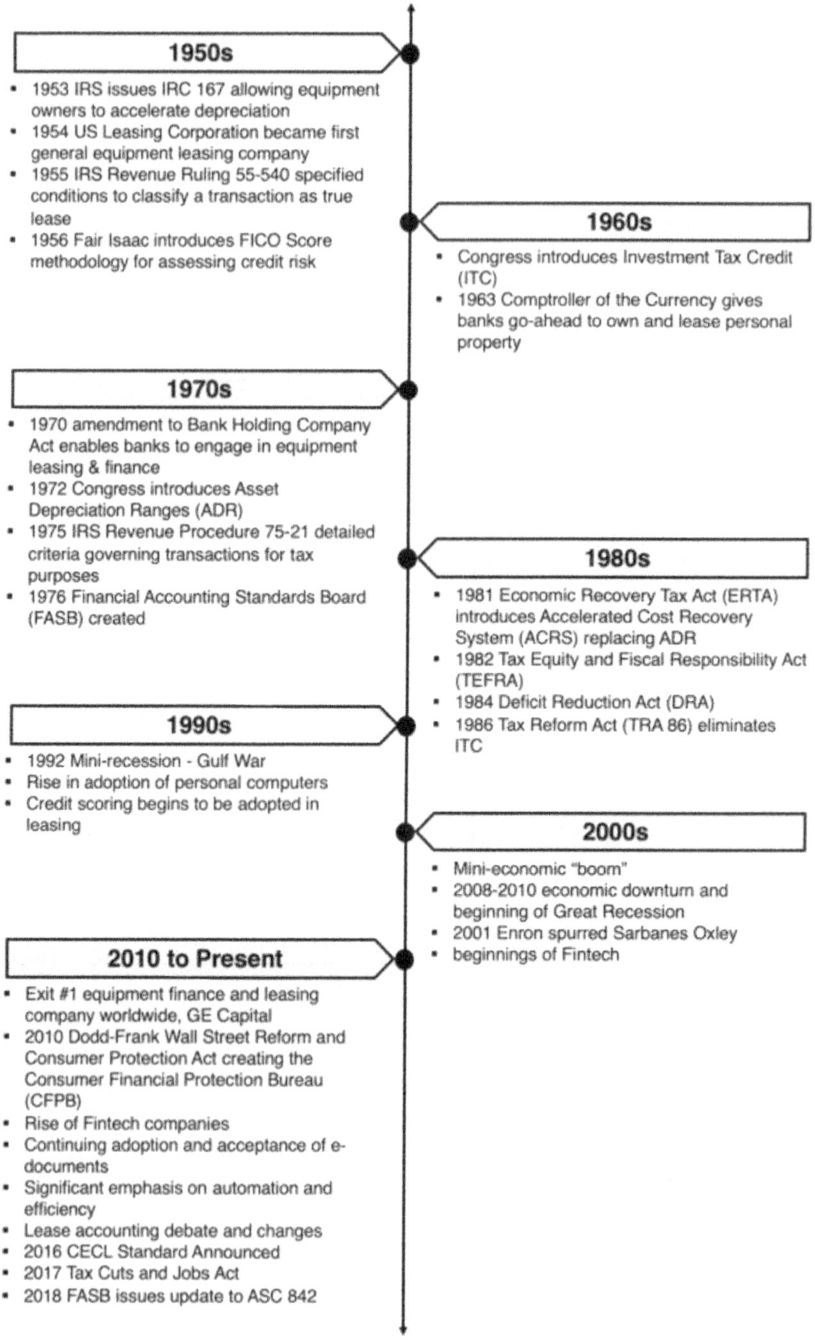

1950s

- 1953 IRS issues IRC 167 allowing equipment owners to accelerate depreciation
- 1954 US Leasing Corporation became first general equipment leasing company
- 1955 IRS Revenue Ruling 55-540 specified conditions to classify a transaction as true lease
- 1956 Fair Isaac introduces FICO Score methodology for assessing credit risk

1960s

- Congress introduces Investment Tax Credit (ITC)
- 1963 Comptroller of the Currency gives banks go-ahead to own and lease personal property

1970s

- 1970 amendment to Bank Holding Company Act enables banks to engage in equipment leasing & finance
- 1972 Congress introduces Asset Depreciation Ranges (ADR)
- 1975 IRS Revenue Procedure 75-21 detailed criteria governing transactions for tax purposes
- 1976 Financial Accounting Standards Board (FASB) created

1980s

- 1981 Economic Recovery Tax Act (ERTA) introduces Accelerated Cost Recovery System (ACRS) replacing ADR
- 1982 Tax Equity and Fiscal Responsibility Act (TEFRA)
- 1984 Deficit Reduction Act (DRA)
- 1986 Tax Reform Act (TRA 86) eliminates ITC

1990s

- 1992 Mini-recession - Gulf War
- Rise in adoption of personal computers
- Credit scoring begins to be adopted in leasing

2000s

- Mini-economic "boom"
- 2008-2010 economic downturn and beginning of Great Recession
- 2001 Enron spurred Sarbanes Oxley
- beginnings of Fintech

2010 to Present

- Exit #1 equipment finance and leasing company worldwide, GE Capital
- 2010 Dodd-Frank Wall Street Reform and Consumer Protection Act creating the Consumer Financial Protection Bureau (CFPB)
- Rise of Fintech companies
- Continuing adoption and acceptance of e-documents
- Significant emphasis on automation and efficiency
- Lease accounting debate and changes
- 2016 CECL Standard Announced
- 2017 Tax Cuts and Jobs Act
- 2018 FASB issues update to ASC 842

Figure 6 Rapid Evolution of Modern Equipment Finance

History of Equipment Finance through the Ages

Ancient History

Equipment leasing could be considered one of the oldest forms of business contracts. Four thousand years ago, the Sumerians produced leases on clay tablets for agricultural tools, land and water rights, oxen, and other animals. The Code of Hammurabi is an ancient record of Babylonian leasing law dating back to 1700 BC. Many ancient civilizations including the Greeks, Romans, Egyptians, and Phoenicians used leasing to enable a party to use equipment owned by another party for fair compensation.

These ancient societies found leasing to be the only viable and affordable way to acquire equipment, land, and livestock. The Phoenicians used a ship charter, which was a way of obtaining the use of a crew and ship. In fact, longer-term ship charters covered the economic life of the vessel requiring the lessee to assume benefits and obligations of ownership. Today when negotiating leases, lessors continue to wrestle with many of the same issues addressed in these ancient ship charters.

Middle Ages

Fast forward 1,000 years, and we see various agricultural, industrial, and even military equipment obtained through leasing. In 1066, the Norwegians and Normans leased ships and crews to form a fleet and invade England. As history continues to unfold, leasing was limited to mostly horses and farming equipment. In 1284 AD, the Statute of Wales (formed the constitutional form of government and introduced English Common Law) was written to deal directly with the leasing of personal property. In 1571, it was clarified by a statute that defined who owned the leased equipment.

Industrial Revolution

In the United Kingdom and the United States, the onset of the Industrial Revolution provided more opportunities for leasing, particularly for railroads. A pattern emerged with investors providing the capital for brand new equipment needed in manufacturing and transportation. Most early railroad companies were able to afford only laying the track, so they sought to finance the locomotives and railcars from private entrepreneurs. With the rise of the railroad industry in the 1800s, the first real growth of leasing was brought to the United States.

Financing was provided by investors for locomotives and railcars through equipment trusts. Set up, issued, and administered by banks or trust companies, equipment trust certificates represented the holder's right to receive a return of principal and interest on funds invested. Administration of the trust included paying the manufacturer for the equipment, selling trust certificates to investors, and collecting rentals from the railroad company, covering the cost of both equipment and interest. The most common form of the trust certificate provided for the transfer of equipment ownership to the railroad company at the end of the contract term. The most popular railroad finance plan was the Philadelphia Plan, a precursor of today's conditional sales contract, equipment finance agreements, and money-over-money leases.

Early 1900s

Independent rail equipment leasing companies formed in the early 1900s. These companies recognized that many railroad companies and other types of end-users were not interested in long-term control or ownership of the leased asset, which was an inherent part of the equipment trust (bank) program. They began to offer more short-term contracts or leases. At the end or expiration of the term, the leasing company retained title and control of the equipment, and the railcar returned to the leasing company. This type of lease financing was the beginning of the true or operating leases still prevalent today.

Other manufacturers, restricted by capital limitations, had few options if they wanted to retain control of their customer or equipment. They turned to independent financing entities to set up vendor finance programs. The independent companies formed to provide vendor financing were called third-party leasing and financing companies. They earned this categorization because they were not related to either the manufacturer or the end-users. Eventually, these independents began to offer leasing and financing services directly to the end-users for other unrelated equipment.

Many manufacturers saw the benefits of providing financing for their products, so they set up their own finance companies (today referred to as captives). Some of these companies felt leasing was a method of retaining control of their proprietary equipment as in the cases of Bell Telephone Company, Hughes Tool Company, and United Shoe Machinery Company; all early leaders in the growth of the equipment finance industry

During the early 1900s, as the economy grew there was a surge of installment credit borrowing as manufacturers desired to sell more equipment by offering affordable payment plans. The Ford Motor Company, for instance, had already begun offering automobile loans for people wanting to buy cars; and other manufacturers began to use leasing to move their products as well.

With the start of World War II, the government used "cost-plus" contracts, allowing government contractors to earn a limited and fixed profit over their costs, once again making equipment leasing attractive. In this type of arrangement, the lease payment became part of the cost, and the contractor lessened its risk by not owning government contract-specific equipment. Today there is an entire specialized field of leasing devoted to the government and suppliers that concentrate on working for governments.

After World War II, as companies sought to upgrade and modernize their operations, leasing as a viable financing tool continued to grow. This growth in leasing led to the modern era of equipment finance.

History of Modern Equipment Finance

During the second half of the 20th century, we saw the equipment finance industry rapidly evolve and advance into what it is today.

In 1953 the nation was in a post-war economic slump, and Congress desired to promote capital formation and manufacturing. To support this policy, the IRS issued **Section 167** of the Internal Revenue Code (IRC or Tax Code), which gave the equipment owner the ability to accelerate depreciation. By increasing tax deductions in the early life of the asset and deferring taxable income to later years, the Tax Code was intended to encourage capital spending and enhance the benefits of ownership.

The 1950s

The shift to modern equipment finance began because of two main trends: the government's efforts to stimulate the economy in the early 1950s and the advancement of technology, both in the area of business equipment and the digital age in general.

Formed in 1954, to take advantage of the tax benefits of equipment ownership while passing on the maintenance expense and right to use equipment to another party, U.S. Leasing Corporation became the first general equipment leasing company. Its contracts typically transferred title to lessees upon their exercise of a nominal purchase option.

By 1955 the use of leasing spread, and several more leasing companies entered the market. While each introduced new products into the leasing arena at a rapid rate, a significant tax issue was surfacing. The Tax Code did not distinguish clearly between a "true lease" and a "conditional sales agreement."

In 1955, intending to define a true lease for tax purposes, the IRS issued **Revenue Ruling 55-540** (Described in more detail later in this chapter). With this ruling, a transaction was classified as a "true lease" only if it met all of the specified conditions. If any of these conditions were not met, the IRS construed the financing to be a conditional sales contract and the tax benefits belonged to the lessee.

The 1960s

The government continued to revise the tax code to stimulate economic development during the 1960s. In 1962 Congress introduced the **Investment Tax Credit (ITC)**, which provided purchasers of capital equipment with a tax credit they could use to offset their total tax liability to the government. The tax credit, initially set at 7 percent, was based on a percentage of equipment cost. This amount could be deducted, in whole, from the net tax due. If the lessor owned a true lease, then it received the benefit of the ITC, resulting in lower tax payments and thereby producing higher net earnings. The ITC became a "give-and-take" option with the government. When the government needed more tax money, it took away the ITC; when it wanted to stimulate capital expenditures, it gave it back.

Previously, banks were not allowed to act as lessor in leasing transactions. In 1963 the Comptroller of the Currency permitted banks to own equipment that, in turn, they could lease to their clients, allowing them to enter the equipment finance markets. This change brought a significant amount of capital held by banks into the leasing market.

The 1970s

In 1970 an amendment to the Bank Holding Company Act was enacted, allowing banks to form holding companies. These holding companies were then allowed to engage in many non-traditional financing activities such as equipment leasing. Initially, banks were only allowed to enter into leases, which were just long-term financing deals.

In 1972 Congress introduced **Asset Depreciation Ranges (ADR)**. This law created hundreds of asset categories and prescribed useful lives for the depreciating assets. Before this, lessors had to guess the useful life of the asset and, if a lessor chose a shorter life than the IRS thought reasonable, they risked losing depreciation benefits. Thankfully, ADR provided the lessor with a method for selecting a useful life that could not be challenged by the IRS.

In the 1970s there were many other government-related actions that had an impact on the industry. IRS rulings and the creation in 1976 of FASB, and their resulting statements and opinions, have had a role in shaping the direction of the industry.

Because IRS Revenue Ruling 55-540 defined a contract of sale and did not include attributes of a lease, the IRS was deluged with requests for advanced rulings to determine if the attributes of specific transactions, especially complex leveraged leases (no longer in existence) qualified a particular lessor to be treated as equipment owner for tax purposes. The resulting **Revenue Procedure 75-21** (further described in Chapter 2 – Financial and Tax Accounting) laid out the six criteria the IRS would use to respond to specific advanced rulings.

Historically there was a great deal of inconsistency in financial statement reporting for leases. In 1976, however, FASB issued **FASB No. 13**. FASB 13 set forth four criteria by which to classify a lease as either a capital lease or an operating lease, and how each is to be treated on the financial statements of both the lessee and the lessor. This provided greater uniformity to the financial reporting of equipment leases. Since 1976, FASB has issued numerous statements clarifying FASB 13 and adjusting for new forms of equipment finance.

The 1980s

The introduction of several notable tax laws affected the industry in the 1980s such as the **Economic Recovery Tax Act of 1981 (ERTA)**; the **Tax Equity and Fiscal Responsibility Act of 1982 (TEFRA)**; and the **Deficit Reduction Act of 1984 (DRA)**. All of these laws related to tax treatment of leases, including methods of depreciation and Safe Harbor Leasing. Safe Harbor Leasing was intended to provide equal investment incentives to companies with different tax liabilities but similar investment opportunities. The assumption was that, sooner or later, income from profitable investments would offset tax deductions and revenue would flow back to the federal government. Safe Harbor Leasing had a significant impact on leasing because it was a method of transferring tax benefits to an unrelated third party, providing tax shelters for investors.

An extensive revision of the 1954 IRC, Congress passed ERTA in 1981, believing that the private sector would spend and invest more money and thereby stimulate the economy if its tax burdens could be sharply reduced (referred to as, "supply side economics"). It was this law, which introduced the **Accelerated Cost Recovery System (ACRS)** and replaced the highly complex ADR depreciation system. This new system had only five classes of assets, ranging from three to fifteen-year life spans and specified the percentage of the cost to be written off in each year. The new system enabled the owner/lessor to fully depreciate an asset without having to estimate useful life and salvage value. ERTA also introduced a ninety-day window for the transference of ITC and a vesting of ITC at 20 percent per year.

TEFRA was passed the following year (1982) to increase the tax revenues lost under ERTA. This new act repealed Safe Harbor Leases, replacing it with "finance leases," which liberalized the true lease guidelines of IRS Procedure 75-21. ITC increased to 10 percent by ERTA and the vesting term of seven years reduced to five years. The taxpayer was required to return 20 percent of the ITC for each of the five years if title passed out of the taxpayers' hands.

The third major tax law revision in four years, DRA, was passed in 1984 as a means of reducing the deficit and again raising tax revenues. DRA affected the industry by introducing the "time value of money" as a method for lessors to adjust uneven rental streams for tax purposes. DRA reduced depreciation benefits on real property, and true tax treatment was disallowed for leases to foreign corporations not subject to U.S. tax. Terminal Rental Adjustment Clause (TRAC) leases, primarily affecting the vehicle industry, were recognized as true tax leases.

The **Tax Reform Act of 1986 (TRA '86)** eliminated ITC with certain limited exceptions. TRA '86 had a significant impact on bookkeeping and companies began keeping two sets of books, one for accounting purposes and another for tax purposes. In simple terms, companies calculated tax liability much like an individual, taking total revenue less allowed expenses and deductions and paying taxes on the difference. Under **Alternative Minimum Tax (AMT)**, a company now needed to do a third calculation using the AMT formula, and then pay the greater of the regular tax calculation or the AMT.

A large deduction for many companies is depreciation. When a company acquires considerable amounts of equipment, it creates a significant amount of depreciation. However, under AMT guidelines, the amount of depreciation is limited. When a company leases equipment, it is not depreciating it; this may produce a reduction in the taxpayer's liability.

In 1987, the **Competitive Equality Banking Act** was passed into law. Among other things, the Act removed the maximum residual value limit for a portion of a bank lessor's business. This law allowed banks to enter into the operating lease marketplace competitively.

The 1990s

The 1990s was a decade of growth and reinvention for the industry as equipment finance activity significantly increased. It was also an important decade for the industry as creativity led to more regulation and revisions to financial reporting and the end of some activities. A valuable lesson learned was that there is a repercussion to the abuse of the tax code, and that is more restrictions.

Credit Scoring Innovations and Acceptance of TPOs

The industry has always thrived on innovation; before the introduction of personal computers, most changes came in the form of products, such as "application-only" programs (also referred to as "app-only"), uncomplicated documentation, and deferred pricing. Most of these innovations aimed at marketing the equipment finance products to vendors and end-users. For many years, however, credit and backroom processes remained tedious and labor-intensive. With the introduction of the computer and the development of credit scoring technology (beginning primarily in the small-ticket leasing segment in the late '80s and early '90s)[2], the dynamics of the equipment finance industry changed dramatically. Independents initially adopted credit scoring followed by some captives; banks seemed to be the last group of lessors to embrace credit scoring widely. Credit scoring, although sometimes used for auto-decisions, more commonly served as another information point for human adjudication (Adjudication is the process of making credit decisions).

Another key driver of the growth of the industry in this decade was the acceptance of **Third Party Originators ("TPO")** by banks. The introduction of scoring models enabled banks and independent lessors to begin looking at the third-party paper in a new way. During this time, the American Association of Commercial Finance Brokers (AACFB) (previously the National Association of Equipment Leasing Brokers (NAELB)) was created to boost the acceptance of TPOs in the industry.

Creative Financing Structures & Large-Ticket Leasing

Adoption of technology was not the only way finance companies were innovating during the 1990s decade. Transaction structures became important and the use of Fair Market Value (FMV), Purchase Upon Termination (PUT), 1st Amendment Leases, and other creative leasing structures grew. To compete with banks, independent and captive leasing companies sought to distinguish themselves by devising unique leasing structures to solve customer problems. In this era, there were a lot of creative and sophisticated large-ticket (over

---

[2] Source: History of Colonial Pacific Leasing by Christopher "Kit" Menkin http://www.leasingnews.org/Conscious-Top%20Stories/CLP.htm

$50mm) transactions for aircraft, subway systems, rail cars, cruise ships, and other high-ticket assets that, within the constructs of the laws at the time, tested the limits regarding what was acceptable concerning the lessor's ownership of equipment and what constituted a lease.

"In the 1990s, very aggressive tax structure transactions turned out to be more creative and entrepreneurial than they should have been."

John C. Deane - Founder & CEO, The Alta Group[3]

Airlines, rail companies, and ship lines financed billions of dollars of equipment through these creative tax transaction structures. Some of these creative large-ticket transaction structures that emerged during this time included:

- **Double-dip Leases**: These transactions were based on standard cross-border leases but were structured to take advantage of tax benefits in both the lessor's country and the lessee's country (the double-dip). One of the countries had to be a form country and one had to be a substance country for these structures to work.

Form and Substance: In a form country, the lessor always is the tax owner of the leased asset. In a substance country (the U.S., for example) the tax ownership of the leased asset is based on who bears the economic/residual risk in the deal.

- **Leveraged Leases**: Leveraged leases contain a unique mix of tax and accounting benefits. The term "leveraged" is used to reflect the high amount of recourse and nonrecourse debt (up to 97%) that is used to finance the assets. This leverage, along with favorable accelerated depreciation rules, long lease terms, and highly-structured rent patterns, created high returns on equity to lessors. This permitted the lessor to offer very attractive financing rates to lessees.
- **LILO** (Lease in Lease Out): A transaction in which an owner of equipment (such as a passenger railroad company in Europe) leased railcars to a bank in the United States, and the bank leased the equipment back to the European rail company. The U.S. bank then prepaid its head lease (primary) obligations to the railway, resulting in section 467 tax benefits to the U.S. bank that were greater than those of tax depreciation. These structures created a net benefit to the railroad of either lower payments or an up-front benefit in a defeased transaction.

  Defeasance occurs when a lender makes a loan to the lessor on a nonrecourse basis for the leased asset with an offsetting deposit made to the lender equal to the sum of the loan payments due for the life of the loan. Concurrently a separate deposit (technically a Guaranteed

---

[3] Source: http://www.monitor-digital.com/monitor/sep_oct_2013/ Title: Leasing Industry Progressions... Perspectives on 40 Years

Investment Contract) was placed which would cover the equity portion of the lease.

- **FSC** (Foreign Sales Corporation) **Transactions:** U.S. leveraged lessors were able to enhance their tax benefits through reduced tax rates when leasing U.S. manufactured goods that were used outside the U.S. (such as Boeing aircraft leased to foreign airlines). The FSC regime was replaced by the ETI (Extra-territorial Income) rules which subsequently also fell out of favor.
- **Synthetic Leases:** The synthetic lease was another product that grew in popularity in the 1990s. It is designed to be a loan for tax purposes and an operating lease for financial accounting purposes. This structure has minimal residual risk to the lessor and is priced like a loan. These transactions can be complicated, and many involved setting up a special purpose vehicle that had minimal equity in the deal, but enough to make it a substantive lessor that was not consolidated by anyone. Synthetic leases continue today, but following the Enron scandal, some of the rules for these transactions changed to make it more difficult to achieve the desired off-balance sheet treatment.

Other complex leasing arrangements during this time included:

- **Sale-in/lease-out (SILO)** which was a combination of a sale of an asset by a tax-exempt entity and a lease back to the same entity.
- **Qualified Technological Equipment (QTE) Transactions** — a SILO for certain classes of high-technology equipment.[4]
- **Tax Benefit Transfer (TBT)**: At the extreme, an unprofitable firm might purchase and own an asset while selling outright for cash the tax benefits typically associated with ownership. Under this arrangement, the firm buying the tax benefits was recognized as "lessor" and owner of the assets for federal income tax purposes only.[5]

Eventually, many of these structures evolved to the point that they looked more like a tax benefit transfer in the form of a financing than a lease. Governments around the world took notice of this activity and tax rules changed such that much of this transaction activity ended by the early 2000s. This market disruption caused some long-term players to exit, but new players emerged.

Another aspect of reinvention during this decade was the acceleration of the asset management professional role. The rise of leveraged leasing and recognition of the importance of asset valuation drove the need for professionals with expertise in both financing and managing equipment risk. This equipment-driven focus continues to the present day; learn more about

---

[4] Source: http://www.woodllp.com/Publications/Articles/pdf/SILOs_and_LILOs_Demystified.pdf

[5] Source: Valuation of Safe Harbor Tax Benefit Transfer Leases, The ....
https://www.deepdyve.com/lp/wiley/valuation-of-safe-harbor-tax-benefit-transfer-leases-H9vnk03BjX

the Asset Management (also referred to as Equipment Management) role in Chapter 9 – Portfolio Management.

The late 1990s saw the emergence of sizeable operating leasing companies, especially in airline industry changing how airlines financed. Lessors entered the aircraft market during this time with the massive need for capital and a need for companies that understood both the equipment and the industry.

As structured finance waned, there was a need for capital to finance large-ticket assets, the flexibility of usage, and industry expertise. Large ticket lessors came on the scene providing financing for rail cars, shipping containers, and more. These finance companies were the asset and industry specialists willing to take equipment risk.

Technology Investment Drives Growth

Around 1998-2000, the "dot com" boom along with the "Y2K" (Year 2000 problem) drove growth in the industry. During this time, Y2K created a panic because companies believed every single computer and digital hardware device likely required upgrades due to the anticipation of potentially harmful consequences resulting from the hardware's inability to recognize dates after December 31, 1999. This led to a boom of investment in new software and hardware.

The rise of internet innovation and technology adoption led to aggressive levels of technology investment driving further growth in the market. In 1995 a lease couldn't be more than 10 percent software, that limit kept rising until there were transactions with 100 percent software during the .com boom and then the bubble burst.

The 2000s

New-Century Lessons

The aggressive level of technology investment rapidly drove the market up. In 2001 when the dot-com bubble burst and software companies failed, software sector transactions failed due to reduction in equipment investment and, in some cases, because there was no equipment to recover.

The early part of the decade was like the Wild West with the continual increase in app-only limits, reduced pricing and relaxing of credit requirements to spur growth became a common practice. These practices along with the advancements in technology and use of sophisticated credit scoring drove industry commoditization.

Enron collapsed during this time, filing bankruptcy in 2001, triggering increased regulatory scrutiny especially for bank lessors and eventually led to changes in accounting rules for leases, financial reporting requirements, and accounting for public companies. Post-Enron, the accounting rules for "special purpose vehicle" companies changed, impacting large-ticket transaction structures. These changes did not have a significant impact on synthetic leases. The most notable effect of the Enron scandal to our industry was how it set the stage for financial disclosures, financial statements, and accounting for public companies. Enron also highlighted the need to enact Sarbanes-Oxley.

During the first half of this decade, the industry faced a harsh lesson with the NorVergence program Ponzi scheme, a massive case of telecom equipment fraud with widespread industry impact. Even though to many companies, the NorVergence business model seemed risky and the value of the equipment questionable, due to attractive pricing and confidence in the Hell or High-Water clause, lenders were enticed to take on more risk than they typically would have. A "crowd mentality" of credit seemed to be pervasive during this time, "if company X approves it, we should be able to as well." This situation significantly impacted the reliance on the Hell or High-Water clause as it did not hold up in many jurisdictions. Many lessors were held accountable by courts for financing equipment that was worth 10 percent or less than the amount financed citing that, as equipment specialists, they should have known this and not assisted NorVergence with its fraudulent abuse of small businesses. This changed the concept of financing for services included in leases and higher levels of due diligence were now required to become comfortable with the ability of a service provider to perform throughout a contract.

Economic Downturn and Industry Resilience

In 2007, the industry started to crack, and in November of that year, we begin to see the first signs of panic. In the past, a typical practice for industry collection professionals, especially in dealing with smaller customers, was to quickly repossess the equipment when customers were in trouble. Eventually, the practice changed and for customers who showed a willingness to make payments during troubled times, equipment values were not as good, and lessors were more inclined to work with lessees to recover more profitably than outright repossession of equipment.

Another significant impact of the downturn was that capital markets disappeared overnight, and capital markets professionals couldn't buy or sell paper at all. A lot of companies failed during this time, and weaker players exited the market.

In response, credit parameters tightened, scorecards seemed to be "thrown out the door," and we went back to "does this transaction make sense" credit approach. Again, this may seem like an overreaction, but the industry still enjoys low delinquency rates for leasing assets as of this handbook's publication.

With the economic slowdown came a financing slow down.

Equipment Financed Annually (in billions)

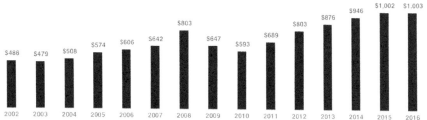

Figure 7 Equipment Financed Annually[6]

The industry paused for about six months and then the focus turned to the app-only, high-velocity business, doing more with fewer people, moving full steam ahead. With increased competition among banks driven by operating ratio numbers, the theme "do more with less" continues and pushes a lot of what is happening in small-ticket and mid-ticket markets. While rapid technology change does enable leasing companies to do more with less, it requires more investment, and the regulatory environment adds complexity.

Another fundamental shift in this decade was the beginning of discussions related to changing accounting rules.

A new business model emerged for banks. Many banks didn't have specialty lending groups focused on equipment financing and saw an opportunity to develop the capacity to offer leasing products to their client base. During this decade, many banks entered the market and became experts on leasing products. Liquidity flowed into the market, expanding the utilization of equipment finance. The expansion of banks in the industry impacted margin and yields over time.

Rise in Technology Adoption

This era saw the internet becoming a primary business tool for leasing companies to stay competitive and new platforms for automation of leasing and equipment finance operations were introduced to the market. The demand for automation, integration, efficiency, and consistency grew in the industry, especially in the small-ticket segment where operating costs were under threat due to margin compression. The ability to manage a leasing business with less overhead and improve efficiency ratio became more critical for small-ticket leasing operations. During this decade, technology providers introduced solutions specific to the equipment finance market; many are still in use. The investment in technology coupled with the availability of advanced technology during this time pushed the adoption of technology in the industry significantly.

---

[6] Source of Data ELFF SEFI Reports 2002 – 2016. Compiled by aggregating amount of equipment financed annually – for each year's report. (Data compiled by Reid Raykovich)

The industry learned many valuable lessons through this decade of significant change when capital markets briefly dried up, and many companies failed. It was like a cleansing as weaker businesses exited the industry resulting in a more resilient and revitalized industry.

2010 to present

Rise in Regulatory Scrutiny

In July 2010, the Dodd-Frank Wall Street Reform and Consumer Protection Act created the **Consumer Financial Protection Bureau (CFPB)**. The CFPB consolidates most federal consumer financial protection authority in one place. Although designed to protect individual consumers, many of the laws are written to apply to smaller equipment financing transactions, sometimes extending to larger ticket transactions as well. The push to bring small-ticket leasing into scope for CFPB may have a potentially disruptive impact on the small-ticket segment of the industry.

Too Large to Fail and the Systemically Important Entity concepts may have contributed to the exit of GE which impacted our industry by creating an opportunity for other equipment finance companies to gain market share especially in the vendor financing space. Bank and independent equipment finance companies were able to buy portions of the portfolio; resulting in a "reshuffling of the deck" in the industry.

Recovery

One of the lessons for the industry stemming from the downturn, "equipment matters." During the recession, more transactions resulted in losses because the lessor or lender didn't understand the equipment. As a lessor, you have to know what to do with stuff when you get it back. Banks, typically equipment finance generalists, are developing more specialization in specific markets.

With the economic downturn, liquidity briefly left the market and by 2012 capital started to flow back into it. Many independent companies that previously weren't competitive from a cost of funds basis became very competitive because the rates at which they were borrowing were significantly lower than before 2010.

With low delinquency rates and exceptional portfolio performance across all asset classes, a lot of capital is flowing into this industry. A significant shift has taken place over the past forty years, and measures of success are changing as companies are no longer measured by how many "assets funded." Instead they are measured by how many assets are under management.

Assets Under Management

An ongoing trend in the industry is the concept of "assets under management" as a measure of success. Many lessors, such as independents, will source, process, and service transactions, which are sold to banks and other investors rather than holding them on their books. Thus, reducing the risk for the lessor and enabling investors to have this asset class on their books without the overhead of end to end processing.

Rather than measuring the size of the portfolio in assets on the books, the trend is to measure assets under management.

Increased Competition and a Significant Shift to Equipment Loan Financing

The industry has shifted from a leasing industry to a finance and leasing industry. We are no longer primarily leasing; a significant portion of transactions are loans or conditional sales agreements and not leases. Small- and mid-ticket equipment finance companies are competing on speed in comparison to bank lenders. Particularly in the small-ticket segment, streamlined documentation, simplified tax requirements, speedy processing, credit understanding of the industry as well as other elements of the transactions are driving growth in financing over leasing.

On the large-ticket side, lease vs. buy considerations and low-interest rates may make leasing less attractive, causing more demand for loans.

Tax Cuts and Jobs Act

At the end of 2017, Congress passed the Tax Cuts and Jobs Act (TCJA) introducing significant changes that affect the industry such as lower corporate income tax rates, bonus depreciation, limitations of deductibility of interest expense, elimination of the Corporate Alternative Minimum Tax (AMT), and more. See chapter 2 for more information about the tax changes.

Current Expected Credit Loss Model (CECL)

In June of 2016, FASB issued the final Current Expected Credit Loss (CECL) standard. CECL is a requirement for all types of lenders and lessors to forecast future credit losses on their current portfolio. Although it is an accounting standard, implementation will be unique for each financial institution and will require a cross-functional approach to implementation.

See Appendix 5 Current Expected Credit Loss Model (CECL) for more information.

Accounting Changes

In February 2016, FASB issued ASC 842 "Leases" as a replacement for ASC 840 "Leases." The largest difference between the old and new standard is the recognition of lease assets and lease liabilities on the balance sheet for those leases classified as "off balance sheet" operating leases under the old standard." See Chapter 2 for more information regarding Accounting.

Advances and Shifts in Financial Technology Adoption

From a technology standpoint, the first part of the 2010s was the beginning of a shift to the adoption of cloud-based technologies across the industry. The democratization of digital capabilities for business is one of the drivers in the rise of fintech startups. Digital savvy companies are taking advantage of the latest technology to offer solutions in the financial services industry.

A lot of the investment in technology in past years has helped equipment finance companies to gain internal operational efficiency, now the shift in focus is leveraging technology to engage with customers. With the rise in advanced technology, more data points are available than ever before. Technology is continuing to change the game for marketing, servicing, and customer experience. Electronic documents are generating a significant lift in efficiency and decrease in operational costs for those equipment finance companies that have adopted the capability. The increase in consistency and accuracy from digital transactions not only improves operational efficiency, and cost, it is enhancing the client experience as well.

Because of the prevalence of cloud-based solutions (provided over the internet), integration required to enable data flow and eliminate redundancy is driving technology investment as well as the need to deliver self-serve digital capabilities for customers.

With changing behaviors and expectations of a multi-generational workforce, equipment finance companies need to be ready to meet increasing customer expectations for interacting digitally.

Industry Drivers
Five drivers of the Equipment Financing and Leasing Industry
1. Economy
2. Cost, availability, and variety of Funding
3. Turnover of plant and machinery
4. Marketplace characteristics (extent and basis of competition and Lessee awareness)
5. Public policy (tax, regulations and law)

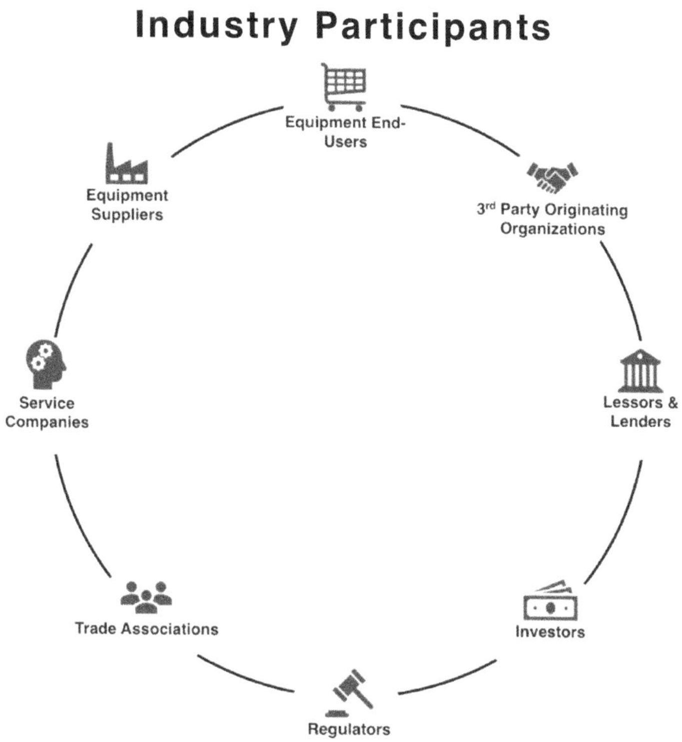

Industry Participants

Figure 8 Industry Participants Ecosystem

The equipment finance industry has a vast and vibrant ecosystem of active participants including equipment suppliers, equipment buyers, third-party originators, lenders and lessors, investors, regulators, trade associations, and service companies. Equipment finance and lease transactions often require the engagement of multiple participants particularly in large, highly structured transaction.

Understanding the variety of participants in this industry will shed light on one the unique attributes of the equipment finance industry. There is a great deal of collaboration that occurs in execution of transactions and business models amongst the industry's many participants. The specialized nature of equipment finance requires expertise and resources that often exist outside of any single participant's capabilities. Considering the many participants in the ecosystem, one may wonder, "Who is the customer in this transaction?" From a lessor or lender perspective, the customer in a given situation could be the buyer of equipment (the "end-user") or the customer may be the vendor who is using financing programs to sell more equipment; the customer may be the third-party originator who is sending the lessor a flow of financing referral business; the customer may also be an investor who is seeking to buy transactions.

Equipment End-Users (Borrower or Lessee or Governments)
Non-consumer end-users of equipment include:

- Small to multinational commercial entities purchasing everything from laptop computers to material handling equipment, to trucks to ships to commercial aircraft
- Governmental agencies, municipalities, universities, schools, hospitals
- Federal government, Native American tribes and nations
- Small to medium enterprises, large corporations, multi-national corporations
- Non-profit organizations

Lessors and Lenders
Suppliers of equipment finance products and services include:

- Banks: community banks, national banks, international, global banks
- Independent lessors and finance companies
- Captive equipment finance companies (a company created and affiliated with a manufacturer or dealer of equipment to finance the sale or lease of its own products to end-users or lessees)

Third Party Originating Organizations
Referral sources of origination for lessors and lenders include:

- Brokers
- Alternative lenders
- Online marketplaces

Investors
Capital market participant buyers & sellers include:

- Multinational institutional investors
- Hedge funds
- Banks
- Wealthy individuals
- Banks (minority investors in private finance companies)
- Private equity

Equipment Suppliers
The suppliers of the equipment that is financed or leased by the end-users include:

- Dealers/vendors
- Manufacturers
- Value added resellers (VARs)
- Distributors
- Private parties (an individual or company selling its own equipment)

Service Companies

A variety of companies provide products and services specific to the equipment finance industry.

- Technology and software companies
- Professional service firms: attorneys, accountants, consultants
- Insurance companies
- Collection/recovery companies
- Equipment appraisal
- Education and training
- Data providers
- Media and publications
- Equipment liquidators

Trade Associations and Foundations

Industry trade associations provide a valuable service to industry participants through education, events, networking, community, and advocacy.

- Equipment Leasing & Finance Association (ELFA)
- National Equipment Finance Association (NEFA)
- American Association of Commercial Finance Brokers (AACFB)
- Association for Governmental Leasing and Finance (AGLF)
- Equipment Leasing and Finance Foundation (ELFF)
- Certified Lease & Finance Professional Foundation (CLFP)

Regulators

A variety of regulatory bodies are involved in setting guidelines for various aspects of equipment finance business with varying levels of impact depending on type and size of transactions and type and size of finance company.

- Consumer Financial Protection Bureau (CFPB)
- Internal Revenue Service (IRS)
- Localities, states, federal government
- Office of Foreign Assets Control (OFAC)
- Financial Crimes Enforcement Network (FinCEN) Bank regulators (FDIC, Federal Reserve and the Office of the Comptroller of the Currency (OCC))
- State agencies and licensing authorities

Government Leasing

Three types of governmental entities often lease required equipment: municipal entities (state and local governments), federal government agencies and Native American tribes. Each is subject to unique tax implications, documentation, structure, and early termination requirements. It is important to remember that from a commercial viewpoint, government leasing is really an installment sale contract, which is called a lease. It is very similar to a loan since to conform structurally to the requirements for tax-free income contained in Section 103 of the Internal Revenue Code, the purchase option must be for $1.00 and the lessor cannot realize the benefits of ownership by taking depreciation.

There are three categories of government leasing:
1. Municipal leasing
2. Leases to the federal government
3. Leases to Native American tribes and nations

"Municipal" refers to states, counties, cities, towns, districts, and authorities, as well as their subdivisions or departments. They are "governmental," in that they have "governmental powers" (as defined by Section 103 of the Internal Revenue Code or IRS). These powers are: 1) taxing power, 2) police power, and 3) the power of "eminent domain."

Not-for-profit entities organized under Section 501(c) of the IRS are not governments even though they may fulfill functions that seem connected to the public good or receive some government funds.

What's a municipal lease; what's not? A state university; not a private college. A public-school system; not a parochial school system. A county hospital; not a private hospital. The distinction is important because the interest paid by a municipal government for public purposes is normally not subject to federal income tax on the recipient. In contrast, a not-for-profit doesn't pay income tax on its normal income, although the interest that it pays is fully taxable to the recipient. For example, if an investor were content with a 4 percent yield on a municipal investment, they would probably need around 5.3 percent to achieve the same net-after-tax yield from a non-municipal obligor.

For more information see Appendix 1 – Government Leasing.

Industry Sector by Transaction Size

Leases are commonly classified based on the value of equipment to be leased. Although specific ranges may vary from company to company, the typical market segment classifications described in the following table will be used for the purposes of this handbook.

Table 1 Industry Sector by Transaction Size

Market Segment	Small-Ticket	Middle-Ticket (also called Mid-Ticket)	Large-Ticket
Typical Transaction Size	Transactions under $250,000	Transactions under $5,000,000	Transactions over $5,000,000
Notes	Transactions under $25,000 are also referred to as "micro-ticket"	Transactions between $250,000 and $1,000,000 are also referred to as "Lower Middle Market"	Sometimes referred to as "Big ticket"
Examples of equipment leased or financed	Micro-ticket: Water coolers, security systems, credit card machines, laptops, computers, phone systems, copiers, software, lawnmowers, trailers, small medical devices, restaurant equipment Small-ticket: Computer networks, trucks, trailers, small manufacturing equipment, forklifts, small medical equipment, small agricultural equipment, restaurant equipment, small construction equipment, small manufacturing equipment	Fleet vehicles, medical equipment (CT, MRI), construction equipment, CNC machine tools, manufacturing equipment, agricultural equipment	Rail cars, aircraft, manufacturing, marine, energy equipment

Competition to Equipment Financing

There are several direct and indirect competitors to equipment leasing and finance in the commercial equipment market depending on the size of the company. Any combination of the alternatives listed in Table 2 may be considered as alternatives to equipment finance or leasing. In the middle market, we are seeing more competition from strong balance sheets and corporate cash.

Table 2 Alternatives to Equipment Finance

Alternative to Equipment Finance	More typically used by Small Business	More typically used by Large Company	Municipalities
Cash	✓	✓	
Unsecured Line of Credit	✓		
Personal or Corporate Credit Cards	✓		
Merchant Cash Advances	✓		
Secured Loans	✓	✓	
Small Business Administration (SBA) Loans	✓		
Home Equity Lines of Credit	✓		
Equity Capital / Public Stock Offering		✓	
Collateralized or Secured Bonds		✓	
Unsecured Bonds		✓	
Capital Budget			✓
Tax Revenue			✓

Alternative finance companies have increased their lending activities, particularly for smaller businesses. Two of the more common business models are entities that provide working capital loans, and third-party "factors." Although some lessors may express concern as to what the impact is of these alternative lenders on the equipment finance industry, many see recent developments in these areas as an opportunity to work together to better serve customers and increase revenues.

Merchant Cash Advance
Many small businesses, namely those that are transactional or retail-oriented, began to use funding sources that offered credit card cash advances. MCA companies consider their funding to be an advance on future credit card receivables and calculate payments based on the total amount to repay. It is generally a percentage based on the borrower's or merchant's credit card volume. Once the merchant takes the advance, their total credit card receivables now cease to go to the merchant and are signed over to the advance company through a process called a lockbox. The MCA company takes its predetermined amount and forwards the remainder to the merchant's bank account.

The cash advance product isn't a fit for many businesses, and there are still significant segments of small businesses without daily credit card receipts. Seeing the need to fill the void for this business owner, the working capital loan industry, as it is known today, was born.

Working Capital
Working capital loans are short-term, unsecured loans for business owners in need of access to funds to run or grow their businesses. More and more, working capital loans are offered to leasing customers as a complement to their lease. For example, a lessor may help a borrower obtain a forklift through a lease. However, the borrower needs additional capital to hire a forklift operator and train that employee, so the equipment may be put to use. A working capital loan can supply the borrower with the needed funds to put the equipment to work, to buy more inventory, to run an advertising campaign, to replace the awnings on the front of the business, etc.

The purpose of a working capital loan is to provide small businesses with a means to obtain capital quickly and is not a substitute for traditional or SBA lending. Traditional and SBA lending are still viable options for business owners, but much like equipment finance borrowers, working capital borrowers are willing to pay a premium for nearly immediate access to funds. Unlike an equipment lease or finance agreement, the loan is unsecured (or non-collateralized), and funds can be used at the borrower's discretion. Since it is not tied to collateral, there is great flexibility in the ways the borrower can use the funds.

Invoice Factoring
Many companies elect to utilize invoice factoring as an alternative funding solution because of its quick and easy setup, ease of use and access to funds. This product is also called accounts receivable financing, invoice financing, or factoring. It doesn't involve any financing; instead, this solution accelerates the cash flow of the business in exchange for a slight discount on the face value of the invoice.

By electing to partner with a factoring company instead of a bank or other traditional lender, a company experiences an off-balance-sheet method of financing. Factoring is not a loan and therefore does not create debt to a company. Further, factoring may enhance a balance sheet by improving debt-to-equity and debt-to-asset ratios. Many companies rely on factoring as a means to accelerate their cash flow and meet their daily operational expenses. For some, it means the opportunity to accept more jobs or fund the upfront costs on the next job.

Equipment Finance Products

A lease is generally defined as a transaction between a lessor and a lessee in which the lessor transfers "possession and use of" property for consideration but retains all right, title and interest in and to the property over a specified term, after which the property is returned to the lessor. For the purpose of this discussion, property is tangible personal property as defined by IRS Section 38 and retention of right, title and interest includes its assignment to another lessor or creditor.

An equipment leasing professional must have an understanding of how a lease is defined and the way it is treated both by the lessor and the lessee. When considering the definition and treatment of a contract, it is helpful to think of the question, **"Through which lens?"**

As depicted in Table 3, these lenses include tax considerations, accounting treatment and how the civil courts view the lease. By revisiting these perspectives, it is possible to determine whether or not a transaction is a lease or another type of financial instrument.

It is important to note that the IRS, FASB, the Uniform Commercial Code (UCC), state sales and use tax authorities, and a variety of courts have chosen to impose their own interpretations of exactly what is and is not a lease for their respective purposes. All of these various jurisdictions are trying to assign "ownership of the asset" to determine individual party rights and obligations for their specific purpose and intention.

Table 3 Three Lenses for Examining Leases

Tax	Accounting	Legal
Internal Revenue Service (IRS) determines eligibility for tax benefits. **IRS Revenue Ruling 55-540** defines what is **not** a lease for tax purposes.	Financial Accounting Standards Board (FASB) **ASC 842** sets forth the criteria to determine classification of the lease for representation on financial statements.	Uniform Commercial Code (UCC) and the Court System **UCC Articles 2, 2A, and 9** are most important to leasing. The UCC determines whether a transaction is a true lease and who owns the equipment.
Is it a "Tax Lease" or "Conditional Sales Obligation?"	Is it a "Finance Lease" or an "Operating Lease?"	Is it a "True Lease," a "Finance Lease," or a "Conditional Sales Contract?"
Why? To understand who gets the tax benefits.	Why? To understand how to represent the lease on financial statements for the lessee and lessor.	Why? Proper handling of warranties and filing of financing statements to perfect interest in the asset. Make ownership of the asset known.
For more detail: Chapter 2 – Financial and Tax Accounting	For more detail: Chapter 2 – Financial and Tax Accounting	For more detail: Chapter 3 – Leasing Law

Tax Lens: Lease or Conditional Sales Contract?

The IRS looks at a transaction for the purpose of determining its eligibility for tax benefits. These benefits generally extend to whether or not the property may be depreciated, how and by what party, whether the acquisition of the property entitles its owner to an ITC (if any is available), and whether the lessee may treat the payments as an operating expense.

To avoid tax abuse, the IRS issued Revenue Ruling 55-540 in 1955, which defined what was not a lease for tax purposes, commonly referred to as a "lease intended as security,"

Given an absence of all of the conditions specified in this ruling, the IRS held the transaction to be a lease and would allow all of the tax benefits to flow to the lessor or to their respective beneficiaries. It is generally assumed that the lessor would take rental revenues into income and be entitled to available tax credits and allowable depreciation. The lessee would be allowed to treat all rentals as an operating expense for federal income tax purposes.

Because Revenue Ruling 55-540 defined what is a *contract of sale* but did not include attributes of a *lease*, the IRS was deluged with requests for advanced rulings to determine if the attributes of specific transactions qualified a particular lessor to be treated as equipment owner for tax purposes. The result was a procedure issued in 1975, Revenue Procedure 75-21, which laid out the six criteria the IRS would use to respond to specific advanced rulings. That has been modified and superseded by Revenue Procedure 2001-28. The definitions and impacts of these revenue rulings and procedures are covered in depth in Chapter 2 – Financial and Tax Accounting.

Accounting Lens: Finance Lease or Operating Lease?

Finance Lease: A finance lease is one that has the characteristics of a purchase agreement and also meets any one of the five criteria as set forth in ASC 842. If the lease is a finance lease, the lessee is required to record a Right of Use Asset and a Lease Liability on the balance sheet at lease commencement. The portion of the payment that is applicable to interest is expensed. Additionally, the amortization of the Right of Use Asset is expensed. The lessor must capitalize the stream of payments (show them on the balance sheet as "lease receivables") and may only take into income that portion of the payment that is applicable to interest. The lessor records the net investment in lease on the balance sheet which is comprised of such components as lease (payments) receivable, residual, deferred income, and initial direct costs. Lessors will record the portion of the payment applicable to interest as income.

Operating Lease: An **operating lease** is one that has the characteristics of a usage (rental) agreement and meets none of the five criteria of ASC 842. If a lease is an operating lease, the lessee is required to record a Right of Use Asset and a Lease Liability on the balance sheet at lease commencement. The lessee will record a lease expense that is comprised of the portion of the payment that is applicable to interest and the amortization of the Right of Use Asset. The lessor must show the property being leased as a fixed asset on the balance sheet and will record depreciation. All of the periodic payments (whether they are paid timely or not) are taken into income, and initial direct costs (further described in Chapter 2 – Financial and Tax Accounting) are capitalized and then amortized over the lease term.

Legal Lens: True Lease, Finance Lease, or Conditional Sales Contract?

UCC Article 9 Secured Transaction

If a transaction is not a lease but rather a secured transaction (a conditional sales agreement, purchase money security agreement, money-over-money transaction, or any of the other nomenclature for a lease intended as security), it is governed by Article 9 of the UCC. Many courts, including the bankruptcy courts, examine the substance of the transaction and the facts of the case very carefully to determine if an alleged lease is, in fact, a disguised secured transaction and therefore subject to the provisions of Article 9. If held to be a secured transaction, the lease would have to meet all of the requirements imposed by Article 9 including perfection of financing statements; amendments and the secured party's right to dispose of collateral after default; and effect of disposition.

UCC Article 2A defines what is not a lease and introduces the term "finance lease"

A finance lease is one in which the

- Lessor is not the manufacturer or vendor ("Supplier") of the leased personal property.
- Lessor does not select the equipment or lease it from an inventory of like items.
- Lessor makes sure that the lessee is apprised of its rights against the supplier with respect to warranties.

Names for Equipment Finance Products

To improve the clarity and consistency of the financial statement presentation and deter possible exploitation of tax incentives, FASB continually redefines the characterization of various debt and lease requirements for Generally Accepted Accounting Principles (GAAP) and accounting treatment.

Semantics True Lease / Tax Lease
Each company has their own preference for describing true lease, some call it true lease, some call it tax lease either way, it's the same thing.

The result of all of this activity is an ever-changing variety of contracts and products designed to serve different objectives. Financing products have names. Some financing products have multiple names. Some names refer to several financing products.

As a result, we may refer to a "true lease" as an operating lease or a tax lease; lessors and lessees are left to wonder what the differences are between a finance lease, a non-tax lease, or even a rental agreement. There also arises speculation on what to call an instrument: a lease intended as security, a money-over-money transaction, a conditional sales contract, a purchase money security agreement, or a loan. Also, what is a sale-leaseback, or a full payout lease? Finally, what difference does it all make and who is affected? The following table illustrates the various terminology used in this Handbook.

Following are some of the names given to equipment leases, conditional sales contracts, equipment finance agreements and various financial instruments. The following list is not meant to be all-inclusive; a quick internet search would reveal a surprisingly large list of synonyms for equipment finance and leasing products.

Commercial Term Loan	A loan agreement between a business and financial institution with a fixed maturity date and stipulated periodic payments.
Conditional Sales Contract	An agreement for the purchase of an asset in which the lessee is treated as the owner of the asset for federal income tax purposes. This entitles the lessee to the tax benefits of ownership, such as depreciation, but the lessee does not become the free and clear owner of the asset until all terms and conditions of the agreement have been satisfied.
Early Buyout Option (EBO)	A lease containing an option for the lessee to pay off the lease and buy the equipment for a premium at a specified point during the contract term. Sometimes called Early Payoff Option (EPO).
Equipment Finance Agreement (EFA)	An agreement, which resembles the structure of a finance lease, but provides for the lender/secured party to lend the obligor/borrower an amount for the purchase of specified equipment. Normally the lender pays the obligor's vendor invoice for the equipment and establishes its security interest by filing a lien against the collateral.
Fair Market Value Lease (FMV)	Fair Market Value (FMV) is the value of a piece of equipment if the equipment were to be sold in a transaction determined at arm's length, between a willing buyer and a willing seller, for equivalent property and under similar terms and conditions. Simply, the actual market value of the leased asset. An FMV Lease is a lease containing an option for the lessee to purchase leased property at the end of the lease term at its then fair market value.
Finance Lease	Finance lease is used in many forms. As most frequently used, a net lease, which has as its purpose in the financing of the use of the property for a major portion of the property's useful life. The term is typically used in reference to leases written by third-party lessors. The term is often confusingly used to refer to a conditional sale in the form of a lease transaction. Finally, the term is a specified lease classification type under ASC 842.
FMV Lease Option	An FMV option provides that at the end of the lease, a determination is made as to the then-value of the equipment, at which point the lessee is given an opportunity to purchase it for that amount. Normally a pure FMV is indicative of a true lease, but the presence of the option does not necessarily ensure a finding that it is a true lease.
Managed Services (Contract Services)	A managed service lease is a service level agreement (SLA) between a managed service provider (MSP) and its client that outlines both parties' responsibilities, including which

	services the MSP will provide, minimum response time and liability protection for the MSP. The contract also specifies the payment structure. Many MSPs, although not all, offer their services on a flat-fee basis, charging a flat-fee per month for each desktop or server, for example.
	A managed service rental/lease is a hardware rental program that matches the MSP's managed IT services selling process and incorporates a standard technology stack bundled with monthly services fees. The equipment and installation are funded to the MSP up front, and the services are billed monthly, collected from the lessee and passed through to the MSP.
	Many other names may be used for this type of lease, including: Bundled Lease, Full-Service Lease, Gross Lease, Maintenance Lease, Service Lease, Wet Lease, and more.
Money-Over-Money Transaction	A non-tax lease or conditional sales contract in the guise of a lease, in which the title is intended to pass to the lessee at the end of the lease term.
Net Lease	A lease in which all of the costs in connection with the use of the property, such as maintenance, insurance, and property taxes, are paid for separately by the lessee and are not included in the rental payment to the lessor.
Nominal Purchase Option	A lease with a purchase option allowing the lessee to purchase the equipment at the end of the lease for $1, or some other minimal payment such that they are extremely likely to exercise the option and the lessor is unlikely to have a "meaningful residual interest." The fact that the lessor has no residual interest in the asset at the end of the term is enough to "re-characterize" it as a secured sale or financing transaction rather than a true lease. (A variety of other names may be used for this type of option including Nominal Purchase Option, Bargain Purchase Option, Buck Out, $1 Purchase Option, $1 Out, $101 Purchase Option).
Non-Tax Lease	Any lease in which the lessee is, or will automatically become, the owner during or at the end of the lease term of the property and, therefore, is entitled to all the tax benefits of ownership. Any lease, which in substance, is, in fact, a conditional sales contract, money-over-money transaction, purchase money security agreement, or other lease intended as security.
Operating Lease	From an accounting perspective, any lease that has the characteristics of a usage agreement, and also fails to meet any of the criteria set forth under ASC 842 for a finance lease.
Purchase Upon Termination (PUT)	An agreement between the lessor and lessee wherein the lessee agrees to buy, and the lessor agrees to sell the leased equipment for a predetermined amount upon termination of the lease.
Rental Agreement	A short service lease, usually less than 12 months in duration.
Sale-Leaseback	A transaction in which the original user sells an asset to a lessor and leases it back. The seller-lessee records either a

	current gain or loss, or a deferred gain from the sale, and classifies the leaseback in accordance with proper lease accounting.
Split-TRAC	A Split TRAC transaction meets the requirements for true lease treatment for tax purposes but may also be classified as an operating lease for GAAP. The Split TRAC provision is structured so that lessor assumes some of the estimated residual value risk. This may be achieved by lessor and lessee taking pro rata portion of the risk or by limiting the risk to the lessee.
TRAC Lease (TRAC)	A lease on a qualified automobile, truck or trailer, which may be considered a true lease for federal income tax purposes even though it contains a Terminal Rental Adjustment Clause (TRAC), which effectively guarantees the lessor the residual value. Note: the mere existence of a TRAC does not, in and of itself, ensure true lease status. To qualify as a true lease for federal income tax purposes, the lessor must also: maintain a minimum at-risk position equal to borrowings used to fund the vehicle (in essence, a non-recourse financing); and obtain a lessee certification that the lessee will use the vehicle more than 50 percent for business.
Tax or True Lease	A lease, which for tax purposes, fails to meet all of the tests for a conditional sales contract under IRS Revenue Ruling 55-540 and therefore entitles the lessor to qualify for the tax benefits of ownership and the lessee to claim the entire amount of the lease rental as a tax deduction.

Equipment Finance Benefits

Customers may choose to lease or finance equipment for a variety of reasons that may fall into the following six categories. For each of the following:

1 Cash Flow or Cash Management

Benefit	Finance Lease	Operating Lease
Financing 100% of equipment cost	✓	✓
Financing 100% of the solution including items such as software, training, and installation		✓
Lower payment owing to residual		✓
Structured leases	✓	✓
Improved cash forecasting	✓	✓
Circumventing temporary budget constraints	✓	✓
Availing of lessor volume discounts via vendor leasing programs	✓	✓
Captive subsidies	✓	✓

2 Tax

Benefit	Finance Lease	Operating Lease
May be a faster deduction from rent expense	✓*	✓
Lower rentals owing to lessor tax benefits	✓*	✓
100% expensing on money-over-money leases	✓	
Circumventing interest expense limitation		✓

* Applicable in some cases

3 Financial Reporting

Benefit	Finance Lease	Operating Lease
Ratio enhancement		✓
Higher earnings		✓
Increased free cash flow		✓
Increase in working capital		✓

4 Hedge Against Obsolescence

Benefit	Finance Lease	Operating Lease
Hedge against deterioration of market value		✓
Early termination option		✓
Technology refresh		✓
Upgrade outdated equipment		✓

5 Convenience and Flexibility

Benefit	Finance Lease	Operating Lease
Full-service – one-stop shopping	✓*	✓
Lower level of decision-making		✓
Priority delivery	✓	✓
End-of-term flexibility		✓
Facilitates planned replacement		✓
Control over vendor lessor	✓	✓
Quicker approval time	✓	✓

* Applicable in some cases

6 Financial

Benefit	Finance Lease	Operating Lease
Availability of financing	✓	✓
No additional collateral	✓*	✓
Fixed rate financing	✓*	✓
Financial diversification	✓	✓
Avoiding single obligor limits	✓	✓
Preserving existing bank lines	✓	✓
Avoiding financial covenants	✓*	✓
Captive financing to "poorer" credits	✓	✓
Less expensive	✓*	✓

* Applicable in some cases

Figure 9 Source: Adapted from Sudhir Amembal's "Benefits of Equipment Finance"

Summary

Through the years, this industry has proven to be most resilient. This industry has shown a unique ability to adapt and thrive in an ever-changing economic and regulatory environment.

A high-level understanding of how the concept of equipment leasing and finance has evolved from ancient times to the present day provides context for a more in-depth study of the fundamentals of the business which will unfold over the next three chapters.

Chapter 2 – Financial and Tax Accounting

Accounting and taxation permeate all aspects of the industry, and each has an integral role to play in the structuring of transactions and the effects on each party. The learning goals for this chapter are to:

- Understand lease classification under ASC 842 for both lessor and lessee.
- Understand the accounting treatment for leases for both lessor and lessee.
- Understand and be able to describe different types of accountants' reports.
- Describe the different types of financial statements and how they reflect leases for lessor and lessee.
- Recognize the impact of the new CECL accounting rules
- Understand the impact of key IRS guidance on classification of leases for tax purposes.
- Understand the different types of sales and use taxes
- Understand the basics of personal property tax applicable to equipment finance.
- Understand depreciation provisions in the tax law applicable to equipment finance.

This chapter covers two foundational topics in the CLFP BOK framework.

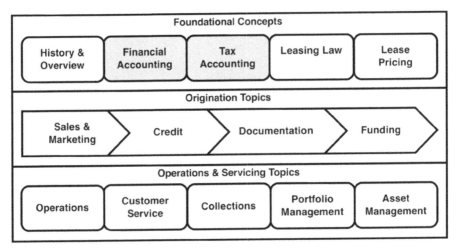

Figure 10 BOK Framework Coverage

An integral part of finance and leasing transactions, financial and tax accounting evolved in response to growth and changes in the equipment finance industry.

In the early years of equipment financing, there were no rules to dictate the proper accounting treatment for a lease transaction resulting in creative methods by accountants to record or omit lease transactions from financial statements. Because GAAP did not require capitalization of leased transactions, lessees could take advantage of off-balance sheet financing, thereby omitting relevant information from their financial reports.

A primary goal of the accounting profession is the reasonable and consistent treatment of similar transactions to allow clarity in presentation and consistency in interpretation of financial statements prepared by various individuals or entities. Since the 1960s, many attempts have been made by multiple standards boards to lay the groundwork for consistent financial reporting of leasing transactions and a brief history follows.

1960s – Accounting Principles Board (APB) issues APB Opinions outlining rules for appropriate conditions under which a lease is recorded as a financing. While consistency of lease accounting treatment was improved, it failed to produce a comprehensive statement on lease accounting.

1970s – FASB establishes a complete set of lease accounting rules for both lessor and lessee resulting in FASB 13 which (together with numerous subsequent FASB issued Statements, Interpretations, and Technical Bulletins) became the rule governing lessors and lessees.

2002 onwards - International Accounting Standards Board (IASB) and FASB work to converge the standards of International Financial Reporting Standards (IFRS) and GAAP into one standard set of high-quality global rules. After working together and establishing similar rules, the long-awaited standard on lease accounting, ASC 842, is issued, effective for fiscal years beginning after December 15, 2018, for public companies and fiscal years beginning after December 15, 2020, for private companies.

Because of the complexities of the numerous sources providing authoritative literature regarding accounting, the FASB approves, on July 1, 2009, the Accounting Standards Codification (ASC) as a single source of authoritative U.S. accounting and reporting standards, other than guidance issued by the Securities and Exchange Commission (SEC). The literature that now governs lessor and lessee treatment of lease accounting may be found in ASC 842 – Leases.

Additionally, as part of the convergence efforts between the IASB and FASB, ASC 326, Financial Instruments - Credit Losses, was issued. ASC 326, generally referred to as CECL, is effective for fiscal years beginning after December 15, 2019 for SEC Filers and all others January 2023. More details about the CECL provisions are discussed in the appendix to this book.

Overview of ASC 842

In response to the increasing interdependency of financial institutions and economies across the globe, the IASB and FASB spent an unprecedented period of time trying to agree upon a consistent and effective financial statement reporting standard for leasing. Under the past guidance of ASC 840, in an operating lease, the lessee never showed the asset or associated lease liability on its balance sheet. On the other side of the agreement, the lessor showed the equipment as a fixed asset, recorded payments as income and depreciated the asset. Consequently, when a lessee was making an equipment acquisition, it could, opt to negotiate terms in the agreement that resulted in either a capital lease, which was reported on the balance sheet, or an operating lease, which was afforded off-balance sheet treatment.

Both the FASB and IASB maintained that the failure of these commitments to appear on the balance sheet resulted in a false impression of a company's liabilities and exposure to financial instruments, so they each issued a new lease accounting standard. The new US lease accounting standard, ASC 842 requires operating leases to be reported on the balance sheet, although it does maintain the distinction between finance (formerly called capital leases) and operating leases. The standard focuses on a right-of-use model and the corresponding liability by the lessee for the lease payment obligation. The new reporting methodology requires lessees to use the term of the lease, the payment stream, and the lessee's incremental borrowing rate to calculate and capitalize the value of the asset's right of use, offset with a corresponding lease liability. For the lessee, this requirement applies to substantially all lease transactions, including real property (office/warehouse space, etc.).

Lessor changes are less significant from an accounting perspective. For the lessor, the most important aspect of lease accounting is that the lessee no longer has the option of off-balance sheet financing, so the lessor may need to take a new approach with regard to sales techniques that focus on the many other benefits of leasing.

Classification under ASC 842

The initial lease conditions dictate proper treatment of the lease on the books of the lessor and lessee, based on the following criteria presented in ASC 842.

1. The lease transfers ownership of the property to the lessee by the end of the lease term.
2. The lease contains an option to purchase the leased property at a bargain price.
3. The lease term is for the major part (75 percent) of the estimated economic useful life of the leased property.
4. The present value of the lease payments and any lessee residual value guarantees equal or exceed substantially all (90 percent) of the fair value of the leased property less any investment tax credit retained by the lessor.
5. The leased equipment is of such a specialized nature that only the lessee can use it without major modifications.

If none of these five criteria are met, the transaction is classified as an operating lease. These criteria are applied by the lessee and are the first part of the two-part test lessors must perform.

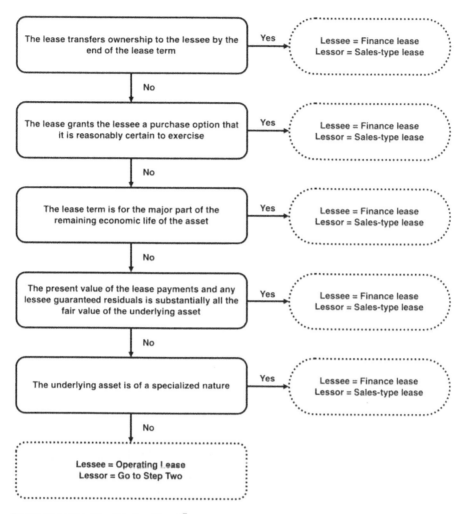

Figure 11 Lease Classification Step 1[7]

---

[7] Source: A New Perspective on Lease Accounting, by Shawn Halladay, used with permission.

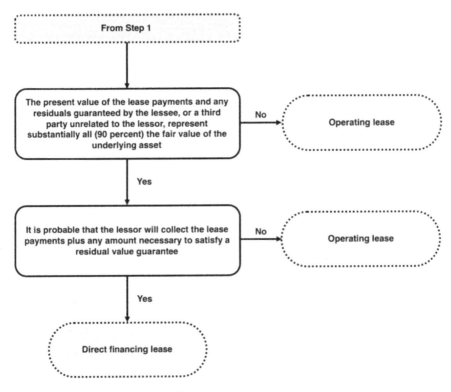

Figure 12 Lease Classification Step 2[8]

Lease Classification for Lessors

The financial statement lease classifications for a lessor are as follows:

1. Operating
2. Sales-type
3. Direct financing

If the lease meets any of the previously discussed five criteria from Step One, it is treated by the lessor as a sales-type lease:

When determining proper lease classification, the accountant looks at the substance of the transaction. Is the lessor lending fixed assets or cash? If the lessor is lending fixed assets, the result is generally an operating lease (think renting a car at the airport). If the lessor is effectively lending cash (financing an asset), the result is typically finance lease treatment.

---

[8] Source: A New Perspective on Lease Accounting, by Shawn Halladay, used with permission.

Sales-type lease accounting rules allow the lessor to recognize sales profit up front if the fair value of the asset is not equal to its cost. Any initial direct costs (IDC), however, must be expensed at that time. A **sales-type** lease also may not have sales profit in it, in which case the IDC is deferred over the term of the lease.

If a transaction meets the classification criteria for a sales-type lease and the 90% test is passed because there is a residual guarantee from an unrelated third party, it is classified as a direct financing lease. If there is any sales-profit in a direct financing lease, it must be deferred over the term of the lease, rather than being recognized up front.

Existing leveraged leases, for accounting purposes, were grandfathered by ASC 842, so some lessors may still have them on their balance sheets. New leveraged leases originated after the ASC 842 effective date are not recognized as a lease type for classification purposes, however.

Accounting for Lessors

For the purpose of this book, the focus is on the booking of sales-type leases and operating leases.

Lessor Accounting for Sales-type Leases

When accounting for a sales-type lease, the net investment in the lease is recorded as an asset on the balance sheet. The net investment consists of:

+	**Gross Investment**	the sum of the minimum lease payments plus the unguaranteed residual value
-	**Unearned Income**	the gross investment less asset costs
=	**Net Investment**	

Debt incurred by the lessor to acquire the property subject to the sales-type lease remains on the balance sheet as a long-term liability.

On the income statement, unearned income is amortized over the lease term so as to produce a constant periodic rate of return on the net investment.

IDC incurred by the lessor are capitalized and then amortized using the interest method to offset income over the lease term as an adjustment to yield. IDC may include fees paid to brokers, and other incremental expenses incurred by the lessor and directly associated with a successful transaction.

ASC 842 embraces a single impairment model that requires the lessor to assess impairment of the net investment in sales-type or direct financing leases using the financial asset impairment guidelines of ASC 326, Financial Instruments—Credit Losses.

Under the single impairment model, the lessor applies the ASC 326 guidance to assess (1) the future collectability of the lease receivable and any guaranteed residuals and (2) the expected value of the residual.

As a result, impairment of the net investment in the lease is estimated considering both credit risk and the non-credit risk relating to the unguaranteed residual asset. A lessor does not separately evaluate the unguaranteed residual for impairment.

Required financial statement disclosures for sales-type and direct financing leases include:
- A general description of the lessor's leasing arrangements, including any major assumptions
- How the lessor manages its residual risks
- The components of the lease income, including variable lease payments
- The components of the net investment in sales-type and direct financing leases as of the date of each balance sheet presented:
  - Lease payments receivable
  - The unguaranteed residual values accruing to the benefit of the lessor
  - Deferred selling profit in direct financing leases
- Significant changes in its residual assets
- A maturity analysis of its lease receivables

Example A: Lessor Accounting for Sales-type Leases

Lease Commencement	1/1/20X1
Equipment Cost	$350,000.00
Payment Structure:	48 monthly payments of $9,500.00, in arrears
Purchase Option:	$1
Lease Yield	13.633%
Borrow to finance equipment:	$300,000.00

Lessor's Balance Sheet at Commencement – Sales-type Lease

XYZ Company, Inc.
BALANCE SHEET
January 1, 20X1

Assets

Cash		50,000.00
Minimum Lease Payments Receivable (MLPR)	456,000	
Unearned Income	(106,000)	
Net investment in leases		350,000.00
Total assets		400,000.00

Liabilities

Long-term debt		300,000.00
Total liabilities		300,000.00

Equity

Common stock		100,000.00
Total equity		100,000.00

Total liabilities and equity		400,000.00

Lessor's Income Statement – First Month – Sales-type Lease

XYZ Company, Inc.
INCOME STATEMENT
For the month ended January 31, 20X1

Lease income	3,976.39
Interest expense	-2,000.00
Net income	1,976.39

Lessor's Adjusting Journal Entries
At Lease Commencement

	DEBIT	CREDIT
MLPR	$456,000.00	
MLPR=$9,500 x 48		
Unearned Lease Income		$106,000.00
Accounts Payable		$350,000.00
Proceeds of Equipment Financing:		
Cash	$300,000.00	
Long-term debt		$300,000.00

Monthly Entries
To record current lease payment receivable:

Accounts receivable	$9,500.00	
MLPR		$9,500.00

To record monthly income amortization (amount will change each month based on amortization):

Unearned lease income	$3,976.39	
Lease income		$3,976.39

To record monthly note payment (portion allocated to interest expense will change each month pursuant to note amortization schedule):

Long-term debt	$5,456.20	
Interest expense	$2,000.00	
Cash		$7,456.20

Please note that recognition of income and receipt of payment are two separate functions. A lessor may not receive a payment in the exact month but still needs to recognize one month of income each month.

Lessor's Annual Financial Statements for First Year

XYZ Company, Inc.
BALANCE SHEET
December 31, 20X1

Assets

	Cash	81,981.80
	Net investment in leases	279,413.95
	Total assets	361,395.75

Liabilities

	Long-term debt	237,940.65
	Total liabilities	237,940.65

Equity

	Common stock	100,000.00
	Retained earnings	23,455.10
	Total equity	123,455.10

Total liabilities and equity		361,395.75

XYZ Company, Inc.
INCOME STATEMENT
For the year ended December 31, 20X1

Lease income	43,413.95
Interest expense	-19,958.85
Net income	23,455.10

Examples of Lessor's Footnote Disclosures Sales-type Lease Accounting

Description of Business	XYZ Company, Inc. (the Company) is engaged in the leasing of equipment to lessees throughout the United States. The Company was incorporated on January 1, 20X1 in the state of Illinois.
Lease Revenue Recognition	The Company accounts for the majority of its leases under the sales-type method. At inception, sales-type leases are recorded at the minimum gross lease payments to be received over the life of the lease plus any future residual value, less unearned lease income. The unearned income is recognized over the term of the lease using the interest method. Management periodically reviews any estimated unguaranteed residual values and records any reductions to market value as deemed necessary.
Net Investment in Leases	The components of the Company's net investment in leases were as follows as of December 31, 20X1:

Minimum lease payments receivable	342,000
Less: unearned lease income	-62,586.05
Net investment in leases	279,413.95

Future minimum lease payments are receivable as follows:

Years Ending December 31	Minimum Lease Payments Receivable
20X2	114,000
20X3	114,000
20X4	114,000
Total	$342,000

Notes Payable

Notes payable consisted of the following at December 31: Installment loan, collateralized by the assets of the company and personally guaranteed by the shareholder; payable in 47 monthly installments of $7,456.20, including interest at 8% per year.

Note payable balance December 31, 20X1	$237,941
Future principal payments are as follows:	
Years ending December 31:	
20X2	73,080
20X3	79,146
20X4	85,715
Total	$237,941

Lessor Accounting for Operating Leases

When accounting for **operating leases**, the leased property is capitalized in the fixed asset section of the balance sheet, at cost, under the caption "Investment in leased property." The leased property generally is depreciated straight-line over the lease term, down to the residual value and must be reviewed for impairment each period.

Rental income is recognized on operating leases in the period the payment becomes receivable. If the rentals vary from a straight-line basis, the revenue is to be recorded on a straight-line basis. Initial direct costs shall be deferred and allocated in proportion to the recognition of rental income.

Financial Statement Disclosures for Operating Leases

Required financial statement disclosures for operating leases include:

- A general description of the lessor's leasing arrangements, including any major assumptions
- How the lessor manages its residual risks

- The cost and carrying amount (if different) of property on lease or held for lease. Major classes of property according to nature or function and the amount of accumulated depreciation in total as of the date of the latest balance sheet presented.

- A maturity analysis of its lease payments

Example B: Lessor Accounting for Operating Leases

Lease Commencement	1/1/20X1
Equipment Cost	$350,000.00
Payment Structure:	48 monthly payments of $8,800.00, in advance
Residual:	$35,000
Purchase Option:	FMV Purchase Option at End of Lease Term
Borrow to finance equipment:	$300,000.00

Lessor's Balance Sheet at Commencement – Operating Lease

XYZ Company, Inc.
BALANCE SHEET
January 1, 20X1

Assets

Cash	50,000.00
Investment in Leased Property	350,000.00
Total assets	400,000.00

Liabilities

Long-term debt	300,000.00
Total liabilities	300,000.00

Equity

Common stock	100,000.00
Total equity	100,000.00

Total liabilities and equity	400,000.00

Lessor's Income Statement – First Month – Operating Lease

XYZ Company, Inc.
INCOME STATEMENT
For the month ended January 31, 20X1

Rental Income	8,800.00
Depreciation expense	6,562.50
Interest expense	2,000.00
Total Expense	8,562.50
Net income	237.50

Please note that the monthly income statement should be the same each month with the exception of interest expense.

Lessor's Adjusting Journal Entries

At Lease Commencement:

	DEBIT	CREDIT
Investment in Leased Property	$350,000.00	
Accounts Payable		$350,000.00
Proceeds of Equipment Financing:		
Cash	$300,000.00	
Long-term debt		$300,000.00
Monthly Entries:		
Accounts receivable	$8,800.00	
Rental Income		$8,800.00
Depreciation Expense	6,562.50	
Accumulated Depreciation		$6,562.50

to record monthly depreciation on a straight-line basis ($350,000 cost - $35,000 residual/48 months)

Long-term debt	$5,456.20	
Interest expense	$2,000.00	
Cash		$7,456.20

to record monthly note payment (portion allocated to interest expense will change each month pursuant to not amortization schedule).

Lessor's Annual Financial Statements for First Year

XYZ Company, Inc.
BALANCE SHEET
December 31, 20X1

Assets

Cash	73,581.80
Investment in leased property	271,250.00
Net of $78,750.00 of accumulated depreciation	
Total assets	344,831.80

Liabilities

Long-term debt	237,940.65
Total liabilities	237,940.65

Equity

Common stock	100,000.00
Retained earnings	6,891.15
Total equity	106,891.15
Total liabilities and equity	344,831.80

XYZ Company, Inc.
INCOME STATEMENT
For the year ended December 31, 20X1

Rental income	105,600.00
Total Income	105,600.00
Depreciation Expense	78,750.00
Interest Expense	19,958.85
Total Expenses	-98,708.85
Net Income	6,891.15

Examples of Lessor's Footnote Disclosures Operating Lease Accounting

Description of Business	XYZ Company, Inc. (the Company) is engaged in the leasing of equipment to lessees throughout the United States. The Company was incorporated on January 1, 20X1 in the state of Illinois.
Investment in Leased Property	Investment in leased property is stated at cost. Depreciation is computed using the straight-line method over the lease term with a salvage value equal to the estimated residual value of the equipment at the end of the lease term.

Lease Revenue Recognition	The Company's leases are classified as operating leases. As such, rental income is recognized over the lease term as it becomes receivable according to the provisions of the lease.

Minimum Future Lease Payments	The Company leases equipment to customers under operating leases. Non-cancelable operating leases are for four-year terms. All leases provide for minimum lease payments and require the lessees to pay executory costs.

Minimum future lease payments to be received during the years ended December 31 are as follows:

20X2	105,600
20X3	105,600
20X4	105,600
Total	$316,800

Notes Payable	Notes payable consisted of the following at December 31: Installment loan, collateralized by the assets of the company and personally guaranteed by the shareholder; payable in 47 monthly installments of $7,456.20, including interest at 8% per year.

Note payable balance December 31, 20X1	$237,941

Future principal payments are as follows:
Years ending December 31:

20X2	73,080
20X3	79,146
20X4	85,715
Total	$237,941

Lessor Accounting for EFA/Loan

The accounting for an **Equipment Finance Agreement (EFA) or Loan** incorporates many of the attributes of sales-type leases, but with less detail. Only the outstanding principal is shown in the EFA/Loan, whereas, in a sales-type lease, the components of the outstanding principal are shown. The EFA/Loan also accrues income on a constant yield basis, just like a sales-type lease.

Example C: Lessor Accounting for EFA

Loan Inception	1/1/20X1
Equipment Cost	$350,000.00
Payment Structure:	48 monthly payments of $9,500.00, in arrears
Loan Yield	13.633%
Borrow to finance equipment:	$300,000.00

Lessor's Balance Sheet at Inception – EFA/Loan

XYZ Company, Inc.
BALANCE SHEET
January 1, 20X1

Assets

Cash	50,000.00
Net investment in loans	350,000.00
Total assets	400,000.00

Liabilities

Long-term debt	300,000.00
Total liabilities	300,000.00

Equity

Common stock	100,000.00
Total equity	100,000.00

Total liabilities and equity	400,000.00

Lessor's Income Statement – First Month – EFA/Loan

XYZ Company, Inc.
INCOME STATEMENT
For the month ended January 31, 20X1

Interest income	3,976.39
Interest expense	-2,000.00
Net income	1,976.39

51

Lessor's Adjusting Journal Entries

At Loan Inception

	DEBIT	CREDIT
Loan receivable	$350,000.00	
Accounts payable		$350,000.00
Proceeds of Equipment Financing:		
Cash	$300,000.00	
Long-term debt		$300,000.00

Monthly Entries

To record current loan payment receivable:

Accounts receivable	$9,500.00	
Loan receivable		$9,500.00

To record monthly income amortization (amount will change each month based on amortization):

Loan receivable	$3,976.39	
Interest income		$3,976.39

To record monthly note payment (portion allocated to interest expense will change each month pursuant to note amortization schedule).

Long-term debt	$5,456.20	
Interest expense	$2,000.00	
Cash		$7,456.20

Please note that, in practice, some lessors choose to present their loans in the same format as sales-type leases.

Lessor's Annual Financial Statements for First Year

XYZ Company, Inc.
BALANCE SHEET
December 31, 20X1

Assets

Cash	81,981.80
Net investment in loans	279,413.95
Total assets	361,395.75

Liabilities

Long-term debt	237,940.65
Total liabilities	237,940.65

Equity

Common stock	100,000.00
Retained earnings	23,455.10
Total equity	123,455.10

Total liabilities and equity   <u>361,395.75</u>

XYZ Company, Inc.
INCOME STATEMENT
For the year ended December 31, 20X1

Interest income	43,413.95
Interest expense	<u>-19,958.85</u>
Net income	23,455.10

Examples of Lessor's Footnote Disclosures for Loans Receivable

Description of Business	XYZ Company, Inc. (the Company) is engaged in the financing of equipment to customers throughout the United States. The Company was incorporated on January 1, 20X1 in the state of Illinois.
Recognition of Income	Interest income on loans is recorded on an accrual basis unless, in the opinion of management, there is a question as to the ability of the debtor to meet the terms of the loan agreement, or interest or principal is more than 90 days contractually past due and the loan is not well-secured and in the process of collection. Loans meeting such criteria are classified as nonperforming and interest income is recorded on a cash basis. Certain direct origination costs and fees are netted, deferred and amortized over the life of the related loan as an adjustment to the loan's yield.
Net Investment in Loans	Loans are aggregated for disclosure purposes by portfolio segment (segment) and by class. A class of loans is a subset of a segment, the components of which have similar risk characteristics, measurement attributes, or risk monitoring methods. Amounts outstanding for loans, by segment and class, as of December 31, 20X1 are as follows:

Net investment in loans   <u>279,413.95</u>

Notes Payable Notes payable consisted of the following at December 31: Installment loan, collateralized by the assets of the company and personally guaranteed by the shareholder; payable in 47 monthly installments of $7,456.20, including interest at 8% per year.

Note payable balance December 31, 20X1	$237,941
Future principal payments are as follows:	
Years ending December 31:	
20X2	73,080
20X3	79,146
20X4	<u>85,715</u>
Total	<u>$237,941</u>

Lessor Accounting for End of Lease Options

There are typically four types of end of lease options. At the end of the lease, depending on the contract provisions, the lessee can choose to:

- Continue to rent the equipment under the existing lease
- Extend the lease agreement
- Return the equipment
- Buy the equipment.

At the end of the lease, there is a residual on the balance sheet and the residual disposition must be addressed before terminating the lease. This is handled differently depending on the end of term option.

For all scenarios, the concept is the same – at the end of the lease term, all lease payments have been collected and all unearned income has been recognized, so the only balance remaining on the books is the residual. The treatment depends on the lessee's end-of-term decision (e.g., continue to rent, buy the equipment, return the equipment, or extend the lease).

Table 4 Accounting Treatment by End of Lease Scenario

End of Lease Scenario	Accounting Treatment
Customer purchases the equipment	The sale transaction would be recorded by debiting cash for the sale price, crediting the entire residual balance to remove it from the books, with the remaining debit or credit recorded to the gain or loss on sale account
Customer returns the equipment	Upon return of the equipment, the lessor brings the asset(s) into inventory at the lower of original cost, book value or fair market value. The lessor should assess whether the assets held in inventory have been impaired. If so, a write-down should be recorded. Write-downs should be assessed on an asset-by-asset basis. Only write-downs are taken; inventory values are never written up.
Customer continues to rent the equipment – no formal lease extension (i.e., month to month)	Generally, any monthly payments received are applied to the residual balance until the residual balance is reduced to zero, with any subsequent payments recognized as continuous billing income.
Customer continues to lease the equipment via a lease extension	The initial lease is removed from the books and the new lease is recorded. The equipment is effectively brought into inventory at its book value, which becomes the "cost" in the new transaction.

Accounting for Lessees

Currently, based on the five lease classification criteria, a lessee classifies its lease transaction as either a finance lease or an operating lease. Equipment acquired under finance and operating leases is recorded as a right-of-use (ROU) asset with corresponding debt.

Lease accounting for the lessee is somewhat less complicated than for the lessor. The lessee uses the same ASC 842 rules to determine proper lease classification between a finance lease and operating lease but does not have to further classify the finance lease as the lessor does on its books.

Lessee	Lessor
• Operating Lease	• Operating Lease
• Finance Lease	• Sales-type Lease
	• Direct Financing Lease

Subtle differences in the application of ASC 842 between lessee and lessor allow for the possibility that the two parties will classify the same lease differently. For instance, differences may occur in applying ASC 842's present value test, as the lessor is required to use the implicit rate in the lease in its calculation, while the lessee uses its incremental borrowing rate.

Additionally, in calculating the present value of the minimum lease payments for purposes of the same test, the lessor includes residuals guaranteed by independent third parties, while the lessee does not. Many leasing companies capitalize on these differences to provide their lessees with the operating lease treatment they desire, while retaining direct financing treatment for their own books.

Lessee Accounting for Finance Leases

The lessee records a finance lease as an ROU asset and an obligation at an amount that equals the lower of:

- The present value at the beginning of the lease term of lease payments during the lease term, or
- The fair value of the leased property at commencement of the lease.

During the lease term, the lessee allocates lease payments between a reduction of the obligation and interest expense.

If the finance lease transaction transfers ownership of the property to the lessee at the end of the lease term or contains a bargain purchase option, the asset amortization is consistent with the lessee's depreciation policy for owned assets. Otherwise, the ROU asset is amortized over the term of the lease.

Disclosure for all leases of a lessee, both finance and operating, should include a general description of the leasing arrangements, information about significant leases that have not yet commenced, a description of significant judgments and assumptions, and election of the short-term lease exception. Other disclosures for lessees, segregated between finance and operating leases, should include:

- Finance lease expense, separated between interest expense and depreciation expense
- Operating lease expense

- Variable lease expense
- Sublease income
- Gains and losses from sale-leasebacks
- A maturity analysis of its finance and operating lease liabilities
- Supplemental noncash information on lease liabilities arising from obtaining ROU assets
- Weighted average remaining lease term
- Weighted average discount rate

Lessee Accounting for Operating Leases

The lessee records an operating lease as an ROU asset and an obligation at an amount that equals the lower of:

- The present value at the beginning of the lease term of lease payments during the lease term, or
- The fair value of the leased property at commencement of the lease.

Rental expense consists of an ROU amortization component and an interest component from the lease liability. These components are calculated in such a way that the operating lease expense is recognized on a level basis over the lease term. If rental payments are made other than on a straight-line basis, rental expense should still be recognized straight-line, unless another systematic and rational basis is more representative of the actual benefit derived from the leased property.

New Standard (ASC 842)

FASB began its lease accounting revision project by addressing lessee accounting, with the goal of eliminating off-balance sheet treatment for operating leases. The new standard results in virtually all leases being recorded on the balance sheet, recognizing both an asset and a liability.

Conceptually, when a business signs a lease for equipment, it has a right to use the asset and a corresponding liability to pay for its use. Under the new lease accounting rules, the value of these two items are recorded on the balance sheet, regardless of lease classification. The only exception is leases in which the lease term, as defined, is equal to or less than twelve months

The distinction between operating and finance leases is maintained under ASC 842, even though they both go on the balance sheet in the same manner that capital leases were booked under ASC 840. A straight-line rent profile is retained for operating leases in the lessee's income statement, however. The liability is shown in Other Liabilities (non-debt) on the balance sheet, at the present value of the rents due under the contract.

This accounting change does not affect the lessee's equity or cash flow and the rating agencies have stated that the new rules will not affect their view of lessee creditworthiness. It does have an effect on lessees' loan covenants with banks or other financial institutions. The required presentation of this liability as "non-debt" in the liability section may eliminate these potential effects to a company's ratios and the covenants often required by lending institutions, if the lending institution understands the concepts and implications of the new standard.

Why are these lessee accounting changes important to lessors? Off-balance sheet financing has been a large draw for lessees and a great selling tool for lessors. The good news is that partial off-balance sheet financing still remains for residual-based leases. With total, off-balance sheet treatment off the table, however, lessors need to rework marketing strategies to highlight the many other benefits of leasing.

Financial Statements

Types of Financial Statements

There are several types of financial statements prepared in today's business environment. With advances in accounting software technology, companies small and large are preparing their own internal financial statements for interim, as well as annual, reporting purposes. A minority of firms, mostly smaller, use external accountants to prepare internal financial statements.

To get a good feel for a company's financial position, it is important to understand the accounting methods used in preparing the financial statements.

Accounting Basis

Most financial statements are prepared on one of three bases of accounting; accrual, cash or tax. GAAP requires accountants to prepare financials on the accrual basis.

- **Accrual Basis**: Under the accrual basis, revenue and expenses are recognized when a service is performed or goods are delivered, regardless of when payment is received or made. This method allows the matching of revenues and associated expenses.
- **Cash Basis**: Under the cash basis, revenues and expenses are recorded when cash is received or paid.
- **Tax Basis**: Under tax basis accounting, transactions are recorded using the same basis and rules used for the company's tax return preparation, which may be either cash or accrual. Tax basis reporting is different than either cash or accrual basis financial reporting in that the preparer uses tax rules to dictate the recording of income and expense items, which may differ from the respective financial accounting method. For example, using the tax method of accounting,

depreciation would be recorded using accelerated tax methods instead of the straight-line method used for book purposes.

To demonstrate the difference between accrual and cash basis, assume legal work is performed for a company in December, and the fees are paid to the attorney in January. On the accrual basis, the legal fees would be recorded as an expense in December, with a corresponding entry to accounts payable. On the cash basis, the legal fees would be recorded as expense in January, when the cash is actually paid. The tax basis entry would depend on whether the tax return was cash or accrual basis.

Accrual basis financial statements are the most informative because they report a company's actual revenues and expenses during a period of time, and also provide information regarding the company's assets and corresponding liabilities at a particular point in time. Looking at an accrual basis financial statement, an individual can get a feel for the liquidity of a company and the magnitude of its current debt. The individual can use this information to determine how likely it is that the company could support additional debt.

Cash basis financial statements are less informative to a reader. Since cash basis statements record only cash transactions that have taken place, a company may have large unrecorded liabilities, such as accounts payable or deferred revenues, which are not presented on the financial statements. This not only understates liabilities and overstates equity on the balance sheet but may also overstate net income on the income statement. It is not recommended that credit decisions be made solely based on cash basis financial statements.

Tax basis financial statements may utilize cash or accrual accounting, depending on the tax filing status of the company. Tax basis financials for a filer using the accrual method for tax would be more informative than one utilizing the cash method, but it would still lack accruals such as loss reserves, which are required by GAAP, but not deductible for tax purposes. In equipment finance, there can be significant differences between GAAP and tax basis accounting. Many leases that qualify as finance leases for GAAP accounting purposes qualify as tax leases for tax purposes, resulting in very different treatment. GAAP depreciation methods are also different from tax depreciation methods, with tax methods allowing for more accelerated depreciation deductions.

It is essential that an individual reviewing a company's financial statements understand the basis of accounting being utilized and how deviations from GAAP accounting can distort a company's financial results.

Accountant's Reports and Level of Assurance for Financial Statements

Equally as important as understanding the accounting method used, one must also consider the level of assurance provided in a financial statement. Internally prepared financial statements may be accurately prepared, but must be viewed with some skepticism, as the preparation is under the control of the entity that benefits by publishing a favorable financial statement. It may be tempting to be less than conservative in reporting transactions. Additional consideration should be given to the level of accounting knowledge of the internal preparer.

Externally prepared financial statements may be compiled, reviewed or audited, each of which provides a different degree of assurance.

Compiled Financial Statements

The preparer of a compiled financial statement presents management's representations in financial statement format. The preparer has no responsibility to verify the accuracy of the information. Compiled financial statement preparation may be on a GAAP basis or an "other comprehensive basis of accounting" (OCBOA). Departure from GAAP, such as utilization of an OCBOA (i.e., cash basis or tax basis), or omission of disclosures or required statements, must be disclosed in the accountant's compilation report.

Reviewed Financial Statements

Reviewed financial statements provide an additional level of assurance. The accountant's review report offers limited assurance that there are no material modifications that should be made to financial statements to conform with GAAP. The preparer of a reviewed financial statement conducts various procedures, including ratio analysis and interviews of company personnel, following Statements on Standards for Accounting and Review Services. Reviewed financial statements are required to be full disclosure financial statements, and any departure from GAAP or omission of required disclosures must be described in the accountant's review report.

Audited Financial Statements

Audited financial statements provide the highest level of assurance. An unqualified auditor's report, with reasonable assurance, that the financial statements present fairly, in all material respects, the financial position of the company. On a test basis, an audit examines the evidence supporting the balances and disclosures in the financial statements. Audit examinations are according to Generally Accepted Audit Standards (GAAS), which require an evaluation of internal control, external confirmations of significant balances such as cash and accounts receivable, inventory observation, and other procedures relevant to the type of business undergoing the audit.

Recent additions to the audit standards now require an auditor to evaluate potential areas of fraud specific to the industry and company, and design audit procedures to test for these potential types of fraud. Departures from GAAP or omitted disclosures may require the auditor to issue a qualified audit report and address the effect of such deviations on the financial position of the company.

Understanding Financial Statements

For many business owners, financial statements appear to be complicated, highly technical documents, which only accountants and loan officers can understand. Further, they seem useful only for borrowing money or when filing taxes. However, because owners themselves are ultimately responsible for the success or failure of their businesses, they must know how well their operations are performing at all times; and to that end, understanding the basic financial statements is imperative.

Among the different types of financial statements, there are two critical reports for all sizes and categories of business. These are the balance sheet and the income statement. The balance sheet presents all of the assets owned and all of the liabilities owed, at a certain point in time — the balance sheet date. The income statement reports revenue minus expenses over a specified period. These universal elements of the enterprise provide a picture of the business' strengths and weaknesses.

By regularly compiling and analyzing financial statement information, business management and owners can proactively detect the types of problems that experts routinely see as chief causes of business failure. These could be problems such as sluggish sales, excessive operating expenses, credit and inventory mismanagement, and underutilized fixed assets. By comparing statements from different periods, management can identify trends and make necessary budget revisions before small problems become large ones. These financial reports also help creditors and investors make decisions on lending and other financial transactions.

The following overview provides a basic understanding of the purposes and components of financial statements. The balance sheet and income statement formats are designed as general models and are not complete for every business operation. This overview applies to an accrual basis, GAAP, financial statement.

To maximize the usefulness of financial statements for management purposes, financial statements are prepared monthly. Timeliness is also important; the timelier the reports, the more effective management can be in acting to reverse negative trends or cure other problems.

Balance Sheet

A balance sheet reports the total assets, liabilities, and equity (net worth) of a business as of a specific day. This statement is divided to provide two views of the same entity: the assets, or what resources the business owns; and the liabilities and owners' equity, or creditor and owner investments that supplied these resources. These divisions are set up in the two-column account form, with assets on the left, liabilities and equity on the right. An alternative, the one-column statement form, lists assets on top, liabilities, and equity below.

The backbone of the balance sheet is the fundamental accounting equation: Assets = Liabilities + Equity (transposed: Assets - Liabilities = Equity). The basis for this equation is the accounting principle that every business transaction, such as selling merchandise or borrowing capital, has a dual effect. Any increase or decrease on one side of the equation always equals a corresponding change on the other side of the equation. If the sides do not balance, faulty arithmetic or inaccurate or incomplete records may be the cause.

<table>
<tr><td>The backbone of the balance sheet is the equation:</td><td>**Assets = Liabilities + Equity**</td></tr>
</table>

To illustrate the principle of balance:

If a business owner purchases $1,000 of new merchandise on credit, assets increase by the cost of the new inventory and liabilities increase by the same amount, representing the balance due to the vendor.

To further illustrate the principle, if the same business used $1,000 of cash to purchase the same inventory, assets would be increased by the inventory value but decreased by the cash outlay. Thus, total assets would be unchanged, and liabilities and equity would also remain the same.

Table 5 Essential Elements of a Balance Sheet

	Essential Elements of a Balance Sheet
Heading	The legal name of the business, the type of statement, and the day, month and year are shown at the top of the report.
Assets	Anything of value that is owned or legally due to the business is included under this heading. In a classified balance sheet, assets are separated into categories such as current assets, fixed assets, and other assets. Many leasing companies use an unclassified balance sheet, which does not separate assets into the various categories.
Current Assets	Cash and liquid assets that can be converted into cash within 12 months of the date of the balance sheet are considered current. Besides cash (money on hand and demand deposits in the bank, such as checking accounts and regular savings accounts), these resources include the items listed below. They are ranked in a generally accepted order of decreasing liquidity - that is, the ease with which the items could be converted to cash; which is the order they should be presented in the balance sheet.

- **Cash**
- **Accounts Receivable**: The amounts due from customers in payment of merchandise or services.
- **Inventory**: Includes raw materials on hand, work in process and all finished goods either manufactured or purchased for resale. Inventory value is based on unit cost and is calculated by any of several methods (see Inventory Valuation).
- **Marketable securities**: Interest or dividend-yielding holdings expected to be converted into cash within a year. Also called short-term investments, they include stocks and bonds,

certificates of deposit and time deposit savings accounts. According to accounting principles, they must be listed on the balance sheet at the lower of their original cost or their current market value.

- **Prepaid Expenses**: Goods, benefits, or services a business buys or rents in advance of use. Examples are office supplies, insurance premiums, and office rent.

Long-term Investments Also called long-term assets, these resources are holdings that the business intends to keep for a year or longer, and that typically yield interest or dividends. Included are stocks, bonds, and savings accounts earmarked for special purposes.

Fixed Assets Expenditures such as buildings, land, machinery, and equipment, office machines and furniture, which are capitalized and amortized, or depreciated over their estimated useful lives. Frequently called plant and equipment, these are the resources a business owns or acquires for use in operations and does not intend for resale. Regardless of current market value, land is listed at its original purchase price, with no allowance for appreciation or depreciation. Fixed assets may be leased rather than owned. Depending on the leasing arrangement, both the value and the liability of the leased property may need to be listed on the balance sheet. For a leasing company, assets held on operating lease are included in fixed assets and depreciated according to the company's depreciation policy.

Other Assets Resources not listed with any of the above assets are grouped here. Examples include tangibles such as security deposits on rental property and intangibles such as patents and trademarks.

Liabilities This term covers all monetary obligations of a business and all claims creditors have on its assets. Liabilities are generally classified as current liabilities or long-term debt.

Current Liabilities All debts and obligations payable within twelve months of the balance sheet date are included here. Typically, they include the following:

- **Accounts Payable**: The amounts owed to suppliers for goods and services purchased in connection with business operations.
- **Short-Term Notes**: The balance of principal due to pay off short-term debt for borrowed funds.
- **Current Portion of Long-Term Debt**: Portion of long-term debt payable within twelve months of the balance sheet date.

- **Interest Payable**: Any accrued fees due for use of both short-and long-term borrowed capital and credit extended to the business.
- **Taxes Payable:** Amounts estimated by an accountant to have been incurred during the accounting period. (Note: Income taxes are business obligations for corporations: proprietorships and partnerships bear personal, but not business, income taxes.)
- **Accrued Payroll:** Salaries and wages currently owed.

Long-term Liabilities   Long-term liabilities are notes, contract payments or mortgage payments due over a period exceeding twelve months. They are listed by outstanding balance net of current portion, which are classified as described above.

Equity   Also called net worth, equity is the claim of the owner(s) on the assets of the business. In a proprietorship or partnership, equity is each owner's original investment plus any earnings, net of withdrawals. In a corporation, the owners are the shareholders; those who have invested capital (cash or other assets) in exchange for shares of stock. The corporation's equity is the sum of contributions plus earnings retained after paying dividends or owner distributions; it is detailed as follows:

- **Capital Stock:** The total amount invested in the business in exchange for shares of stock at values up to the par value. Par is the per-share price assigned to the original issue of stock, regardless of subsequent selling prices. (In the case of a partnership, this would be Partner's Capital, in the case of an LLC, it would be Member's Equity).
- **Excess Paid in Capital:** The amount in excess of par value that a business receives from shares of stock sold.
- **Retained Earnings:** The total accumulated net income minus the total accumulated dividends declared since the corporation's founding. These earnings are part of the total equity for any business.
- **Total Liabilities and Equity:** The sum of these two amounts must always match the total assets.

Sample Lessor, LLC
BALANCE SHEET
December 31, 20X2

ASSETS

ASSETS

Cash	$	32,850
Accounts receivable		12,940
Net Investment in leases		3,458,612.00
Property and equipment (at cost, net of Accumulated depreciation of $76,276)		58,652
Assets held on lease (at cost, net of accumulated depreciation of $328,555)		141,445
Member advances		12,000
Prepaid expenses		8,500
TOTAL ASSETS	$	3,724,999

LIABILITIES AND MEMBER'S EQUITY

LIABILITIES

Line of credit loan	$	120,000
Notes payable		3,068,813
Accounts payable, trade		86,160
Customer deposits		6,840
Security deposits, leases		28,000
Sales/use tax payable		18,526
Accrued expenses		8,435
State income taxes payable		1,329
Total Liabilities	$	3,338,123
MEMBER'S EQUITY		386,876
TOTAL LIABILITIES AND MEMBER'S EQUITY	$	3,724,999

Sample Lessee, Inc.
BALANCE SHEET
December 31, 20X2

ASSETS

ASSETS

Cash	$	49,394
Accounts receivable		6,503,605
Inventory		2,870,853
Property and equipment (Net of Accumulated Depreciation)		19,561,649
Prepaid expenses		956,743
Other Assets		759,229
TOTAL ASSETS	$	30,701,473

LIABILITIES AND STOCKHOLDER'S EQUITY

LIABILITIES

Accounts payable	$	3,592,982
Line of credit loan		5,251,452
Current portion of long-term debt		2,604,992
Current portion of long-term debt - leases		148,952
Long-term debt, net of current portion		10,667,313
Long-term debt, net of current portion - leases		145,077
Other liabilities		200,000
Total Liabilities	$	22,610,768

Stockholder's Equity

Additional paid in capital		3,266,762
Retained earnings		4,823,943
Total Stockholder's equity		8,090,705
TOTAL LIABILITIES AND STOCKHOLDER'S EQUITY	$	30,701,473

Income Statement

The income statement shows business revenue, expenses and the resulting profit or loss over a given period. The income statement represents activity during the fiscal year of operations, which may or may not coincide with the calendar year. For example, the fiscal year could be July 1 to June 30.

Essential Elements of an Income Statement	
Heading	The legal name of the business, the type of statement, and the period of time covered in the report are shown at the top of the report.
Column Headings	Including both current month and year-to-date columns on the income statement allows management to review trends from accounting period to accounting period and to compare previous similar periods. Also, it is often helpful to show the dollar amounts as percentages of net sales. This helps owners in analyzing the company's operation and comparing its performance to similar businesses.
Revenue	All sources of trade revenues flowing into a business for services rendered or goods sold come under this category. In addition to actual cash transactions, the revenue figure reflects amounts due from customers on accounts receivable as well as equivalent cash values for merchandise or other tangible items used as payment. Revenues are generally reported net of any sales returns and allowances.
Cost of Sales	Cost of sales represents the total cost allocated to goods sold during the period covered in the income statement. This might include the cost of inventory sold during the period, including costs of manufacturing or warehousing products. Service businesses generally do not have a cost of sales.
Gross Profit	Also called gross margin, this figure is the difference between the cost of goods sold and net revenue. It is the business' profit before operating expenses and taxes.
Operating Expenses	The expenses of conducting business operations generally fall into two broad categories: selling and general/administrative. Note: manufacturers normally allocate a portion of operating expenses, such as rents, utilities and labor, and machinery depreciation, as part of their cost of sales.
Total Operating Income	Total operating expenses are subtracted from gross margin to show what the business earned before financial revenue and expenses, taxes, and extraordinary items.
Other Revenue and Expenses	Income and expenses that are not generated by the usual operations of a business and that are not considered extraordinary are recorded here. Typically included in this category are financial revenue, such as interest from

	investments and financial expenses, such as interest on borrowed capital.
Pretax Income	Also called pretax profit, to derive this figure, total financial revenue (less total financial expenses) is added to total operating income. From pretax income, taxes are subtracted if the business is a corporation. Proprietorships and partnerships do not pay business taxes on income: the income is reported on the owners' personal returns.
Net Income (Loss)	This figure represents the sum of all revenues minus the sum of all expenses (including taxes, if applicable). Net income (loss) is commonly referred to as the bottom line.

Following is an example of an income statement.

Sample Lessor, LLC
STATEMENT OF OPERATIONS AND MEMBER'S EQUITY
For the year ended December 31, 20X2

		Amount	Percent of Revenue	
REVENUE				
Finance lease income	$	497,761	66.9	%
Rental income		125,085	16.8	
Gain on lease discounting		14,487	1.9	
Documentation and late fees		38,492	5.2	
Gain (loss) on sale of assets		68,025	9.1	
TOTAL REVENUE		743,850	100.0	
OPERATING EXPENSES		586,934	78.9	
INCOME BEFORE OTHER INCOME		156,916	21.1	
OTHER INCOME				
Interest income		380	0.1	
TOTAL OTHER INCOME (EXPENSE)		380	21.1	
INCOME BEFORE PROVISION FOR INCOME TAXES		157,296	21.1	
PROVISION FOR INCOME TAXES		36,178	4.9	
NET INCOME		121,118	16.3	%
MEMBER'S EQUITY, January 1		330,758		
MEMBER DISTRIBUTIONS		(65,000)		
MEMBER'S EQUITY, December 31	$	386,876		

Sample Lessee, Inc.
STATEMENT OF OPERATIONS
For the year ended December 31, 20X2

		Amount
SALES AND GROSS PROFIT		
Sales	$	46,559,787
Cost of Sales		37,799,605
GROSS PROFIT		8,760,182
OPERATING EXPENSES		6,686,122
INCOME (LOSS) FROM OPERATIONS		2,074,060
OTHER INCOME (EXPENSE)		
Interest and dividend income		6,932
Gain on Sale of Assets		336,689
Loss on interest rate contracts		(122,830)
Interest expense		(769,145)
Miscellaneous expense		(31,595)
TOTAL OTHER INCOME (EXPENSE)		(579,949)
INCOME BEFORE PROVISION FOR INCOME TAXES		1,494,111
PROVISION FOR INCOME TAXES		373,528
NET INCOME		1,120,583

Statement of Cash Flows

The third chief document of financial reporting is the statement of cash flows. Many small operations omit the statement of cash flows from internally prepared financial statements. However, according to GAAP, the statement of cash flows is required in audited financial statements. Once a business owner familiarizes themselves with the format of the statement of cash flows, it can become a useful economic tool.

A significant purpose of the Statement of Cash Flows is to show the sources and uses of cash from the beginning to the end of the accounting period, and what caused the change. The statement accomplishes this by listing the sources (such as from revenue, borrowed capital, and investors' contributions) and the uses of cash (such as for equipment purchases, repayment of long-term debt, and declaration of cash dividends or owner distributions).

By understanding the amounts and causes of changes in cash flow, management can realistically budget for continued business operations and growth. For example, the statement of cash flows helps answer such questions as "Will present cash flow allow the business to acquire new equipment," or "will financing be necessary?"

Sample Lessor, LLC
STATEMENT OF CASH FLOWS
For the year ended December 31, 20X2

CASH FLOWS FROM OPERATING ACTIVITIES		
Net income	$	121,118
Adjustments to reconcile net income to net cash provided		
by operating activities		
Depreciation and amortization		116,805
Gain on sale of assets		68,025
Changes in assets and liabilities:		
Decrease in accounts receivable		1,733
Increase in net investment in leases		(285,150)
Increase in prepaid expenses		(500)
Decrease in accounts payable, trade		(3,089)
Increase in customer deposits		1,500
Decrease in sales taxes payable		(586)
Increase in accrued expenses		1,875
Increase in state income taxes payable		329
Net cash provided by operating activities		22,060
CASH FLOWS FROM INVESTING ACTIVITIES		
Purchase of property and equipment		(4,290)
Purchase of assets held on lease		(88,900)
Proceeds on sale of assets		186,952
Advances to member		(12,000)
Net cash used in investing activities		81,762
CASH FLOWS FROM FINANCING ACTIVITIES		
Net repayments on line of credit loan		(30,000)
Proceeds from notes payable		685,295
Repayment of notes payable		(765,835)
Member distributions		(65,000)
Net cash used in financing activities		(175,540)
NET DECREASE IN CASH		(71,718)
CASH, January 1		104,568
CASH, December 31	$	32,850
SUPPLEMENTAL DISCLOSURES OF CASH FLOW INFORMATION		
Cash paid during the year for:		
Interest	$	118,125
Income taxes	$	30,000

Sample Lessee, Inc.
STATEMENT OF CASH FLOWS
For the year ended December 31, 20X2

CASH FLOWS FROM OPERATING ACTIVITIES

Net income	$	1,120,583
Adjustments to reconcile net income to net cash provided		
by operating activities		
Depreciation and amortization		2,770,229
Changes in assets and liabilities:		
Increase in accounts receivable		(756,254)
Increase in prepaid expenses		(500,000)
Decrease in inventories		251,368
Decrease in accounts payable		(333,659)
Decrease in accrued liabilities		119,332
Net cash provided by operating activities		2,671,599
CASH FLOWS FROM INVESTING ACTIVITIES		
Purchase of property and equipment		(3,074,649)
Proceeds on sale of assets		536,294
Net cash used in investing activities		(2,538,355)
CASH FLOWS FROM FINANCING ACTIVITIES		
Net repayments on line of credit loan		(276,003)
Payments of Shareholder Dividends		(50,000)
Payments on Lease Obligations		(756,123)
Net cash used in financing activities		(1,082,126)
NET DECREASE IN CASH		(948,882)
CASH, January 1		998,276
CASH, December 31	$	49,394

SUPPLEMENTAL DISCLOSURES OF CASH FLOW INFORMATION
    Cash paid during the year for:

Interest	$	500,000
Income taxes	$	25,000

Reconciliation of Retained Earnings or Net Worth

The reconcilement of retained earnings reconciles the changes in retained earnings during the financial statement period being reported on. The reconcilement beings with the beginning balance of the retained earnings account. The reconcilement then adds or subtracts such items as net income, net loss, and dividends paid to arrive at the ending retained earnings balance.

The calculation of the reconcilement can generally be described as follows:

Beginning Retained Earnings + Net Income or – Net Loss – Dividends Paid = Ending Retained Earnings

Sample Lessee, Inc.
Reconcilement of Retained Earnings
For the year ended December 31, 20X2

Retained Earnings at January 1, 20X2	$ 3,400,025
Net income for the year ended December 31, 20X2	1,473,918
Dividends paid to shareholders	(50,000)
Retained Earnings at December 31, 20X2	4,823,943

Notes to Financial Statements

Financial statement notes are crucial to developing an understanding of the accounting methods and policies applied by a company. They are required to report items significant to the reader in evaluating the financial position and results of operations of any business. In addition to disclosing accounting methods and policies, the notes provide relevant information regarding the makeup of various account balances, such as the details and repayment terms of long-term debt.

Tax Accounting

Taxation of leases and conditional sales contracts goes beyond that of lessor and lessee income taxes. Both parties also are affected by the imposition of sales or use and personal property taxes. Awareness and understanding of all aspects of taxation is essential knowledge for the leasing professional.

Lease classification criteria are different for book and tax purposes. While leases are classified as sales-type or operating for book purposes, transactions are classified as tax leases or conditional sales for tax purposes. Consistency of treatment is not required between book and tax. This fact can present surprises for the unprepared lessor and opportunities for the well-informed lessor.

Tax classification criteria are not as straightforward as accounting criteria. Unlike accounting criteria where one body (FASB) by and large sets the accounting rules, tax rules are based on the tax code, on the results of tax court case litigation (which sometimes is not consistent with the code or other cases), and on IRS private letter rulings and administrative rules. As such, tax rules can be more confusing and ambiguous than accounting rules.

For federal income tax purposes, the leading exposition of the analysis to determine if a lease qualifies for tax lease treatment is in the United States Supreme Court's decision in *Frank Lyon Co. v. United States*, 435 U.S. 561 (1978), 1978-1 CB 46, rev'q 536 F. 2d 746 (8th Cir. 1976). Among other things, the Court there concluded:

> *"... so long as the lessor retains significant and genuine attributes of the traditional lessor status, the form of the transaction adopted by the parties governs for tax purposes. What those attributes are in any particular case will necessarily depend upon its facts."*

This test suggested that a balancing be performed among the various attributes of the transaction, i.e., the "bundle of sticks" theory with the decision being rendered on the basis of whether the transaction had more attributes of a lease or a financing.

What is "Bundle of Rights" Theory?

The concept that compares property ownership to a bundle of sticks with each stick representing a distinct and separate right of the property owner, e.g., the right to use real estate, to sell it, to lease it, to give it away, or to choose to exercise all or none of these rights.[9]

---

[9] Source: https://thelawdictionary.org/bundle-of-rights-theory/ accessed January 11, 2018

Revenue Rulings and Procedures

Revenue Ruling 55-540

Revenue Ruling 55-540 states that a transaction may not be a lease for tax purposes if one or more of the following conditions are present:

- Any portion of the periodic lease payment is applied to an equity position in the asset to be acquired by the lessee.
- The lessee automatically acquires title to the property upon payment of a specified amount of "rentals" he/she is required to make.
- The total amount, which a lessee is required to pay for a relatively short period of use, constitutes an inordinately large proportion of the total sum required to be paid to secure the transfer of the title.
- The agreed "rental" payments materially exceed the current fair rental value.
- The property may be acquired for a nominal purchase option in relation to the value of the property at the time the option may be exercised.
- Some portion of the periodic payment is specifically designated as interest or its equivalent.

This builds on the history described in Chapter 1 – History and Overview. In its Revenue Ruling 55-540, the IRS provides its own guidelines to be used to determine whether a particular contractual arrangement constitutes a conditional sales contract or a tax lease. Revenue Ruling 55-540 states that whether an agreement, which in form is a lease, is in substance a conditional sales contract depends upon the intent of the parties as evidenced by the provisions of the agreement, read in light of the particular facts and circumstances existing at the time the agreement was executed—intent is in no sense subjective as used here.

In 1984, in the Congressional Record of the House, in the "Joint Explanatory State of the Committee of Conference" Congress stated that:

"… tax rules generally are not written in the Internal Revenue Code. Instead they evolved over the years through a series of court cases and revenue rulings and revenue procedures issues by the Internal Revenue Service."

Additionally, the reader should take note that the *burden of proof* lies with the taxpayer, i.e., the lessor or lessee, to prove that the transaction is a tax lease. The IRS need only object and does not have to prove it is not a tax lease.

While the IRS does not provide explicit rules, the following guidelines can be utilized in evaluating the lessor's tax classification in a lease transaction. Generally speaking, to be considered a tax lease, a transaction should *not*:

- Pass title to the lessee at the end of the lease term for no additional consideration. If title passes at the end of the lease term, the lessee is considered to have an ownership interest, and the transaction would be considered a conditional sale, allowing the lessee the tax benefits of ownership.

- Contain a bargain purchase or renewal option. In order to be considered a true tax lease, the agreement should include a purchase option that approximates the reasonably predictable fair market value of the asset at the end of the lease term, taking into account the intended use of the equipment.
- Cover a lease term substantially equivalent to the useful life of the asset. The IRS contends that if the lease term approximates the economic useful life of the equipment, then the lessor has not retained any significant interest in the asset.
- Be entered into solely for tax avoidance motives. The IRS requires that a transaction have a legitimate business purpose. In other words, the lessor must realize a profit in the transaction, independent of the tax benefits; the transaction must have "economic substance."
- Minimize the lessor investment in the transaction. The IRS attempts to ensure that the lessor has something to lose if the residual value is not realized. If the lessor does not suffer any loss, if a residual value is not realized, the substance of the transaction would be more reflective of a conditional sales contract. This does not mean the lessor must assume a residual, which is supported by later tax cases that used the useful life test to support lessor investment in the lease.

If the transaction is in substance a sale and not a tax lease, the lessor will recognize interest income to the extent the total lease payments exceed the equipment cost, as it is not entitled to the tax benefits of ownership. The interest income is amortized over the lease term, with each lease payment allocated between return of principal and interest income.

What is the proper treatment of a tax lease? A tax lease is treated for tax purposes much the same as an operating lease for book purposes; rental payments are recognized as income and the leased assets are capitalized and depreciated. The difference between book and tax treatment, however, is that IRS depreciation methods, rates, and asset lives must be utilized for tax purposes.

Since Revenue Ruling 55-540 defined a contract of sale and did not include attributes of a lease, the IRS issued Revenue Procedure 2001-28. It provides that "for advance ruling purposes only," the IRS will consider the lessor to be the owner of the property if all of the factors in the procedure are met including the following:

- Risk: The lessor must maintain a minimum unconditional at-risk equity investment in the property (at least 20 percent of the cost of the equipment) during the entire lease term.
- Right to Buy: The lessee may not have a contractual right to buy the property from the lessor at less than fair market value when the right is exercised.
- Investment: The lessee may not invest in the property.
- Loans: The lessee may not lend any money to the lessor to buy the property or guaranty the loan used by the lessor to buy the property.

- Profit: The lessor must show that it expects to receive a profit apart from the tax deductions, allowances, credits, and other tax attributes.

Failure to meet the guidelines of Revenue Procedure 2001-28 does not necessarily mean the transaction is not a lease for federal income tax purposes. In fact, it states, "These guidelines do not define, as a matter of law, whether a transaction is or is not a lease for federal income tax purposes and are not intended to be used for audit purposes."

Failing to meet the requirements set forth in Revenue Ruling 55-540 and Revenue Procedure 2001-28 may render a transaction to be deemed a "mere financing." The contract may be labeled variously as a conditional sale contract, a capital lease, a finance lease, a lease intended as security, money over money transaction, a purchase money security agreement, or a loan or a non-tax lease. Whatever its designation, the IRS does not consider it to be a lease for tax purposes, and the lessor is therefore deemed a creditor and not entitled to the tax benefits of ownership.

For more detail on the revenue rulings and procedures discussed here, see the toolbox page of the CLFP Foundation website (www.clfpfoundation.org).

Modified Accelerated Cost Recovery System (MACRS)

The Tax Reform Act of 1986 enacted the Modified Accelerated Cost Recovery System (MACRS) as the predominant method for tax basis depreciation for assets placed in service after January 1, 1987. (Other available options include utilizing the MACRS 150 percent declining balance method, straight-line basis over the MACRS asset life or the Alternative Depreciation System.) MACRS provides eight depreciation categories, six for personal property and two for real property. Personal property cost recovery categories include 3, 5, 7, 10, 15 and 20-year classes.

The basis for 3, 5, 7 and 10-year categories is 200 percent declining balance, and the basis for 15- and 20-year categories is 150 percent declining balance. Each method utilizes a switch to straight-line at the point that straight-line depreciation maximizes the current deduction. Further, one-half year of depreciation is recognized in the year of acquisition (the half-year convention), so an asset qualifying in the five-year MACRS category is depreciated over a six-year period (A link to sample depreciation tables may be found on CLFP Toolbox page of the CLFP Foundation website). One-half year of depreciation also is allowed in the year of disposition, should disposition take place prior to an asset being fully depreciated for tax purposes.

The 200 percent declining balance depreciation for a five-year asset is calculated as follows:
First, straight-line depreciation is calculated as the asset cost divided by the life of five years, for a straight-line rate of 20 percent. This 20 percent is doubled to provide for the "double declining" basis of MACRS depreciation resulting in a depreciation rate of 40 percent, which is applied to the undepreciated asset balance each year except the first and last year.

One-half of a year's depreciation is taken in the year of acquisition and disposition.

First year	40% x ½ first year depreciation	**20%**
Second year	40% x 80% undepreciated balance (100% less first year's 20%)	**32%**
Third year	40% x 48%	**19.2%**
Fourth year	40% x 28.8%	**11.52%**
Fifth year	40% x 17.28, or 6.91% double declining depreciation, or 11.52% straight-line (17.28/1.5 years remaining)	**11.52%**
Sixth year	straight-line of 11.52% x ½ year	**5.76%**

If more than 40 percent of assets are acquired in the fourth quarter of the company's tax year, the mid-quarter convention must be utilized. The effect of the mid-quarter convention is to limit the present value benefit of the tax depreciation.

Bonus depreciation, originally put in place by the Job Creation and Worker Assistance Act of 2002, provides lessors with additional tax benefits through increased acceleration of depreciation deductions. The bonus depreciation rules allow an up-front depreciation deduction in the year of purchase, followed by the application of MACRS depreciation on the asset cost adjusted by the bonus depreciation deduction. The bonus depreciation percentage has ranged anywhere from 30 percent to 100 percent over the years. Unlike Section 179, which applies to new or used assets, bonus depreciation only applied to new asset purchases.

As an example, the 50 percent bonus depreciation allowed in 2017 would be calculated as follows for five-year property with a cost of $200,000:

- $200,000 x 50 percent = $100,000 bonus depreciation
- $200,000 - $100,000 = $100,000 basis for MACRS deprecation
- $100,000 x 20 percent first year MACRS rate = $20,000

Total first year depreciation = $100,000 + $20,000 = $120,000, in effect, effectively creating a 60 percent deduction in year one.

The Tax Cuts and Job Act of 2017 allows bonus depreciation of 100 percent, effective September 27, 2017, and also designates used equipment as eligible for bonus treatment. Under the 100% bonus depreciation rules, the entire cost of the asset may be expensed as depreciation in the year it is acquired.

Depending on the type of equipment and the lease term, utilizing non-bonus IRS depreciation rules may present both opportunities and challenges to the lessor. For example, most personal computer leases do not exceed thirty-six months in duration, yet the IRS normally requires computers to be depreciated over a five-year period. For a thirty-six-month computer lease with a 10 percent residual, a lessor realizes 100 percent of rental payments as income over thirty-six months, but at the end of the thirty-six months, may only have deducted 71.2 percent of the asset cost as depreciation. At the end of the lease term, the lessor will recognize a loss on the sale of this asset when its remaining 28.8 percent of tax basis is sold for the 10 percent residual amount. In this example, the lessor is taxed on income in the early years of the lease in excess of the income that will be realized over the entire lease and then realizes a loss on the sale of the equipment at the end of the lease term.

Section 179

In addition to MACRS depreciation, the IRS offers other incentives for accelerating the deductions related to equipment purchases, namely Section 179.

Section 179, like 100% bonus depreciation under MACRS, allows a company to immediately deduct 100% of the cost of an asset in the year of acquisition. The Section 179 deduction is allowed on both new and used equipment. Intended to provide a benefit for small business, the provision is phased out after a certain amount of total asset acquisitions during the year.

In the past several years, the amount of equipment eligible for immediate deduction under Section 179 was significant. For example, in 2017, the Section 179 deduction was $500,000 and began phasing out $1 for $1 after $2 million of total asset acquisitions. This trend continued with the Tax Cuts and Job Act of 2017, under which the Section 179 deduction was increased to $1 million for the tax year 2018, with the benefit phased out $1 for $1 by the time total asset purchases exceed $2.5 million.

Alternative Minimum Tax (AMT)

There existed essentially two parallel universes of taxation under prior tax law - the regular tax law with a series of deductions for businesses and the alternative minimum tax rules. The AMT was enacted to make sure that every entity paid its fair share of taxes and was applicable to both individuals and businesses. The thought was that some taxpayers could utilize tax deductions under the regular tax law to the point where they were paying little to nothing in taxes. AMT utilizes a calculation that differs slightly from the regular calculation to ensure that some level of taxes (the minimum) is paid.

The Tax Cuts and Job Act did away with the AMT and provided a timeline for recovery of AMT credits held as of December 31, 2017. Under this phase-out, any AMT credit available in 2020 is eligible for a 50% refund, while any remaining AMT credit is eligible for a 100% refund in 2021.

Net Interest Limitation

The Tax Cuts and Jobs Act of 2017 created a new concept that limits the amount of interest a business can deduct in its tax return. Under this provision of the tax code, the deduction for interest expense is limited to the sum of (1) the taxpayer's business interest income, (2) 30 percent of its adjusted taxable income and (3) any floor planning interest.

Any interest expense disallowed as a current deduction is carried forward indefinitely. Adjusted taxable income (ATI) is basically an EBITDA calculation, except on a tax basis, so it is taxable income computed without regard to business interest or business interest income, Net Operating Losses

(NOLs), and deductions for depreciation, amortization, or depletion. Table 6 illustrates the lessor's calculation of its adjusted taxable income for purposes of determining the interest expense limitation.

Table 6 Adjusted Taxable Income Calculation

Adjusted Taxable Income Calculation	
Rent	5,047,928
S, G, &A	(2,248,470)
Other income	2,019,171
Adjusted taxable income (A)	4,818,629

Table 7 shows that the lessor's interest expense in this example is fully deductible, even in this extreme case in which the lessor does not have any interest income.

Table 7 Interest Expense Limit Calculation

Interest Expense Limit Calculation	
Business interest income	0
ATI add back (30% x A)	1,445,589
Floor plan financing interest	0
Interest expense limit	1,445,589
Actual interest expense	(1,338,340)
Nondeductible interest	-

The impact of this tax provision on lessees is that the cost of buying equipment may go up relative to the cost of leasing because of the lessees' inability to deduct interest payments under the net interest rules.

Sales and Personal Property Tax

Equipment leasing and finance companies are subject to the sales and personal property tax requirements of the jurisdictions of their equipment location. As most lessors hold assets in multiple states, reporting requirements may be cumbersome. The variety of sales and personal property tax rules and rates mandated by each state further complicates the compliance burden.

Sales Tax

Some lessors believe that if a lease is a net lease, or if their lease agreement indicates such, that remittance of the appropriate sales or property tax is the lessee's responsibility. While these companies may be successful in delegating responsibility for these filings to their lessees, most governmental agencies do not agree with the assignment of this burden and maintain that the lessor is ultimately responsible for the tax liabilities. Lessors following this practice should be aware of the tax liabilities that may await them if their lessees do not meet their tax filing and payment responsibilities. As owner of the equipment, the lessor will be held financially responsible.

The concept of sales tax is simple — withhold and remit the appropriate amount of tax — but the actual assessment of the tax is not as simple. For sales tax filings, states may require monthly, quarterly, semi-annual, or annual filings, dependent upon the company's filing history with the state or the amount of sales tax liability customarily incurred. Some states require tax to be paid on certain types of lease transactions up front, while others require sales tax to be collected and remitted over the lease term.

States may charge use or rental tax instead of sales tax for specific lease financing transactions. Localities within a state, such as counties, cities, or parishes, may tack on an additional tax amount, which may or may not require supplemental filings. Some states may assess sales tax on personal property taxes invoiced to a lessee, and a select few states do not assess sales tax at all.

Certain types of equipment may be exempt from sales tax within a state or within designated areas of a state. The lessee also may be sales tax-exempt, but if the lessee is leasing the equipment and does not own it, occasionally the lease still may be subject to sales tax.

Exemption Certificate

When a lessor purchases equipment to be leased, it generally does not have to pay sales tax on the purchase, as it is purchased for resale. In these instances, the lessor files an exemption certificate with the taxing authority. Other examples in which the lessor may file an exemption certificate occur when certain assets, such as manufacturing equipment, are statutorily exempted from tax in that jurisdiction.

Typically, a lessor provides a resale exemption certificate to the vendor (which is normally obtained when the lessor registers to do business in a state) and, by doing so, takes the responsibility for sales tax collection and remittance. Valid exemption certificates may allow the lessee to be exempt, but the lessor should take due care to maintain documentation and verify the validity of any exemption certificate, whether it applies to resale, type of entity, or equipment use.

Personal Property Tax

A majority of states assess personal property tax on assets held as of a specific date, referred to as the assessment date. Personal property tax renditions are typically filed annually at the county level. Personal property, and in most cases the soft costs associated with it (e.g., delivery, installation, etc.), are subject to tax if the item is located within the state on the state's assessment date, regardless of how long it has been at or remains in that particular location. For example, a lessor holds equipment on a lease in California with an assessment date of December 31, 20X1. On March 25, 20X2, the lessee purchased the equipment. As owner of the equipment on the assessment date, the lessor is responsible for filing and payment of 20X1 personal property taxes. To avoid being left with the personal property tax liability for property sold during the year, the lessor needs to remember to include an estimate of the personal property tax amount in the payoff calculation.

Personal property tax filing and payment is a multi-step process.

1. First, file a personal property tax rendition in the taxing jurisdiction of the equipment location. The rendition reports the type, cost, purchase date, and location of the equipment.
2. The taxing jurisdiction responds by sending the leasing company an assessment notice, which indicates the value on which the asset is taxed. Most states adjust the asset cost for items such as depreciation and/or inflation to arrive at the assessed value. The leasing company has a specified period to protest the assessment if they feel the asset is incorrectly valued.
3. Once this period has expired, the taxing jurisdiction determines the tax rate applicable for that year and issues a bill, allowing a period to pay the tax before assessing penalties and interest on the amount due. Most leasing companies use that time to invoice and collect payment from the lessee. By the time the tax is paid, enough time has passed that it is usually time to start the process again!

Like sales tax, personal property tax rules vary from state to state. States have a variety of assessment dates, filing dates, equipment exemptions, assessment methods, and tax rates. Additionally, in some states, personal property taxes collected from a lessee are considered a form of rental payment, subject to the same sales tax treatment as the regular lease payments.

Lessee Exemption

Certain entities may be exempt from personal property tax. In most jurisdictions, government and nonprofit entities typically are exempt from paying taxes on the property they own. A lessor that owns property that is leased to such entities, however, generally is not exempt and, therefore, must still pay the property taxes.

In consideration of the complexities of sales and personal property tax filing requirements, many leasing companies find that employing professionals knowledgeable with the various states tax rules and filing requirements, or outsourcing this function, is a good investment.

Leasing companies are in the unique position of managing both financial statement and tax treatment of income by the proper structuring of lease transactions. To do so, however, it is imperative that such companies understand the intricacies of the accounting and tax rules related to lease accounting. Ever changing tax rules, like bonus depreciation provisions, can have a significant impact on leasing companies and these provisions are a perfect example of why it is crucial for leasing professionals to stay current with tax changes.

Summary

Accounting and taxation permeate all aspects of the equipment leasing and finance industry. Each has an integral role to play in the design of a leasing transaction and the effect on its parties. A leasing professional's understanding of both the tax and accounting consequences and treatment of a lease is of primary importance. By applying knowledge of this area, leasing professionals can perform at advantageous levels in their careers

Chapter 3 – Leasing Law

A well-rounded understanding of leasing requires an understanding of the basics of law as it applies to equipment finance. The intent of this chapter is not to provide a comprehensive instruction in law, rather, to point out the legal considerations that are crucial for a foundational understanding of leasing and equipment finance. This foundational understanding of law sets the table so to speak for understanding lease documentation and collections requirements later in this book.

Note that, unless otherwise stated, this chapter will often include equipment leasing within the term "equipment finance." We will also use the term "secured financing" to mean a loan secured by a security interest in the financed equipment. Often a secured financing is in the form of a "lease intended as security," meaning a "lease" that is legally considered a secured financing because of its economic substance. Other names for such a "lease" include "buck-out," "security," "conditional sale," "dirty," "not-true," or "financing" lease. The term "finance lease" is still used for a secured financing but it should never be used in this way because the UCC now uses "finance lease" to mean something entirely different.

Learning goals for this chapter:

- Understand the different sources of law (federal and state law, statutory, regulatory and case law), how they interact and how they may affect equipment finance.
- Understand generally those sections of the Uniform Commercial Code that apply to equipment finance, including those relating to financing statements and perfection of security interests.
- Understand the difference between true lease and a lease intended as security, and the meanings of each term.
- Understand why it is important to know the difference between various types of businesses, such as corporations and limited liability companies, and how to deal with each as a borrower or lessee.
- Understand the fundamentals of bankruptcy law, types of bankruptcy, and applicability for leasing and equipment finance.

Equipment finance as a means for the acquisition and financing of goods is a vital component of both American and global economies. The explosion of activity in the industry since the 1980s has prompted a variety of legislative responses as lease financing transactions (and the relevant legal responses) have become increasingly complex.

In the context of the BOK framework, this chapter is considered one of the "Foundational Concepts."

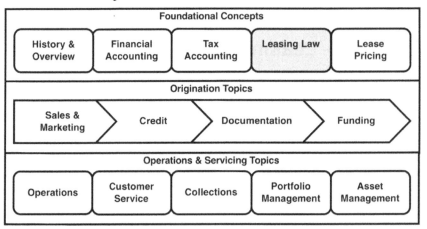

Figure 13 CLFP BOK Framework Coverage

The following information is intended to provide a general overview of the legal issues involved in leasing personal property for use in business. Readers are advised to consult an attorney to determine the applicability and to obtain clarification when confronting specific problems. This text does not offer legal advice and is not a substitute for consultation with a licensed attorney-at-law.

Basis for U.S. Leasing Law

There are many types of U.S. law originating from the following sources.

Table 8 Sources of U.S. Law

Statutory Law	• Statutory law includes law enacted by legislative bodies such as state legislatures and the U.S. Congress. • The Uniform Commercial Code or UCC is a body of state statutory laws adopted in whole or part by all 50 states and the District of Columbia, sometimes with important variations.
Case Law	• Case Law is a matter of "precedents," which are cases that apply the statutory law or the results of prior cases to particular sets of facts. • The type of law created by applying these precedents is called "common law." • Many cases interpret the UCC and other state and federal statutory laws, and such cases are essential to understanding the meaning of statutory law. Additionally, cases articulating the common law may resolve questions not addressed explicitly by the UCC or other statutes.

Regulatory Law	<ul><li>Regulatory law consists of regulations adopted by state and federal government regulatory agencies.</li><li>Examples: regulations issued by the IRS or the SEC.</li><li>Regulatory laws are not binding upon the courts in the manner of statutory laws and may be subject to a judge's interpretation. They can, however, influence the outcome of a court case and represent statements of policy that are often binding on the issuing agencies.</li></ul>

The two categories of statutory law are federal law and state law. Federal laws are those adopted or otherwise created by Congress, the federal courts and federal regulatory agencies, and state laws are those laws adopted or created by state legislatures, courts and regulatory agencies.

Table 9 Federal and State Law

	Federal Law	State Law
What are some examples?	The Internal Revenue Code, The Bankruptcy Code, and federal court cases interpreting or applying them.	The UCC and state tax laws (sales, use, and rental taxes and property taxes), together with state court cases interpreting or applying them.
How does it apply to leasing and equipment finance?	Although federal case precedents may be necessary for interpreting federal statutory laws, federal common law has little application to equipment finance transactions.	State law is more relevant to day-to-day equipment finance operations. It is important to remember that federal courts, such as bankruptcy courts, will often look to state law for answers to certain questions, such as whether a transaction is a lease or a secured financing and whether an injured person can sue a lessor.

General Principles of Contract Law

Contract law is generally a matter of state law. Although specific statutes (principally the UCC, discussed below) are essential to contract enforcement or interpretation, case law plays a significant role in each state.

Requirements for a valid, enforceable contract include an offer and acceptance evidencing a mutual agreement on principal terms and consideration, or something of value, given or promised by each party. In some cases, actions of the parties may be sufficient indication of this mutual agreement. Past dealings between the parties and general practice in a given industry may also indicate a mutual agreement, despite the absence of a clear offer and acceptance as to various terms.

Capacity is also required, meaning that each of the parties must be legally able to enter into the contract and naturally includes prohibitions on contracts by minors and incompetents, as well as contracts by corporations and other entities that have not acted correctly within legal requirements. Of particular concern are lease agreements by municipalities and other public bodies, and leases by corporations that have not authorized the contract by appropriate Board of Directors' actions.

Legality is a requirement often used to prohibit enforcement of secured financings that exceed the legal usury limit, but also available to prevent leases of equipment used in illegal activities, such as gambling where not permissible by applicable law.

Statute of Frauds: the law provides that certain types of contracts are not enforceable unless in writing. This is not merely the so-called "parole evidence rule," under which oral statements may not be used to modify certain writings or are treated as poor evidence of the parties' intent. Rather, it is an absolute prohibition on the enforcement of unwritten contracts.

Under UCC Article 2A-201 a lease contract involving payments over $1,000 (excluding renewals and options) is unenforceable unless in writing. Some states have similar laws concerning other types of contracts, including guarantees of performance by other parties.

The Uniform Commercial Code

An example of state statutory law, the UCC plays an important role in equipment finance.

The UCC is a comprehensive body of model (suggested) statutory laws, including many laws addressing key aspects of commercial transactions. Most of the UCC, including virtually all of the provisions applicable to equipment finance, have been adopted by all 50 states and the District of Columbia, as well as Puerto Rico and the U. S. Virgin Islands, although many states have adopted different versions of certain UCC provisions, or have altered the language. Each state adopting the UCC incorporates it into the state's own statutory system, so that the state law citation might be "Section 11-2A-103" or "Section 2-A-103" instead of "Section 2A-103."

The UCC includes three articles that are crucial, three of which, to equipment finance, include the legal distinction between a true lease and a lease intended as security for state law purposes.

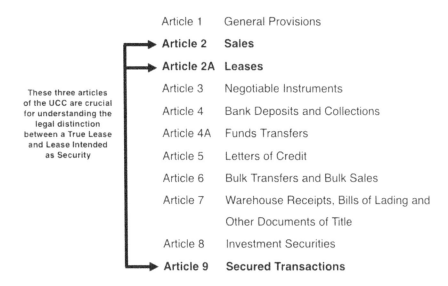

Figure 14 Articles of UCC Pertaining to Equipment Finance

It is important to have a basic understanding of the following three articles of the UCC.

- **UCC Article 2** deals with the sale of movable property (called "goods" in the UCC).
- **UCC Article 9** deals with secured transactions, including loans secured by goods as collateral and leases intended as security, and is generally not applicable to true leases.
- **UCC Article 2A** deals with true leases.

The term "Conflicts of Law" refers to inconsistencies in laws from state to state. For example, the UCC is not uniform across all fifty states. Because state laws are not consistent (even though all fifty states have adopted some version of the UCC), the concept of conflicts of law often comes into play. Under this concept, a court chooses to apply the law of one state over that of another. The purpose of the UCC is to reduce conflicts of law by presenting uniform laws to the states.

"Choice of law" refers to a voluntary choice of the law of one state to apply to a contract for certainty and to avoid having a judge make a conflicts of law decision. The choice of law can be very important because some state laws favor lessor or lessee. The right to choose which state's law applies to a given lease or other contract has its limitations. One is that the laws of most states require the contract or parties to bear some relationship to the chosen state. For example, a lessor whose principal place of business is in Georgia could choose Georgia law under its lease documentation, even though the transaction is with a lessee located in Texas. On the other hand, a lessor based in New Jersey and doing business with a Texas lessee could not ordinarily choose Georgia law (although the laws of some states now permit just such flexibility).

Courts sometimes refuse to apply a choice of law provision where the application would result in violation of strong public policy. An example of this sort of analysis would be a lease, which is a secured financing arrangement and involves an interest rate significantly more than the usury limit permitted by the state in which the lessee's principal place of business is located.

Choice of law is not the same as "Choice of Forum," often called "Forum Selection" or "Consent to Jurisdiction." These terms refer to a provision in a contract allowing (or requiring) litigation between the parties to be situated in courts located in a specified state and/or county. Choosing a convenient location for any lawsuit can save a lender or lessor a great deal of money, avoid travel and delay and place the litigation before a judge likely to uphold a choice of law provision allowing them to apply the laws of their own state.

Legal Definition of a Lease

It is essential to distinguish between the legal definition of a lease primarily used for state law purposes and those definitions that exist for federal (and sometimes state) tax law and accounting purposes. While there is substantial overlap, each involves its specific analysis and rules.

For UCC and state law purposes, the general definition of a lease is found in Section 2A-103, but the more important definition is in Section 1-203, in which a lease is distinguished from a security interest. Section 1-203 is the section likely to be applied by a judge when determining whether a transaction labeled a lease by the parties is actually a lease intended as security creating a security interest.

Briefly, UCC Section 1-203 provides that a transaction always creates a security interest and is not a lease if **the lessee cannot terminate the lease** (without paying off the lease) **and**

(1) **the lease term equals or exceeds the equipment's economic life**, which means the time during which the equipment will have value, **or**

(2) at the end of the lease term, **the lessee is required to buy the equipment or has the option to buy it for a nominal (insignificant) amount or automatically owns the equipment, or**

(3) at the end of the lease term, **the lessee is required to renew the lease or has the option to renew it for a nominal (insignificant) amount, if the renewal will cause the lease term to equal or exceed the equipment's economic life**.

These rules boil down to something simple: if the lessee has all the benefits and risks of ownership and the lessor has no realistic residual value risk or benefit, the transaction is the same as a loan for all practical and economic purposes.

Example 1: You lease a computer, which will be worthless except for scrap value, after 10 years, to a lessee for 25 years. The lessee has all the benefits of ownership, there is nothing for you except rent. How is this different from a sale with a 25-year payout of principal and interest? (Note: The UCC assumes you are getting payment in full, with interest, of the purchase price of the equipment in all these examples, or you are making a deal that makes no sense).

Example 2: You lease the same computer for only three years, but the lessee has the option to buy it for $1 at the end of the lease, or the lessee must buy it for any amount. Again, how is this different from a loan, perhaps a loan with a mandatory balloon payment at the end?

Example 3: You lease the same computer for only three years, but the lessee is required to renew the lease for another seven years or has the option to renew the lease for another seven years for $1.

These are not the only evidence that a transaction creates a secured financing rather than a lease. It is also important to note that Section 1-203, unlike earlier UCC sections, does not mention the parties' "intent." The economic substance of a deal, not its form or what the parties think they are doing, is what governs whether the transaction creates a lease.

Section 1-203 goes on to say that other criteria used by judges and commentators over the years to distinguish leases from secured financings may be relevant but are not automatically determinative. For example, a transaction does not fail to be a lease merely because a lease is a full-payout lease (where the lessee is paying 100 percent of the purchase price of the equipment with interest over the term as rent). There must be some other indication that the transaction is a secured financing, such as one of those listed above.

These distinctions are crucial to the legal treatment of a transaction as a lease or secured financing, which may be the most important issue in any dispute. Among other things, this distinction can determine whether the lessee or lessor owns the equipment, whether a third party's claim against the equipment is superior to the lessor's, and whether a defaulting lessee can continue to use the equipment after filing for reorganization in bankruptcy court without curing defaults.

UCC Article 2: Sale of Goods

Introduced in the early 1960s, the oldest article of the UCC, Article 2 deals exclusively with the sales of goods, which are generally defined as tangible personal property (as opposed to real estate or intangible property, such as securities and promissory notes).

Article 2 comes into play where a lessor may be deemed a vendor or "supplier" under a secured financing, as opposed to a lessor under a lease. Article 2 also affects transactions between the supplier and the lessor as buyer, or between the supplier and the borrower as buyer. Article 2 is the source of "implied warranties," under which a merchant who sells goods (in this case the lessor) is deemed to warrant that they are fit for ordinary purposes, in overall good condition, and fit for the particular use the lessee/buyer contemplates.

Implied warranties may be excluded by a conspicuous disclaimer stating that the lessor does not make the implied warranties. In a UCC finance lease (discussed below), the lessor is not charged with making implied warranties, whether or not it disclaims them in the lease. Note: the law also recognizes "express warranties," which are affirmative representations regarding the equipment made by a party. If such statements are made, the UCC disclaimer may not effectively nullify them.

UCC Article 9: Secured Transactions

Article 9 of the UCC deals exclusively with the creation of security interests in personal property. As such, Article 9 does not have any direct effect on true lease transactions; it is important only for secured financings. Article 9 sets up a system, not unlike the state mortgage recording system for real property, in which a lender taking a security interest in personal property may file a financing statement (designated a UCC-1 financing statement).

Financing Statements

A financing statement contains key information that lenders considering advancing credit to a borrower should know to avoid confusion as to the original lender's security interest. This information includes the name and address of lender and debtor, and a description of the equipment.

Financing statements for most types of equipment are filed with the Secretary of State where the lessee was incorporated (if a corporation) or organized (if a partnership or limited liability company). In some cases, however, financing statements must be locally recorded with real estate records. In particular, a local real estate filing is required for equipment affixed to real estate (a "fixture").

Filing a financing statement for a secured financing causes the lender's security interest to be "perfected" for that equipment, meaning that its interest usually takes priority over those of other creditors who filed financing statements later and a trustee in bankruptcy. Without such a filing, or if the filing is improperly made, the lender may be treated as an unsecured creditor.

As a general rule, the first lender to file a financing statement wins if there is a dispute because more than one security interest is claimed in financed equipment. There are several exceptions, most notably purchase money security interests (discussed below). Bear in mind that none of this affects the ownership of a lessor in a true lease, as opposed a lease intended as security.

A key issue is where to file a financing statement. In the case of a corporation, LLC, limited partnership, or other entity created by filing with a state (discussed below), that state's Secretary of State maintains the UCC records. Filing should be there, regardless of where the equipment is being used or where the borrower's offices are located. If an individual (sole proprietor) is the borrower, the individual's state of residence is the place to file. If a general partnership other entity that is not formed by a filing with a specific state is the borrower, the sole or principal place of business is where to file.

In any event, the name of the "debtor" (borrower) on the UCC financing statement must be perfectly correct if the lender is to be safe. Only filing in the exact legal name of the debtor is certain to perfect the lender's interest;

anything else can be ineffective if the state's computerized records system does not pick up the error. Omitting an individual's middle initial, using "Corp" instead of "Corporation" (or vice versa), and any use of a trade name (dba) have resulted in loss of perfection. In some states, a driver's license is sufficient proof of the correct name for filing against an individual, but use of only the trade or business name for a person or entity whose legal name is different renders a filing ineffective.

Security Interest

A "**security interest**" refers to the interest granted to the lender/lessor and is analogous to a lien or other encumbrance. A transaction in which a secured party extends credit to a debtor and takes a security interest in personal property is called a "secured transaction" for UCC purposes.

Purchase Money Security Interest (PMSI)

There is an exception to the general UCC rule of first-to-file-wins for **purchase money security interests (PMSIs),** which are advances to finance the lessee/borrower's acquisition of the equipment (as opposed to sale leasebacks). A PMSI is given a grace period, usually twenty days under state law, to file a financing statement.

This is important because many banks and other lenders file financing statements that attempt to perfect interests in property the borrower will acquire in the future ("after-acquired property"). A properly filed PMSI takes priority over these older financing statements, but if the PMSI financing statement is not filed in time, or if the funds advanced by the lender do not actually enable the borrower to acquire the equipment, the lender's interest will not qualify for PMSI protection and the security interest perfected by the earlier-filed financing statement will have priority. For this reason, if a lender will not have PMSI protection, or if a lessor is buying equipment from its lessee and leasing it back to the lessee, it is highly advisable to search the UCC records before funding.

Again, this analysis only applies to secured loan financings, but it is generally a good idea to file a financing statement within the statutory period for any lease-type financing.

Key points for UCC Article 9

1. **Article 9 does not apply to true leases and it is not necessary to file a financing statement for a true lease**. However, it is a good idea to do so in most instances because anyone checking the lessee's credit will be informed of the lessor's ownership of the equipment and the filing may avoid an examination of whether the lease is actually a secured financing in case of bankruptcy or a claim by another creditor.

2. **The UCC does not cover all types of claims and equipment.** The UCC does not apply to interests in aircraft, vessels, and certain other types of property. Financing statements are not used to perfect interests in motor vehicles and other properties covered by certificates of title, unless such items are held as inventory

3. **File in the lessee's state of organization**. The UCC-1 financing statement should be filed in the state where the lessee is incorporated.

4. **UCC Article 9 terminology** includes the use of the term "secured party" for the lender (or lessor under a secured financing-type lease) and "debtor" for the borrower (or lessee under a secured financing-type lease).

UCC Article 2A: True Leases

Introduced in the 1980s, just as Article 9 deals only with secured financings, Article 2A deals only with true leases and not secured financings.

Article 2A is modeled on Articles 2 and 9. Article 2A includes implied warranties virtually identical to those provided under Article 2. As with Article 2, Article 2A permits the lessee to waive implied warranties through a conspicuous disclaimer, which should be included in any well-drafted lease document.

Because true leases are governed by Article 2A and not Article 9, it is not necessary to file a financing statement for a true lease; there is no "security interest" to protect. Most lessors, however, file financing statements for true leases for a couple reasons:

1. In case the lease is held by a court not to be a true lease.
2. To give others actual notice that a lease exists and avoid confusion.

Article 2A introduces the term "finance lease," a true lease in which:

- The lessor is not the manufacturer or supplier of the leased personal property.
- The lessor does not select the equipment or lease it from an inventory of like items.
- The lessor makes sure that the lessee is aware of its rights against the supplier concerning warranties.

Finance lease designation is very important to the lessor for several reasons, including:

1. All warranties provided by the supplier are automatically deemed assigned to the lessee, but the lessor is specifically absolved of any responsibility with respect to equipment malfunction or failure to meet the lessee's expectations. This means the lessor does not make any implied warranties regarding the equipment.
2. The "Hell-or-High-Water" clause found in any well-drafted lease is automatically made a part of the lease and legally enforceable, meaning that the lessee must make rental payments for the equipment irrespective of any claim it may have against the lessor and without setoff.

Contrasting the True Lease and Lease Intended as Security

Leases and leases intended as security differ in many respects, but there are also many similarities. The table below illustrates some of their *similarities (shown in italic text)* and differences.

Table 10 True Lease Vs. Lease Intended as Security

	True Lease	**Lease Intended as Security**
Distinctions in Bankruptcy	• *Lessor not permitted to ignore the bankruptcy altogether and recover the equipment or sue for damages* • Lessor has better rights to recover equipment in event of lessee default because lessee must cure defaults to keep lease in place • Lessee cannot pursue a "cramdown" plan	• *Lender not permitted to ignore the bankruptcy altogether and recover the equipment or sue for damages* • Borrower may force a "cramdown" in which the reorganization plan will limit the lender's recovery to the fair market value of the collateral – not the agreed upon loan repayment
Interest/Usury	• Rent includes an interest factor rather than charging a separate interest amount • Usury laws do not apply in most states • Lessee pays all or a significant portion of the cost of the equipment to the lessor together with an implicit interest factor or "rent factor"	• Because interest is charged, payments may be subject to state usury limitations
Collateral	• Inappropriate to refer to leased equipment as collateral • *Lessee required to maintain equipment in good repair*	• Appropriate to refer to financed equipment as collateral. • *Borrower required to maintain the equipment in good repair*

	True Lease	Lease Intended as Security
Liability of Lessee and Lessor	• More exposure to the lessor for liability to third parties caused by faulty or improperly maintained equipment	• Less exposure to the lender for liability to third parties caused by faulty or improperly maintained equipment
UCC Rights	• Governed by UCC Article 2A • Lessor owns the equipment	• Governed by UCC Article 9 • Lender has security interest in the equipment
Perfecting Security Interests in Different Types of Collateral	• Lessor is not required to file a UCC-1 financing statement for a true lease • Motor vehicles, aircraft, and other titled equipment leases require that the lessor be shown as the owner on titles and similar documentation	• Lender should file a UCC-1 financing statement for secured loan • Motor vehicle financings require notations on certificates of title and similar documentation to indicate the lender's interest
Residual	• A lessor in a lease expects a profit from the combination of a portion of the rents and residual value	• A lender (even if called "lessor" in the documents) looks only to the interest (or interest factor in the "rent") during the term

Bankruptcy Law

Federal bankruptcy law is one of the least understood and most important areas of the law pertaining to this industry. There are different types of bankruptcies typically referred to by their respective chapters in the U.S. Bankruptcy Code. The Federal Rules of Bankruptcy Procedure are the rules governing how bankruptcy courts operate.

Chapters of U.S. Bankruptcy Code[10]

Bankruptcy Chapter	Description
Chapter 7	Individual or businesses entities may file Chapter 7 to liquidate; that is the entity will stop doing business, and its assets will be sold to pay its creditors
Chapter 9	Cities, towns, villages, taxing districts, municipal utilities, and school districts may file Chapter 9 to reorganize.
Chapter 11	Reorganizations. Businesses may file Chapter 11 to reorganize, a proceeding in which the debtor (usually a corporation) has a hope of continuing to do business and returning to profitability. A Chapter 11 debtor may propose a "Plan of Reorganization" that provides for liquidation of the business.
Chapter 12	Provides debt relief to family farmers and debtors engaged in commercial fishing.
Chapter 13	Applicable to bankruptcies by individuals. Relevant to bankruptcies by guarantors and sole proprietors.
Chapter 15	Bankruptcy filings involving parties from more than one country.

Table 11 Bankruptcy Types (based on info from usbankruptcycode.org)

Individuals, corporations, and most other legal entities may file for bankruptcy protection to give them time to reorganize and restructure their debts. Bankruptcies may either be liquidating or reorganization.

A liquidating bankruptcy (a "Chapter 7") is one in which the entity will stop doing business, and its assets will be sold to pay its creditors. A "reorganization" (a "Chapter 11") is a proceeding in which the debtor (usually a corporation) has a hope of continuing to do business and returning to profitability. To confuse matters (and result in delay), however, a Chapter 11 debtor may propose a "Plan of Reorganization" that provides for liquidation of the business.

Before looking at these two chapters of bankruptcy, note that Chapter 9 of the U.S. Bankruptcy Code applies to reorganizations of government instrumentalities such as cities and counties, and Chapter 12 applies to certain "family farmers." Chapter 13 is the Bankruptcy Code chapter applicable to bankruptcies by individuals. This chapter is relevant to bankruptcies by guarantors and, in certain situations, businesses operated by sole proprietors (known by the fictitious name DBA). These proceedings require liquidation of most of the debtor's personal assets, but the debtor is usually permitted to retain his or her home and certain personal items.

Liquidating Bankruptcy or Reorganization

In a Chapter 7 bankruptcy, a trustee is appointed to liquidate the debtor's assets and pay its debts. In a Chapter 11 reorganization, the debtor generally

---

[10] source: https://www.usbankruptcycode.org

stays in control of its business and is called a debtor-in-possession for this purpose.

Voluntary and Involuntary Bankruptcy

Bankruptcies may be voluntary or involuntary, depending on whether the debtor seeks relief, or a group of its creditors places it in bankruptcy. In either event, the filing of a bankruptcy petition is the first step in the process.

Bankruptcy Procedures

Following the filing of the bankruptcy petition, the "**automatic stay**" goes into effect, prohibiting parties from taking action against the debtor or its assets other than through the bankruptcy court. Even if a lessor merely wants to repossess property it owns or a secured party wants to foreclose on assets in which it has a security interest, the bankruptcy court has the right to be involved. In order to obtain permission to take action, the lessor or secured party must file for relief from the automatic stay with the bankruptcy court.

The debtor-in-possession in a Chapter 11 proceeding must prepare a "**Plan of Reorganization**," which proposes to repay all or a portion of its debts according to a specified schedule.

Assumption/Rejection: The debtor is permitted to assume or reject "executory" contracts, including equipment leases, before confirmation of the Plan of Reorganization. Where equipment leases are concerned, a lease that is assumed will continue, but the lessee must remedy all defaults (paying back rent and reinstating lapsed insurance or maintenance arrangements), continue to make all payments, and render all performance in accordance with the terms of the lease. If a lease is rejected, the lessor is permitted to recover equipment and to make a claim for its back rent and other damages.

The same protection does not exist for secured loan financings; the debtor may wait several months before curing defaults and commencing to retire the debt unless the bankruptcy court, on motion of the creditor, orders that monthly payments be made. Defaults might not be cured until the Plan of Reorganization is approved.

Claims for back rent and other charges due before the petition date should be made on a Proof of Claim form supplied by the court on or before the "bar date" or deadline for filing claims. Because the bar date may precede the deadline for assuming or rejecting the lease, the lessor should make a practice of filing a timely proof of claim for any unpaid pre-petition charges.

Charges occurring between the petition date and rejection may be entitled to priority as an "administrative expense" claim and an application may be filed seeking payment. An additional claim for post-rejection damages (i.e., future rentals) may also be filed, but such a claim is treated as a general unsecured claim.

Preferences in Bankruptcy

Many lessors are concerned about "preferences," which are basically payments within ninety days prior to the filing of the bankruptcy petition (one year in case of payments made to the debtor's owners or those in control of its business). The theory is that a debtor's preference of one creditor over another is unfair. Such payments are required to be returned into the bankruptcy estate (the debtor's overall assets) for apportionment among the creditors.

A notable exception to the rule about preferences is that timely payments made in the ordinary course of business are not considered preferences. For this reason, regular rent payments made within ninety days prior to the petition in bankruptcy should not be deemed preferences. However, lessors may find themselves returning payments where they have permitted the lessee to fall behind and to catch up with a single payment, which can no longer be said to be an ordinary-course rent payment.

Legal Entities

Before doing an equipment finance transaction with any business or organization, it is essential to know the type of business entity that will be the lessee, borrower, guarantor, or otherwise involved. There are many instances where equipment finance professionals will use this knowledge; a few examples include the following:

- Business type is a fundamental element of the credit application, a driver of the financial and credit information required, and the level of analysis and due diligence conducted during underwriting.
- The rules for the accurate filing of the UCC financing statement pertain to the entity type. For example, one must file the UCC in the state of organization for a corporation, and for a sole proprietor, the legal name for the filing must match the valid driver's license in most states.
- Entity type plays a role in both the kind of documentation to be used and the requirements for authorization and signing.
- The type of business entity may dictate compliance with regulatory and other legal requirements as well as significant tax planning issues.
- The type of business entity plays a key role in the procedures followed in the event of customer bankruptcy.

There are several common types of business entities involved in equipment finance transactions. Each is organized in a different way and present different challenges as well as opportunities. A high-level comparison of business types is summarized in Figure 15 and explained in more detail in the following sections.

	Sole Proprietor	Partnership	Ltd. Partnership	C Corporation	S Corporation	LLC
Minimum Number of Equity Owners	1	2	2	1	1	1
Equity Owners of the business are personally taxed for business' profits	Yes	Yes	Yes	No	Yes	Yes
Lessor can go immediately and directly after equity owners if company defaults on a lease	Yes	Yes	No*	No	No	No
Continues in existence as is if one or more equity owners die	No	No**	Yes	Yes	Yes	Yes

* can go after general partner only
** but partnership agreement might affect this answer

Figure 15 Business Type Comparison

Corporations

A corporation is a legal entity separate and distinct from its owners (shareholders) and officers in the view of other businesses, the law, and taxing authorities. Investors who buy shares of a corporation, common, preferred, or both, own the corporation. Investor liability is limited to the extent of their investment plus any debts they individually guarantee. Shareholders are typically individuals; however, a corporation can form a subsidiary corporation, owning the shares of that subsidiary corporation. Investors draw money from the corporation through either salaries or dividends, which are both taxable to the recipient. The corporation files a separate tax return and pays taxes on the profits of the business. Dividends are distributed from after-tax dollars.

Corporations are formed by filing Articles of Incorporation with the Secretary of State of the state under whose laws they are incorporated. They are governed by bylaws that, together with the Articles of Incorporation, control how transactions such as equipment leases and financings are authorized, and the documents executed.

Generally, the Articles of Incorporation will provide for a board of directors to be elected by the shareholders. The Board of Directors must approve any transaction not pre-approved in the Articles or bylaws unless it is in the "ordinary course of business" of the corporation. For example, board approval is not required for a bakery to purchase flour or sign a contract to provide bread to a supermarket; board approval would most likely be required for the bakery to purchase an airplane or agree to open a video arcade.

If approved by the board of directors or in the ordinary course of business, contracts may be signed and performed by the corporation's officers. Officers provided by statute in each state include a president and one or more vice presidents, a secretary, and a treasurer. Officers are elected by the board of directors.

Key issues in dealing with corporations are:

- Whether a transaction must be approved by a "resolution" of the board of directors (generally, equipment finance transactions are not considered within the ordinary course of business and the best practice is to obtain board approval, but this is often waived in smaller transactions);
- Whether an officer signing a document is who he or she claims to be (addressed by an incumbency or secretary certificate showing specimen signatures and certifying as to the signer's title);
- Whether the information obtained about the corporation is accurate and the corporation is in existence and able to transact business.

The last of these is addressed by obtaining a good standing certificate or certificate of existence and other information from the secretary of state of the state of the corporation's incorporation.

There are several types of corporations as illustrated in Table 12.

Table 12 Types of Corporations

"C" Corporation	This is the basic corporate form. There are no limits to the number of shareholders. Profits are taxed to the corporation itself and distributions to the shareholders are also taxed.
"S" Corporation	A corporate entity that elects under specific IRS guidelines to be taxed in the manner of a partnership is known as a "Sub S" corporation. The number and types of shareholders are limited by IRS regulations. All profits and losses flow to the individual shareholders and are reflected in the shareholders' tax returns.
Non-profit Corporation	A non-profit corporation is an entity usually formed to provide some services, such as a hospital or a charity and whose purpose and motives are not profit oriented. Many are known as 501(c)(3) or 501(c)(6) entities, which refer to the IRC section applicable to them. Non-profits issue their own financial statements and have the legal ability to borrow money.
Professional Corporation ("PC")	In most states, individuals in specific professions such as physicians, dentists, and attorneys, can incorporate as a professional corporation. This business structure provides certain tax and pension benefits and limits the individual's personal liability for normal business matters. For the individual shareholder(s) to be liable for the business obligations of the corporation, they must sign a personal guaranty.

Limited Liability Company

Limited Liability Companies (called "LLCs") are similar to Sub "S" corporations in that their profits or losses flow through to the owners' ("members") tax returns. Unlike a Sub "S" corporation, however, the owners may be individuals or corporations, and the number of owners is not limited.

An LLC is similar to partnerships in that they are governed by an agreement among the members and do not generally have boards of directors. LLCs are formed by filing Articles of Organization with the secretary of state of the state where the LLC is organized. LLCs are governed by Operating Agreements. The terms of these documents govern whether the LLC is managed by one or more managers ("manager-managed") or by the members directly ("member-managed"). It is important to determine who has authority to bind the LLC to equipment finance agreements: a single or group of managers may be sufficient or the vote of all members or a special group of members may be required.

There is no personal liability for the LLC members unless they personally guarantee the debts of the LLC.

Some states provide for "Limited Liability Partnerships." These are general partnerships that have been recast as limited liability entities, similar to LLCs but governed by their partnership agreements, as modified to create the LLP. They operate much like partnerships, but the partners all enjoy protection from LLP debts and obligations like members in an LLC.

As with corporations, closing documents will evidence the identity of managers and officers designated by the Articles of Organization, and the approval of the necessary parties.

Partnerships and Limited Partnerships

As the name suggests, two or more people or entities doing business consists of a partnership, usually documented with a partnership agreement. Although partnership tax returns are prepared, income and losses are generally taxed directly to the partners rather than at the partnership level.

A general partnership is merely a partnering of persons, corporations, LLCs, or other business entities. The general partnership may or may not have a formal partnership agreement and some states do not provide for any type of registration or filing for general partnerships. Absent a binding partnership agreement with specific voting provisions, the consent of all partners should be obtained when dealing with a general partnership. All partners in a general partnership are liable for all partnership debts, usually without regard to the portion of the partnership they own (although they may be able to obtain partial reimbursement from other partners).

A limited partnership is a statutorily created type of partnership in which only the "general partner(s)" are liable for partnership debts. "Limited partners" have no such liability and are protected similarly to corporation shareholders and LLC members.

A limited partnership may only be formed by filing Articles of Limited Partnership or similar documents with the secretary of state in the state in which it is organized. The limited partnership is governed by an Agreement of Limited Partnership, which specifies the powers and rights of the general and limited partners, including the power to sign equipment finance documents.

Table 13 Types of Partnerships

General Partnership	Two or more people, or entities, with each one being legally liable for all activities and obligations of the business.
Limited Partnership	Two or more people or entities that come together to do business. At least one person or entity must be the general partner, and all others may be Limited partners (LP). General partners are legally liable for all activities and liabilities of the business. Liability of limited partners is usually limited to the extent of their investment.

Sole Proprietors

The simplest business entity is a Sole Proprietorship in which one individual owns the business. There are no legal requirements to start the business apart from a standard business license and specific licenses that apply to the industry. If the owner of the business is using a business name other than his/her own personal name, he/she usually must file a "Doing Business As" (DBA) certificate with the local county, town, or state office. This gives that individual the right to use that trade name. There may not be a separate financial statement for the business and there is only one tax return: the individual's Form 1040, with business income and expenses reflected on a Schedule C. Income is reported before the owner's draws and taxes. When doing cash flow calculations, the income must be calculated after taxes and after the owner's draws.

Dealing with sole proprietors is a matter of dealing with the individual as if the sole proprietorship does not exist. The trade name is disregarded completely for UCC purposes; only the individual's name is used. This can be dangerous as the exact correct legal name must be on the financing statement or the statement will be invalid. The customer's driver's license will determine the UCC filing name in some, but not all, states and state law must be checked.

Some states have usury laws applicable to sole proprietors and there are other issues that make dealing with individuals operating under tradenames somewhat risky.

Other Variations of Business Entities

While corporations, partnerships, LLCs and LLPs may be more common business entities encountered in equipment financing and leasing, there are many other variations of business entitles also encountered in our industry.

Joint Venture

Two or more companies set up a joint venture entity for a specific project or set up to provide a vehicle to handle a certain type of business in which the creating entities have a common interest. A separate financial statement is prepared for the entity and the joint venture members share the resulting profits or losses. Joint ventures are dissolved at some future date.

Association

This type of entity is used mostly by organizations that are not generally in a commercial enterprise, (e.g., a local civic association, a club, etc.). These are usually non-profit organizations with little if any assets. If an association requests a lease, their bylaws should be reviewed to ensure that the association has the authority to borrow money and to determine who can commit the association to the indebtedness.

Trust

A trust is formed to hold assets for the benefit of others, such as an equipment trust, to which is assigned certain equipment to be used as collateral for an obligation. A Trust Agreement shows the name of the trust, identifies the trustee, the responsibility of the trustee, the beneficiary of the trust, and the powers of the trustee. It is important to review the Trust Agreement before entertaining any type of credit request.

Municipality

This is the name generally given to a local government entity. It could be a state, city, county, or town government, a local school district, a fire district, or any kind of community under municipal jurisdiction. Municipalities use what is called "fund accounting." They usually issue their own budgets and financial statements. Such financial statements look different from financial statements issued by a typical corporation. Municipal financial statements reflect expenses and income, which is usually derived from taxes and grants from other municipalities or the federal government. Any excess of revenues over expenses flows to a "fund balance" rather than to a "stockholder's equity account" (as in a typical corporation).

In most cases, a municipality cannot commit to a lease or loan for more than one year. When they do execute longer-term obligations, however, they are subject to what is known as "fiscal funding clauses" or "non-appropriation" language. This allows the municipality to cancel the obligation if funds are not provided for that obligation in subsequent budgets.

Federal Government

The government of the United States of America can borrow funds as needed, subject to whatever laws or regulations Congress puts in place. As is the case with municipalities, the federal government typically does not obligate itself for long-term lease obligations. There are some instances, however, where they are authorized to commit to more than one-year leases.

The government is also authorized to issue long-term bonds in the form of Treasury bonds. Different agencies of the federal government have different methods whereby they lease equipment. Some do it through purchase orders only; others execute lease documents written to their specifications.

Qualification to Do Business

Any consideration of this topic must involve an understanding of the penalties involved in making the wrong judgment call. It is almost universally true that the penalty for failure to qualify to do business is minimal. There is a financial penalty involving chiefly the payment of all annual report and registration fees since the foreign corporation began doing business and the corporation is required to retroactively "cure" its error by registering with the secretary of state. After this, the corporation is treated as if it had performed its obligations correctly and obtained a Certificate of Authority at the time it commenced doing business.

So long as a corporation, LLC, or other type of business that is required to qualify to do business has failed to do so, it may not sue or make any use of the courts in the state. (Again, this can be cured retroactively allowing refiling of lawsuits so long as the statute of limitations has not expired.) Such corporations may be served legally by service of process on the secretary of state, which does not always reach the corporation and can result in default judgments.

As to the lessee or borrower, failure to qualify to do business primarily means that the lessee cannot obtain written confirmation from the state that it has the legal right to transact business in the state, has not dissolved, or failed to pay its taxes properly. Note: this is often a matter of maintaining qualification or, in the case of a corporation that is formed under the laws of the state, continuing to file its annual reports and pay its franchise taxes. These actions, by foreign or domestic corporations, are called "remaining in good standing."

The failure to be in good standing, or to obtain qualification to do business, does not mean that the lessee does not exist, or does not have the right to enter into contracts enforceable against it. Instead, it means that the lessee may owe additional taxes and fees, and that the lessor cannot obtain assurances as to the lessee's legal viability or information about its officers and directors.

In the case of a lessee that has failed to qualify to do business, certain of the lessee's legal rights in the foreign jurisdiction may be impaired until the lessee retroactively cures this failure. It is common for lessors to insist that lessees qualify to do business and be in good standing in all foreign jurisdictions in which they conduct a material part of their business or in which they will use the leased equipment. It is also a good practice for the lessor to insist that the lessee be entirely up to date on all filings in the state in which it was incorporated so that the lessor can obtain proper information and assurances that the lessee has not filed for dissolution and is a viable business concern.

Taxes

Qualifying to do business as a foreign corporation involves the payment of franchise taxes but does not in itself affect certain other taxes. Property taxes are payable for property location irrespective of whether the owner has registered with the secretary of state or any separate legal entity. The presence of equipment in a state allows the state (or local government) to assess property taxes. Sales and use Taxes are payable on equipment purchased (financed with a lease intended as security) or leased (on a true lease) in the state. These laws vary markedly from state to state, and lessors are required to obtain a separate registration with the state tax authority anywhere that sales or use taxes will be payable (rental taxes).

Income taxes are payable generally wherever a lessor's business generates taxable income, although this process and the interplay of credits for taxes paid to foreign states varies from place to place. Most state tax authorities hold that they have the authority to tax and enforce taxes against corporations wherever those corporations are either doing business or have property located. It is not uncommon for lessors to be unpleasantly surprised by being assessed income taxes where they merely have one or more leases in place.

Licensing and Being in "Good Standing"

There are many ways states regulate and license commerce, from organizational documents and city licenses to permits and tax registration. In addition to maintaining good standing and active status in the state of incorporation (by paying annual franchise taxes and filing annual reports), all states require that foreign corporations (those formed outside the state) "qualify to do business." Businesses achieve this by obtaining a Certificate of Authority if the corporation is "doing business" within the state.

"Doing business" is defined differently in each state. In most, having an office or an agent that regularly transacts business in the state is required. In some, merely having a significant number of leases, or other business, or obtaining a sales tax or other registration is enough to require the corporation to "qualify to do business." The good news is that in every state now, including Alabama, the corporation can retroactively cure the failure to qualify if it is found to be necessary. In Alabama contracts made by companies required to qualify that did not are voidable by the other contracting party.

Most businesses are likely familiar with how states are permitted to regulate licensing requirements for occupations and trades, for example, as it may apply to insurance agents, mortgage brokers, real estate agents, various contractors, and engineers. For many years, only certain micro-ticket lessors and automobile lessors were required to be licensed, in addition to qualifying to do business (if necessary, under state law) and obtaining tax registrations.

Some state laws require licensing for making high-interest or very small-ticket loans; leasing or selling motor vehicles; buying installment sale contracts from vendors; or other lessor activities. As discussed in Chapter 8 – Funding and Operations, California is the only state that requires licensing of commercial lenders generally (as opposed to lessors engaged in leasing only).

Other states may also set forth requirements as it pertains to loan brokers and advance fees. It is always worthwhile to look into the laws and rules applicable to the states where conducting business. This is a very brief introduction addressing state licensing requirements concerning finance lenders. Consult an attorney when it comes to advising on the advantages and disadvantages of meeting the criteria to invest in and transact business in individual states.

Summary

Understanding of the basics of law and legal considerations applicable to leasing is part of a well-rounded knowledge of this industry and provides context for the entire equipment finance lifecycle.

Knowing the difference between various types of legal entities and how to deal with each as a borrower or lessee is a key component of credit and documentation. A solid understanding of the articles of the Uniform Commercial Code specific to equipment leasing and finance also forms the basis for comprehending many of the documentation, funding, and regulatory concepts discussed later. Finally, grasping the fundamentals of bankruptcy law, types of bankruptcy, and applicability for leasing and equipment finance helps form a basis for understanding collections processes and other topics covered in this book.

Chapter 4 – Lease Pricing

Learning goals for this chapter:

- Understand time value of money concept.
- Understand the concept of cash flow diagramming and how it applies to leases.
- Understand the different types of pricing tools and how to use a financial calculator for basic lease pricing.
- Know the basic elements of a lease transaction.
- Understand basic formulas underlying pricing and how and why they are used.
- Understand fixed monthly payment scenarios compared to structured payment scenarios.
- Understand the tax impact on lease pricing.

Within the BOK Framework, pricing is considered a foundational concept.

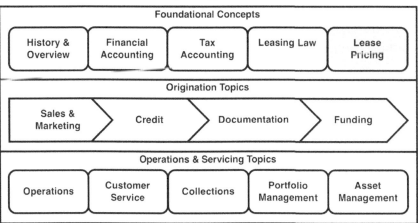

Figure 16 BOK Framework

A sound understanding of lease pricing is essential for the equipment finance professional. By being able to confidently "do the math" as well as "check the math," the lessor is able to protect their company and their customers, and detect simple errors, intentional "mistakes," and even fraud.

More importantly, the lessor can assure lessees that they are getting the best lease finance deal to meet their needs.

Knowing how to calculate a lease rate; how to discount to financial institutions; and how to quote a rate factor, including broker's points from a buy rate, all are different aspects of one of the most critical areas of the leasing business. Familiarity with the math of leasing helps you to compete against a lower rate or a lease with a different structure, and to meet any particular cash flow needs the lessee may have, such as seasonal payment requirements.

Figure 17 Lease Pricing Building Blocks

This chapter covers the building blocks of lease pricing. By the end of this chapter, if you practice the exercises described here, you should be able to perform a variety of lease pricing calculations using a financial calculator.

Although the mathematics of lease pricing can seem overwhelming at first, it helps to break the concepts down into separate parts and practice the various calculations.

Appendix 3 – Pricing Sample Problems provides various lease pricing practice problems, referenced by the sections covered in this chapter.

This chapter is laid out in the following learning progression:

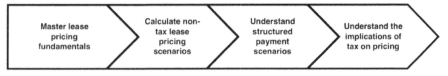

Figure 18 Pricing Learning Progression

Lease Pricing Fundamentals

This chapter deals with the mathematics behind leasing. Lease calculations become less complicated when the problem is broken down into numerous small parts or cash flows. The computations discussed range from simple interest to complex lease calculations. The reader needs to be aware that tax implications affect yields, but tax is not the focus of this chapter; therefore, these implications are ignored. This chapter also discusses the use of financial calculators and software, and how to use them in the equipment finance industry. It is expected that the reader already possesses a basic understanding of these tools.

There are many concepts involved in lease pricing. Concepts are introduced one at a time, and a few examples and problems are included with each new introduction to make sure the concept is understood. The concepts build upon one another and as new concepts are added, the lease pricing examples and problems become more complex.

Time Value of Money Concept

All pricing problems involve the time value of money. This concept means that a dollar today is worth more than a dollar tomorrow, and money gained in the future is worth less than money earned in the present. The following examples help to explain the time value of money.

Which is preferable: a) $100 today, or b) $100 a year from now? The answer should be obvious: $100 today is more valuable.

But which of these is preferable: a) $100 today, or b) $105 one year from now? It depends on the current market interest rates. If you can earn 8 percent per year in an interest-bearing CD account, then the answer should be a): $100 today because, with investment, that money would end up as $108 one year from now. But if the current interest rate is only 3 percent, then the answer should be b), $105 one year from now, because you will end up with more money by waiting a year for the money than by taking it now and investing it.

One hundred dollars today invested in some fashion so that it pays 8 percent interest per annum, compounded annually, becomes $108 in one year. This process is the concept of compounding. For the same example, let's say one holds that $108 invested at 8 percent per annum for another year, it then becomes $116.64. Albert Einstein is credited with saying,

*"Compound interest is the eighth wonder of the world.
He who understands it earns it… he who doesn't… pays it."*

The inverse of the concept of compounding is the concept of discounting. Rather than investing $100 for a year, what if someone promised to pay another individual $100 one year from now? How much would that individual be willing to lend them (i.e., pay them) today in return for that $100 received after a year? Something less than $100! If the preferred interest rate is, for example, 7 percent, then the amount must be "discounted" by 7 percent to determine its value today.

Compounding and discounting make up the concept of the time value of money. This idea underlies all of the lease and loan calculations that lessors work with every day. Determining the value of future dollars today is called the "present value of money." The "present value" is the current equivalent of payments, or a stream of payments, to be received at various times in the future. The present value varies with the interest rate applied to future payments.

Terminology

Before proceeding to actual calculations, it is useful to familiarize yourself with the following definitions which explain the standard terms used in pricing calculations:

Yield	The total value of all cash flows, e.g., rent, residual, and tax benefits stated as an annual percentage rate. Note that this chapter does not discuss calculating yield for true tax leases because the calculators are not capable of taking into consideration the impact of taxes.
Implicit Rate	The value of rent (or payments) and residual stated as an annual percentage rate.
Running Rate or Stream Rate	The amount of the rent stated as an annual percentage rate without consideration of other factors that affect the actual interest rate.
Lease Rate or Lease Rate Factor	The monthly payment stated as a percentage of the original equipment cost.
Discount Rate	The interest rate used when discounting a series of payments to the present value.
Internal Rate of Return	The interest rate that makes the present value of the cash flow(s) equal to the investment (i.e., equipment cost or loan amount). Also known as the discounted cash flow rate of return, which is just a long title that answers the question "what discount rate must be used to get the net present value to equal zero?" It is the most common method used to compute yields.
Points	A term that refers to the percentage of profit or commission that is "priced in" or "to be paid" to a broker, originator, or seller of a transaction. For example, a $30,000 transaction with two points priced into it has $600 profit or a commission (2 percent of $30,000).
Basis point	One-hundredth of 1, is usually used when discussing differences in interest rates. For example, if the cost of funds is 6 percent and the yield is 7.5 percent, then there is a 150-basis point spread between the cost of funds and the yield.

Calculating Present Value

Financial calculators such as the Hewlett Packard 17BII, HP 12c, and others are preprogrammed to do present value calculations. These calculators are menu driven. On some, the present value program is found by choosing the function button labeled finance (FIN) from the main menu and then choosing the function button labeled time value of money (TVM) from the finance menu. Others have buttons right on the calculator for the time value of money variables.

Major Variables

There are five standard variables used in any present value calculation. If any four of the variables are known, then the calculator can figure out the remaining fifth variable.

Term	"N"	The number of payments (number of months)
Rate	"I"	The implicit rate per year or internal rate of return to be achieved by the lessor (note that some calculators may require the interest rate to be entered per month rather than per year)
Present Value	"PV"	The cost including fees or other upfront expenses.
Payments	"PMT"	Payments made periodically during the term of the lease, usually monthly.
Future Value	"FV"	Payments made at one time during the lease, usually the residual.

Minor Variables

In addition to the five major variables, there are quite a number of minor variables, which can also impact the cash flow and yield of any given transaction. These include the number of advance payments and any one-time fees or expenses added to or deducted from the cost such as security deposits, broker fees, indirect costs, and other fees/costs.

Example: PV Calculation
The following example shows how the present value calculation works. Before beginning, the calculator must be in "**begin mode**" and set to "**monthly**" payments. (Note: variations on these concepts are addressed later in this chapter.)

Suppose the amount received will be twelve monthly payments of $1 each. Further, assume that all of this money is going to a piggy bank with no interest received. How much is that stream of twelve-monthly payments worth today (i.e., if someone wanted to buy the rights to collect that stream of payments, how much would it be worth)?

- Four of the five variables are known:
  N = 12 monthly payments
  I%/YR = 0 (receiving no interest)
  PMT = $1
  FV = 0 (after the twelfth payment, nothing more is going to be received; therefore, the value of what will be received 12 months in the future is zero).
- Enter all these variables into the calculator and press the "PV" button.
- The screen should read, "PV = -12" meaning that the present value of a stream of twelve-monthly payments of $1 each, discounted at 0 percent, is $12.
- Why does the present value say "negative' $12?" Keep reading to find out in the section titled, "Practice exercises

> for this **section are in Appendix 3 Pricing Sample Problems #1-8.**
> - Positive & Negative Values."

Using a Financial Calculator

A convenient method for calculating lease variables is the use of a programmable financial calculator. The exercises in this chapter are written for the HP 17BII calculator.

Use the following steps[11] to store and use the solve program for the HP17-BII:

Enter the following program in the "solve" menu:

0=(-LEASE-FEE+CLOSFEE+SECDEP+(#ADVxPMT))+ (PMTxUSPV ((I%÷12):(TERM-#ADV)))+(SPPV((I%÷12):TERM)x(RESID-SECDEP))

Input
Enter the following variables into the program. Enter an amount into each variable, except for the variable being solved for.

TERM	Total number of lease payments. Include any payment that will be made in advance
I%	Annual yield
# ADV	Number of advance payments
FEE	Dollar amount of the broker fee, if any
LEASE	Lease amount or equipment cost
CLOSFEE	Closing fees, if any
SECDEP	Dollar amount of the refundable security deposit, if any
RESID	Dollar amount of the residual
PMT	Dollar amount of the monthly payment

Solve for the variable needed.

Solve for an unknown element in a transaction

Practice exercises for this section are in Appendix 3 Pricing Sample Problems #1-8.

Positive & Negative Values

In the PV Calculation example earlier in this chapter, the present value came out as a negative value because the variables in the calculator represent cash flows, and the positive and negative signs represent the direction that the cash is flowing. For the lender, the payments flow *to* the lender and the present value (i.e., the loan amount) flows *away from* the lender. Conversely, for the

---

[11] Source: Terey Jennings, Financial Pacific Leasing - ALFP Instructor

borrower or lessee, the payments flow *away from* the lessee, and the present value, representing the money paid for the equipment or the loan, flows *to* the lessee. Since the positive and negative signs represent the direction of the cash flow, then if stating the payment as a positive value, we must state the present value as a negative value, and vice versa. For the lessor perspective, the monthly payments (PMT) are paid to the lessor (a positive value), and the equipment cost (PV) is paid by the lender (a negative value). For the lessee then, the monthly payments (PMT) — a negative value — are being paid by the lessee and the cost of the equipment (PV) is paid to the lessee (a positive value).

In actual practice, it does not matter if the practice of always having the PV as a positive or negative value is adopted as long as the individual doing the calculation remembers that the PMT and the PV must always have opposite signs. Thus, if trying to solve for the interest rate, when entering the PV and the PMT, either the PV or the PMT must be input with a negative sign. DO NOT FORGET: THE PAYMENT MUST BE NEGATIVE IF THE PV IS POSITIVE! Some custom formulas like the one above for financial calculators are programed in a way that negative variables are not needed.

Finally, we must recognize that the future value (FV) represents another payment; this is cash flow to the lessor/lender at the end of the term just like the payments (PMT) are cash flows to the lessor/lender during the term. Therefore, the FV *always* has the same sign as the PMT. The PMT and FV will both be negatives values if the PV is a positive value. The PMT and FV both have positive values if the PV is a negative value. Note: the future value variable is discussed later in the chapter.

Cash Flow Diagrams

One fundamental skill for a leasing professional is to understand and be capable of diagramming lease and loan transaction cash flows. The flow of funds both "in" and "out" helps to visualize the life of the transaction and understand the entries made in a pricing calculator or program. The flows of cash in a transaction are the basis of all pricing products. A cash flow diagram consists of a horizontal line representing the timeline from the beginning (or even before the beginning) of the transaction to the end (or after the end) of the transaction.

Building on the ancient history discussed earlier in this book, let's imagine a Sumerian is leasing a plow to work their farm in 2010 BC, and they rent the equipment for three months in the spring. The horizontal cash flow timeline might look like this:

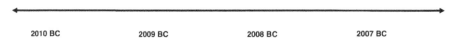

Figure 19 Cash Flow Timeline

Vertical lines are used in a cash flow diagram to help show the scale of the time period involved. In this case, we might use lines to show the months around springtime, like this:

Figure 20 Cash Flow Scale & Time Periods

Now suppose that Sumerian agrees to pay three Sumerian shekels per month to rent the plow. Vertical arrows point up and down to represent cash inflows and cash outflows. Upward arrows represent cash inflows and downward represent cash outflows.

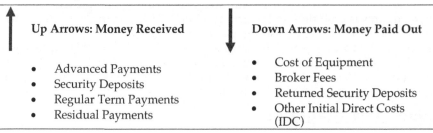

In our example, since the payment is three shekels per month, the cash flow diagram shows cash inflows for those three months:

Figure 21 Cash Outflows

Now fast forward a couple of thousand years to 25 BC and suppose that a brand-new fishing merchant in Rome is about to acquire their very first vessel. The merchant has managed to save 200 denarii, but the ship costs 900 denarii. Fortunately, a Roman ship supplier has offered to loan the other 700 denarii to the fishing merchant with a promise to repay 800 denarii at the rate of 200 per year for the next four years. The fishing merchant's cash flow diagram starts with an upward arrow representing the cash inflow of 700 denarii, and then shows downward arrows for each of the next four years of the cash outflows of 200 denarii per year:

Lessee's Perspective

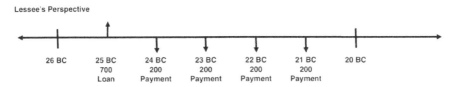

Figure 22 Cash Flow Diagram Lessee Perspective

Fast forward to the modern age, and the descendant of the Roman fishing merchant working for a leasing company wishes to demonstrate their knowledge of cash flow diagrams. They produce the following to show a lease for a $100,000 piece of equipment, which requires a 10 percent down payment, 60 monthly payments of $1,800 each, and then a 20 percent residual at the end.

Lessor's Perspective

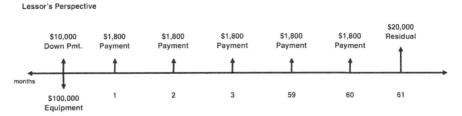

Figure 23 Cash Flow Diagram Modern Lease - Lessor Perspective

Amortized Lease - Principal & Interest

An amortized lease is one with a scheduled periodic payment that consists of both principal and interest. An amortized lease payment pays the relevant interest expense for the period before any principal is paid and reduced. Similar to mortgage payments, lease payments are "level payment" instruments, which means the total payment is constant throughout the term. A different amount each month is allocated to principal and interest, but always adds up to the same amount each month. For example, a $12,000 lease for 60 months at an interest rate of 10 percent (and with no residual) would have a fixed monthly payment of $252.86 Beginning of Period (BOP); $254.96 End of Period (EOP).

For leases or these types of loans, lessors first calculate the amount of interest due on the outstanding balance and then allocate the rest of the payment towards the principal balance. The amount of interest in each payment declines over time, but for the total payment to remain fixed, the principal component increases over time. Therefore, interest and principal have an inverse relationship with the level payment amount over the life of the amortized lease or loan.

A graphical representation of this lease/loan looks like this:

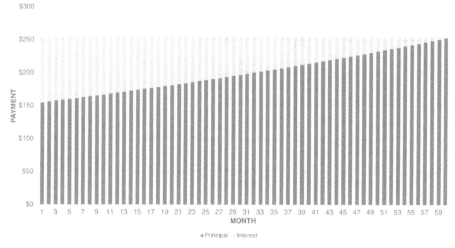

Figure 24 Payment Amortization

Non-Tax Pricing

Lease Rate Factors

Practice exercises for this section are in Appendix 3 Pricing Sample Problems # 9-18.

Another tool for quickly calculating lease pricing is the lease rate factor (LRF). Lessors will often set lease rate factors for various program relationships, allowing the vendor to quickly and simply calculate the payment amount by multiplying equipment cost by the lease rate factor.

LRF is merely an expression of the payments as a percentage of the cost. The LRF is calculated dividing the monthly payment by the equipment cost and expressed as a decimal. For example, if the monthly payment is $2,340 and the cost is $100,000, then the LRF is:

$$\frac{\$2,340}{\$100,000} = .02340 \qquad \frac{PMT}{PV(Cost)} = LRF$$

In this case, we express the LRF as dollars per hundred thousand. Some people prefer to show it as dollars per hundred (which would be 2.340) or even as percentages (which would be 2.34 percent). The way in which a lessor expresses its rate factors is unimportant as long as the concept is understood and used correctly.

In simple math, the formula for the LRF can be changed to read: PV (equipment cost) x LRF = PMT.

Once the LRF is understood and calculated, it becomes a useful concept. It enables the lessor to have a tool to quote and calculate payments in situations in which the exact equipment cost is either unknown or may change. The LRF can be calculated instead of an exact monthly payment, and the vendor or customer can multiply the LRF by the exact equipment cost to determine the exact monthly payment. If equipment costs should change somewhat, the vendor or customer can calculate exactly how much the payment will change by using the same LRF with the new equipment cost.

If you know two of the three LRF variables (Equipment Cost, Monthly Payment, Lease Rate Factor) you can easily determine the unknown variable using one of these three equations:

$$\frac{PMT}{Equipment\ Cost} = LRF$$

$$Equipment\ Cost * LRF = PMT$$

$$\frac{PMT}{LRF} = Equipment\ Cost$$

Beginning of Period (BOP) vs. End of Period (EOP)

Practice exercises for this section are in Appendix 3 Pricing Sample Problems #19-23.

All of the problems completed so far have been figured with the payments billed in advance (BOP). For the reader's convenience, answers for the sample problems are in both BOP and EOP. Some lenders, however, do not bill until the last day of the month (billing in arrears). On a financial calculator, there is a button or menu with the words "BEG/END," a toggle button, which changes the calculator's setting back and forth between begin mode (BOP) and end mode (EOP).

If all of the variables in a given transaction remain unchanged when the user switches from BOP to EOP, what then happens to the true interest rate?

 Example: BOP and EOP Modes

Place the calculator in BOP (Begin) mode and enter the following variables:

N=60
PV=100,000
PMT=-2203

Press the "I%YR" function button.
The interest rate should be 12.01 percent.

Now set the calculator to EOP (End) mode.
All of the variables should still be in the calculator's memory just as entered before. (If deleted, reenter the variables listed above).

> Press the "I%YR" function button.
> This time the calculator figures the interest rate in EOP instead of BOP.
> The End of Period interest rate should be 11.57 percent.

The cost of financing (interest rate) is lower when the payments are due on the last day of the month instead of the first day of the month. If the payment is not due until the last day of the month, then the money can be put in a savings account and earn interest for thirty days before it is needed to make the payment. Conversely, for the lessor or lender, they are not receiving the payment until the last day of the month, so they do not have that money to invest during those first thirty days, making their return on the whole transaction (i.e., interest rate) lower.

Effects of Down Payments, Advance Payments, and Residual Values/End of Term Payments

Practice exercises for this section are in Appendix 3 Pricing Sample Problems #24-32.

All of the examples discussed thus far have not incorporated any down payments, advance payments, or end of term payments.

Down Payments

Down payments are fairly self-explanatory. The only effect of a down payment is to reduce the total finance amount. The value entered as the PV will be Total Equipment Cost – Down Payment.

Advance Payments

Advance payments are similar to down payments. The term "advance payment" refers specifically to a scheduled lease payment, which is at the beginning of the lease term. With the calculator set to BOP, then it makes calculations assuming that the first lease payment *is* at the beginning of the lease. With the calculator set to EOP, it makes calculations assuming that the first lease payment is *not* at the beginning of the lease. Many leases require the first *and* the last payment to be made at the beginning of the lease. In fact, there is no reason why a lessor and lessee cannot negotiate a lease, which requires the first and last two lease payments at the beginning of the lease; or the first and last three, etc.

Advance payments must be taken into account when calculating present values. If a transaction has no payments due in advance, then simply do the present value calculations with the calculator set to end mode. And if the transaction has only the first payment due in advance, then do the present value calculations with the calculator set to begin mode.

When the first *and* last payments are due in advance, then some adjustments must be made to the present value calculations. The calculator should be set to begin mode to account for the fact that the *first* payment is due at the beginning of the lease. Treat the last payment in advance similar to a down payment. Subtract the last payment in advance from the equipment cost or loan amount. Also, shorten the term (i.e., the number of payments in the present value calculation) by one month. In other words, we calculate a thirty-six-month lease with first and last payments in advance as a thirty-five-month lease in begin mode with the PV, or equipment cost, reduced by one payment (last payment in advance).

An examination of a cash flow diagram demonstrates what is happening:

This cash flow diagram shows the cash flow for a thirty-six-month lease with the first payment due in advance:

Lessor's Perspective

Figure 25 Cash Flow Diagram 36-month Lease 1st Payment in Advance

The following cash flow diagram shows the *last* payment moved to the beginning of the term for a lease with the *first and last* payments due in advance.

Lessor's Perspective

Figure 26 Cash Flow Diagram 36 Month Lease 1st and Last Payments in Advance

This diagram shows the thirty-sixth payment moving all the way to the beginning of the cash flow. It has the effect of reducing the lender's/lessor's initial cash outlay (i.e., equipment cost or loan amount), and it also has the effect of leaving only thirty-five remaining payments (including the first payment, which is also due at the beginning).

Interestingly when the first payment is due in advance, then that first payment *can* be treated as a reduction in the loan amount or equipment cost and shorten the term (i.e., remaining payments) by one. When doing this, the remaining payments must be calculated in EOP.

Note: in the following two examples, we are using the Time Value of Money (TVM) formula for the HP 17BII calculator not the previously mentioned formula.

Example: First and Last Payments in Advance

Let's examine a thirty-six-month lease for $40,000 with monthly payments of $1,245 with the first and last payments due in advance.

Set the calculator to begin mode, and enter the following:
PV = $40,000
PMT = -$1,245
N = 36
Solve for I% and the answer should be 7.99 percent.

Now with the calculator set to end mode, enter the following:
PV = $38,755 (which is $40,000 - $1,245 because the last payment being paid in advance from the cost is subtracted)
PMT = -$1,245
N = 35 (subtract one payment from the term because the last payment is in advance).
Solve for I%, and the answer once again is 7.99 percent.

Residual Value/End of Term Payments

Many leases and sometimes loans have a payment due at the end of the term such as a fixed buyout or a residual value for a lease or a balloon payment for a loan. In doing present value calculations, enter the end of term payment as the future value (FV). The sign (positive or negative) of the future value is always the same as the sign of the monthly payment (PMT) because the FV represents another payment of cash flowing in the same direction as it does for all of the monthly payments.

Example: Effect of an End of Term Payment
To see the effect of an end of term payment, enter the following variables with a calculator in begin mode:

N=60
PV=$100,000
PMT=-$2,300

When you press the interest rate button, the answer should be 14 percent.

Suppose now that this transaction was the same except that there is a 10 percent buyout or balloon at the end.

Enter FV=-$10,000

When you press the interest rate button, the interest rate on the transaction goes up to 16.16 percent due to the residual/balloon.

Determining Profit

Practice exercises for this section are in Appendix 3 Pricing Sample Problems # 33-39.

Leasing and financing transactions generate profit by the difference between the buy rate or funding rate (the rate at which the leasing professional can "buy" the money for the transaction), and the sell rate (the rate at which the leasing professional can "sell" the transaction to the customer). Alternatively, for a direct lender, it would be the difference between the cost of funds (similar to a buy rate) and the yield on the transaction (i.e., the sell rate to the customer). To make a profit, the lessor must sell the customer a rate that is higher than the funding rate or cost of funds.

Once the lessor has negotiated an exact monthly payment with the customer, the lessor already knows how to determine the exact interest rate of the transaction, taking into account any down payment, buyout, advance payment, etc. Both the cost of funds or buy rate, and the sell rate must be known to determine the profit on the transaction.

Looking at a prior problem, assume that a manufacturing company has agreed to lease a $100,000 CNC machine from a lessor. They have agreed to a five-year, one-dollar buyout lease, with nothing down, at 9 percent, with billing at the end of the month. What is the exact monthly payment? The payment should be $2,075.84. Now, what if a bank could approve this transaction at the incredible funding rate of 3.5 percent? This would mean that the bank will "buy" this transaction from the lessor by discounting the stream of payments at 3.5 percent (alternatively, if the lessor works directly for the bank, then assume that the cost of funds is 2 percent).

	Example: Discounting a Stream of Payments Enter 3.5 percent as the interest rate to determine how much the bank will pay for this stream of payments (the lease). Enter the term as 60 months, the payment as -$2,075.84, and set the calculator for EOP, then compute the present value. The answer should be $114,108.90.

The stream of payments of $2,075.84 is worth $114,108.90 today discounting the payments at 3.5 percent. Of course, $100,000 must be spent to pay the vendor for the CNC machine. So that leaves $14,108.90 as profit on this transaction.

Steps for determining profit on a transaction:
1. Determine the exact cost, monthly payment, and term.
2. Determine the buy rate or cost of funds.
3. Determine the present value of the stream of payments by discounting the stream of payments at the funding rate.
4. Determine the profit by subtracting the cost of the equipment from the present value of the stream of payments.

Deposits, Fees, and Other Costs

Thus far, the five major variables that go into every present value calculation are the term (N); the interest rate (I%); the equipment cost (PV); the payment (PMT); and the residual (FV).

In addition to the five major variables, there are quite a number of minor variables, which can also impact the cash flow and yield of any given transaction. Minor variables include indirect costs, security deposits, number of advance payments, and other fees/costs.

A previous example in the section, "Effects of Down Payments, Advance Payments, and Residual Values/End of Term Payments," included last payment taken in advance. In some cases, a lease may even have two or more of the payments scheduled at the end of the lease that are required to be paid in advance at the beginning of the lease. The more payments that are "moved" from the end of the payment schedule to the beginning of the payment schedule, the more the yield increases.

A **security deposit** is another common variable that can affect the yield of a transaction. Security deposits may be required in place of, or in addition to, advance payments. Security deposits may be necessary to enhance the yield of a transaction, to help mitigate the risk of a transaction, or both. On a lender/lessor's cash flow diagram, the security deposit would be represented by an up arrow at the beginning of the term (representing a cash inflow) and by a down arrow at the end of the term (representing a cash outflow).

In actual practice, when computing present value calculations companies treat a security deposit in many different ways. The most common treatment is to deduct it from the equipment cost at the beginning of the lease and show it as returned to the lessee at the end of the lease. Other treatments include not valuing the deposit at all in the PV calculation and valuing the deposit at a rate different than that in the lease.

Most lease transactions have other costs or fees, such as a documentation fee (doc fee), inspection fee, or other closing costs. These types of fees represent income to the lessor/lender. Many lessors/lenders do not account for this type of fee income in their present value calculations and merely book it as fee income in the current period. FASB Statement No. 91 specifies that loan origination fees shall be recognized over the life of the related loan as an adjustment of yield. Therefore, following FASB accounting, a cash flow diagram as a lender/lessor would show an up arrow at the beginning of the term in the amount of the doc fee or other origination fees, showing the cash inflow. For calculation purposes, this would have the effect of offsetting a part of the cash outflow, which is the down arrow at the beginning of the term representing payment for the equipment cost. Imagine, therefore, if a lessor had an equipment cost of $10,000 and charged a $500 doc fee. Without taking the doc fee into account, the transaction might have a 9 percent yield. However, when taking the doc fee into account over the life of the lease, the same present value calculation would be performed, using a $9,500 PV (net of $10,000 cash outflow for the equipment purchase and $500 cash inflow from the doc fee) instead of a $10,000 PV.

Example: Pricing with and without a documentation fee

Examine the following example *without* a documentation fee:
N = 36
PV = $10,000
PMT = $318.00
FV = $0
Solve for I percent (answer should be 9 percent)

Now the example *with* documentation fee:
N = 36
PV = $9,500
PMT = $318.00
FV = $0
Solve for I percent

On a thirty-six-month term, the inclusion of the documentation fee would increase the yield from 9 percent to 12.54 percent.

In addition to direct fees, like doc fees, transactions can have direct costs associated with them, such as sales commissions and filing fees. **The term used to refer to the costs incurred by a lessor/lender at the inception of a transaction is the IDC.** In actual practice, some lessors/lenders do not account for these types of costs in their present value calculations and merely book them as expenses in the current period. FASB Statement No. 91, however, specifies that certain direct loan origination costs shall be recognized over the life of the related loan as a reduction in the loan's yield. The PV calculation for loan costs would be the inverse of that was just reviewed for documentation fees. In other words, the loan costs are added to the equipment cost to come up with the amount of the PV in the calculation because they both represent cash outflows at the beginning of the term. That is to say, the IDC amortize over the life of the lease or loan.

Computing Unusual Payment Structures

There are a variety of reasons why a leasing professional may need to calculate unusual payment structures. Some of the more common unusual payment structures include:

- Seasonal payment structures;
- Payment structures with delayed or skipped payments at the beginning of the term;

- Stepped up or stepped down payment structures where the amount of the payment either increases or decreases during the term of the transaction;

- Hi-Low payment structures where payments are higher for the first part of the term and then decrease later in the term; and

- Contact payments (also referred to as touch payments) are often used in annual payment scenarios where the bulk of the lease payment is made annually and for the rest of the year, the customer is billed smaller monthly payments to keep the customer in the habit of receiving and paying invoices.

All of these types of structures are much more difficult and complicated to compute using a financial calculator. Instead, they are best calculated using simple pricing programs such as T-Value™ or other similar pricing programs, which break the cash flow diagram or timeline apart with each part entered as a separate, sequential line entry. (See the section on Lease Pricing Tools later in this chapter).

Delayed Payments at Beginning of Term

For example, suppose an organic farm company wanted to lease a $30,000 tractor, but it was the middle of winter, and they didn't want their payments to start until four months later. If trying to compute the monthly amount that would give an 11 percent yield, with a $1 buyout and their first payment due in four months, then the cash flow diagram would look like this:

Lessor's Perspective

Figure 27 Delayed Payments at Beginning of Term

The corresponding lines that entered into the pricing program would probably look like this:

Event	Date	Amount	Number	Period	End Date
Lease	12/01/20X0	$30,000.00	1		
Payment	01/01/20X1	$0.00	3	Monthly	03/01/20X1
Payment	04/01/20X1	Unknown	33	Monthly	12/01/20X3

If 11 percent was entered in the field for the yield and then solved for the unknown (in this case the payment amount for the thirty-three-month portion of the thirty-six-month term), then the result should be $1,086.99 per month. The thirty-six-month term is split it up into a three-month period with payments of zero, and a thirty-three-month period with payments calculated to obtain the desired yield.

Step Payment Schedules

A similar pattern of logic can be followed to calculate payments or yields on step payment schedules. Let's imagine the organic farm company example changes, and instead of asking for no payments until the fourth month, they wanted lower payments until the spring, leaving it up to the lessor to propose something specific. If the lessor wished to offer them a structure where their payment for the first five months was one-third of the "normal" payment for the rest of the term, and the lessor collected the first payment in advance, then the cash flow diagram would look like this:

Lessor's Perspective

Figure 28 Stepped Payments

The corresponding lines entered into the pricing program would probably look like this:

Event	Date	Amount	Number	Period	End Date
Lease	12/01/20X0	$30,000.00	1		
Payment	12/01/20X0	.33x	5	Monthly	04/01/20X1
Payment	05/01/20X1	1.000x	31	Monthly	11/01/20X3

In this case, the unknown variable is still the payment, but we enter the unknown payment in two lines. The full payment calculates for the thirty-one-month portion of the term, and one-third of the payment (i.e., .33x) calculates for the five-month portion of the term. If 11 percent is entered in the field for the yield and then solved, the result should be $1,089.52 per month for the thirty-one-month portion of the term and $359.54 per month for the first five months of the term. Essentially, the thirty-six month term has been split up into a five-month period and a thirty-one-month period, with payments, which, during the first five months are one-third of the payment during the thirty-month period.

Seasonal Payments

We can take the organic farm company example one step further. Suppose they wanted their lease structured so that they had no payments for every December, January, February, and March throughout the lease term. Once again, we split the term into its parts based on the structuring needs. In this case, the requirements are to split up each twelve-month period into two segments – a four-month segment (December to March) with no payments and an eight-month segment (April to November) with regular payments. The cash flow diagram would look like this:

Lessor's Perspective

Figure 29 Seasonal Skipped Payments

The corresponding lines entered into the pricing program would probably look like the table below:

Event	Date	Amount	Number	Period	End Date
Lease	12/01/20X0	$30,000.00	1		
Payment	12/01/20X0	$0.00	4	Monthly	03/01/20X1
Payment	04/01/20X1	Unknown	8	Monthly	11/01/20X1
Payment	12/01/20X1	$0.00	4	Monthly	03/01/20X2
Payment	04/01/20X2	Unknown	8	Monthly	11/01/20X2
Payment	12/01/20X2	$0.00	4	Monthly	03/01/20X3
Payment	04/01/20X3	Unknown	8	Monthly	11/01/20X3

Once again if we enter the yield as 11 percent and unknown payment is the number in question, the result should be $1,487.16 per month. Thus, during the entire thirty-six-month term, the organic farming company has twenty-four months when they will make payments of $1,487.16 and twelve months when they will make payments of zero.

Contact Payments

Continuing to build on the organic farm company example, let's suppose you want to set up contact payments for this customer. Instead of setting payments as $0.00 each December, January, February, and March, the lease would be structured with a low amount such as $100.00 during those months to keep the customer in the habit of receiving and paying invoices for the contract.

Hi-Low Payment Scenarios

An example of when Hi-low payment structures may be beneficial, consider a customer that has been in business for a short time. The company may currently have a lot of cash, but as you look toward the future, there is less certainty and you believe the customer's cash burn rate may be faster than they anticipate. So, you establish a three-year lease where the payments are higher for the first year and then drop down later in the term. It's a way of structuring the payments for a credit that may not be as pristine as we would like.

Agricultural Leasing – Payment Structures

Unlike most industries, agriculture has a unique cash flow cycle. Many grain farmers have one or possibly two harvests per year, leading to irregular cash flow. For this reason, most agricultural entities require annual payments coinciding with the sale of their crops. There are some exceptions to this cycle, such as in the animal husbandry and dairy segments. These types of entities have a more even cash flow, conducive to monthly payments.

A typical Midwest grain crop cycle begins in the spring with the planting of crops and ends in the fall with the crop harvest. By the time the farmer receives payment from the harvest, it can be late in the year or early in the next. For this reason, it is common for lenders to offer a "harvest plan" structure. With a harvest plan, an entity borrows money for equipment early in the year when it is required and skips several months before making an annual payment. Typically, the borrower pays the lender an advance payment that is greater than or equal to the accrual of interest during the period between funding and when the first annual payment is due (referred to as the "skip period"). This advance payment keeps the loan from negatively amortizing before receiving the first payment and mitigates some of the lender's initial risk.

Since payments are only made once a year, some lenders require a monthly "contact" payment which consists of a small amount, for example, $50 or $100 per month. These payments allow the lender to keep in frequent contact with the borrower.

Some industry segments such as logging are seasonal. Loggers usually work only during the warm months, so lessors and lenders adjust payment schedules to suit. Payments are made only during the work season, for example, eight months of the year, with no payments during the four months of the off-season.

As mentioned before, companies that are involved in dairy farming or animal husbandry are typically candidates for a more traditional monthly payment structure. These types of entities produce products that can be sold any time during the year. For example, a dairy farm may have several hundred head of cattle that are producing milk on a daily basis. Or a poultry farmer may steadily bring thousands of chickens to market.

Payment Frequency

The previous scenarios are examples of payment frequency. Payment frequency (also referred to as payment periodicity) refers to the recurrence of payments at regular intervals. Payment frequency can be monthly, quarterly, semi-annual, or annual.

Monthly payments are common, in some cases, quarterly, semi-annual, or annual payments make more sense for a customer's situation and cash flow. For example, in an agricultural business, to match timing of the payment stream to the timing of the customer income stream, you would set up annual or seasonal payments coinciding with crop harvests.

Lease Pricing Tools

All of these types of structures are much more difficult and complicated to compute using a financial calculator. Instead, they are best calculated using simple pricing programs such as T-Value™. In T-Value™ or other similar pricing programs, the cash flow diagram or timeline is broken apart into its component parts and each part entered as a separate, sequential line entry.

This chicken-and-egg problem is solved by a computer, which starts with a formula that is too high and one that is too low. It interpolates until it gets an answer that solves the question. This kind of complicated pricing can be done today with computer programs such as SuperTRUMP™ by Ivory Consulting Corporation, or InfoAnalysis™ by International Decision Systems, and others.

There are a variety of tools on the market for calculating lease pricing each has its benefits. Some equipment finance and lease processing platforms on the market today also include proprietary embedded pricing calculation engines. With an understanding of the formulas underlying lease pricing calculations, you could even create a lease pricing tool within a spreadsheet.

Table 14 Lease Pricing Tools

Tool Type	Example	Common Uses
Tax-Oriented Pricing	• SuperTRUMP™ by Ivory Corporation • InfoAnalysis™ by International Decision Systems	Tax-based pricing and complex pricing
Non-tax Pricing	• T-Value™	Small-ticket, structured, non-tax pricing scenarios
Financial Calculator	• HP 17B • HP 12C (as of this writing, an emulator for this calculator is available as a mobile app for IOS and Android)	Calculate any of the five unknowns (Major Variable) of lease pricing for a constant stream of payments You can program the financial calculator with custom formulas to expand the variables beyond PV calculation to make pricing simpler. Although it is possible to calculate structured payment scenarios with a financial calculator, it can be more complicated and time consuming to do so compared to the software pricing tools described above.
Custom Spreadsheet	Microsoft Excel	With an understanding of the formulas and basic math of lease pricing, you can use functions within Microsoft Excel to create a lease pricing tool.

Using a financial calculator is convenient and quick. Also, you can program the calculator with custom functions to include additional variables to make pricing easier.

In contrast to a financial calculator, where you do the calculation and it displays a result, using a tool such as T-Value™, InfoAnalysis™, or SuperTRUMP™ produces a report. These reports not only provide a visual of what you calculated, but you can also include them with the transaction documentation as a record of how you priced.

An example of where spreadsheets come in handy for pricing as a lessor is when you need to calculate the present value and net present value of a portfolio of transactions to come up with the purchase price for the collection of transactions.

In addition to the tools used by lessors internally to calculate lease and equipment finance transaction pricing, many lessors are also providing online tools to interact with customers such as end-users, vendors, and dealers, via online portals. Quick pricing and quote calculation tools are often a feature of these online portals. Some companies even provide mobile pricing tools to allow their customers to calculate lease pricing quickly on the go.

True (Tax) Lease Pricing

Comparison of Tax Implications for Lease Pricing

In this chapter, thus far, we ignored any impact of taxes on pricing calculations. These pricing strategies and skills work just fine for loans or leases treated as conditional sales contracts. But for transactions classified as a true tax lease, many lessors integrate the effects of their tax benefits into their lease pricing.

In a true tax lease of this sort, the lessor recognizes the full amount of the lease payments as rental income; however, the lessor is also entitled to recognize the depreciation expense of owning the equipment. In most cases, MACRS depreciation exceeds the rental income in the early years of the lease, giving the lessor a net taxable loss. In the later years of a true tax lease, the rental income exceeds the MACRS depreciation, giving the lessor net taxable income. In the end, the total amount of income to the lessor is the same whether the lease is a true tax lease or a conditional sales contract, but the timing of the income and loss can affect the lessor's yield.

Consider the following example comparing nearly identical transactions when one is a true tax lease, and one is a conditional sales contract:

Infinispace Transport, Inc., a growing space industry transportation supply company, is acquiring an autonomous shuttle bus for their growing West Coast technology engineering campus. The following example compares nearly identical transactions, one structured as a conditional sales contract and the other as a true tax lease.

Conditional Sales Contract Scenario

Infinispace Transport, Inc. acquires a shuttle at the cost of $100,000. It negotiates a sixty-month lease at $1,879 per month with payments in advance and a $10,000 balloon payment.

Over the life of the contract, Infinispace Transport, Inc. pays a total of $122,740 (60 x $1,879 plus $10,000). The lessor's total income over the life of the contract is, therefore, $22,740. In other words, Infinispace Transport, Inc. repaid $100,000 of principal and $22,740 in interest. The interest income recognized by the lessor would look like this:

	Income	Cumulative Income
Year 1	$6,737.05 interest income	$6,737.05
Year 2	$6,141.99 interest income	$12,879.04
Year 3	$4,780.38 interest income	$17,659.42
Year 4	$3,305.71 interest income	$20,965.13
Year 5	$1,708.68 interest income	$22,673.81
Year 6	$66.19 interest income	$22,740.00
TOTAL	$122,740	

True Tax Lease Scenario

Infinispace Transport, Inc. acquires a shuttle at the cost of $100,000. It negotiates a sixty-month lease at $1,879 per month with payments in advance and with a purchase option at the then Fair Market Value (estimated at $10,000 for pricing purposes).

Assuming that Infinispace Transport, Inc. exercises its purchase option at the end, then over the life of the contract, it pays a total of $122,740 (60 x $1,879 plus $10,000). The lessor's total income over the life of the contract is $122,740. However, the lessor also recognizes depreciation expense.

According to IRS Publication 946 (How to Depreciate Property) if the equipment is a five-year MACRS asset, depreciation could be recognized on the half-year convention at 20 percent in the first year, 32 percent in the second year, 19.2 percent in the third year, 11.52 percent in the fourth year, and 11.52 percent in the fifth year, leaving a basis of 5.76 percent at the end of the five years.

The lessor's income and expense would line up year by year like this:

	Income	Expense	Net Income (Loss)	Cumulative Income (Loss)
Year 1	$22,548 rental income	$20,000 depreciation	$2,548	$2,548
Year 2	$22,548 rental income	$32,000 depreciation	($9,452)	($6,904)
Year 3	$22,548 rental income	$19,200 depreciation	$3,348	($3,556)
Year 4	$22,548 rental income	$11,520 depreciation	$11,028	$7,472
Year 5	$22,548 rental income	$11,520 depreciation	$11,028	$18,500
Year 6	$10,000 sale price of asset	$5,750 book value of asset sold	$4,240	$22,740
TOTAL	$122,740		$22,740	

Now lay the cumulative lessor income for each year side by side for the two different scenarios:

	Conditional Sales Contract Cumulative Income	True Tax Lease Cumulative Income (Loss)
Year 1	$6,737.05	$2,548
Year 2	$12,879.04	($6,904)
Year 3	$17,659.42	($3,556)
Year 4	$20,965.13	$7,472
Year 5	$22,673.81	$18,500
TOTAL	$22,740.00	$22,740

Clearly, the lessor who writes a conditional sales contract has more cumulative taxable income, and therefore, pays more income tax every single year of the life of the contract until the very end when they even out. In the case of the true tax lease, the lessor is not avoiding income taxes but is deferring income taxes. The value in deferring income taxes once again has to do with the time value of money. If a lessor can hold onto its money longer by paying its income taxes later, then it can make use of that money in the meantime to earn additional income.

Elements Affecting True Lease (Tax Lease) Pricing

Determining the effect of deferring income taxes on yield and pricing depends on many factors, some of which include:

- Federal income tax rate of the lessor
- State income tax rate of the lessor
- Local income tax rate of the lessor
- Federal MACRS depreciation term for the equipment
- Lessor's state's treatment of depreciation
- Lessor's IDC
- Lessor's amortizable fees (i.e., doc fees, etc.)

> Note: When the benefit of a tax deduction is assumed in pricing, keep in mind the impact of corporate tax rate changes. If the tax rate changes to a lower amount, the benefit is decreased.

Pricing with tax benefits is complicated. The challenge is that it is not possible to know the payment until the value of the tax benefits is known, but the tax benefits are not known until the payment is known.

A computer can solve this chicken-and-egg problem by starting with a formula that is too high and one that is too low. Then interpolating solving the question.

Residual Value Estimation

The FMV residual estimate is a determination of the value of the equipment at some later date such as the end of the term. This valuation helps the lessor to get comfortable with the return and sale of the asset on the back end of the transaction. The reason for this structure is to minimize the payment stream for the initial lease term, during which the lessor is financing a lesser amount because the equipment is expected to come back with some value.

In the context of true tax leases, there are several approaches for estimating the residual value for purposes of pricing calculation.

- If the residual is unknown, use $0 residual.
- Establish a floor that you can be comfortable with such as 10 percent or 5 percent residual.
- For large-ticket lease transactions, obtain a forward appraisal estimate for the fair market value at the end of the lease term.
- For large-ticket lease transactions, consider obtaining residual value insurance (RVI).

For more details on how these upfront residual value estimates are determined, see the Asset Management section in Chapter 9 – Portfolio Management.

Sinking Fund Rate

A sinking fund rate is the earnings rate applied to the balance of investment during sinking fund (or disinvestment) phases and is an essential element of yields based on after-tax cash flows (such as the Multiple Investment Sinking Fund (MISF). Such yields break the calculation into investment and sinking fund phases. The yield is the earnings rate during the investment phase (when the investor has an investment balance), and the sinking fund rate is the earnings rate in phases when the investor has temporarily received extra cash back from the investment, in anticipation of future outflows. Usually, these are for paying taxes on the residual value. The sinking fund rate is a low rate (often 0 percent) on those temporary cash balances.

Summary

A sound understanding of lease pricing is necessary for the equipment leasing and finance professional. The ability to confidently "do the math" as well as "check the math," enables lessors to protect their company and their customers, identify simple errors, and even detect signs of fraud. More importantly, the lessor can assure customers that they are getting the best finance deal to meet their needs.

Although the mathematics of lease pricing may seem overwhelming at first, as stated in the introduction to this chapter, it helps to break the concepts down into separate parts and practice the various calculations. Multiple lease pricing practice problems are included in the appendix.

Chapter 5 – Sales and Marketing

The learning goals for this chapter:

- Understand the difference between sales and marketing and how they work together.
- Understand how transaction size, customer type, and origination model affects both sales and marketing.
- Understand the purpose for each of the three origination models, the different approaches, benefits, and drawbacks to each.
- Understand that sales and marketing vary from one equipment finance company to the next.

In the context of the CLFP BOK Framework, sales and marketing is the beginning phase of the origination lifecycle.

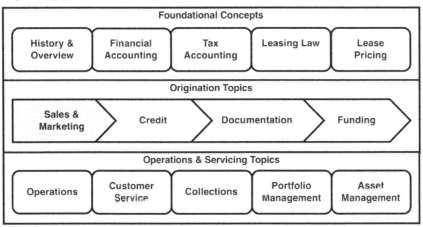

Figure 30 CLFP BOK Framework

Role and Purpose of Sales and Marketing

Approaches for sales and marketing vary widely across our industry and even within the same equipment finance organization. Some lessors have the benefit of an organized marketing group and can do high-level objective planning. However, smaller companies may not have that same capability. Keep in mind that in all of the examples and approaches covered, your company structure and culture may be different from what is represented here. In the equipment finance industry, sales and marketing fundamentals apply regardless of company size and situation. There are plenty of resources and tools and entire books available to go deeper into the details of sales and marketing techniques. The purpose of this chapter is to broadly cover sales and marketing in the context of equipment finance and more specifically speak to the common types of origination channels used in our industry.

Although there are many overlaps, it is it is necessary to understand the difference between marketing and sales and how they fit into an equipment finance company. Sales and marketing professionals have different focuses and methods, but ultimately, they are working toward the same organizational goals.

Marketing Role & Purpose	Sales Role & Purpose
• Big picture marketing strategy and brand identity.	• The act of influencing a customer to buy a product or service.
• Generate awareness of the company, products, and solutions.	• Convert the leads generated through marketing into sales.
• Use a variety of methods to generate leads.	• Sales role requires utilizing your company strengths/goals to determine your target market. This includes identifying prospective customers by the type of account, by company size or structure (public, private, small or medium business, etc.), industry, equipment type, average transaction size, credit quality, and location.
• Marketing activities support the sales effort and play a significant role in stimulating the sales process.	
• Marketing efforts occur before a sale is made and after the sale to pave the way for future referrals and sales.	
• Marketing activities may be employed throughout the equipment financing and leasing lifecycle to retain and encourage return customers.	
• Marketing team may provide handouts, sales and/or customer promotions, and collateral materials.	

Sales and Marketing Coordination and Collaboration

Whether you are a single broker working out of a home office or a multi-billion-dollar financial institution, the concepts of marketing and sales have to be integrated. Having a sales and marketing plan is vital. From the big picture marketing plan, you can distill it down to identify the daily sales activities required to achieve business goals.

In a smaller equipment finance company, these activities may be performed by the same person, while larger companies may have an entire department dedicated to marketing and supporting the efforts of the sales force. Marketing activity assists sales in creating new products and programs to overcome lease avoidance and maintaining regular contact with customers and prospects.

Some typical examples of the integration of sales and marketing efforts in an equipment finance company are listed below:

- **Brand:** Marketing focuses on the big picture, creating and differentiating the company brand. These branding efforts enable the sales professional to have an audience with the prospect. When associated with a strong brand, it is easier for the sales professional to get in the door with potential customers.

- **Top of Mind Awareness:** Marketing efforts generate appeal for potential customers, generating trust and brand name recognition and helping sales professionals to stay top of mind with their audience of prospective clients.
- **Continuous Contact:** Continual contact and follow up with customers, even a soft touch matters. Regardless of origination channel, relationships are vital for the sales process.

Equipment Finance Origination Channels

The three most common origination channels are direct, vendor, and third-party origination (TPO). Portfolio acquisition is also considered an origination channel for some finance companies. Sales and marketing approaches and tools employed may vary by origination channel.

Who is your customer? In the direct origination channel, the customer is the end-user of the equipment. In the vendor and third-party origination channels, the customer relationship is on multiple levels. In vendor origination, the primary customer is the vendor who is the source of financing opportunities for the lessor as well as the end-user of the equipment (the lessee). Similarly, in third-party origination, the lessor's primary customer is the source of financing opportunities (referral source) and, depending on the third-party relationship, the lessee. Table 15 is an "at a glance" comparison of key characteristics of the three most common origination channels. (Each origination channel is explained in more detail later in this chapter).

Table 15 Comparison of 3 Common Origination Channels

Characteristic	Direct Origination	Vendor Origination	Origination via TPO
Sales Force	• The lessor's internal sales professionals	• The vendor's salesforce or dealer representatives	• Referral sources generate sales.
Training	• Lessors focus on training internal sales professionals on credit requirements and products.	• Lessors focus on educating internal staff, the vendor organization, and sales force on the program particulars.	• Lessors educate the referral source on financial products and credit requirements.
Customer Interaction	• The lessor's customer is the end-user of the equipment whom the lessor interacts with through the entire origination process.	• The vendor's or dealer's sales representatives generate transaction flow for the lessor. Many vendors have a lease administrator or "finance department" that interacts with lessor's and the vendor's sales staff to request credit checks and coordinate financing transactions.	• Although this may take many forms, typically the third-party originator interacts with the end-customer and lender to coordinate the transaction.
Relationship Objectives	• Meeting the needs of the customer by differentiating on customization, customer experience, and relationship. The value for the customer is a tailored, specific, and complete solution working with a single organization.	• The objective for the vendor is not financing, but to sell more equipment using financing as a sales tool. The lessor aims to generate a reliable quality flow of business that fits the goals of the organization. • Vendors may also receive a referral fee from the lessor or build in additional margin. • Lessors may provide the vendor with private labeled documents, online tools, residual sharing, etc.	• For referral sources, the goal is to increase their reputation with lenders. • For the end-customer, working with a TPO gives them specialized attention to meet their business needs and additional sources of funding. • For the lender, the relationship helps to generate a flow of business to fit portfolio goals.

Characteristic	Direct Origination	Vendor Origination	Origination via TPO
Relationship Agreement	• In some direct relationships, lessors may establish a Master Agreement custom program to meet the specific repeat buying needs of the customer.	In both vendor origination and TPO, the lessor typically establishes some level of written understanding between the source and the lessor, which can range from an email to a formal document outlining how the parties will work together.	

Even though each company does it slightly different, the basic process of originating a lease or equipment finance transaction typically follows the same high-level phases as illustrated in Figure 31.

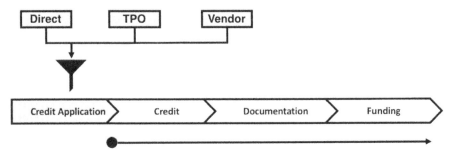

Figure 31 Origination Channel Impact on Deal Flow

It is important to understand the nuances of each origination channel because the source of the transaction is a fundamental contributor to variations in how transactions flow through the remaining phases of the origination lifecycle.

Variations in Approach

Approaches vary by leasing company type, origination channel, industry, customer size, and even customer need. Large corporate direct sales are different than meeting with a small to midsized company that needs lease financing to move them to the next level in their company growth. For example, a large institutional customer may not need financing so much as they need solutions and that is where a knowledgeable equipment finance sales professional can bring value to the relationship.

Across the industry, equipment finance companies use a wide variety of approaches for marketing and sales. For instance, banks or other large lessors working with manufacturer relationships may require meetings between c-level executives to establish a formal vendor relationship and program agreement. Whereas, a lessor serving a specialized industry may use pre-approved credit lines to use as a marketing tool. Depending on complexity, this may lead to very different marketing needs compared to the needs of a broker serving a specialized industry niche. A technology captive finance company working with large corporations may use creative financing programs explicitly tailored to solve the customer's pain points. Imagine, for example, a high-tech company that always needs to have the latest notebooks, storage, or servers; they may benefit from a "refresh" program that allows them not only to replace their hardware but also to take care of the recycling of the old equipment on their behalf.

A bank equipment finance executive who needs to serve customers across multiple business lines may look at it like this,

"essentially you are marketing to your internal team first; yes, you have external communication, but you are marketing to your employees to ensure awareness of equipment financing products as well as process and solutions. Doing this equips your internal staff to talk about leasing with their customers and prospects."

An independent lessor might choose to target advertising to end-users of equipment within their selected markets. Regardless of company size, origination channel, and method, as a lessor, sales and marketing strategies and tactics all tie back to what you offer, what makes you competitive, and what will resonate with markets that you serve.

Marketing

The American Marketing Association defines marketing[12] as "the activity, set of institutions, and processes for creating, communicating, delivering, and exchanging offerings that have value for customers, clients, partners, and society at large." (AMA Approved July 2013) Simply stated, marketing is the process of finding, developing, and profiting from opportunities.

A vital component of this process is the marketing plan. Each equipment finance company regardless of size develops its specific marketing plan. By understanding customer needs, interests, and desires, the company can supply a product, service, or support in a way that both attracts potential customers and generates a profit. A necessary aspect of this planning process includes target identification, market analysis, and segmentation.

Target identification is sometimes a matter of luck. A sales professional may call on businesses in an industry and start to have success; then they continue to go deeper into that industry. More often targeting is, a matter of strategic market research, industry experience, and expertise.

Once a lessor identifies a target market, market research is conducted to understand further its particulars, such as buying trends, seasonal aspects, market needs, and growth. This information provides a basis for sales projections regarding new lease volume, pricing flexibility, profit margins, advertising, and staffing. The definition of a target market includes more consideration than just the industry. Other questions to consider: Is the focus

---

[12] Source: https://www.ama.org/AboutAMA/Pages/Definition-of-Marketing.aspx
Accessed 2/10/18

on equipment vendors or mostly marketing directly to lessees? Is the emphasis on referral sources (banks, CPAs, brokers, etc.)?

Market Segmentation Strategies

Having segmented a market, the task is then to determine which segments are profitable to serve. The business can adopt one of three market segmentation strategies:

- Undifferentiated marketing, in which the business attempts to go after the whole market with a product and marketing strategy intended to have mass appeal
- Differentiated marketing, in which the business operates in several segments of the market with offerings and market strategies tailored to each segment
- Concentrated marketing, in which the business focuses on only one or a few segments with the intention of capturing a large share of these segments

Source: American Marketing Association, AMA Dictionary[13]

Market segmentation for an equipment finance company is about knowing where you want to invest energy to generate business. Lessors look at this in a variety of ways such as industry expertise, pricing, speed, and flexibility (technology capabilities). There are various levels of equipment and financing structures that could suit the strengths of many different lenders. Looking at segmentation allows you to determine where to invest resources to originate business.

Each equipment finance company looks at segmentation and target markets slightly differently. Banks often have industry segment expertise in which cases, the markets are defined. From a captive perspective, the market is defined based on the businesses that are acquiring the type of equipment sold by the company.

A third-party originator may look at it like this,

"Targeting is funding source driven and begins by looking at sources of capital and their credit criteria, restrictions, and availability of capital. The segments may develop by equipment type, industry, geography, transaction size, or credit strength. We are frequently asking the question When my transaction gets to the approval desk, is it acceptable?"

In all origination segments, it is important to understand the customer's business landscape. Knowing the industry and the business of the customer goes a long way toward enabling sales professionals to meet the customer's needs with financing solutions.

There are many considerations for lessors involved in developing market segments, and a few are listed here:

---

[13] Source: http://www.marketing-dictionary.org accessed 2/10/2018

- What are we selling? Are we selling rates? Are we selling based on collateral? Are we selling competitive credit? Are we selling credit or structure flexibility?
- What are our strengths? Are we great at technology? Are we great at speed? Is our expertise centered on a specific transaction size such as small-ticket? Is our advantage in developing new relationships? Do we have specialized industry knowledge?
- What is our understanding of the industry? For lessors, the better you understand the market you are in, the better portfolio performance you will have over time.
- How invested are the end-users of the equipment in this market? The more investment your end-user has in the industry, the better it is for you. For example, if the customer has to be licensed, certified, and accredited, they have "skin in the game." Look for customers that are committed to the business and industry in which they operate.

Components of a Marketing Plan

The marketing plan is a document allowing a lessor to achieve consistency in the critical areas of product, price, distribution channels, and promotion. The marketing plan sets the direction of the company and typically contains extensive research and information about the company's past triumphs and challenges.

A typical marketing plan consists of the following components to help the equipment finance company target the markets in which it wants to operate.

- **Executive Summary:** Sets the purpose and direction of the entire organization and includes research highlights, future company direction, and may also include the company's mission statement and overall goals.
- **Situation Analysis**: This analysis typically includes a market summary, environmental audit, funding, keys to success, critical issues, credit quality, and historical results.
- **Market Summary/Analysis:** The market summary determines the "go-to-market" strategy and defines the target markets in which the lessor has chosen to operate. A good market summary starts with an investigation of the size, scope, and strength of the market.
- **Environmental Audit:** Once the target market is defined, a company must determine how it fits within that environment. The environmental audit forces a leasing entity to look at a variety of factors that may influence its success.

Keys to Successful Execution

Once the marketing plan is in place, it is beneficial to list important factors that make the difference between success and failure for the organization.

- **Critical issues:** These are challenges to address for the plan to work; for instance, hiring needs, how to ensure availability of sufficient capital, training needs, equipment requirements, and competition to overcome.

- **Historical results**: These detail past plans, successes, failures, and performance measurements. Showing historical results provides transparency and enhances the plan's credibility.
- **Marketing strategy**: Once a company has an understanding of the landscape of the marketplace and its relationship to that market, a comprehensive strategy is developed to reach the goals set for the company.
- **Financials**: The financial section of the plan covers the specifics of projected volume, revenue, expenditures, profit, and rates of return as well as balance sheet concerns. It should provide details sufficient to allow the company to monitor performance on a periodic basis.

4 Ps of Marketing

The marketing strategy integrates the four traditional elements of marketing: product, price, promotion, and place.

- **Product**: The product must be completely and thoroughly defined. In doing so, it is necessary to understand what you are selling. Consider that equipment finance companies are not just selling "financing;" instead they are usually selling a means to an end. In most cases, the product is more about the equipment than it is about the financing. Considerations for product may include the following types of questions. What is the size range of expected transactions? What are servicing and support is necessary for the overall product? What payment structures, funding, and residual assumptions do we anticipate? How is our product strategy influenced by the availability of funding or the risk appetite of funding sources?
- **Price**: The development of an effective pricing strategy is the most important and complex factor in the design of a marketing plan. Considerations include the cost of funds, estimation of future losses, expense coverage, competition, and desired profit. A variety of internal and external issues may affect pricing. The pricing plan should have the flexibility to deal with change and respond accordingly.
- **Promotion**: The purpose of promotion is to educate the targeted prospect about the company's products and services, and to differentiate it from competitors. Products are advertised, promoted, or publicized through a variety of methods which, due to technological advances, are continually evolving.
- **Place/distribution**: Place refers to how the product reaches the customer. In the equipment finance industry, these distribution methods are called origination channels.

Monitoring and Measuring Success of the Marketing Plan

There are a variety of methods to monitor the marketing plan and measure success. The financial section of the plan typically includes projected goals for selected measurements. Such measurements could be in the form of total volume, market penetration, market share, return on investment, return on equity, return on assets, margin, and many others, depending upon the goals.

The environment in which an equipment finance company operates is not static; thus, marketing plans should be used and referred to regularly. When there are changes to this environment, the most well thought out plan could become a recipe for financial problems unless it is altered to respond to such changes. It is a good practice to build the discipline of ongoing monitoring and control into the plan and establish who has accountability and responsibility for each area of the plan. A common practice is to set up reporting and tracking, checkpoints, and regular reviews to ensure that the plan is working as desired.

Sales

The purpose of sales is converting the prospect into a customer. At the core of selling is matching the benefits and features of the lessor's products to the prospect's needs and approaches vary by industry, origination channel, customer size, and customer need. There are numerous resources available that teach sales methods, strategies, and techniques that are beyond the scope of this manual. In this section, we focus on sales within the equipment finance context. The typical sales process of converting a prospect to a customer may include the following activities.

Marketing
- Campaigns
- Social media
- Events
- E-mail

Prospecting
- Trade shows
- Commercial databases
- Associations
- Public records
- Prior customers and vendors

Qualify Leads
- Finding prospects that find the product appealing
- Contacting, communicating, and evaluating prospects

Discover
- Understand needs of prospective customer
- Information gathering

Value Proposition
- Tailoring the benefits of the product specifically to the prospect's wants and needs
- Presenting the product to the prospect

Figure 32 High-level Sales Process

The time and level of activity to convert prospects to customers vary widely ranging from minutes in a highly automated small-ticket scenario to months for a complicated large-ticket opportunity.

Filling the Prospect's Need

A key to filling the prospect's need is to put yourself in the customer's shoes and having a product or solution that the customer feels is tailored to meet their needs. Understand the customer's pain points. For example, in the health care market, customers require programs explicitly tailored to health care to help them deal with the rapidly changing landscape of their industry such as security on IT products and digitization of medicine. Ask yourself, how might we help our customers to stay relevant when things are changing so rapidly?

"As a sales professional for a captive lessor, I think the outside world believes that we sit here with the catcher's mitt and wait for our teammates who sell the equipment just to funnel transactions or customers to us. While that's true in some instances, it doesn't often happen.
– Sales Executive and CLFP, Captive Lessor

Mind the Portfolio

Sales professionals, especially in the direct origination channel, need to keep an eye on their portfolio of clients and prospects as well as the alignment of their sales activities with the overall company objectives to hit their personal and organizational sales targets. For sales professionals, it is essential to understand the economics of their portfolio. How many of your clients will need financing this year? How many of your current client contracts are nearing the end of their term? How many new clients do you need to bring on to hit your targets? These questions and more can be answered through the use of smart Customer Relationship Management (CRM) and analytical tools widely available today.

In any origination channel, the sales professional must collaborate with credit and portfolio so that you are bringing in the right type of business that aligns with your company strategy, achieves profitability goals, avoids concentration issues, and preserves credit quality.

Sales Participation Throughout the Origination Lifecycle

In the context of the equipment finance origination lifecycle, sales activities typically take place before and during the credit application phase of the process. Depending on company structure, process, and origination channels, sales professionals participate in the origination process until the funding stage of the transaction is complete. From a customer relationship standpoint, depending on the situation (especially in direct origination), the sales professional may continue to be involved in the customer relationship after funding. As an example, a broker sales professional coordinates between the lessee and the lessor and may remain engaged in the customer relationship for the life of the transaction. At the other end of the extreme, in a small-ticket vendor origination scenario, sales professionals may be involved in establishing and maintaining the vendor relationship, but with the benefits of automation and streamlined processing, they may have little to no involvement with individual transactions originated through the program.

Communication and Customer Experience

Communication methods vary widely depending on the origination channel and scale of leasing. As an example, micro-ticket transactions may be largely technology driven with little to no human interaction. The other extreme is large-ticket leasing, which is highly customized, requires specific domain knowledge and development of deep relationship to become a solution provider for the customer. Small-ticket and mid-ticket leasing fall somewhere in between.

146

Other factors that add to the variation in communication with customers are the customer company size, management structure, and level of technology adoption. Technology and event-driven communications vary with triggered automated responses to communicate status updates, self-service portals, and both proactive and reactive phone calls. Even with so much technological capability, human interaction, outside sales, building relationships, and building trust is still highly valued. Specifically, in the development of vendor programs, consistency is important to the vendor relationship and the lessor views the vendor as customer.

While we rely heavily on technology today, with multiple channels for communication, it can be frustrating for the customer. The sales professional must identify customer communication preferences and understand that not everyone has the same communication preferences in this digital age. There is no single way to interact and communicate with customers – everyone has new preferences these days. It is important to listen well and pay attention.

The challenge is to identify and create systematized approaches to communicate with customers in their preferred manner. This results in the need for ongoing system enhancements as technology continues to evolve. The opportunity is to make sure that you are taking advantage of technology and continually improving. Smaller financial institutions with less regulatory oversight are sometimes nimbler where technology adoption is concerned, creating an advantage.

The Necessity of the Niche

The fitting together of a product with a specific sector of the market is developing a "niche." When a lessor focuses on a market segment, whether that segment is large or small, the sales process is simplified. A company cannot be everything to everybody. It is typically small-ticket, middle-market, or large-transaction driven. Even within these categories, the focus needs to be on a few areas. Medical is different than yellow iron, which is different from computer, copier, or telephone systems. By concentrating on a few areas, the leasing company develops expertise in that market enabling it to fund more transactions and to be a better fit for its customers.

For instance, brokers might service one or two niches, while larger institutions might develop several niches via different divisions. Aircraft, transportation, medical, construction, and high-tech are some of the more common examples of specialized niche markets.

Tailoring the Benefits of the Product to Prospect Needs

A sales professional should strive to know the customer and the outcome they want to achieve as well as the financing options to help them achieve their end goal.

When preparing the proposal, this means understanding how the prospect expects to evaluate the offer, i.e., by lowest rate, lowest all-in cost, lowest payment, residual disposition assistance, etc. Consider what you will offer to meet the customer's needs.

Proposals

Presentations of proposals range from an email notifying the prospect of their online application approval to a formal boardroom presentation. Typically, a written format is the best method to present the offer to avoid disputes and misunderstandings. While proposal formats vary widely, a written proposal typically includes the following types of information:

- Parties to the transaction (lender-lessee/borrower and/or guarantors)
- Type of transaction (finance lease, operating lease, tax lease, loan, etc.)
- Payment Terms (seasonal rentals, low-hi, hi-low structures, advance payments)
- Purchase/renewal terms at the end of lease
- Credit Requirements
- Residual Treatment
- Tax/insurance requirements
- Equipment description
- Equipment cost and expected delivery/funding dates
- Fees/miscellaneous transaction costs
- Expiration Date of the Proposal
- Documentation requirements
- Any additional requirements such as additional collateral, pre-payment penalties, rate indexing
- A disclaimer that the document is just a proposal and not a commitment, and that by accepting this proposal the client is making an application for the approval of the facility
- A place for the prospect to formally accept the proposal and commit to the facility. Often a fee is collected at this time to consummate the acceptance in which case the proposal includes an explanation of the specific use and application of that fee.

Typical Sales and Marketing Tools

Modern technology and tools are reshaping the approach to marketing across the industry. With the rapid rise in advances in marketing innovation today, technology is frequently used in marketing and sales to generate leads, manage marketing campaigns, develop relationships, and more. Lead generation and sales methods vary across origination models and lease company types. Table 16 lists some examples of modern tools employed in leasing and equipment finance sales and marketing.

Many equipment finance companies today see technology as vital for increasing sales volume. For instance, a sales professional may be able to process five to ten transactions in a week with the manual approach; however, using technology they can scale to 30 or more transactions a week and track the statistics for all of them. Scaling volume without technology is challenging.

"I'm in small-ticket leasing, and for ten years, I've been telling people that we're a technology company that happens to lend money. If you think about the direction in which our business is heading, technology is the fundamental underpinning of small-ticket leasing.

We use it in our scoring and credit adjudication; we use it in the documentation, we're a full electronic signature shop. We use technology for storage and sharing of information that we use throughout the organization. We are a technology company that focuses on how we scale our business. We can't do that by throwing people at it.

Fifteen years ago, you might have an accounting staff of 25 people. Today you do not need that simply because of the technology used everywhere in our business. The same is true on the marketing side. If we are not talking about how we're leveraging technology to effectively market and to drive sales, then I think we're missing the context of the world we live in today.

There are some companies still using traditional approaches like direct mail marketing, and frankly, some of them do well with that, but they're very few and far between."

Bank Equipment Finance Company Executive and CLFP

The abundance of options for marketing innovation is vast and beyond the scope of this handbook. Specific to equipment finance companies, sales and marketing technology typically comes into play with CRM, communication, and analytics. The following table lists a few examples of the sales and marketing tools and technology used in the equipment finance industry today.

Table 16 Examples of Sales and Marketing Tools

Tool Type	Examples Tools & Technology Commonly Used in Equipment Finance
Market and Lead Research Tools	• LinkedIn Sales Navigator • D&B • UCC
Customer Relationship and Contact Management Tools	• Spreadsheets • Contact management software CRM platforms (e.g., salesforce.com, Microsoft Dynamics, and more)
Email Platforms	• MailChimp • ConstantContact

	• ConvertKit
Industry Specific Software	• Broker software specific to managing equipment finance vendor and customer relationships
	• Various origination platforms
Communication	• Email
	• Mobile phone
	• SMS/texting
	• Conference calling
	• Web Meetings
	• Video conferencing
Analytics	• Visual desktop and cloud-based analytic tools
	• Analytics embedded in CRM platforms
	• Excel
Social Media	• HootSuite
	• Twitter
	• Instagram
	• Facebook
	• LinkedIn

Contact and Customer Relationship Management

Tools used for contact and customer relationship management range from spreadsheets, email contact management, to sophisticated CRM platforms. Regardless of the tool used, sales professionals must have some means to manage contacts, capture information on interactions with those contacts, and a mechanism to stay on top of following up. Whether you keep your contacts on a spreadsheet or in CRM platform, the key is to track them.

Across the various origination channels, contact and relationship management is necessary on a variety of levels. Some examples are listed here:

- Vendor origination requires managing relationships with vendors, vendors sales reps, end-users of equipment as well as the programs offered to each vendor.
- Direct origination requires the management of direct customer relationships.
- Third-party origination requires management of lender relationships, referral source relationships, as well as end-user relationships.
- Portfolio acquisition requires managing preferences and relationship parameters for lender, investor, and source relationships.

The Direct Origination Channel

Direct Origination: Direct equipment finance origination is a relationship where a lessor's staff works with the end-customer throughout the entire origination lifecycle from proposal to credit application through underwriting, documentation, and funding; thus, the lessor maintains control of the customer relationship.

Direct origination often fulfills a very particular customer need. The key to direct sales is understanding the customer's pain points and helping to solve business problems through financing solutions. With larger companies, it is often about financing solutions to help them achieve their business objectives within budgeting constraints.

"My customers do not need financing; they need solutions,
so that is what I develop for them. It's about solving their problems."
~Sales Executive and CLFP – Technology Captive Equipment Finance Company

Understanding the customer's pain points is the key to developing these tailored solutions. What is it that is difficult for the customer? How might you make their business life simpler with your financing solution? How might you help the customer acquire the equipment they need to achieve business objectives within their budgetary constraints?

In another example, consider hospitals and the challenges they often face with accounting, payables, and administration. When you understand the nuances and niches of these organizations, you can come in with a financing solution that makes their life easier. Understanding what is difficult for a customer and then having a solution allows you to come in and offer unique value.

Meeting the needs of a large corporate client

As an example of working with customers to solve their specific business problem, you may work with a large corporate client, and they do not necessarily need cash, but you can still find out what they do need and tailor a financial solution to meet the need.

Let's say a large company leases servers for a three or more-year term. As you get to know them, you find out that their real pain point is not the need for cash as much as the coordination pain involved in staying current with the technology and the process of recycling technology equipment at the end of its life. You could approach this with a financing solution that saves them money and also solves the headache of recycling equipment needing replacement.

As one CLFP leasing executive stated, "Generally, the larger the organization, the more difficult it can be to work with them. Understanding how to help the customer deal with their 'chaos' can often help you to earn their business."

For direct client relationships, some lessors set up customer-specific financing programs. These customer-specific programs are different from vendor programs. In these cases, the lessor sets up a Master Agreement type arrangement for multiple transactions with a particular customer relationship.

While one may assume that small-ticket leasing is more typical in vendor and TPO channels, there is value to direct origination of small-ticket leasing within banks to serve the needs of existing customer relationships. In these cases, the benefit to the organization is not in the volume of transactions; it is in solidifying and strengthening the customer relationship. Direct leasing origination capability also enables banks to expand their footprint and provide financing solutions in addition to other banking products to meet specific customer needs.

Following are some of the challenges that impact equipment financing and leasing within institutions having multiple commercial finance lines of business:

- **Exposure and Concentration Limits**: Limits for credit exposure and concentration may be a challenge for banks that have other lines of commercial lending business. (Commercial Real Estate, Commercial and Industrial (C&I) lending, etc.)

- **Relationship Management**: Bank lessors often face the challenge of relationship management across multiple lines of business. Relationship managers for other lending lines, C&I lending, for instance, may inadvertently set mixed expectations with the customer on the rate or other elements of the transaction due to differences in approach between C&I lending and equipment finance. Internal communication among relationship managers is important for customer relationships which cross lines of business.

- **The domain of expertise**: A challenge for captive leasing sales reps is the limitation on what types of equipment they can finance. For example, a computer company may not be able to do leases for the furniture and fixtures the client may also need.

Benefits and Drawbacks

There are a few other benefits and drawbacks to consider for direct origination.

Benefits

- Efficiency in targeting the right type of business.
- Control over the resources involved in selling the financing product.
- Selling directly to the lessee can be cleaner because you have direct contact with the lessee.
- The lessor can provide more service to the lessee because there are no intermediaries; the lessor is not going through a broker to deal with the customer.
- In the case of banks, having a direct origination sales force enables expansion of the relationship with its banking customers.

Drawbacks

- May be less efficient to obtain business through cold calling.
- For larger financial institutions exposure limitations and compensation challenges that cross lines of business can become an issue.
- If you have that one "golden goose" customer and they go away, it hurts. The ebbs and flows of direct business may be emotional; it is possible to spend a lot of time working an opportunity without

results. It is not a flow business like a TPO or vendor transaction. In the direct channel, you establish the relationship and then have to get another relationship to get another transaction.

- Limitation of a single funding source may lead to lack of solution variety.

The Vendor Origination Channel

Vendor: A purveyor of equipment from whom a lessor purchases equipment at the specific request of a lessee for a lease to that lessee; a supplier.

Vendor Leasing: Lease financing offered to an equipment end-user in conjunction with the sale of equipment. Vendor leases may be provided by the equipment vendor (two-party lease) or a third-party leasing company with a close working relationship with the equipment vendor.

Vendor Program: Vendor programs are a relationship with a manufacturer and seller of equipment.

Vendor relationships can be an excellent way for a lessor to establish a stream of consistent, profitable volume in which the vendor becomes a lessor's sales agent. Before entering into such relationships, lessors typically perform due diligence on the industry, type of equipment, and the potential vendors. Nurturing and regularly evaluating vendor relationships ensures that they are producing the desired results for all parties involved.

Many equipment finance companies choose to develop vendor relationships as a major part of their go- to-market strategy. Additionally, potential lessees are more likely to work with a lessor when it comes with a recommendation from a vendor; such referrals simplify the sales process. However, there are many aspects of developing and maintaining vendor relationships that the successful lessor needs to evaluate when considering this approach.

Building the Vendor Relationship

Regular communication with various stakeholders within the vendor's organization is central to forming a long-term relationship. The approach for communications depends on where you are in building the relationship. When initially developing a relationship with a prospective vendor, the interaction is more likely to be face-to-face at trade shows. Once the relationship is established, the communication may vary by regular text, calls, emails, or occasional face-to-face meetings.

Many vendors will have a lease administrator or finance department that works with the salesperson to perform credit checks, etc. This approach varies by type of vendor. Determination of which lessor the vendor works with depends on the parameters that drive their business – example: creative financing options, speed, lowest rate, risk appetite, and more.

Vendor relationships may be developed and managed on multiple levels. First, it can be with the manufacturer or seller of the equipment, the vendor organization. Second, it can be with the vendor or manufacturer's sales force. Unless the relationship is exclusive and mandatory, these sales reps are the ones who will determine where the transaction goes. If they like doing business with you, it will lead to more transactions. The third level for managing relationship is with the operations or finance department staff who often interact with the lessor for vendor program transactions. Their primary interests are generally speed of payment and ease of doing business with you.

Developing Vendor Programs

Vendor programs are the lifeblood of successful vendor relationships. They allow the vendor to differentiate themselves from their competition and help the lessor defend its relationship from other lease companies that also solicit this vendor. Programs cover the spectrum from basic referrals and simple offerings of sales-oriented marketing material about leasing, to integrated website links and online portals and blind discounts. Many vendor programs include risk-sharing agreements that include remarketing agreements, vendor guarantees of residual positions, ultimate net loss sharing, and repurchase agreements.

Some of the keys to good vendor programs are making sure there is a clear understanding of the expectations about what the program can do for all the parties involved. This includes management and sales on the vendor's side as well as expectations of fundable volume on the leasing company's side. It is important to revisit the program and manage expectations regularly. This ensures that all stakeholders evaluate whether the program is meeting the needs for which it was designed and whether the program should be improved or modified to meet needs or respond to changing market conditions. Good communication is a must; on the front end of the sales cycle, on the back end in the event of delinquencies and defaults, and over time as conditions change.

From a broker perspective, a vendor program is much like a TPO for a lessor. It is a source of business that is a manufacturer, dealer, or reseller of equipment. These types of programs help equipment resellers to meet their need for consistent sales. Financing programs also help them to sell to clients who do not necessarily have cash or for whom using cash is an objection. As an example, a broker may offer a 0 percent financing program which the vendor helps to support through subsidies, and then the vendor sales staff aggressively sells their product with that financing option. This is commonly referred to as a blind discount,

As one bank lessor stated,

"From our perspective, a vendor program is either a manufacturer or value-added reseller (VAR) engaged in selling technology to end-users that we would partner with to provide financing for that end-user. The strategic purpose and value of vendor programs is scale. We develop a relationship with one customer, the vendor, with whom we can do multiple millions of dollars per year. Operational efficiency and technology capabilities are required to scale vendor business."

In developing programs, it is important to know the pain points of the customers in that market. From the captive sales and marketing standpoint, it's about having a product that the customer is interested in and that they think has been tailored to them. Programs fit the needs of specific markets. For example, health care programs will be different from retail programs. Health care companies may keep some of their medical equipment for a long time; in which case, they wouldn't want a three-year refresh cycle. They may also have "hot buttons" like the need for security on their IT equipment, the need to update other equipment that is changing as things are becoming digitized, and financing solutions that can help them to stay relevant in their marketplace.

The leasing sales professional works with the vendor to develop a mutually beneficial arrangement that enables them to offer financing to their customers so that they can sell more equipment.

"Helping the vendor to sell more; helps the finance company to finance more."

~Leasing Sales Executive and CLFP

The agreement between the funding source and reseller ranges anywhere from a handshake to a guaranty of performance or Right of First Refusal document that requires that lessor has the right to review and accept or refuse to accept all new applications from the vendor. The level of documentation for a program agreement ranges from an email to a multi-page document depending on the scenario. Ideally, program relationships have some degree of written understanding of what will happen and how the program is mutually beneficial. Sometimes a vendor relationship begins informally, financing one-off transactions for a period of time and eventually evolving into a formal vendor agreement.

Even though the approach to program development varies across the industry, in all cases, the common thread is that vendor programs are about generating a flow of business by consistently helping the vendor to sell more equipment with financing.

Vendor Program Types

- Referral Program
- Risk Sharing Program
  - Residual Guaranty
  - Ultimate Net Loss (UNL)
  - Repurchase Agreement
- Third Party
- Private Label
- Virtual Joint Venture
- Joint Venture

Vendor Program Features

Vendor program structures vary widely in both sophistication and formality and cover the spectrum from basic referral and simple offerings of sales-oriented material about leasing, to website links and online portals, to sophisticated fully developed programs. Lessor marketing strategies for programs are typically aligned with the vendor. Some of the methods and features that lessors include in structuring vendor programs are listed below:

- Vendor programs may be product, industry, or vendor specific
- Financing structures to help vendor's product be more attractive to market
- Co-branded programs where lessor and vendor are both represented in the documentation and financing experience
- Online portals for vendors to interact with the lessor to streamline origination.
- Financial merchandising training for vendor salespeople (how to sell financing in your products' market)
- Online self-service portals for lessees to manage their contract obligation
- Risk Sharing Programs:
  - o Remarketing Agreement: Agreement where the vendor manages or assists in the remarketing of assets
  - o Residual Guarantee: Agreement that the vendor guaranties all of, or a portion of the residual position priced into the structure
  - o Ultimate Net Loss (UNL) Agreement: Agreement where the vendor guaranties a portion of the potential loss, generally in a pooled structure for all contracts in that pool
  - o Repurchase Agreements Agreement where the vendor agrees to purchase contracts under specific circumstances
- Private label where the lessor provides financing in the name of the vendor.
- Blind Discount Program: Subsidized rate arrangements such as 0 percent financing for the customer
- Specialized invoicing features: Promotions, Look and Feel
- Lease contract documentation specific to the vendor program agreement

Risk-sharing programs transfer risk from the funding source to the vendor. Given this, the vendor should be underwritten as to their ability to support that risk financially. Often, the vendor will not be able to support any or all of this financial liability. When this occurs, the means of funding this liability may move from a vendor accounting guaranty to a funded guaranty. This may take many forms, including a holdback of a percentage of the funding amount at the time of contract funding, an initial seeding of cash held by the funding source as security for this risk, and/or a combination of these methods.

Segmentation and Targeting Specifics

- In targeting markets, it is essential to know the options you can offer. For a broker, this depends on your funding source's programs. It is important to understand what is and is not acceptable to know what aspect of the market to target. For example, can you target startup businesses?

- Know the options that the competition offers. Is your competition able to match your offers? How does that impact your customer base?
- What are we interested in doing? Where do we have industry knowledge and expertise?
- Do we have access to where potential vendors are, for instance, industry tradeshows and associations?
- What is the demand for essential use equipment? What does it do for the business and how important is it to the business that it remains? What is the incentive for the business to pay for the equipment when times get tough?
- Program opportunities may be scalable, but they still need to make sense. The end-users of the equipment have to need the equipment and want to pay for it. It is also important to look for vendor program opportunities and profiles that match credit appetite and pricing policies.

Marketing Methods

Beyond the typical marketing methods common for any origination channel, there are a few additional methods used by lessors to generate leads for new vendor relationships and stimulate sales within existing vendor programs:

- Trade show attendance is one of the most effective methods for marketing to find new vendors.
- Lessors often collaborate with their vendor relationships to develop marketing collateral to support finance program offers.
- Using online tools, co-branded landing pages, and marketing tools such as links to leasing offers.
- Strategic training of the vendor's organization through sales meeting presentations, continuing education on financial products and benefits of leasing, and training on how to use leasing as a tool for selling equipment.

Benefits and Drawbacks

Benefits

- Vendor origination may be the best way to leverage your sales team, enabling a lessor to scale the sales effort with a higher return on time investment.
- The strategic value of vendor programs for lessors is scale. With vendor programs, the lessor acquires a customer with whom they may potentially generate multiple millions of dollars each year.
- It creates "stickiness" to drive return customer business to both the vendor and lessor.

- Financing programs help vendors to move more of their product so that they can control the sale. Sometimes they may avoid discounting through the added value of convenience through financing.
- By focusing on a monthly payment, vendor salespeople can often increase or "upsell" the customer creating the opportunity for a larger sale.
- It may generate a steady stream of business in an industry that you know and like for the type of business that fits your portfolio goals regarding geography, equipment types, transaction size, and type of credit.
- When compared to other origination channels, vendor programs generally perform better.
- For the vendor, the ability to offer financing options can be a competitive advantage when compared to other vendors.
- For the vendor, financing programs create a relationship with a familiar entity and reliable funding; the ability to avoid "slow pay" situations with unfamiliar leasing companies eliminates uncertainty which enables the vendor to provide a better all-around solution to their customer.

Drawbacks

Unfortunately, fraud is a fact of life in the equipment finance industry, and much of it happens with vendor involvement. There are numerous instances of company-wide fraud by vendors totaling hundreds of millions of dollars. There is also fraud that occurs with collusion of vendor sales representatives and lessees, vendor sales representatives and leasing sales representatives, and fraud by lessees alone. It can be difficult to determine who the perpetrator is and who the victims are. Not only does fraud destroy vendor programs, but it can also ruin unwitting lessors.

In developing vendor programs, there is always the temptation to lessen credit and documentation standards to provide a simpler, easier approval process for lessees. It is critical to review any changes in the credit, documentation, and funding process because fraud is always a possibility. The lessor should remain alert for indicators of fraud, including changed or unusual invoicing, mismatched credit information, problems on verbal confirmations and site inspections, and an unusual push by the various parties to rush the funding process. As with the rest of vendor programs, continued regular communication with the various stakeholders within the vendor's organization can help deter these incidents.

Following are some other drawbacks to be aware of for this origination channel.

- From the outside looking in, it may seem that it is easiest to develop business in the vendor space, but vendors can be fickle. It is essential to find a niche and maintain a diversity of vendors.

- The vendor relationship could put pressure on the lessor to approve transactions they usually wouldn't in the interest of the broader relationship. You must remain disciplined in underwriting.
- Many vendors partner with large lessors to do vendor programs which can take a lot of resources on the part of the lessor. To cover all of the needs of a sophisticated vendor program, the lessor has to have the resources to offer help with promoting the program, supporting unique market needs like seasonality and ultimately remarketing and repossession.
- A lessor may become too dependent on a vendor, if not diversified enough by industry and vendor. Lessors should continually manage concentration and strategically bring on vendor relationships that allow for their targeted levels of diversity in the portfolio. Establishing vendor programs in one industry may lead to the ability to expand to satellite industries or adjacent markets.

The Third-Party Origination Channel

TPO: Companies such as equipment finance brokers, independent lessors, and other types of organizations that refer equipment finance opportunities to finance companies for funding.

Referral Source: Attorneys, CPAs, anyone with insight into a client's need for your financing product could be a referral source of business.

Third-party origination is the process by which external parties bring funding opportunities to the equipment finance company. TPOs are any third-party companies/individuals originating transactions indirectly with the lessor. There is a wide variety of approaches to third-party origination. In some larger financial institutions, portfolio syndication (selling portfolios) is considered a form of third-party origination. More often, when we speak of TPOs, we are referring to other companies such as equipment finance brokers, independent lessors, and various types of organizations that refer equipment finance opportunities to finance companies for funding. Related to third-party origination is the concept of the "Referral Source," these are professionals with a unique capacity to bring business to lessors because of their client relationships. Attorneys, CPAs, anyone with insight into a client's need for your financing product could be a referral source of business, which is different in comparison to a vendor sales representative selling a piece of equipment.

The purpose of third-party origination is to widen transaction origination opportunities and increase portfolio diversity without having a direct sales group. For example, a captive lessor may work with TPOs to acquire certain types of transactions to satisfy portfolio requirements, for instance, buying transactions for minority- or women-owned businesses.

Dealing with TPOs does not necessarily lower the cost, often the cost for third-party origination is higher because of the cost to buy the third-party business. For example, if a lessor's direct origination team looks at the same transaction as the lessor's third-party origination team, the direct origination team may often do it at a lower cost.

Due to the variety of third-party origination scenarios, it is useful to consider perspective to understand this origination channel. From the broker's perspective, as a TPO, their primary role is to coordinate the end-to-end (inception to funding) details of a transaction origination on behalf of the customer. In some cases, they get involved in resolving servicing issues with the lessor. Brokers serve a crucial role as the primary contact in the relationship with the customer, and a key focus is continual attention to the relationship between lessee, lessor, and equipment supplier (vendor).

Similarities to Vendor Origination

In both origination channels, there is often some written understanding, ranging from an email to a formal legal document, which outlines the expectations for how the parties will work together to keep everything above board and ethical. Written understanding not only helps to clarify expectations, it is auditable. As a leasing sales professional, it is helpful to fall back to the relationship agreement whenever there is a question.

Similar to vendor origination, training is a fundamental component to the success of these relationships, and it is essential for lessors to educate referral sources on the types of financial products and credit parameters that may benefit the source's customers. The style and techniques of working with TPOs and referral sources may overlap with vendor origination concerning what you do on a daily basis.

Market Segmentation and Targeting Specifics

There are a variety of ways to segment business in this origination channel. For the TPO, it is imperative to focus in specific industry specializations and niche segments and develop an in-depth understanding of particular markets, such as machine tool or medical, and to develop expertise in distinct equipment and credit types. Another important component of segmentation is to understand the hard assets and what is involved in remarketing it.

TPO (Day in the Life of a Broker)

TPOs must know the business they are in by developing an understanding of the industry, how to serve the needs specific to customers in that sector, as well as identifying quality transactions to send to funding sources. Brokers develop an intuitive ability to understand which financial product and program best suits the customer's need and which lender is best suited to receive the credit application for each customer scenario. Table 17 is an example of what a typical "day in the life" might look like for a broker originating transactions and the interactions with all parties.

Table 17 Typical Broker Origination Activities

Lifecycle Phase	Activities
Opportunity	• The **broker** is contacted by a customer and interviews the customer to understand their situation and provides a quote that meets their need.
Credit Application	• The **broker** processes a credit application and obtains necessary supporting documentation (Credit Bureau Report, tax statements, financials, etc. depending on the situation). • Based on the scenario, the **broker** determines lender placement and submits the application to the **funding source**. Primary considerations for funding source placement may include price, process speed or complexity, credit parameters, transaction type and size, and/or equipment vendor.
Credit Decision	• The **funding source** receives the application from the **broker**, performs their underwriting process, and upon approval, delivers documentation.
Documentation	• The **broker** follows up with the customer to ensure documentation is in order and when the customer fully executes all documents, delivers the documentation package to the **funding source**.
Funding	• The **funding source** receives the documentation package, audits documents and performs necessary due diligence. They then issue a purchase order and fund the equipment purchase. The **broker** may assist to coordinate and follow-up for items such as insurance. Once the **funding source** funds the transaction, the broker's primary involvement in the transaction is complete. • The **funding source** pays commission to the **broker**.
Ongoing Customer Relationship	• Although the **funding source** services the transaction, if there are issues with non-payment, the **broker** may be involved in resolving issues with the customer. • Even though the **broker** is mostly finished with the transaction at funding, they ideally maintain the relationship with the customer and may assist in customer relationship matters at any time throughout the transaction lifecycle.

Communication

It is vital for funding sources to stay in touch with third-party originators and understand when the industry changes by remaining in contact at least quarterly. With continuous communication and follow-up, you are not cold calling when you are reaching out for business. Presence at various industry association events helps TPOs and funding sources to continue to build relationship and rapport.

Broker/Lender Relationship Keys
For brokers, it is important to develop and cultivate good relationships among lessees, lessors, and vendors. One of the most important things a broker can do is promote a good relationship with their lenders.

- Understanding lender credit requirements and appetite for volume
- Build trust
- Prove performance

Submission to Approval and Approved to Funded ratios are vital measures for these relationships. As a broker, it is helpful to develop relationships with many lenders to whom you are important.

Benefits and Drawbacks

Benefits

There are many benefits to all parties in the third-party origination channel. First, for the lessor, it is a means to outsource the sales effort, providing value and solutions for end-customers while controlling costs. At the same time, TPOs enable the lessor to generate a consistent stream of business that meets credit and portfolio criteria from an experienced partner that understands both the industry and the asset niche.

Because of the importance of relationship and reputation, the documentation may also be more reliable, and the chance that the customer meets the lessor's credit criteria is much higher. The TPO is incented to manage the customer relationship and solve problems by coordinating the transaction (resulting in fewer headaches).

For the TPO, the ability to fund transactions without having to incur debt or use cash as well as helping clients with multiple financing options is a benefit. Because the TPO is not servicing the transactions, there is less overhead and administration once the transaction funds.

This channel enables the development of a network of sources to solve client needs that you may be unable to resolve directly and contribute to portfolio diversity. Many TPOs have extreme domain expertise and have developed good reputations in specific industries enabling them to meet particular needs of an end-user.

For the funding source, having a network of referral sources leads to an abundance of transactions to look at without cold calling. The relationships between TPOs and funding sources may be long-lasting.

Drawbacks

Fraud is a reality in equipment finance, and since the lessor is once-removed from the end-customer, perception is that the risk of fraud is higher in this origination channel, resulting in a need for more stringent due diligence to vet referral source relationships as well as individual transactions. TPOs who understand how the business works can perpetrate more complex fraud, which can be harder to detect. Verification and adherence to standards are key. There may be some reduction in fraud risk for small-ticket business with higher levels of automation and fraud detection technology.

Both lessors and TPOs must be efficient and generate a lot of transaction volume (especially for small-ticket business) to profit from this origination channel. Concentration issues may arise when a large TPO sends a high amount of business to a lessor, therefore, monitoring is crucial.

From a customer experience standpoint, there may be less specialization and more pressure to deliver. For the lessee, the customer experience may be more transactional than relational when fee driven. Since the TPO manages the customer relationship, to reduce risk, lessors often insist on speaking directly with the end-customer without circumventing the TPO relationship.

For lenders and lessors receiving TPO business, it is a common practice to have some level of written agreement in place that outlines how the parties will work together.

Marketing Strategies

Although all origination channels have similar approaches to marketing, here are some of the specifics for the third-party origination channel. The marketing approach is often identical to lessor/lender marketing and may include activities such as those listed below:

- Trade show and industry association event attendance
- Referrals
- Trade show advertising for specific industry specialties
- Prospecting for vendors with whom they can work out deals to provide financing
- Direct mail or email campaigns
- Web advertisements

Similar to the vendor origination channel, the key to marketing in this origination channel is relationship over transactions, and it is crucial to build and maintain relationships with sources of business. In these cases, the relationship with the source takes priority over the lessee relationship.

Lease Syndication
A form of indirect origination, lease syndication is the sale and/or assignment of all or part of a lease or loan transaction and may include newly originated deals or groups of transactions from seasoned portfolios. Equipment finance companies set up separate functions to deal with the buying (Buy Desk) and selling (Sell Desk) of transactions.
Syndication sales professionals build relationships with institutional buyers often meeting with buyers and sellers at industry funding conferences. Developing these types of relationships can lead to a flow of transactions (similar to the flow of transactions generated in vendor program relationships).

Some lessors choose to sell a specific portion of their deals as part of their business strategy. When syndication is part of the business strategy, the salability of the transaction is a key consideration early in the origination process. The earlier the decision is made, the better. The lessor chooses whether to sell the transaction in whole or in part. For large-ticket transactions, the lessor may also sell the transaction as a participation either at the contract level (where participants share in the collateral) or as individual schedules with distinct assets.

Benefits:
Syndication allows the equipment finance company to manage risk by credit or segment and to continue to service customer relationships and provide complete solutions for customers while managing risk to exposure limits and concentration for customer, asset classes, industry segments, and more. It may be less expensive to originate indirectly as it requires less staff to build this origination channel. Syndication may also be a means to gain market intelligence to understand the terms and conditions that are accepted in the market.

Drawbacks:
On the sell-side, there may be an administrative burden depending on whether the equipment finance company chooses to sell or retain the servicing of the contract. While continuing to provide service for syndicated transactions is a value-add to customers through continued provision of capital and consistent seamless end-to-end customer service, it may be an administrative burden for the equipment finance company to service the contract without retaining the exposure due to the need for coordination between the customer and investor. The servicer has to provide service to both the buyer of the paper as well as the end-customer. On the buy-side, the equipment finance company buying transactions is not client-facing and has to work through the syndication source first, rather than directly with the customer's company (unless there is a default or other exception scenario).

Considerations:
A key consideration for setting up this function is the separation of duties and information access between the sales teams to preserve relationships with sellers. Depending on the nature of the equipment finance organization, the need for separation of duties could span across multiple functions including sales, pricing, credit, documentation, portfolio management, and servicing.

Portfolio Acquisition as an Origination Channel

Another means for finance companies to originate business is to acquire portfolios from other finance companies (banks, independents, and captives). The arrangement of acquisitions can be on a one-off basis or an ongoing basis. Some lessors systematize the process and form relationships to periodically buy contracts from the same key partners on an ongoing basis.

Benefits and Drawbacks

Benefits

There are many benefits to portfolio acquisitions. First, it allows the organization to scale at a rapid pace while controlling employee overhead and operational expenses. Secondly, it can be an effective approach to increase your asset base with lower infrastructure investments. Additionally, portfolio acquisitions can provide valuable information about industries, equipment types, and vendors.

Drawbacks

Pricing is aggressive for strong performing portfolios thus expect less interest income when purchasing portfolios with similar risk attributes compared to other origination channels. Because you are acquiring a larger number of contracts from a given origination partner, there can be a performance downside if you do not correctly assess the partner risk, credit risk, asset risk, geography risk, and industry risk that can have material effects on your overall portfolio performance. It is important to understand these dynamics before acquiring portfolios.

Considerations

It is valuable to have set guidelines for portfolio acquisitions that help maintain a consistent risk and performance profile. For example, will you purchase newly originated contracts or only aged portfolios? Additionally, it is imperative to understand who you are purchasing portfolios from and their track record. Following are additional considerations for portfolio acquisitions:

- How does the originator find its business?
- Are they asset class experts? Do they have recourse and remarketing agreements with vendors that will be assigned? What is their static pool portfolio results in the assets, geography, origination channel, and industries over the last ten years that you will be purchasing?
- Will the originating party retain servicing, or will they assign it with the contracts?
- If the contracts contain tax and equity positions, will you be purchasing those or merely the remaining stream of rentals?
- Will the portfolio acquisition be a one-time event or an ongoing relationship?

Portfolio acquisitions can be complicated, yet when done well this origination channel can have material effects on the growth of your asset base.

Summary

While specific approaches to sales and marketing vary widely across our industry and even within the same equipment leasing and finance organization, sales and marketing fundamentals apply regardless of company size and situation.

Whether it be the approach to credit decisions, documentation requirements, funding processes, or portfolio segmentation, understanding the different types of origination channels provides context to understand the rest of equipment finance lifecycle.

Equipment leasing and finance companies of all types combine a variety of origination channels, program designs, marketing, and sales strategies to create unique business models. This variety and creativity are contributors to the resilience and innovation mentioned earlier in this book

Chapter 6 – Credit

This chapter builds on the previous chapters of this handbook focusing credit-specific concepts. Following are the learning goals for this chapter:

- Be able to describe the role and purpose of credit and the five Cs framework for credit analysis.
- Understand similarities and differences between credit processes for small-, medium-, and large-ticket transactions.
- Recognize the critical aspects of credit due diligence and why they are essential.
- Understand the information required for making a sound credit decision and some of the tools typically employed in data gathering and credit analysis.
- Understand what credit scoring is, the value it can bring and how it fits into the credit process.
- Understand the fundamental purpose and types of financial statements as well as the key ratios used in credit assessment.
- Know the typical enhancements for structuring credit transactions.

In the context of the CLFP BOK Framework, credit is the second phase of the origination lifecycle.

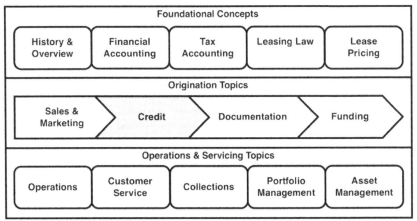

Figure 33 Credit Chapter BOK Framework Coverage

It has been said, "Like it or not; credit is the language of our industry." It's where the landmines are. The role of a credit analyst in an equipment finance company is to make decisions within the parameters of an organization's credit policies. Part of credit analysis is developing an understanding of the creditworthiness of potential lessees and borrowers.

Role and Purpose of Credit

Fundamentally, credit risk is the chance of not receiving money back in a timely manner and as agreed. The underlying purpose of all of these credit processes is to evaluate credit risk.

Evaluating credit risk and granting credit (also referred to as underwriting) is the process in lending that determines the acceptability of a proposed transaction based on the inherent risk of the deal and the lender's or lessor's credit policies.

Before addressing the topic, one must understand the difference between the sales process and the credit process. Salespersons are paid to find fundable transactions, accentuate the positives, and help gain as many approvals as possible. Compare the sales process to the credit process of which the credit analyst gathers the right level of data to understand the big picture, assess risk, analyze credit, be suspicious of anything about the transaction that might be vague, and make sound decisions. It is almost as if they are coming from opposite directions in looking at the transaction, even though, in a sense, they are working toward the same ultimate goal.

Sales Lens	Credit Lens
• Paid to find fundable transactions. • Accentuate positives. • Help gain as many approvals as possible.	• Understand the big picture to determine acceptability of a proposed transaction based on inherent risk and credit policy. • As if playing the role of detective, be suspicious, require clarity and transparency. • Assess risk and make the right decisions. • Evaluate the transaction in light of itself and in relation to the overall portfolio.

Another important element of credit is portfolio level credit risk management. Beyond the prediction of the likelihood of a new customer to pay, it is important to monitor the performance of deals that are already on the books. Ongoing credit review and monitoring is discussed in Chapter 9 – Portfolio Management.

The new CECL standard impacts credit risk on a strategic portfolio level. See Appendix 5 - Current Expected Credit Loss Model (CECL) for more information.

The Five Cs of Credit

The role of a credit analyst in an equipment finance company is to make decisions within the parameters of an organization's risk appetite. The ultimate question to be answered: does the transaction make sense? Considering the five "Cs" of credit can help in answering these questions.

| Character | Cash Flow | Capital | Collateral | Conditions |

"**The five Cs of Credit**" is a common framework for evaluating characteristics of the borrower and the transaction to estimate chances of default and the sensibility of the transaction. These components are assessed qualitatively and quantitatively using a variety of tools such as credit reports and scores, financial statements, and other documents to understand the borrower's financial situation. In addition to the borrower analysis, the credit analyst considers specifics of the transaction itself. The weighting of each of these factors in the credit decision may vary by credit analyst experience, finance program, risk appetite, policies, procedures, guidelines, and credit focus.

- **Collateral**: Some credit analysts focus on collateral first to determine if they are even interested in a transaction and this comes into play when there is a weakness in one of the other Cs for the transaction. When considering the equipment, the credit analyst wants to know, "in the event of repossession, what is the value of the asset on the secondary market? What is the strength of the secondary market? What is the potential cost of repossessing the equipment?" Are we dealing with hard collateral or soft collateral (software, furniture, fixtures)? Even if the credit is not stellar, the collateral may be what convinces you to do the transaction.

- **Character:** Character refers to the borrower's reputation and performance on past financial obligations. The credit review involves assessing past behavior to predict future behavior, honesty, and reliability to answer the question, "Can we trust this borrower?"

- **Cash Flow:** What is the cash flow? Does the borrower have the capacity to repay the proposed loan or lease? The methods for this assessment vary by scenario, but may include credit bureaus, PayNet™ reports, as well as financial statement review.

- **Capital:** Capital deals with the ability for the borrower or lessee to withstand unexpected negatives. Credit analysts assess the business owner's investment into the business, retained earnings, or assets of the business owner. In small-ticket transactions, bank statements may be reviewed to assess whether there is enough liquidity to withstand a downturn in the economy while larger transactions may involve financial statement analysis.

- **Conditions**: Conditions refers to the terms of the contract as well as economic conditions that might affect the lessee or borrower. Key to this assessment is the overall economy and the specific purpose of the transaction. It is important to understand the reason for financing: Is it working capital? Is it equipment to drive expansion? Is it paying off debt or a tax lien? Is the business financing equipment that is essential use or non-essential use?

Example of Essential Use vs. Non-essential Use - the Dozer vs. Motorhome
Imagine the owner of a construction company who is looking to finance a bulldozer vs. a fancy motorhome that allows them to travel around to work sites and save money on hotel costs. While the motorhome provides a convenience for the business owner, it is not essential for the construction business in comparison to the bulldozer. Work may go on without the motorhome but cannot go on without the bulldozer. In a time of financial distress, the construction company owner would more likely pay for the asset that helps to generate revenue on projects such as the bulldozer, rather than the motorhome.

Variations in Approach

Credit analysts use different approaches and weighting of the five Cs for different scenarios. When evaluating character, for instance, a bank credit professional might think about a large-ticket transaction like this:

"As a bank, we must consider character; just because financials are impeccable, doesn't always mean we can trust the borrower. Even if all of the rest of the 'Cs' are good, if I am not satisfied with character, for example, not comfortable with the industry (cannabis, gambling, etc.) I am not going to do the transaction. There are plenty of bad players that have corporate jets."

For federally regulated financial institutions, the credit professional must be aware of the legalities of various industries and how they vary from state to state. A small-ticket credit professional, on the other hand, may look at it like this:

"Let's say you have a prospective borrower; we are trying to assess whether they are willing to pay when their back is against the wall. When reviewing credit history and other public records, we ask questions like: Are they sloppy with their taxes or having cash flow issues? If there is a bankruptcy or financial hardship in their history, how hard did they fight? Did they show willingness to work with lenders?"

Risk Appetite Framework

One way to think about credit in a lending organization is within the context of a "risk appetite framework" of which credit policy is a component. This framework is a foundation for making decisions considering risk appetite, policies, procedures, and guidelines.

The diagram below is one way to visualize the relationship among the various elements of the risk appetite framework.

Figure 34 Risk Appetite Framework

Each equipment finance company sets its credit policy within its risk appetite framework; some policies are more stringent than others. Regulated institutions, for instance, do not have the luxury of changing policies rapidly. Independents, on the other hand, may often enjoy more entrepreneurial agility with the ability to revise credit policy more quickly, allowing them to enter new industries faster.

Assessing Collateral and Expected Loss for Large-Ticket Transactions
For bank equipment finance companies every large credit must have probability of default "PD" and loss given default "LGD" risk ratings as a part of the credit package.

The expected loss for a transaction varies because the amount to be repaid declines over time and the value of the underlying asset or pledged collateral also changes over time at a different rate from the outstanding loan value. (Basel II requirement for banks).

The following equation is used to determine the expected loss and takes into account the variables below.
$$\% \ PD * LGD * EAD = \text{Expected Loss}$$
PD: Probability of default provides an estimate of the likelihood that a borrower will be unable to repay debt obligations.
LGD: Loss given default refers to the amount of money a bank or other financial institution would lose should a borrower default on loan.
EAD: Exposure at default

For example, on a corporate jet, the recovery rate is better, therefore, loss given default is less.

Credit Process

Credit process varies from company to company by risk appetite framework, organization type, organizational structure, business model, and ticket size.

While each equipment finance company does things slightly differently, at the highest level, we can visualize the credit process for a transaction as flowing through these four stages. Each contains a variety of activities, tasks, and sub-processes depending on the variables mentioned above.

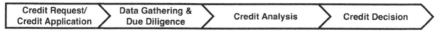

Figure 35 High-Level Stages of a Typical Credit Process

Variations by Transaction Size

Although each company may define these ranges slightly different, for our purposes, we will use the definitions of small-ticket, mid-ticket, and large-ticket as introduced in Chapter 1.

Table 18 Excerpt of Industry Sector by Transaction Size Table from Chapter 1

Market Segment	Small-Ticket	Middle-Ticket	Large-Ticket
Typical Transaction Size	Transactions under $250,000	Transactions under $5,000,000	Transactions over $5,000,000
Notes	Transactions under $25,000 are sometimes called "micro-ticket"	Transactions between $250,000 and $1,000,000 are sometimes called "lower middle market"	Sometimes called "big ticket"

The extent of the evaluation in a credit decision is generally dependent on transaction size. Lessors may have different standards and policies for the amount of information required for a small-ticket, a mid-ticket, and a large-ticket transaction. Some lessors make decisions without financial disclosure and process transactions on an "app-only" basis, up to a certain dollar amount (sometimes referred to as an "App-Only Limit").

Typically, as the size and complexity of the transaction increases, the data and due diligence requirements, analysis activities, and time to assess the credit also increase. Lessors rely on well-defined credit policies, experienced credit professionals, and robust technology tools to continually refine this process to drive down costs and reduce time to make decisions while managing risk and satisfying necessary regulatory requirements. Continual attention to technological and process innovation in this aspect of processing is vital in today's highly competitive environment with rapidly changing customer expectations for speed and service.

- **Small-ticket:** Transactions are often credit scored and may even use automatic decisions. In most instances, a credit application is completed, which usually requires the disclosure of the lessee or borrower organization, the ownership structure, and details of the transaction. Because of the importance in "scoring the transaction," most applications also require the owner's personal information. The credit decision is made by machine ("auto-decision") or by humans (Credit Scoring is covered later in this chapter). Because the transaction sizes are small, low-touch credit processes from both customer interaction and internal processing standpoint are necessary for profitability. The computer has become a useful tool in automating, streamlining, and adding consistency to the credit process. That said, even the most advanced software programs may have difficulty tolerating exceptions (also called "exception handling") hence the value of experienced credit staff.

- **Middle-ticket:** This credit process is more involved than the app-only credit scored transaction. In addition to knowing some of the primary information required for the small-ticket request, other factors come into play such as receipt and analysis of financials. Depending upon the dollar amount and the lessor's/lender's credit policies, usually two- or three-years' worth of financial statements are required to be submitted and analyzed as well as background information on the company and its principals. Some of this background information is available from services such as D&B (Dun & Bradstreet). Sometimes, trade and bank references are required. *Note: this process may also be utilized for small-ticket transactions if they are "rejected" from the app-only model or for lessors that do not process transactions on an app-only basis.*

- **Large-ticket:** These transactions often involve a major corporation, either publicly traded or privately owned. For publicly traded companies, more detailed financial information is available. Such information may be obtained from published annual reports as well as from financial information a company is required to file with the SEC The 10Q (quarterly) and 10K (annual) reports filed with the SEC are available to the public. These usually contain more information than what is available for privately owned firms. For privately held companies, it is common to request three years of audited/reviewed financial statements and interims. Depending upon the size of the request, copies of bank agreements containing the covenants may also be needed. Projections may be required so that the lessor can see that the lessee is able to meet its current obligations, both short-term and long-term, as well as to meet the new money request.

While the details and nuances of data requirements, due diligence, and credit analysis activities may vary by transaction size and company policy, at a high-level, the credit process follows a standard framework. The following diagram shows how the typical credit processes for app-only (usually small-ticket), mid-ticket, and large-ticket transactions compare regarding the extent of credit evaluation and processing.

A High-level Comparison of Credit Processes

Diving a bit deeper into activities that typically happen within each of the stages of the credit process, Table 19 shows the level of activity involved and how it may vary by transaction size.

Table 19 High-Level Comparison of Typical Credit Process by Transaction Ticket Size

Credit Request/Credit Application	Small-Ticket	Middle-Ticket	Large-Ticket
Credit application or request	✓	✓	✓
Data Gathering & Due Diligence	Small-Ticket	Middle-Ticket	Large-Ticket
Automatically request data for credit review	✓	✓	✓
Regulatory and fraud checking	✓	✓	✓
Credit reports (consumer and/or commercial)	✓	✓	✓
Financial statements		✓	✓
Other data requirements based on credit policies		✓	✓
Review equipment management evaluation of future residual estimates		✓	✓
Gather and review public information			✓
Review bank agreements with covenants			✓
Review projections			✓
Credit Analysis	Small-Ticket	Middle-Ticket	Large-Ticket
Automated algorithms, calculations, scores, and analysis performed by human or computer	✓	✓	✓
Human or computer evaluates asset and transaction specifics	✓	✓	✓
Manual credit analysis	✓*	✓	✓
Financial statement analysis		✓	✓
Credit enhancements, structuring	✓	✓	✓
Credit Decision	Small-Ticket	Middle-Ticket	Large-Ticket
Automated algorithms make a credit decision	✓		
A human renders and records the credit decision	✓	✓	✓
Multiple credit authorities may be involved in the credit decision		✓	✓
May require committee-based decision			✓

* *Applicable in some cases*

As you can see in the table above, there are some aspects of credit analysis and decision processes that are applicable for all transaction sizes (as always, the applicability of each varies by company). A competitive differentiator these days is the speed of these processes and whether humans, technology, or humans augmented by technology are performing elements of these processes (see section later in this chapter, "The Future of Credit Scoring").

Credit Request/Credit Application

In most instances, in an app-only/small-ticket credit processing scenario, the vendor, broker, lessor, or lessee will submit a credit application, which requires the disclosure of the lessee, business organization, ownership structure, and transaction details. Since most small-ticket, app-only transactions rely on credit scoring to reduce time and cost of processing, the owner's personal information is also required (e.g., Social Security number, home address) to pull consumer credit reports. As well, middle-ticket and large-ticket transactions can begin with an initial credit request or application; the difference is in the extent data elements typically required up front for each transaction size as illustrated in Table 20 Comparison of Typical Credit Data Requirements by Ticket Size.

Data Gathering and Due Diligence

When it comes to "due diligence," how much diligence is due?

The level of due diligence for a credit evaluation will vary based on the origination channel (source of business), the size of the transaction, and the risk appetite framework of the lessor/lender.

Information Requirements for Successful Credit Evaluation

Many factors go into the credit evaluation, and we should consider no single factor in isolation. The table below compares the typical data elements required for processing a credit for various transaction sizes. Several types of data are universally needed regardless of transaction size, and as the complexity of the transaction increases so does the amount of credit data required for thorough analysis. Table 20 lists data elements typically needed by ticket size, although lessors and lenders determine the degree of importance of each.

Table 20 Comparison of Typical Credit Data Requirements by Ticket Size

Credit Data	Small-ticket	Middle-Ticket	Large-Ticket
Time in business	✓	✓	✓
Lessee's industry	✓	✓	✓
Type of equipment	✓	✓	✓
Average bank balances *Applicable in some cases	✓*	✓	✓
Business credit reports	✓	✓	✓
Owners' / principals' names	✓	✓	
Personal credit bureau reports of the principals	✓	✓	
Quality of the vendor	✓	✓	✓
Structure of the lease	✓	✓	✓
New or used equipment	✓	✓	✓
Equipment location	✓	✓	✓
Credit reports of outside reporting agencies		✓	✓
Receipt and analysis of lessee's financial statements		✓	✓
Public corporation annual report			✓
10Q and 10K reports filed with the SEC			✓
Privately held corporation – 3years of financial statements and interims		✓	✓
Bank agreements containing covenants			✓
Projections			✓

All of this data is gathered to help the credit analyst develop the big-picture understanding of the customer and transaction and support making a sound decision to extend credit.

Know the Origination Channel

Knowing the origination channel is important when evaluating credit. Chapter 5 – Sales and Marketing describes the three most common equipment finance origination channels, Direct, TPO, and Vendor. Those concepts come into play in the credit phase as credit guidelines, and the level of due diligence performed may vary based on the source of the transaction and how closely the lender/lessor interacts with the end-user customer.

Table 21 Comparison Typical Customer Interaction by Channel

Channel	Levels of Customer Interaction
Direct Origination	Lender → End-user Customer
TPO	Lender → (Source) Broker → End-user Customer
Vendor	Lender → Manufacturer/Dealer Sales Rep → End-user Customer

For example, as shown in Table 21 with direct origination, the lender/lessor is directly interacting with the end-user customer. With third-party originators, the lender/lessor is once removed from the end-user customer and relies on the third-party originator for much of the customer interaction. The level of communication with the end-user customer in this origination model will vary, and it may not be as intimately connected to the customer as direct relationships. With vendor origination, depending on the structure of the vendor program, the lender/lessor may be even further removed from the end customer.

The most important reason to know where a transaction is coming from is the inherent risk in various origination channels.

Third Party Origination (TPO)

Consider a broker scenario as an example: if the lender books the transaction originated by a broker, the broker receives a fee. In a majority of cases, there is very little recourse to the broker (if the transaction goes wrong, the broker still keeps the fee and the lender takes on all of the risks). Because the broker is not holding any risk in the transaction or employment risk, they may be a bit more aggressive at closing deals since their incentives for transaction performance are not the same as the lender. In addition, they may not have the same level of credit expertise as there is another level of due diligence needed to originate business from someone who is not part of your company.

An additional level of due diligence for the TPO channel is the broker approval process (also called source approval process). Just like a borrower, the lender or lessor evaluates the broker through a credit process. Due diligence includes understanding how long they have been in the business, industry experience, background searches, industry trade association involvement, and references from other lenders.

From transaction to transaction, credit policy in this channel may be more conservative with higher credit scoring requirements and lower app-only limits.

Direct

These are transactions that are originated by lessor's own sales representatives working directly with the customer. In this channel, sales reps know their company's credit policy, risk appetite, know what to look for, and with a portfolio perspective in mind, understand that the transactions they bring in must perform. Often, direct sales representatives will go through some credit training to get a basic understanding of what internal credit expects. Usually focused on industries favorable to the leasing company, the direct sales representative can speak the language of the customer.

In this channel, credit guidelines may be more aggressive compared to others.

Scaling Vendor Origination with Credit Automation
It is possible to generate a high volume of transactions through vendor origination, with some large lessors seeing hundreds of thousands of transactions flow through this channel. Lessors often employ credit scoring and automation to scale vendor origination volume.

Vendor Origination

For transactions originated through vendor programs, remember that the sales force in these vendor organizations may have some understanding of credit, but it is not as extensive as the lender. Depending on the nature of the vendor program and relationship, the credit guidelines may be more aggressive to enable development of strong transaction flows and may vary by transaction size. With vendor programs, you may encounter more exceptions to help the vendor take care of their customers since, in this case, the primary customer relationship is with the vendor, your source of flow business. There are ways to address this challenge such as recourse arrangements, rate subsidies, net loss programs, remarketing agreements, and buy back agreements. Refer to Chapter 5 – Sales and Marketing for more details on vendor program development.

The vendor program relationship is key to developing flow business and it is important to balance sound credit decisions with generating transaction flow. Similar to the TPO channel, there is an added level of due diligence in setting up a new vendor relationship and program. Depending on the volume expectations and nature of the vendor, this due diligence may include reviewing public records, background checks, credit checks, and financial review.

Indirect Origination Channels

From a bank perspective, indirect origination channels, the "Buy/Sell" function, allow a bank to offer a solution to a client without holding all of the exposure. This capability enables the lessor to dial the business volume up or down while managing concentration in geography or other characteristics of the portfolio as well as earnings and credit exposure. See Chapter 5 – Sales and Marketing for more detail about Portfolio Acquisition as an origination channel).

Concentration: Concentrations of credit risk occur within an equipment finance portfolio when a common characteristic links otherwise unrelated transactions. These pools of individual transactions may perform similarly because of a shared characteristic. If this shared characteristic becomes a source of weakness for the pool of transactions, these transactions together could pose considerable risk to earnings and capital even regardless of the underwriting quality of individual transactions.[14] Examples of concentration: geography, industry, transaction type, and origination source.

Know Your Customer "KYC"

KYC stands for Know Your Customer, and you will learn more about the regulatory aspects in the Regulatory Compliance section of Chapter 8 – Funding and Operations.

From a credit processing standpoint, KYC comes into play in a couple of different ways, again depending on perspective and scenario. Regardless of the type of financial institution, you must understand the entity to whom you are granting credit.

In the small-ticket and independent equipment financing world, KYC focuses on knowing you are accurately identifying the owners of the business. The requirements may be less stringent for non-regulated lessors. In small-ticket transactions, lessors typically do not ask for organizational documents or tax returns, and instead rely on a secretary of state lookup, PayNet™, D&B™, and other data sources to understand and identify principals and owners of the business.

The key is knowing who the legal owner, operator, and decision maker for a business is. There is a delicate balance between due diligence vs. cost vs. risk and customer and vendor relationship. Often, there can be more sensitivity to having to go back to vendor clients for added documentation. The goal is to do the right level of due diligence without negatively impacting transaction flow.

For bank-owned lessors, the requirements for customer background checking and identity verification are far more rigorous than they might be for a non-regulated institution. The significant expense and attention to due diligence processes, and regular and extensive training of employees on the topics of ethics and anti-money laundering are an essential focus for bank lessors.

The KYC-related background checks are critical to the credit process for ensuring the lender is not aiding and abetting terrorists or financing illegal activities. In large-ticket transactions, the level of this due diligence increases, and the nature of the due diligence varies by size of the company and whether

---

[14] Source: https://www.occ.gov/publications/publications-by-type/comptrollers-handbook/concentrations-of-credit/pub-ch-concentrations.pdf Website Title: Safety and Soundness - OCC: Home Page Date Accessed: March 05, 2018

it is public or private. Many methods and tools are employed to perform KYC due diligence.

Bank Lessors & Regulatory Impact for KYC
Another element of the KYC implications specific to bank lessors is the "Beneficial Ownership" requirement. Banks are held accountable to ensure that they are not financing nefarious activities. They must file suspicious incident reports with the FBI when necessary and remember that they are always in service of doing the right thing, preventing the financing of criminal activities, and staying "out of the news." Aforementioned is an added level of criteria for bank credit analysts to consider. All of this sometimes makes a bank a little less competitive because others do not have the same rigor applied to due diligence and can do the deals somewhat faster or require slightly less information.

Fraud Prevention

Comprehensive due diligence can help to reduce the potential for fraud. Unfortunately, fraud is a fact of life in the equipment finance industry, and much of it happens with vendor involvement. There are numerous instances of company-wide fraud by vendors totaling millions of dollars. There is also fraud that occurs with collusion of vendor sales representatives and lessees, vendor sales representatives and leasing sales representatives, and fraud by lessees alone. It can be difficult to determine who the perpetrator is and who the victims are. Not only does fraud destroy vendor programs, but it also can ruin unwitting lessors.

In developing vendor programs, there is always the temptation to lessen credit and documentation standards to provide a more straightforward, more accessible approval process for lessees. It is critical to review any changes in the credit, documentation, and funding process because fraud is always a possibility. The lessor should remain alert for indicators of fraud, including changed or unusual invoicing, mismatched credit information, problems on verbal confirmations and site inspections, unusual UCC filing activity, and a significant push by the various parties to rush the funding process. As with the rest of vendor programs, continued regular communication with the various stakeholders within the vendor's organization can help deter these incidents.

For banks, from an Anti-Money Laundering (AML) (see Chapter 8 - Funding and Operations) standpoint, let's say a law firm applies to lease a backhoe. When we look at due diligence from a KYC perspective, if the law firm is purchasing a backhoe, credit scoring may not likely catch that. Human touch allows for a pause to ask questions about whether a transaction makes sense.

Techniques commonly used to combat fraud:

- To ensure that you are not dealing with someone who has personal credit that is posing as owner on paper on behalf of the operator that might not have personal credit, verify the business owners and their active involvement in the business.
- Perform adequate vendor due diligence to vet vendors for transactions of all sizes to assess reputation and business credit.

- Perform UCC searches to determine whether another lender has filed on the equipment.
- Perform criminal background searches and public record searches on owners/vendors.

Know the Legal Entity

Before doing a lease-financing transaction with any business or organization, it is necessary to know the kind of entity under consideration. The type of business entity whether, a sole proprietor, LLC, partnership, corporation, or other, makes a difference from credit standpoint in the financial and background information required as well as requirements for adequately documenting the transaction after approval. To review the definitions of each type of legal entity, refer to Chapter 3: Leasing Law.

Know Your Risk Appetite

Most people do not think of credit as a creative process, but those experienced in this field applaud the "art" involved along with the science of analysis. Varying degrees of both exist in app-only and financial analysis models. Regardless of company particulars, the end goal of the credit process is to make a sound credit decision and suitably structure a lease or equipment loan transaction that is appropriate and acceptable for both the marketing style and risk appetite of the lender/lessor.

Credit Analysis

Credit Evaluation Tools

Credit professionals use a wide variety of tools to evaluate credit and select the appropriate tools for analysis based on the type and size of transactions. The following table lists examples of tools typically used in credit analysis.

Category	Examples
Credit Scores	Credit scores can be commercially available scores from various bureaus such as FICO and other data providers or proprietary scores built on a combination of personal and business scores plus additional data elements. Scoring models often include key data elements such as time in business, industry (NAICS code), and personal and business credit scores. • Proprietary credit and risk scoring models • Personal credit score (FICO, Beacon, or other) • Business credit score (D&B™, PayNet™, etc.)
Credit Bureaus	• Consumer bureaus Experian, Equifax, Transunion • Business bureaus Experian, Equifax • D&B™ • PayNet, a key business credit report for this industry
Financial Statement Analysis	• Ratios • Specialized financial spreading software or spreadsheets

Category	Examples
	• Centralized or outsourced financial statement spreading service (sometimes used by large banks) • Financial statement spreading is sometimes an embedded feature or functionality in advanced lease and loan origination systems.
Non-Traditional Data Sources	• Social media • Internet searches • Industry specific online sources • Quick online check to see if the customer is "in the news" • Online reviews and reputation • Some lessors have even developed "online presence" scores for specific industries
Risk Ratings and Risk Scores	• Agency ratings such as Moodys, S&P, Fitch • PD, LGD, Expected Loss • Proprietary spreadsheets • External risk ratings are not typical for small-ticket transactions; some lessors use internal risk ratings • Risk rating models
Industry Peer Comparison	These sources are helpful for credit analysts to assess the borrower and determine whether they are better or worse than industry standards. • D&B™ • TROYs • Value Line • IBIS World • RMA

Financial Statements

In Chapter 2, we discussed the purpose, construction, and content of financial statements, as well as the appropriate classification of equipment finance transactions for financial reporting. Financial statements play a crucial role in assessing the financial condition of an entity and help build the big picture of the credit under review.

A snapshot of an entity's financial condition as of a specific date, financial statements are made up of several components each providing different information. It can be seriously misleading to view individual components in isolation. As described in Chapter 2 – Financial and Tax Accounting, there are varying degrees of quality of financial statements depending on who prepares them and how.

The following list represents the varying degrees of quality of a company's financial statements:

- Audited statements with an unqualified opinion
- Audited statements with a qualified opinion
- Reviewed statements
- Compiled statements

- Tax returns may be used in place of statements, either prepared by outside CPAs or someone able to do so
- Statements prepared by public accountants (not certified), enrolled accountants, and financial consultants
- Statements prepared by in-house accountant
- Statements prepared by management

Whenever possible, it is best to ask for a statement with the original signature of the accountant and evaluate the reputation of the accounting firm preparing the statements. The preparation of quality statements does not require a multinational accounting firm, but the smaller accounting firm does need to have systems in place to perform audits, etc.

If using a small CPA firm, which may be less expensive for the customer, the following questions should be asked: What is their level of expertise? Do they need special knowledge with this customer? Are they independent? It is common practice when using unknown firms to verify their membership in local or national accounting societies and confirm that they prepared the statements.

A complete financial statement includes the accountant's letter, balance sheet, income statement, statement of cash flows, reconciliation of shareholder equity, and financial footnotes. When reviewing financial statements for a credit, if the transaction is missing any of these, there may be a reason for concern. Keep in mind, however, that certain levels of statements, such as "compiled" (see explanation in Chapter 2 – Financial and Tax Accounting), do not usually contain all of the components of an audited statement.

The credit analyst evaluates the relevance (timeliness) and the reliability (verifiability, representational faithfulness, neutrality) of the financial statements. Utilizing financial statements for lending decisions has limitations because it is historical data, but such financial statements are the most objective and concrete information available. There are other ways to evaluate a potential lessee further. For example, data from the financial statements can be manipulated and related to additional data, such as industry averages, to assess a company's performance.

Components of the Key Financial Statements

Chapter 2 describes the components of key financial statements, following is a typical approach used by credit analysts to review them:

- **Accountant's letter**: An accountant's letter is usually the opening page of a financial statement. It is addressed to the board of directors of a corporation, the general partner of a partnership, or the owner of a sole-proprietorship. The letter confirms that the statements are prepared in accordance with GAAP and, if not, explains any deviations. It also should alert a reader if the information is missing from a complete statement, i.e., the elimination of notes. For a publicly traded corporation, it is not uncommon for the accountant's letter to declare that management is responsible for the preparation of the statement; the accountants performed such tests, audits, etc. to confirm the soundness of the statement, and the financial statements were prepared in accordance with GAAP.

- **Audited and unqualified opinion**: a letter confirming that a full audit has been performed, that statements are prepared according to GAAP and fairly represents the company's financial status.
- **Audited and qualified opinion**: This is a letter confirming that a full audit has been performed, that statements are prepared according to GAAP and fairly represent the company's financial status, except for certain noted items.
- **Reviewed**: A letter stating that management supplied the information, but the CPA firm performed some basic tests to confirm the authenticity of the information. In this instance, the CPA firm did more than compiled financial statements but did not perform an audit nor express an opinion.
- **Compiled**: The date of the letter, indicating the time required to complete the financial statement, should be compared to the date at the bottom of the letter, which reflects the last day of fieldwork. If work was done on the books after the date of sign off, management should be questioned about these subsequent events.
- **Balance sheet:** It is important to look at the nature of the assets and liabilities on the Balance Sheet. A company with a large amount of inventory looks different than one with a large number of fixed assets. For example, a school bus operator has a large fixed asset base and very little inventory, which affects the company's working capital ratio; whereas a company that sells a product most likely has a better working capital base since its main assets are of a current nature.
- **Income statement and net income:** The income statement is a presentation of the revenues and expenses for a specific period reflecting the total of the company's profits or losses from date of inception to the statement date.
- **Statement of cash flows:** A requirement of the annual report, the statement shows a company's cash receipts and cash payments during the specific accounting period, summarizes non-cash expenses such as depreciation and amortization, and reconciliation between net income and cash flows from operations. Note to credit analysts: This is an accounting tool that reflects a reconciliation of cash. It does not provide a credit view of cash flow or the more sophisticated "cash throw-off."
- **Accountant's notes:** Many credit analysts read the accountant's notes first. These are a listing of significant points, in most instances, regarding specific balance sheet or income statement accounts that need to be understood when analyzing the other parts of the financial statement.

Financial Statement Analysis Techniques

When using financial statements in the credit analysis, usually the first step is to input them into a spreading program (accounting software). The output commonly utilized when making the evaluation include:

- Assets and liabilities listed in summary form in dollars and also calculated as a percentage of assets or liabilities ("common sized").
- A projected balance sheet which shows the effect of the asset acquisition and the new lease or loan.
- The capsulized income statement, giving a specific note of extraordinary incomes and expenses, and dividends or other distributions (common sized presentation).
- Interim statements annualized for trend analysis. This calculation may be very misleading, as it does not take into account the seasonality of the business. A proper analysis would call for the comparison of interims at similar times in the prior years.
- A calculation of cash flow.
- A calculation by the program of cash throw-off.
- A calculation of reconciliation of net worth.
- All calculation of the key ratios.

These graphic presentations help visualize the trends. As noted in the bullets above, when spreading the financial statements, it is essential that there is a reconciliation of net worth year over year. This proving process confirms that statements tie together from one year to the next. The method used is:

1. Total net worth at the end of previous fiscal year end (FYE).
2. Add current income after tax, dividends, and distributions.
3. Should equal ending net worth of current FYE statement.

Any discrepancy should be explained and understood. The accountant's notes to financial statements should explain differences.

Financial statement analysis involves judgment in evaluating and interpreting the data, and deciding which areas are the most important to focus on and analyze, and with what degree of emphasis. Analysis commonly takes into consideration:

- Earnings stability of the enterprise
- Earnings stability of the industry
- The kind of asset investments
- Liquidity
- Debt maturities (size and spacing over time, look for balloon payments and impact)
- Purpose of debt and whether it matches outcome
- Interest costs

- Identifying contingent liabilities and off-balance sheet liabilities
- Capital structure and solvency
- Cash flow coverage

The ability to conduct a thorough and insightful analysis lies at the heart of the credit analyst's job. In "Financial Statement Analysis; Theory, Application and Interpretation," internationally recognized professor and writer in financial analysis, Leopold A. Bernstein[15] states,

"There is no mechanical substitute for the process of judgment; however, the proper definition of the problem and of the critical questions that must be answered, as well as the skillful selection of the most appropriate tools of analysis available, goes a long way toward meaningful interpretation."

Industry Review and Comparison

There are several tools that credit analysts can employ in comparing the customer to industry peers. For example, if you have a $2 million construction company on the East Coast, you can use industry comparison tools to plug that in and see how they stack up against peers in their area for a variety of statistics such as income, revenue, financial ratios, and more.

One example of an industry review and comparison tool is the industry average tables prepared by the Risk Management Association (RMA), which makes the data available online through their market intelligence tool, eMentor® (www.rmahg.org). It is necessary to understand the methods for compiling industry tables. The data in RMA is from businesses that have relationships with commercial banks. Companies which do not need banks or are non-borrowing companies are excluded from the positive end of the scale. Companies that do not qualify for bank credit, or those that borrow from finance companies et al., are excluded from the negative end of the scale. Other industry peer assessment tools and data sources include ELFA, D&B™, as well as others indicated in the credit tools section of this chapter.

By tracking the North American Industry Classification System (NAICS) code (or in some cases, its predecessor the Standard Industry Classification (SIC) code), you can look up the standard indicators for a type of business to compare the company you are analyzing to industry standards such as typical gross profit margin, typical net profit margin, and typical receivable turnover.

The North American Industry Classification System (NAICS)[16] is the standard used by federal statistical agencies in classifying business establishments for the purpose of collecting, analyzing, and publishing statistical data related to the U.S. business economy.

---

[15] Source: <u>Financial statement analysis: theory, application, and interpretation</u>. McGraw-Hill accounting series. Authors: Leopold A. Bernstein, John J. Wild. Edition: 6. Publisher Irwin/McGraw-Hill, 1998

[16] https://www.census.gov/eos/www/naics/ Website Title: North American Industry Classification System (NAICS) Main. Date Accessed: January 22, 2018

The Big Picture: Factors Involved in Evaluating Company Credit

Before going into the details of commonly used ratios, it is important to note that within this process, a single ratio means nothing by itself. Given the variety of ratios, an experienced credit analyst knows the appropriate ratios to use for the unique issues of each credit request. Ratio analysis is only one tool for evaluating a company and must be combined with various factors, including knowledge of the industry, management, competitors, technological developments, government actions, geographic location, business practices, sources of labor, etc.

The analysis should also include the comparison of specific statement ratios and calculations to industry averages. If large enough, some lessors may compare the ratios to other companies in the same industry within their portfolio.

Industry "guidelines" are just that — guidelines. Be alert for regional impacts, large company impacts, and other unusual circumstances.

Ratios should be viewed both in the light of the specific figures compared to the industry average and in light of trends. Not all ratios move in the same direction at the same time. Seldom are credit profiles all good or all bad.

Trend Analysis

In addition to current ratios and cash flow calculations, analysts should evaluate trends over a three- or four-year period. Although it is important to note changes year over year, any trend analysis done with less information is considered very limited.

↑ Increasing ratios that reflect positive trends:	↓ Decreasing ratios that reflect positive trends:
• Return on Sales (Gross Profit Margin) • Net Profit Margin • Current Ratio • Quick Ratio	• Accounts Receivable Turnover in Days • Inventory Turnover in Days • Accounts Payable Turnover in Days • Total Liabilities to Net Worth

The following ratios cannot be viewed by themselves, as either positive or negative: Return on Assets and Return on Equity.

Financial Ratios

This section covers four categories of financial ratios commonly used in evaluating equipment finance credits. See Appendix 4 Financial Statement Review Sample Problems for exercises that will allow you to practice calculating various ratios (Ratios with * indicate ratios that are included in the practice exercises).

Profitability Ratios

Gross Profit Margin *

Gross profit is the result of the cost of goods sold subtracted from net sales, or net revenues, after returns and allowances. Steady or increasing trends are positive. Declines need specific justification.

$$\frac{\textbf{Gross Profit on Sales}}{\textbf{Net Sales}}$$

Operating Profit Margin

The Operating Profit Margin shows product costs and markups as well as relevant expenses and is agnostic as to how a company finances.

$$\frac{\textbf{Earnings Before Interest and Tax (EBIT)}}{\textbf{Net Sales}}$$

Net Profit Margin (also known as Return on Sales or Profit on Sales)

Net profit margin is the ratio of net profit, after taxes and/or S corporation distributions, divided by net sales. Proper analysis requires an understanding of management's philosophy of paying taxes. Note: especially with Sub S corporations and closely held corporations, net profits after taxes and distributions may be artificially low because some shareholders take out large distributions and then lend funds back to the corporation. A steady to increasing percentage is positive.

$$\frac{\textbf{Net Income (after taxes)}}{\textbf{Net Sales}}$$

Return on Assets (ROA)

Return on assets (ROA) is the after-tax return on assets employed. This ratio expresses the after-tax return on total assets and measures the effectiveness of management in employing those resources available to it. This ratio is calculated using profit after taxes to total assets. Steady to upward trends are important.

$$\frac{\textbf{Net Income (after taxes)}}{\textbf{Total Assets}}$$

*Return on Equity (ROE)**

Return on equity (ROE) is the after-tax return on the equity capital (net worth) of the company. It should be steady or growing in comparison with industry data. ROE increases that are combined with increasing leverage may not be a positive indicator.

$$\frac{\text{Net Income (after taxes)}}{\text{Net Worth}}$$

Liquidity Ratios

*Current Ratio**

This Current Ratio is a general gauge of a company's ability to meet short-term liabilities coming due in the next operating period. The ratio should be compared with industry norms. The higher the ratio the better, but generally, a ratio of more than 1.25:1 is preferred.

$$\frac{\text{Current Assets}}{\text{Current Liabilities}}$$

*Quick Ratio**

The Quick Ratio is also known as the "Acid Test." Quick assets are readily convertible to cash items like accounts receivable and marketable securities. It consists of most of the current assets less inventories and prepaid expenses. A ratio over 1:1 is good and a better indicator of a company's ability to pay its current liabilities than the Current Ratio.

$$\frac{\text{Quick Assets (current assets} - \text{inventory)}}{\text{Current Liabilities}}$$

*Accounts Receivable Turnover**

The Accounts Receivable Turnover ratio determines the number of days accounts receivable are paid and re-established during the accounting period. The higher the turnover, the faster the business is collecting.

$$\frac{\text{Average Accounts Receivable}}{\text{Net Sales}} * 365 = \text{days}$$

Inventory Turn Over*

The Inventory Turn Over formula yields the number of days inventory turns over in one accounting period. This ratio is valuable for spotting understocking, overstocking, obsolescence, and need for merchandising improvement.

$$\frac{\textbf{Average Inventory}}{\textbf{Cost of Goods Sold}} * 365 = \textbf{days}$$

Accounts Payable Turnover

The Accounts Payable Turnover Ratio is the number of days a business will take to pay for purchases made during an accounting period. It is measured by the relationship of purchases to existing accounts payable.

$$\frac{\textbf{Average Accounts Payable}}{\textbf{Purchases}} * 365 = \textbf{days}$$

Leverage Ratios

Total Liabilities to Net Worth* (aka Debt to Equity)

The Total Liabilities to Net Worth ratio, also called Debt to Equity or Debt to Worth, is a relationship of borrowed funds compared with owners' capital. An increasing trend may suggest a leverage problem.

$$\frac{\textbf{Total Liabilities}}{\textbf{Net Worth (owners'equity)}}$$

Debt to EBITDA

The Debt to EBITDA ratio is a measure of a company's ability to pay its debts; however, there are differing views as to what should be included in the ratio. From a banking perspective, the analyst may look at senior funded debt only and ignore subordinated debt whereas an ultraconservative approach would include all debt in the ratio.

$$\frac{\textbf{Liabilities}}{\textbf{EBITDA}}$$

Long Term Debt to Capitalization

The Long-Term Debt to Capitalization ratio measures the relative importance of long-term debt in the company's capital structure.

$$\frac{\text{Long Term Debt}}{\text{Long Term Debt} + \text{Net Worth}}$$

Cash Flow and Coverage Ratios

EBITDA/EBITDAR

EBITDA:
Earnings before interest, tax, depreciation, and amortization (EBITDA) is a measure of a company's operating performance. Essentially, it's a way to evaluate a company's performance without having to factor in financing decisions, accounting decisions, or tax environments.[17]

EBITDAR: This is similar to EBITDA but adds back in the rent. This ratio is a leverage test to answer the question, "How much debt can the business support considering the level of cash flow?" In practice, each company does this slightly differently.

Traditional Cash Flow Analysis

Cash flow is the evaluation process to determine if the company can pay for the new equipment acquisition out of historic profits plus non-cash expenses. This calculation concentrates on the income statement of the company. Another approach commonly referred to as "cash throw-off" (see explanation below), considers increases and decreases in assets and liabilities in addition to the traditional method. This analysis looks to see if last year's cash flow is sufficient to make the future payments. Although there is no guarantee that last year's cash flow is going to remain the same in future years, it is still an indicator.

For situations where historical cash flow does not cover the payments for a new lease, the credit analyst must then make adjustments to the analysis. If historical cash flow is burdened with twelve months of lease payments for the new contract, with no benefit of deductibility of the payments (tax reduction) or MACRS, or interest, the analyst could make a case for adding back the tax benefit generated by making the lease payments. Or the analyst could make the point that the acquisition of this new equipment is needed to service a significant new contract, which is expected to generate additional income,

[17] Source: http://www.investinganswers.com/financial-dictionary/financial-statement-analysis/earnings-interest-tax-depreciation-and-amortization

profits, and cash flow to cover the lease payments. In this case, cash flow projection from the lessee is helpful.

A shortfall in the cash flow calculation is often a "deal killer" for many financial institutions and lessors. Others, however, use credit enhancements to improve the transaction.

Cash Throw-off

As noted above, cash throw-off is a more sophisticated approach to the traditional cash flow analysis. The method involves the same steps for the above analysis plus an additional evaluation of changes in balance sheet accounts. This analysis takes into account cash drivers, such as revenue growth and profitability, and operating factors, such as how the entity manages its assets as evidenced by its operating cycle (accounts receivable, accounts payable, and inventory changes) and capital expenditures. There is an interrelationship between sales, profitability, and cash flow. The only real source of cash from operations is sales. Finished goods represent the accumulation of all costs and expenses. Profit enhances the inflow of liquid funds in the form of receivables and cash. When doing a cash throw-off analysis, the higher the profit margin, the higher the potential for cash. The impact of changes in an entity's balance sheet is summarized below.

Table 22 Balance Sheet Impacts

Additions to Cash Flow (sources of cash):	Reductions of Cash Flow (uses of cash):
• Reductions of current assets • Reductions of fixed assets • Increases in current liabilities • Increases in long-term liabilities • Increases in net worth	• Increase of current assets (other than cash) • Increases of fixed assets • Reductions in current liabilities • Reductions in long-term liabilities • Reductions in net worth

Global Cash Flow Analysis

Global Cash Flow analysis is used to assess the combined cash flow of a group of people or entities and build a global picture of their ability to pay for new equipment acquisition. Global cash flow analysis may factor in both business and personal cash flow of guarantors.

Debt Service Coverage Ratio (DSCR)

The Debt Service Coverage Ratio (DSCR) is a measure of the cash flow available to pay current debt obligations. The ratio states net operating income as a multiple of debt obligations due within one year, including interest, principal, and lease payments.[18]

$$\frac{\text{EBIT}}{\text{Total Debt Service}}$$

Fixed Charge Coverage Ratio

The Fixed Charge Coverage Ratio (FCCR) measures a firm's ability to satisfy fixed charges, such as interest expense and lease expense. Because leases are a typically a fixed charge, the calculation for determining a company's ability to cover fixed charges includes earnings before interest and taxes (EBIT), interest expense, lease expense and other fixed charges[19] (which include items like maintenance).

$$\frac{\text{EBIT} + \text{Fixed Charge (before tax)}}{\text{Fixed Charge (before tax)} + \text{Interest}}$$

Personal Financial Statements

When credit analysts require personal guarantees as added credit support, they will review the personal financial statements of guarantors. But analysts need to be careful when evaluating such statements. If the statements are joint; that is, created with someone else (such as a spouse), it may not be possible in the event of a default to consider all of the guarantor's assets as available to repay the lease.

The personal cash flow of the guarantor must also be factored into the analysis and whether they can meet their obligations. This is when a "global cash flow," which combines the business and the guarantor(s) excess or cash flow deficiency, is commonly utilized.

Deal Structuring

Changing the terms and conditions of the approval may reduce risk on specific lease transactions. Some possibilities include:

---

[18] source: https://www.investopedia.com/terms/d/dscr.asp

[19] Source: https://www.investopedia.com/terms/f/fixed-chargecoverageratio.asp

Table 23 Common Credit Enhancements

Credit Enhancement	Purpose
Shortening the approval term	Recovery of money lent is much quicker at 24 months than at 60 months. There is less time for unexpected events to occur (car accidents, divorces, illnesses, etc.). The shorter term usually generates a quicker improved equity position in the equipment for the lessor.
Increasing advance payments	Increasing advance payments helps to reduce the risk in the same manner as above.
Addition of outside guarantors to the transaction	Although this may reduce risk, there must be economic consideration benefiting the outside guarantors. If not, there is a chance that a court will not allow the lessor to collect from the guarantors.
Additional Collateral	Additional collateral may be in the form of equipment or various types mentioned below to strengthen the loan to value ratio.
Security Deposits	If structured and appropriately documented, interest-bearing (or non-interest bearing in some cases) security deposits, which are under the control of the lessor, may be used to offset a possible loss on the transaction in the event of default.
Yield	By increasing the inherent rate (yield) in a transaction, a lessor may help to compensate itself for any added risk to a transaction.

Additional Collateral and Other Credit Enhancements

If appropriately documented, the following also can be used to reduce the risk of a transaction:

- **Certificates of deposits from banks or other financial institutions**. One must factor in the risk of that institution making a mistake and releasing the collateral, or the risk of that institution going out of business.

- **Publicly traded stocks may be pledged**. The potential fluctuation in price is another risk to be assessed. The lessor may decide to consider only counting a certain percentage of the stocks' value as added collateral.

- **Take assignment of either trade notes receivable, accounts receivable, or specific notes receivable**. Evaluate the repayment source and the underlying collateral, if any.

- **Take assignment of inventory**. Each of the different forms such as raw materials, work-in-process, and finished goods, all create different liquidation concerns. Monitoring is recommended.

- **Take a security interest in other equipment either as a blanket or specific lien**. An evaluation is recommended.

- **Real estate, either residential or commercial property, may be pledged**. Caution should be exercised with different state and local laws as well as federal regulations regarding flood insurance. The appetite for real estate as additional collateral varies by lessor. It is increasingly difficult for regulated institutions to take real estate as additional collateral to support a lease or equipment loan transaction.

- **Standby letters of credit** can be easily drawn and represent the bank's agreement to repay should the lessee default. Most banks only write a one-year standby letter of credit with the option to renew at the reduced lease balance each subsequent year. Evaluate the financial condition of the bank as an additional risk.

- **Cash surrender value of life insurance** may be pledged.

- **Vendor guarantees arranged by the lessor with the vendor**. The vendor may provide a full or partial guaranty of the lease or purchase of the equipment (a recourse agreement).

- **Credit life/health insurance** may be added as a requirement when leasing to individuals such as doctors, dentists, etc. It specifies that life insurance protection is included for the lease and/or disability insurance. In the event of death or disability, the lease may be paid via insurance. This requirement is particularly important when the company is dealing with a business owned by one individual.

- **Co-lessees** add another obligor to the transaction, which increases the source of repayment. The co-lessee, however, must have an economic benefit in being a co-lessee.

- **Other**: Many creative credit people reduce risk by taking various other pieces of collateral or a combination of collateral. These may include:
  - **A pledge of the company's stock**: If a default occurs, the lender may control the company. However, the lender should be concerned about taking over the control of a company that may create liability for the lender. For example, the lender may be held liable for payroll and payroll taxes, etc., if not paid.
  - **Diamonds, gold, or other commodities**.
  - **Assignment of the premises**: this kind of lease also provides the lender control of the operation if there is a default.
  - **Vendor re-marketing**, etc. In this case, assistance from the vendor may be different from that of a guarantee.
  - **Reserve programs** from several sources: vendor, broker/lessor, or increased loss reserve internally, may offset losses.

Lenders must be careful to structure additional collateral pledges correctly. Questions to ask include: are we taking collateral to secure the lease additionally or are we securing the guarantee? Having proper documentation gives significantly more comfort in taking additional collateral.

From a critical viewpoint, some credit analysts may structure a lease without fully understanding the underlying risks. For example, it is easier to ask the lessee for additional advance payments, or a high security deposit rather than taking free and clear equipment. It is also easier to shorten the term from sixty months to twenty-four months. But such actions by the lessor put additional pressure on cash flow reducing the lessee's operating cash and may increase the risk of default.

Credit Decision

The decision process is a mathematical modeling procedure coupled with human judgement. Past prejudices, both positive and negative, may be added to the weighing. Most lenders do not disclose their exact model; some even feel it is a trade secret.

Rendering the credit decision itself may be performed by either a human or increasingly, by computer. The technology used in credit processing continues to evolve allowing lessors to make consistent decisions, significantly streamline credit processing, reduce time to decision, and enhance customer experience and increase the ability to offer equipment finance at the point of sale. Even with credit scoring and advanced tools, human involvement or sophisticated algorithms may be required to handle exceptions to credit scoring results.

Large-Ticket Credit Decisions

Large-ticket credit decisions are often processed manually and require more attention to risk mitigation activities. These decisions may require multiple credit authorities to weigh in on the decision.

Before mitigating a risk, the risk must be understood. The better trained the company's staff, the better those individuals can understand and evaluate the risk. Continual training and self-improvement in areas of new laws, the new interpretation of existing laws or changes in governing body rules is always positive. Salespersons should be given basic credit training so that they can initially assess a transaction when they are in front of a lessee discussing or negotiating a transaction.

It is not uncommon for a lease request to have identified challenges. Examples include:

- Deteriorating revenue base
- Decreasing profitability
- Entity is within what is considered a "higher" risk industry with a negative outlook or deteriorating trends
- Insufficient cash flow coverage
- Tight liquidity
- High leverage position
- Substantial distributions and owners unwilling to provide guarantees
- Requested term isn't supported by the financial strength of the lessee or the collateral

The above list is not all-inclusive but is meant to provide common examples of some challenges. Most credit decisions incorporate taking on some calculated risk. The next step in the process is to try to mitigate those risks.

Improvement in three areas may reduce risk on leases: portfolio policies, structuring of specific leases, and education of personnel.

- **Portfolio:** A lessor can reduce risk by adjusting credit guidelines in the areas of credit and cash flow (ratios, trends, quality of statements, etc.). The more conservative a company is at setting its various policies, the more conservative the credits approved. A company's credit policy may also exclude lending to specific industries. A company can adjust required cash flow coverage through credit policy. Many credit analyses require a specified amount of coverage minimums, for example, that profits plus depreciation exceed current maturities of long-term debt plus twelve payments on the proposed lease by at least 120 percent. Adjustments may also be made in the evaluation of the components of the numbers, i.e., elimination of any extraordinary income, etc.
- **Structure:** Changing the terms and conditions of the approval may reduce risk on specific transactions.
- **Education/Training:** Before a risk can be mitigated, the risk must be understood. The better trained the company's staff, the better those individuals can understand and evaluate the risk. Continual training and self-improvement in areas of new laws, the new interpretation of existing laws, or changes in governing body rules is always positive. Salespersons should be given basic credit training so that they can initially assess a transaction when they are in front of a lessee discussing or negotiating a transaction.

Small to Mid-Ticket Credit Decisions

For scalability and cost control, as transaction ticket size decreases the necessity for automation of credit decisions increases. Although not all lessors use automation in the decisions for small and mid-ticket transactions, the adoption of credit decision automation is increasing. Credit scoring and analysis techniques are often used to automatically render a decision or to present the credit analyst with information that helps them to make consistent manual decisions. Manual credit decisions for these transactions are usually processed by a single credit authority but mid-ticket transactions may sometimes require more than one authority depending on transaction size and company policy.

Credit Scoring and Analysis

Originally implemented in response to a shortage of trained labor, the value of credit scoring today may be summarized as quicker, cheaper, more objective, and oftentimes more accurate than manual analysis. With increasing pressure to respond to vendors and customers as rapidly as possible, credit scoring has its obvious benefits. Credit scoring may reduce the time to process credit applications to a matter of minutes, although the time savings vary depending on whether a lender adheres strictly to a credit score cutoff or whether it reevaluates applications with scores near the cutoff. An adequately deployed scoring system may also significantly reduce the time needed to work through the approval process. Such time efficiencies translate to cost savings for lenders as well as advantages to the customer. Since customers only need to provide credit application information required for the scoring model, applications are shorter. Even if a lender does not want to depend solely on credit scoring for making its credit decisions, scoring may increase efficiency by allowing loan officers to concentrate on the less clear-cut cases.

Credit scoring also provides improved objectivity in the loan approval process. Such objectivity helps lenders ensure they are applying the same underwriting criteria in credit decisions to all borrowers regardless of race, gender, or other factors prohibited by law. Other benefits of credit scoring include improved consistency from one credit approver to another as well as allowing managers to more easily tighten or loosen scoring parameters.

There have been numerous statements by banking regulators concerning the objectivity of credit scoring systems. Credit scoring may help lenders comply with the conventions of Regulation B and other fair lending regulations. (See Chapter 8 – Funding and Operations). A properly deployed credit scoring model makes it easier for a lender to document the business reason for using particular factors that may have a disproportionately negative effect on certain groups of applicants protected by law from discrimination. The weights in the model give a measure of the relative strength of each factor's correlation with credit performance.

The idea behind credit scoring and decisioning is that history repeats itself when it comes to borrower behavior; that is future credit applicants display "characteristics or attributes" that are substantially similar to those credit applicants from a historical data pool. By using historical data and statistical scoring models, developers of a scoring model isolate the effects of various applicant "characteristics" on delinquencies and defaults.

This method of statistical analysis produces a score that a lender may use to rank its applicants or borrowers regarding risk to the portfolio. The score may not specifically identify an applicant that may pose delinquency or default-risk. The score may, however, place applicants with similar characteristics into discreet "pools" within the portfolio. The "rank ordering" predicts, with an astounding degree of accuracy, a certain percentage of any pool of applicants expected to be delinquent or subsequently default. For example, a score may indicate whether an applicant is high or low risk. The score doesn't say with certainty which borrower will default, but if, for example, a score pool historically averages a 20% default rate, one out of five borrowers in that pool will probably default.

Within a given portfolio, once a lender has identified which applicants belong in which pools, they can make adjustments in pricing and collection strategy. Such adjustments compensate for any increased or decreased risk posed by an applicant or group of applicants ("risk-based pricing").

Risk-based pricing is a method adopted by many lenders and lessors where the rate on a transaction is determined not only by the time value of money but also by an estimation of the probability of default and/or the probability of loss.

Building and Using a Scorecard

To build a scoring model, or "scorecard," developers analyze historical data on the performance of previous applicants to determine which borrower characteristics are useful in predicting whether the applicant performed as expected.

Model developers begin by culling the "characteristics" from the customer's application, their credit bureau reports, and in some cases, subjective data from the lender's underwriting guidelines. The historic portfolio being used to build the scoring model must be of sufficient size to provide a statistically valid sample of transactions. To develop a thoroughly predictive scoring model, developers need a sample of both good (non-defaults) and bad (defaults) transactions.

The development of models geared toward small business decisions includes characteristics of both the business and, sometimes, the principals of the business. Potential factors that may relate to the future performance and used in a consumer credit scorecard may include:

- Business owner's monthly income, outstanding debt, and financial assets
- How long the applicant has lived at the same address
- Whether the applicant has defaulted or was ever delinquent on a previous loan
- Whether the applicant owns or rents a home
- Applicant's type of bank account

For commercial credit scores, there are additional factors relating strictly to business performance such as time in business, NAICS or SIC Code, average bank balances, past performance on business loans and lines of credit, handling of trade credit and suits, liens or judgments, and more.

Risk Acceptance Criteria & Making Decisions

In most (but not all) scoring systems, a higher score indicates lower risk. The lender sets a cutoff score based on the amount of risk it is willing to accept. Strictly adhering to the model, the lender then approves applicants with scores above the cutoff and denies applicants with scores below the cutoff. Many lenders, however, take a closer look at applicants that score below the cutoff in an attempt to broaden their approval window. Some lenders, by approving applicants that score below the cutoff, may empirically test the validity of the model. This approach makes it possible for the lender to establish the criteria for adding risk-based pricing to offset the additional risk posed by approving applicants that score below the scoring system cutoff or to make future adjustments to the model.

Scoring Methodology

Much of the theory behind scoring methodology comes from the work of John von Neumann and Oskar Morgenstern[20], authors of "The Theory of Games and Economic Behavior." The book was the first definitive work that demonstrated the use of mathematics and statistics in business decision-making. Many of the models described below come from their game theory.

There are several statistical methods used to develop credit scoring systems. A few of these include linear probability models, logit models, probit models, and discriminant analysis models. The first three are standard statistical techniques for estimating the probability that an applicant will default based on historical performance of the portfolio and the individual characteristics of the borrower (both business and personal). The linear probability model assumes there is a linear relationship between the probability of default and the factors; the logit model assumes that the probability of default is logistically distributed; and the probit model assumes that the probability of default has a (cumulative) normal distribution.

Instead of estimating a borrower's probability of default, discriminant analysis divides borrowers into high and low default-risk classes.

Implementation Considerations

Implementation considerations for both the art and science of building a credit scoring model and auto decision capabilities include building, validating, testing, governance, and ongoing maintenance. Additionally, it is wise to take the following into consideration:

- **Regulatory Compliance**: Bank lessors undergo a higher degree of regulatory scrutiny than other lessors when implementing scoring models.
- **Security**: It is vital to consider the security implications and safeguard customer data and meet regulatory requirements.
- **Ongoing Monitoring and Maintenance:** Depending on the application, implementing auto decisioning may require commitment to ongoing periodic monitoring for the predictiveness of the score, stability of the population, and performance of the score in light of market conditions. It's not a "set it and forget it" type of implementation.
- **The Human Element:** How will you help your staff to get to the point where they trust machine-generated decisions? How will you help them to think differently about their role to avoid undermining or overriding the machine generated results?

---

[20] Originally published in 1944 by Authors: John von Neumann, Oskar Morgenstern. Princeton University Press

- **Data Sufficiency and Extraordinary Circumstances:** Under which circumstances might you implement rules to prevent automatic decisions? For example, data may be insufficient to be confident in a score, or there may be an extreme circumstance such as bankruptcy.

While implementation of credit scoring and auto decisioning could lead to job worries among staff, the addition of auto decisioning often allows a company to increase capacity and generate more business. Tom Ware of PayNet™ states,

"I have never seen a company lay people off
because of adding credit scoring."

With these considerations in mind, most companies start small with a targeted portfolio, learn from it, and then expand over time.

The Future of Credit Scoring

What may be on the horizon for credit scoring? From a modeling standpoint, with increasing adoption of configurable digital platforms and greater digital maturity across the industry, we may see companies take advantage of their ability to access internal data in combination with commercially available scores along with other data elements to create hybrid proprietary scores unique to a lessor and its products.

Automatic decisioning with credit scoring can significantly increase efficiency and consistency in credit processing and lead to reduction in the cost of doing business. Applying artificial intelligence capabilities such as machine learning could lead to streamlining credit processes such that customer experience becomes a competitive advantage. Although machine learning may not be an immediate game-changer, it could add more predictive value to scoring and decisioning and as the volume of data increases, models will continue to improve over time.

Robotic Process Automation ("RPA"), another branch of artificial intelligence, enables improving speed and accuracy of repetitive business tasks like credit data analysis and synthesis from various sources such as bank records, rating agencies, and financial statements. Applications running automated scripts can perform these types of activities faster than humans without error, enabling credit analysts to process credit analysis and underwriting tasks more quickly, thus improving customer experience.

While it is exciting to think about future possibilities, we must also consider the human element when applying advanced technologies to credit. The workforce of the future may require new skillsets and mindsets with less focus on tedious, repetitive tasks and more focus on meaningful thoughtful work and the ability to collaborate with machine intelligence. [21] As the

---

[21] See: 4 ways the rise of the machines can work for humans https://www.weforum.org/agenda/2018/01/how-to-make-the-rise-of-the-machines-work-for-humans/

application of advanced technology to credit automation continues to evolve, the credit professional of the future will need the ability to collaborate with machine intelligence to transcend human-only capabilities, creating a sort of "super credit analyst" for the future.

The "Black Box Problem"

When it comes to the application of machine learning to automated decisions, the transparency and traceability of decision-making algorithms become a challenge; it is vital to be able to explain how an AI makes a particular decision. Some AI methods, such as deep learning, a fundamentally different way to program computers, use techniques that may obscure the reasoning behind a particular result thus making it difficult to determine how the AI arrived at a particular decision[22]. This lack of transparency in machine learning-enabled decision making is the "black box problem." While there is work underway to address this challenge and develop AI applications for decisioning featuring built-in explanations, this is a problem that must be solved before we will see a wide-spread implementation of AI for credit decisioning, especially for banks.

Summary

While some may not think of credit as a creative process, those experienced in this field applaud the "art" involved along with the science in the area of credit analysis. With the rise of technology tools to aid in automation and financial analysis, varying degrees of both art and science exist across the broad spectrum of transaction types and sizes. The end goal of the credit function is to make sound credit decisions and properly structure a lease or equipment loan transaction that is appropriate and acceptable for both the marketing style and risk appetite of an equipment leasing and finance company. The output of the credit function has a far-reaching impact on the remaining stages of origination processing as well as the monitoring and servicing of booked contract portfolios.

---

[22] See: https://www.technologyreview.com/s/604087/the-dark-secret-at-the-heart-of-ai/

Chapter 7 – Documentation

The learning goals for this chapter:

- Understand the three basic forms of lease contracts.
- Understand various types of standard lease documents and their purpose.
- Understand typical elements and provisions of lease contracts
- Understand purpose and types of schedules and exhibits.
- Understand the considerations for municipal and agricultural leasing due diligence and documentation.

In the context of the BOK Framework:

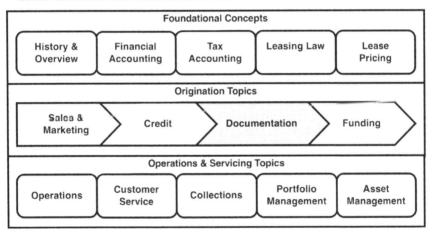

Figure 36 BOK Framework Coverage

The single most important facet of documentation is clarity. While legalese has become the language of contracts, careful reading of all documentation generally yields an understanding of the intent of that particular clause or paragraph. Clear language is easier for all parties to understand and, if necessary, it is more likely to be enforced by a court. In a proper presentation, a set of documents is discussed as to each item's intent and its specific set of responsibilities.

A good understanding of documentation facilitates the lessor's presentation and aids in the documentation process. As an added benefit, such adherence to good practice helps maintain the CLFP standards of ethical conduct

NOTE THAT THE FOLLOWING INFORMATION IS INTENDED TO PROVIDE A GENERAL OVERVIEW OF THE LEGAL ISSUES INVOLVED IN PERSONAL PROPERTY LEASES AND FINANCINGS. WHEN CONFRONTING SPECIFIC FACTUAL PROBLEMS, LESSORS ARE ADVISED TO CONSULT AN ATTORNEY ACCOUNTANT OR OTHER APPROPRIATE PROFESSIONAL TO DETERMINE THE APPLICABILITY OF THESE ISSUES AND OBTAIN CLARIFICATION.

DISCLAIMER: THE CLFP FOUNDATION DISCLAIMS ANY LIABILITY BASED UPON THE CONTENTS HEREOF AND URGES THE READER TO LIMIT ANY RELIANCE ON THE FOLLOWING INFORMATION, EXCEPT FOR THE GENERAL GUIDELINES PROVIDED HEREIN.

Documentation Process

Before we dive into the details of documentation content, let's step back and understand where we are in the lifecycle of a transaction. Within the lifecycle of a lease or loan, the documentation phase of the origination process includes crucial tasks that are required for due diligence, data verification, document preparation, and coordination of information and tasks across a range of stakeholders involved in the transaction process. All of this is done to ensure adequate documentation of the transaction.

Documentation processes vary from company to company for reasons such as policy, organizational type, organizational structure, business model, industry served, equipment, transaction type, ticket size, and level of automation. While each equipment finance company does things slightly different, at the highest level we can visualize the documentation phase of origination as four stages each containing a variety of activities, tasks, and sub-processes depending on the variables mentioned above.

Depending on the aforementioned differences, the time it can take to perform all of the tasks that go into properly documenting a transaction can range from minutes to months. For instance, in some origination channels, the process is very automated for small-ticket transactions with automated document preparation and digital delivery within minutes of credit approval. On the other end of the spectrum, a large complex transaction may require additional due diligence and negotiation as well as collaboration with legal counsel to prepare documentation.

The following diagram is a framework for understanding what goes into the typical documentation process which can be extrapolated to a variety of scenarios.

Documentation Due Diligence	Data Validation	Document Preparation	Document Delivery & Receipt
• UCC searches • Name verification (e.g., SOS lookup) • Invoices • OFAC check • KYC process	• Party identification • Equipment details • Vendor verification • Tax treatment • Pricing calculations	• Prepare documents appropriate for transaction type and credit approval	• Deliver documents in a variety of ways, or execute in person • When all documents are received, submit package for funding

Figure 37 High Level Documentation Process

When we refer to "documentation package," we are talking about all of the various documents that must be executed, received, and examined in the process of closing a transaction before funding, a process covered in the next chapter.

While there are a lot of variations in how these documents are prepared, there are consistent standards for what is typically included in lease documentation packages. The remainder of this chapter will help you answer the following questions:

- What does it take to adequately document a lease or equipment finance transaction?
- What are the elements typically included in a lease document package?
- Why are they necessary?

The language, format, and content of each document will vary; however, typically, lease contracts will include the following fundamental elements:

- Lessor identification
- Lessee/co-lessee identification
- Suppliers
- Contract terms
- Equipment description and location
- Clauses and provisions
- Signatures
- Attachments, schedules, addendums

3 Typical Forms of Lease Contracts

Equipment leases can be written in many different ways, but the following are the three basic forms of lease contracts.

- **Standard "One-off" Lease Agreement:** A lease that governs only one transaction and explicitly describing the equipment and accompanied by all the additional documents normally involved in a lease transaction is known as a standard or "one-off" lease agreement.
- **Master Lease Agreement**: This document is an umbrella agreement for a series of lease transactions and provides a template simplifying the documentation process for each. It usually provides for a schedule to be attached listing the particular equipment involved in each lease transaction (called a "Master Lease Schedule"). Depending on size or nature of subsequent schedules, lessors may or may not wish to make a provision that some documents normally part of the process may be bypassed due to the existence of the Master

Lease Agreement. When appropriate, all documents should refer throughout to "the accompanying and all subsequent, schedules."

- **Plain Language Agreement:** This is a lease document (or any agreement) that is written for purposes of avoiding "legalese," making it shorter and more easily understood, and presenting provisions in an easy-to-understand format. Such agreements have increased in popularity as courts increasingly try to assure that parties can read and understand legal documents. Care should be exercised, however, in structuring "plain language" documents to ensure that provisions that may have significant importance to lessors are not omitted.

13 Standard Lease & Financing Documents

There are thirteen standard lease and financing documents utilized in our industry summarized here and described in more detail later in this chapter.

1. **Lease:** A lease is a fundamental document by which a lessor agrees to provide equipment or other personal property or rights to a lessee in return for rental payments. An Equipment Finance Agreement (EFA) is a markedly different type of financing document discussed at the end of this chapter.
2. **Lease Schedule:** Often simply called "Schedules" or "Supplements," these are documents used with Master Leases. The Lease Schedule incorporates the terms of the Master Lease or, in some forms, are incorporated into the Master Lease, adding specifics about the transaction such as equipment descriptions, rent amount, and term. They should not be confused with the exhibit-type "Schedules" discussed below.
3. **Exhibits & Schedules:** Exhibits are formal additions to the lease (sometimes referred to as "Schedules").
4. **Delivery & Acceptance Certificate (D&A):** This is a document signed by the lessee indicating that the lessee has unconditionally accepted the equipment.
5. **Guaranty:** This document contains all credit support provided by third parties that are not primary lessees.
6. **Corporate Resolution:** A Corporate Resolution demonstrates that the lessee has appropriately authorized the signers to validly bind the corporation to the lease. The document also may provide valuable UCC filing information by specifying the state of incorporation.
7. **Real Estate Waiver:** This document is the acknowledgment by an owner (landlord) or mortgagee of real property that the leased equipment belongs to the lessor and they can remove it (in agricultural leasing, this is often referred to as a Severance Agreement/Easement).
8. **Fixture Filing:** This is a filing similar to a UCC financing statement, filed in real property records to provide notice to third parties of the lessor's ownership interest in the equipment.
9. **UCC Filings:** These papers are filed in the Office of the Secretary of State where the lessee is incorporated (or organized if not an

incorporated entity). UCC filings preserve priority lien rights of a creditor and notice to inquiring parties of a lessor or secured party's interest in the equipment.

10. **Cross Default Agreement:** This agreement provides that if a creditor/lessor has multiple agreements with a debtor/lessee and one goes into default, they all become in default.

11. **Purchase Order:** Issued by a lessor indicating the lessor intends to purchase the equipment from the vendor upon fulfillment of certain conditions by the vendor and lessee.

12. **Invoice:** The vendor of the equipment issues invoices to the lessor seeking payment for the equipment. The invoice also demonstrates the passage of title from vendor to lessor.

13. **Advance Funding/Prefunding Agreement:** Sometimes referred to as "pre-delivery Hell or High-Water agreements," these describe terms and conditions under which a lessor may advance part, or all of the equipment cost to a vendor before full delivery and acceptance of all the equipment by lessee. See "Advance Funding/Prefunding Agreement" below.

14. **Purchase Option:** This language is sometimes contained in a lease and sometimes it is a separate agreement. It deals with whether, how, and for what consideration a lessee may be able to acquire ownership of the equipment at the end of lease term. The manner in which this is done, and the price set can significantly impact characterization of the lease as a true lease or lease intended as security.

31 Elements of a Lease Agreement

Lease agreements are made up of numerous components, the inclusion of which vary from company to company. Following are thirty-one provisions commonly found in lease agreements as well as their purposes

As a CLFP, it is essential to understand the purpose and use of these provisions. Because legal treatment of leases and financings varies from state to state, and due to the complexity of legal analysis, we recommend experienced counsel be consulted if legal questions arise involving these provisions and lease documentation generally. Many of the following elements have specific variations from state to state, and these are pointed out for the purposes of this manual. In matters of state law or concerning application to your particular situation, seek local counsel.

Identification of Parties

Parties in a lease document must be identified by their correct legal names to create legally binding contracts. See Chapter 3 - Leasing Law for more information. Lessors may rely on the business formation documentation or check the secretary of state for name verification. Determining the exact names of entities (the filed names, including accurate punctuation) such as corporations, LLCs. and other registered organizations also ensures the effectiveness of UCC financing statements, which is vital for ensuring the reliability of any future searches by a creditor or bankruptcy trustee.

Identification and Address of Vendor/Supplier

If a lease document is being used to attain UCC finance lease status (see Chapter 3 – Leasing Law), and other arrangements meeting the definition are not made, it is especially important to identify all suppliers. If there are multiple suppliers, all names and addresses should be included, using an exhibit, if necessary. To avoid claims that the lessor and supplier are acting together, a common practice is to list this information on the Exhibit and not as a pre-printed form.

Equipment Description

The description must accurately reflect the equipment; it is especially crucial for titled equipment because, if not accurate, it can call into question perfection of the lien.

A complete equipment description includes:

- Indication whether equipment is new or used
- Year, manufacturer, make, and model
- Serial number or Vehicle Identification Number (VIN)

Equipment Location

Specifying the equipment location ensures that the lessor knows where to find the equipment and that sales and property taxes are paid to correct entities. It is common to include a provision that prohibits movement of the equipment without written consent.

Terms

Terms set forth the correct amount, number, and frequency of lease payments. The tax amount or the phrase "plus applicable taxes" must be stated separately to avoid confusion and comply with taxing regulations.

Purpose/Intent of Agreement

This provision states that the lessee is, in fact, paying rent to the lessor in return for possession and use of the equipment; that parties intend for the transaction to be a lease and not a loan (if true); and that all provisions should be interpreted to give effect to this intention.

Acceptance of Equipment by Lessee

In the acceptance document, the lessee represents that it will accept the equipment when fully delivered and operational, after which time the lease is in full effect.

If the equipment condition becomes an issue in court, there is nothing as useful as a lessee's signature on the document indicating the equipment to be satisfactory, the testimony of the lessor that it relied on that representation, and a verification call confirming when lessor paid for the equipment and entered into the lease.

CONSPICUOUS DISCLAIMERS
Statutes and the courts require certain disclaimer language to be "conspicuous"
(E.G., CAPITALIZED, IN BOLD PRINT, IN LARGER PRINT, DIFFERENT COLOR, ETC.).
A common practice is to have lessees specifically sign or initial such provisions so the lessor can say, "if they did not read the whole lease, they should have at least read that part." However, if there is a provision for such signature or initials, ensure they are filled in, or there could be an argument that by not signing or initialing, the lessee specifically did not agree to those provisions.

Disclaimer of Warranties

The Disclaimer of Warranties is an essential provision in any lease. The UCC provides that a seller (including a lessor under a lease intended as security) or lessor who sells or leases equipment or other goods automatically makes "implied warranties" that those items are merchantable (in generally saleable condition) and fit for their intended use or purpose. These implied warranties give the purchaser or lessee remedies if the equipment is defective (for this purpose, meaning not in saleable condition or unfit for the intended use) unless the seller or lessor expressly disclaims such warranties.

A Disclaimer of Warranties must be "conspicuous" to be effective and usually specifically states that the lessor "expressly disclaims all warranties, including warranties of merchantability and fitness for use or purpose."

Warranties of Merchantability or Fitness for a Particular Purpose may be considered as given, if not specifically disclaimed, by a conspicuous provision. Lessors may also wish to include "as-is where-is" language" that states:

> *The lessee's duty to make rental payments is unaffected by issues about the equipment; claims about the equipment will be made against, and only against, the supplier; There will be no offset against rental payments. So long as the lessee is not in default, the lessor assigns to the lessee the benefit of all warranties extended by the supplier.*

Article 2A Provisions

As we learned in Chapter 3 – Leasing Law, Article 2A of the UCC defines a "finance lease." Lessors should include provisions reciting compliance with the process needed to qualify for statutory finance lease treatment.

There are other such provisions to note. If it is required that the lessor specifically purchase the equipment for purposes of the lease, the wording should say so. Because the intention of the parties may be considered, the lease should state that the parties intend that the lease qualify under the applicable law as a finance lease, as defined in Article 2A.

There are several provisions of Article 2A that lessors may wish to have lessees specifically waive, most notable UCC 2A -517 - 522. When waiving provisions, it should explicitly state that provisions are waived, and that the lessee has knowingly agreed to waive them.

Assignment

Lessors usually wish to prohibit assignments by lessees to unknown entities, or at least, require a lessor's written consent. The validity of such provisions under Revised Article 9 may be an issue. In the modern era of lease syndications and securitizations, it is imperative to most lenders that leases be freely assignable and include a "Waiver of Defenses" clause (see Lessor Assignment, Waiver of Defenses Clause, below). Such waivers prohibit lessees from asserting most claims against one who buys the lease from the lessor. In this way, a funding source can purchase a lease, knowing it will not face defenses or claims that may have arisen against the lessor.

Rental Commencement and Other Payments

Often, this information links to the equipment delivery date. It should specify the date first and when subsequent payments are due. This is done either by specifying or by setting forth a method to determine the amount (such as an agreement by the parties). A common practice is to confirm the actual due date with the original invoice during a verification call.

Non-cancellation

A lease should state that it may not be canceled unless the lessor agrees in writing. Non-cancellation specifies that merely returning the equipment to the lessor does not excuse the lessee from making payments or other obligations unless the lessor agrees to this in writing.

Lessee/Lessor Signatures

Signatures are vital to the formation of a valid contract. These may be written or electronic. Under some legislation, electronic signatures are valid if a party has agreed that they will be; under other legislation, electronic signatures meet the requirement of a "written signature" without the necessity of further action.

To ensure that electronic signatures are considered valid, contact a qualified legal adviser. In any event, the document should specify that an electronic or facsimile signature may be used and constitutes a valid signature.

An incumbency certificate signed by another lessee officer and a copy of Corporate Resolutions (explained later in this chapter) are often used to ensure the identity and authority of the person signing on behalf of the lessee. It is also a good idea to require a witness to the lessee's signature.

To head off an eventual dispute as to the original condition of equipment, it is in the interest of both parties to have the lessee's signature on a document explicitly setting out the condition of the equipment when received. The lessor will want this document to confirm the lessee's satisfaction with the equipment's condition at that time. In the event of a dispute as to the equipment's original condition, the lessor's case can be further strengthened by evidence that the lessee knew that the lessor relied on the lessee's representations as to satisfaction upon receipt and that the lessor had made a timely verification call confirming when the lessor had paid for the equipment and entered into the lease.

Electronic Signatures

If dealing with "electronic chattel paper" (a document stored in an electronic medium), the concept of "control or possession" is similar to the taking of possession of paper originals. The term "chattel paper" means a document that is a promise to pay and is either secured by personal property (such as equipment) or gives the person obligated to make payments the right to possess and use personal property. An EFA and a lease, therefore, meet the definition of chattel paper. For purposes of perfection of an assignee's or rights in an EFA or lease, chattel paper is either the only copy of the document that is either manually signed by the parties or is the copy the EFA or lease specifies qualifies as the chattel paper. Possession of any other copy does not affect the security interest of the holder of the copy that is designated the chattel paper by law or the document itself.

Electronic signatures are covered in more detail in Chapter 8 – Funding and Operations.

Choice of Law/Jurisdiction/Venue

These provisions ensure that the law chosen by the parties governs the interpretation of most provisions of the lease. (In the case of many lessors, the laws of the state with which it is familiar.) Some provisions are not subject to the choice of law provisions, but in large part, choice of law clauses are honored so long as the state whose law is chosen to govern has a reasonable relation to the transaction, and the legal question is not a matter of prevailing public policy.

"Consent to jurisdiction and venue" states that the parties agree that courts in certain states, perhaps the lessor's home state, may or must be used to decide matters arising out of the lease.

For more detail on the "Choice of Law" concept, refer to Chapter 3 – Leasing Law.

Security Deposits

There are various cautions related to security deposits:

- If there is a security deposit, the provision should specify it as such, as well as permissible uses.
- If the lessor is allowed to commingle funds (blend assets together from more than one account) and/or is not required to pay interest, such provisions should be spelled out.
- If the lessor is allowed to use security deposits to cure defaults, this should be specified as well as the duty of the lessee to replenish the security deposit if applicable. It is crucial to spell out conditions under which the lessee is entitled to receive any remaining portion of the security deposit. Typically, such conditions are the full and satisfactory performance of all duties, including non-monetary duties such as returning the equipment.

Authorizations, Power of Attorney, Amendments

Although provided by law, many leases and EFAs state that the lessor or lender may file UCC financing statements without the signature of the lessee or borrower.

If the lessor is to be permitted to take certain actions on the lessee's behalf (e.g., filing UCC financing statements or vehicle titles, negotiating insurance settlement checks, etc.), this provision may be used to provide to the lessor a Power of Attorney to act as attorney for the lessee for the specified actions. Some lessors also define circumstances under which a lessor is allowed to modify a lease without the signature of the lessee (e.g., modification of payments if the cost of the equipment changes). Use caution in changing any terms or specifics of the lease, even in the presence of such a provision. This is why some lessors specify in their documents that certain changes are restricted to obvious errors.

Location and Use of Equipment

For tracking and tax purposes, specifying the equipment location is essential. Movement without notice to or consent by lessor should be prohibited for the same reasons. In some cases, location may also be relevant concerning UCC filing issues. There should be specific provisions that the equipment is to be used only by the lessee and that such use must at all times be in conformance with the lease provisions and applicable law. What if the lessee is in the business of renting equipment? This sometimes prompts the use of a "Rental Yard Addendum" if the customer is in the business of renting out the equipment they are financing. Said addendum is acknowledgement by the lessor that they are aware and allowing under certain circumstances.

Ownership

The lease should specify that the equipment is personal property and not part of any real estate where it might be located. The lessee agrees it is personal property in any event and is solely the property of the lessor.

Renewal

Most renewal clauses give the lessee the <u>option</u> to extend the term of the lease.

Many lessors feel they are due compensation if the lessee holds the equipment rather than immediately returning it at the expiration of the initial term of the lease or fails to notify the lessor that the lessee does not wish to exercise a purchase or renewal option. It has become common practice to extend the term from month-to-month or for a longer period if the lessee fails to return the equipment and wrongfully "holds-over." This provision ensures that the lessor will continue to receive the bargained-for rent or another acceptable amount, rather than relying on the courts to set the holdover rent. This is often called an "evergreen" clause or an "automatic renewal" clause. It is crucial to specify the lease renewal conditions, and that the lease will continue until each of the requirements of the lease, including any notice and actual return of the equipment to the lessor, have been completely satisfied.

In other leases, the lessee's failure to notify the lessor of its intention to return the equipment within the prescribed time, or the failure to return, results in a longer renewal period. This practice has come under legal scrutiny in recent years. Renewal payments in perpetuity, in the same amount as during the base term of the lease, might be viewed by some courts as harsh and, therefore, suspect.

Over the years, scrutiny of renewal clauses has increased in some states. Some have gone as far as legislating required advance notification periods for lessors. Lessors are required to notify lessees before any contractually required notification by the lessee regarding their intent for the equipment at the end of the lease term. It is necessary to be aware of various state requirements before executing or acting on any renewal clause.

Insurance Requirements

There are various requirements "set forth for coverage" in a lease. The lessee typically is required to carry property insurance (comprehensive all-risk). The policy names the lessor as the loss payee, which may require the insurance company to deal separately with lessor to adjust their interest, in an amount sufficient to compensate lessor for loss of its equipment. A provision may be included stating that the insurance settlement will be applied toward, but does not satisfy, the lessee's obligations under the lease.

A loss and damage provision typically requires the lessor to be fully compensated not only for the value of the equipment but also for the benefit of its bargain (that is, the benefit derived from its use and income obtained from its use). In the event of catastrophic loss, insurance may be a vital source of funds to enable the lessee to fulfill that obligation.

Most equipment has the potential to cause physical injury. Lessors should always require the lessee to carry liability insurance, naming the lessor as additional insured. Although in the case of a mishap involving the leased equipment, lessors are not usually the primary cause of injury, it is not uncommon for lessors to be named as defendants in actions arising out of such injuries. This is called "vicarious liability." The additional insured endorsement ensures not only that insurance will cover eventual losses, but, the costs of defense, which can be very substantial, will also be covered.

Vicarious Liability: Liability imposed upon a person even though they are not a party to the particular occurrence (e.g., the owner of a motor vehicle is vicariously responsible for injuries even though they are not driving the car at the time of the occurrence). In the case of a lease, the lessor is considered the owner of the vehicle.

Most lessors require insurance binders or certificates demonstrating that adequate, active coverage is maintained at all times during the lease term. In the case of liability insurance, the lessor may consider declaring a default of the lease if the lessee fails to provide adequate proof of insurance or if insurance lapses. Even the cost of defending a suit by a party or many parties injured can be catastrophic.

Many lessors reserve the right to use "force-place" or "automatic" insurance, (covered in more detail in the insurance section of Chapter 8 – Funding and Operations) which requires additional disclosures in the lease.

Loss and damage provisions provide for the obligation of the lessee to the lessor if some or all of the equipment is destroyed. It should be structured so that if the equipment must be either repaired or replaced, the lease continues as before; if it cannot be repaired or replaced, sufficient payment is provided to the lessor as if the lease had been fully performed. (This is called making the lessor "whole.")

A typical formula for what is considered "sufficient payment" provides for payment to the lessor of all payments now due (rental and other), plus the present value of future payments, plus the present value of future residual (if any), which may be discounted at some rate. This payment is also referred to as the Stipulated Loss Value.

The provision also states that this amount will be due to the lessor despite any limitations on recovery from insurance.

Responsibility for Liens and Tax Liability

A lease should specify that the lessee is responsible for any and all taxes of any kind imposed on the possession, use, value, or payment for the equipment. A common practice is to specify that these include personal property taxes, which can be very expensive. Provisions may be added requiring lessees to pay personal property taxes directly, although the lessor may want some control over this process since unpaid taxes on equipment could subject the equipment itself to levy. Also, because the lessor is technically the owner of the equipment on a lease, they could be held liable by the jurisdiction for any unpaid property tax amounts. Whatever the method (e.g., payment and reimbursement, prorated payments with each rental, or other), specify this along with a clear statement of who assumes this responsibility. The lessee should also be required to keep the equipment free of liens at all times.

Lessee Indemnification of Lessor

A vital provision, this provides for any claim made regarding the equipment or its use by any party (including the lessee and any third parties) other than relating to lessor's improper conduct.

Indemnification means that the lessee will indemnify (compensate for damage or loss) and hold lessor fully harmless from and against any such claim, including all costs of defense and attorney fees.

By requiring such indemnification, the lessor has somewhere to turn for defense against such claims; and ultimately, if the lessor were to be found to be liable, there would be a method to recover any required payments by the lessor. It should be clear that this provision covers anything occurring during the life of the lease and afterward. This provision protects the lessor against any claim asserted during or after the term of the lease.

Lessor Assignment, Waiver of Defenses Clause

Assignments typically give the lessor permission to assign the lease, or any portion of the rights and duties under the lease, to third parties with or without notice to the lessee. This provision is necessary if there is a chance that at any point in the future the lease might be assigned to a funding source, syndicated, or securitized.

The "waiver of defenses" clause goes hand in hand with such assignments, essentially providing that any defenses to collection, which a lessee might have, must be asserted only against the original lessor, not against any assignee down the road. Most funding sources, syndicators, or securitizers insist on this. It ensures that if they take an assignment, they can collect the rental stream without being subject to claims the lessee might have against the supplier, the original lessor, or other parties.

Service Charges/Late Fees, Interest

A lease document should spell out the charges for late payments. It is common to allow a short "grace period" following the due date, after which the charge is imposed. The late charge should be reasonable, and the lessor should be able to demonstrate that the charge is related to additional costs and servicing because payment is late. If it is determined that the lessor is simply attempting to generate extra revenue, it may be deemed to be a "penalty" and therefore unenforceable. Even worse, if it is deemed to be an interest charge, it could trigger a finding that the rate in the entire lease is usurious and could potentially trigger unenforceability of the entire lease and various civil and criminal penalties. Lessors should take care to be able to defend the charge as related to additional costs, and to allow a reasonable grace period to forestall such claims.

If the late charge is reasonable, the lessor should also be entitled to charge interest on the amounts not received since the lessor must replace the cash it would have received. This provision should be enforceable as long as the rate is reasonable and accrues for only so long as the payment is outstanding. Many lessors make provision for such interest charges, but because of the difficulty of calculation and administration (and to avoid the appearance of being overbearing), they only calculate the charge once a lease is seriously in default.

"Time is of the Essence" Provisions

Some state courts still look for this language to indicate that it is expected and part of the contract that all payments and other performance must be completed in a timely manner. To further ensure enforcement in such states, it is typical to insert the wording: "Time is of the essence of this lease and acceptance on occasion of late payments or performance shall not be deemed to waive this provision."

Default Provisions

These provisions set forth those events that are deemed to be a "default" under the lease, triggering the remedies allowed by the lease contract and by law. They should include provisions when some or all of the following takes place:

- Failure to pay rentals when due
- Failure to pay other amounts when due
- Failure to meet non-monetary obligations (e.g., insurance)
- The lessee makes any false or misleading statement in the documents

215

- The lessee is a debtor in bankruptcy or reorganization (but see below)

There are other defaults found in some leases, for example, failure to keep financial covenants, death, or restructuring of lessee. Most include filing bankruptcy as an event of default although such provisions are generally not enforceable.

Some lessors agree to allow a grace period during which a formal default is not declared. In this way, the lessee can cure the default and avoids giving the appearance the lessor is poised to pounce at the first hint of a mistake by the lessee.

Similarly, concerning notice, provisions are often included that allow a lessor to declare a default "without notice." In practice, it is common to notify a lessee when they are in default and why, and allow them to cure the default, before pursuing remedies. Failure to notify, even if permitted under the lease, might appear to be overreaching or unfair. Most lessors would prefer a performing (or active) lease over a default, even though the situation is less than desirable.

Remedies

The Remedies section sets forth the lessor's rights in the event of a lessee's default, as defined in the default section. The lessor may repossess the equipment with or without a court order, but it is common not to repossess unless it can be done peacefully. If a lessee insists on a court order, the lessor should get one. Remedies typically include the following, with language making clear that they are "cumulative." This means that one or more may be pursued simultaneously or consecutively without closing off the possibility of pursuing others:

- The lessor may require the lessee to return the equipment to the lessor upon receipt of instructions (this is the ideal option)
- Cancellation or termination of the lease (this is not typical unless the equipment value exceeds the balance owing)
- Acceleration of all future rentals
- Payment of damages by formula, e.g., full payment of damages by formula; present value of future rental payments; present value of future residual value, etc.
- Any other remedy allowable by statute or other law with reference made to provisions elsewhere allowing recovery of costs of enforcement (legal costs and attorney fees) as well as interest at rates referred to elsewhere in the lease.

Note: Take caution in drafting clauses setting out payment by formula. They are typically brought to bear only if the equipment is repossessed and sold or re-leased since in such event the lessor will not receive it back at the end of the term. The formula should credit the defaulting lessee with any net proceeds of resale or re-lease. Also, whether spelled out in the document or not, all aspects of any disposal of equipment always should be "commercially reasonable."

Any measure of damages provided here should be reasonably related to the amount it would take to make the lessor whole, as if the entire lease had been performed. If the equipment is picked up, credit should be given to the lessee for proceeds. Otherwise, a clause allowing the lessor to pick up and sell the equipment and receive all future payments could be found to be an unenforceable penalty.

Specific language that these remedies are cumulative and that failure to exercise any of them in a particular default situation does not constitute a waiver of the default or of the remedy concerning any future defaults.

Cross-Default Clause

Lessors include a cross-default clause when they want to provide that a default under any other contract or lease between the lessee and lessor also constitutes a default under the present lease. The provision may help to avert a default by a lessee under one lease (e.g., the computer lease) while at the same time the lessee retains the use of other mission-critical equipment (e.g., the assembly line) to keep up payments. Some cross-default clauses also provide that a default under any contract with any third party constitutes a default while others limit the cross default to certain sized obligations or specific types of contracts. These cross defaults protect against a lessee's financial condition weakening while the lessor is unable to act.

Attorney Fees/Enforcement Expense

These expenses may only be recoverable if agreed by the parties. Fees can be made available to the "prevailing party" instead of just to the lessor since many statutes and courts imply this in any event. Additionally, the language can state that any additional costs of enforcement are recoverable. Ensure that costs recovered are not the same amount as those used to justify the late charge on any late payments.

Severability

This provision states that if any provision of the lease is unenforceable under state law or found by a court to be so, all other provisions of the lease are to be enforced as if the offending provision were not included. As an example, a late charge may be found to be an unenforceable penalty. Severability helps to avoid the danger of an entire lease being unenforceable just because one provision was improper under the particular state's law or if it was being viewed as "overzealousness" by the lessor in the eyes of the judging court.

Exhibits & Schedules

Schedule and Exhibit documents are used as formal additions to the lease.

For instance, when the description of the leased property is too lengthy to fit into the space allotted on the lease contract, it is typically detailed on an exhibit document with the following wording in place of the equipment description:

"See Exhibit A, attached hereto and by this reference incorporated herein."

The exhibit itself might include wording such as:

> This Exhibit is made a part of the lease dated _____ between [lessee] and [lessor].

It is a common practice to have the lessee initial or sign an equipment exhibit to clarify what equipment is included and acknowledge that the exhibit is part of the lease.

Other types of exhibits and schedules might consist of additional terms or provisions that require extra space, such as payment schedules, schedules of suppliers, or non-standard payment structures like contact payments. In each case, these documents should be physically attached and contain references to and from the lease.

Note: exhibits should not be confused with "Lease Schedules" used in connection with Master Leases described earlier in this chapter.

Delivery and Acceptance Certificate (D&A)

The D&A allows the customer to acknowledge that the equipment is received, installed, and working properly, and that they are ready for the contract to commence. Historically this document is one of the most useful and practical documents in equipment finance. This is especially so with the advent of UCC 2A "statutory finance leases" and the emphasis on unconditional acceptance. Under an equipment lease, the lessor is required to confirm delivery to and possession of the equipment to the lessee; the acceptance certificate should prove that the lessor did so.

The D&A should state that the lessee is completely and unconditionally satisfied with the equipment since unconditional acceptance is required to achieve "Statutory Finance Lease" treatment for the lease (see Chapter 3 – Leasing Law)

- The D&A indicates to the lessor that the lessee is fully satisfied with the equipment and that it has accepted it for purposes of the lease.
- The D&A should be executed by the lessee after the lessee has received the equipment and had an opportunity to inspect it.
- It is imperative that the date on this document, if any, is after the date the lease is signed and that the lessee has, in fact, signed after receiving the equipment. Note: many lessors make a "verification call" by telephone to the lessee to confirm the lessee's representation.

In other words, this document is an independent representation by the lessee that the lessor has already entirely performed its obligations under the lease. Having this may efficiently forestall later claims by the lessee that it didn't receive the equipment or shouldn't have to pay because the equipment was unacceptable or didn't perform. Having this document is a form of protection for lessors because the lessee has already made a representation to the lessor, in writing, that the equipment, was acceptable.

D&A Nuances: Sometimes equipment suppliers require equipment to be paid prior to delivery, but the customer doesn't want to sign the D&A because equipment isn't delivered yet. The prefunding authorization has similar language to the D&A where the customer is acknowledging that the lessor is paying before they receive the equipment.

The D&A may include the following elements, some of which may instead be included in the lease or lease schedule.

- **Acceptance and Representations Regarding Equipment**: The document should state that by signing, the lessee indicates it has fully received all the equipment and finds it acceptable in all respects for purposes of the lease.

- **Instructions to Pay Supplier:** The lessee states that because the equipment is entirely acceptable, the lessee wants the lease to begin and the lessor to pay the supplier/vendor for the equipment. After paying the supplier, the lessor and possibly the lessee have no enforcement tool against the supplier. It is to the advantage of the lessor to be in a position to ensure that when they paid the supplier and started the lease, it was in reliance on this representation by the lessee. This document places the lessor in this position.

- **Unconditional Nature of Acceptance**: With this language, the lessee states that its acceptance is unconditional and without reservation. Such action adds credence to the lessor's reliance on the document and representation. It also corresponds to language in Article 2A regarding attaining statutory finance lease treatment, under which the lessee must pay its obligations regardless of issues, which might later arise respecting the equipment or other matters.

- **Verify the Delivery Date:** Occasionally, the lessee may date the D&A in error when signing documentation, therefore, it is important to verify the actual delivery date. The lease records should always accurately reflect information regarding delivery date. If the lessee failed to date the D&A when they signed it, the lessor should consider noting the date elsewhere in the lease records. (Sometimes this is done to make it appear that the lessee inserted it when signing.) If not noted on the lease record, the date should be noted on the D&A to show that the date was inserted by someone else, based on information provided directly by the lessee.

- **"Acceptance" in Advance of Delivery:** Exercise caution concerning so-called "acceptance in advance." This occurs when the lessee purports to unconditionally accept the equipment before it has been delivered. The same issues arise in "progress payment" or "advance payment" scenarios. Whether the document so provides or whether the lessor knows that in practice such documents are signed before delivery, the legitimacy of the unconditional acceptance of the equipment may be jeopardized, which can have significant consequences. It is important for the customer to acknowledge the release of funds and commencement of contract even though equipment is not yet delivered. (See "Advanced Funding/Prefunding Agreement," below.)

Cautionary Note

On occasion, lessors have engaged in the practice of inserting the date on the D&A to match either the date of the verification call or the date identified by the lessee during that call as the actual date of delivery. When practical, the preferred practice, is not to have the D&A signed until the equipment delivery is complete.

Personal and Corporate Guaranties

As described in Chapter 6 - Credit, a Guaranty may be desired to make an additional person or entity other than the primary lessee responsible for the obligation. The law often treats guarantors as somewhat unusual and worthy of special protections, as described below. This is because, traditionally, guarantors might be third parties not as directly involved in the affairs of the lessee as those active in the lessee's company.

Following are considerations for preparing guaranty documentation:

- **Consideration**: There must be "consideration" (value) of some sort to the proposed guarantor to make the agreement enforceable. This demonstrates that the guarantor received value in return for becoming obligated. It also makes it clear that the lessor would not enter into the lease with the lessee were it not for the guarantor being bound as well. It should be ensured when dealing with corporate guarantees that there is a relationship such that the guarantor (e.g., parent company) receives a benefit from the transaction. Not all corporations that are loosely related necessarily have the kind of relationship where one significantly benefits from the wellbeing of another. Mere common ownership should be closely examined.

- **Authority to Guaranty**: As in the case of a corporate resolution to lease, authorization should be obtained to demonstrate the authority of parties signing a corporate guaranty to do so; this is often in the form of a "Corporate Resolution to Guaranty."

- **Obligation Guaranteed**: This should specify that the guaranty is a guarantee of performance, not of collection; the guarantor is primarily liable for any obligations, and the lessor is not required to pursue or attempt to recover from the lessee before proceeding against the guarantor.

- **Waiver of Suretyship Defenses**: This should state that obligations of the guarantor are not subject to some traditional defenses to guarantees such as the lessor is obligated to exhaust remedies against the lessee. The waiver should do the following:

- Waive the right to require pursuit of other parties.

- Waive the right to notice of each and every change or modification to the underlying obligation (although efforts should be made to keep them informed nonetheless).

- Consent that the guaranty is valid despite changes to the underlying obligation such as renewal, modification, acceptance of occasional late payments, etc.
- Provide that the guaranty is absolutely enforceable despite any underlying defenses or claims the lessee might have against the lessor or its assignee.
- **Standard Provisions:** Rather than attempt to piggyback on lease provisions, these should include attorney fee/recovery expense, jurisdiction and venue, integration, and other standard provisions.

Corporate Resolutions

In order for a registered entity such as a corporation to enter into a contract, the signing individual must be authorized to do so. This document is a certification by the corporate secretary or another officer that the person signing is authorized. It is a more efficient way to ensure authorized signatures than a review of the articles of incorporation and bylaws.

A typical certificate provided by a corporate secretary includes incumbency statements attesting to the official position of any person signing on behalf of the lessee, often with specimen signatures. Certificates, where an officer authorizes themselves, are not advised unless others are unavailable, e.g., in the case of smaller companies. If possible, notarize these.

A Corporate Resolution demonstrates that the lessee has appropriately authorized the signers to validly bind the corporation to the lease. The document may also provide valuable UCC filing information by specifying the State of Incorporation.

This document is used when a lessor enters into a lease with an organization other than a natural person to ensure the following:

- Identifying information regarding the entity is true and correct.
- The organization has validly authorized the lease.
- The signers hold the positions they purport to hold.
- The signers have been authorized to bind the organization.

It is possible for a corporation to enter into "normal course of business" transactions without a resolution. However, exercise caution, since the lessor will not usually know (without obtaining Articles of Incorporation or Bylaws) what is considered the normal course of business or what defines the specific authority of officers.

Some lessors are willing to assume this risk in smaller transactions if the signer is known to be an officer; some are not. From time to time, the existence of so-called "apparent authority" can become the subject of litigation.

Resolution to Lease language may be a separate document or in some cases is combined with the Guaranty. Resolution to Guaranty Lease is used in cases where another entity (due to ownership or some other interest) is agreeing to guaranty a lease as a corporate guaranty.

Real Estate & Landlord Waivers

Real Estate Waivers are similar in purpose to a fixture filing except a waiver is specifically signed by parties having an actual interest in the property and contains rights that go beyond protecting the lender's security interest. Unlike fixture filings, however, Real Estate Waivers are not binding on third parties unless the waivers are filed, as discussed below. This document increases the protection to the lessor in that parties with existing interests have specifically recognized and consented that the property belongs to the lessor and may be removed by the lessor in the event of default on the equipment lease. A waiver can protect in addition to the protection of a fixture filing because the landlord/mortgagee has acknowledged the lessor's interest, whether or not the technical rules about fixture filings were met. It is therefore much less likely that a landlord's lien for rents could be successfully asserted.

> **Example of Real Estate Waiver:** Imagine the leased equipment is a walk-in freezer that is going to be bolted to the wall, or otherwise permanently affixed to a piece of real estate. This waiver documents the acknowledgment that even though the equipment is affixed to the wall, the equipment belongs to the lessor.

The Landlord Waiver is used for instances where equipment is going to be on the property or in a building owned by someone else. In this document, the owner of the building or the landlord acknowledges that even though the lessor's equipment is on their property the lessor owns the equipment.

> **Example of Landlord Waiver**
> Imagine your lessee is operating a fitness club and defaults on the lease. The lessee is locked out of the building. As the lessor, you do not want the landlord to sell your equipment to a new tenant or to recoup past due rents to them.

The form has similar formalities to a fixture filing. Most county recorders require sufficient legal description to enable filing in the official real estate records. They often require an "acknowledged" signature (such as a notarized signature) and requirements vary by jurisdiction. Lessors should pay attention to where the forms originate, for example, from the party in possession, owners/landlords, institutions, or individuals who may have an interest such as a mortgage; then use precisely the right forms for each circumstance. This ensures written records are clear and makes a difference in how well a business is protected.

Filing Requirements

In larger transactions and where the equipment might be deemed a fixture, lessors often want to file the landlord waiver with the real estate records where the equipment will be located. This will generally make the waiver binding on future property owners. It is important for lessors to strictly comply with all filing requirements, which may vary from county to county if recording the agreement in real estate records. The real estate waiver is usually filed with the county, the landlord waiver is not.

Landlord waivers typically include the following elements:

- **Identification of Parties** identifies the lessor and holder of an interest in the property (for indexing purposes). It is critical to provide the correct legal name of entities and individuals because this is how the filing information is indexed for searches.

- **Agreement on Subject and Nature of Fixture** states that the parties agree the equipment, whether deemed to be a fixture or personal property, is nonetheless continually owned by the lessor.

- **Waiver of Rights by Landlord/Mortgagee** is an agreement that the lessor has the continual right to remove its property even if the law, mortgage, or lease would otherwise allow the real property interest-holder to take the equipment in the event of default or at the end of the real property lease.

- **Permission to Claim Property** is an agreement by the mortgagee or landlord that in the event of default under the equipment lease, the lessor has the right to repossess and remove the subject equipment, despite any contrary provisions in the real property lease.

- **Acknowledgement** could consist of a notarized signature and/or other special requirements (see local requirements).

Legal Description of Property Filings

Accurate legal description is essential for property filings. Legal description is not the street address. It is by reference to township and section numbers followed by what is known as a plat map description or "metes and bounds." Such descriptions are recognizable by paragraphs that include measurements such as 3' to the north, then 2' to the west.

Pay attention to the following when preparing a Real Estate Waiver filing:

- **Documentation:** The document should contain legal description of the property and the name of holders of interests in the real property. This document must be signed and notarized.

- **Filing Requirements:** Take care in identifying local requirements. Usually, filings are in the real estate records for the equipment location's county. Note: this is quite different from the location of filing of financing statements. Additional items may be required (e.g., legal description).

- **Protections Provided:** It serves as notice to third parties contemplating the purchase of the property, so they cannot claim that when they bought the property, they thought they were also purchasing lessor's equipment.

- **In the case of Mortgaged Property:** Sometimes it is advisable to go beyond the landlord (owner) of the real property and obtain similar rights from the landlord's mortgagee, a "Mortgagee Waiver." It is often advisable where the real estate is owned, rather than leased, by the lessee but is subject to a mortgage. Unless the mortgagee agrees otherwise, it might become an adversary if it forecloses on the real property, creating issues similar to those discussed above vis-a-vis landlords. The problem can be more serious if the mortgagee sells the real estate to a third party unaware of the lessor's rights. For this reason, it may be advisable to record the Mortgagee Waiver.

- **Taxes:** In some states, real estate mortgage taxes as well as nominal filing fees, may be payable if a fixture filing or other document is filed. This should be researched in advance.

Fixture Filing

A fixture filing makes the lessor's ownership of the equipment that might be perceived or deemed to be part of the real estate (e.g., a machine bolted to the floor) a matter of record. It also preserves the lessor's rights in the equipment, as opposed to a holder of an interest in the real property, such as a bank or other mortgage holder. Note: the question of what constitutes a fixture is far from clear, and there have been widely varying results in the courts.

In general, if an item is physically attached to the building and/or if there is any indication that a purchaser of the building assumes they are also acquiring the equipment, "fixture" status might be an issue. If this is the case, consideration should be given to obtaining a fixture filing or a real estate waiver.

Fixture filings function similarly to UCC financing statements. They serve notice to anyone researching the property that the lessor has prior rights in the equipment, and when they acquire the real estate, they are not acquiring the lessor's property.

Pay attention to the following when preparing a fixture filing.

- **Form**: The form is a UCC-1 filing statement including a UCC-1 Addendum which contains the legal land description and real estate owner, if not the debtor.
- **Filing Requirements:** Take care in identifying local requirements. Usually, filings are in the real estate records for the equipment location's county. Note: this is quite different from the location of filing of financing statements. Additional items may be required (e.g., legal description).
- **Protections Provided:** A proper and timely filed fixture filing should preserve the lessor's rights to its equipment (as opposed to a mortgage holder or other party with interest in the property). It also serves as notice to third parties contemplating the purchase of the property so they can't claim that when they bought the property, they thought they were also purchasing lessor's equipment.
- Timing: the timeframe for filing matches the state UCC filing, typically 20 days from the date of delivery.

UCC Financing Statements

In secured lending, a UCC filing "perfects" the lender's interest in the leased property as against all other parties. Under this system, usually, the first party to file a valid financing statement for a particular property or equipment has the superior right to all other parties to reclaim the property in the event of default. As well, financing statements are in the public records. Having a financing statement on file protects lessors from claims that a third party purchased their equipment from the lessee without knowledge of the lessor's interest because it puts the purchaser on duty of inquiry.

What does it mean to perfect security interest?
Also called "perfected lien," a lien is perfected by registering it with appropriate statutory authority so that it is legally enforceable and any subsequent claim on that asset is given a junior status or priority.

What is a lien position?
When a lender is in a first lien position, they are in the first or priority position to benefit from any liquidation of the collateral which secures the loan, if property is to be sold in the event of default.

Refer to Chapter 3 – Leasing Law for more details on this topic.

The two main forms of UCC filing statements are UCC-1 and UCC-3.

- **UCC-1:** This is the most basic form of financing statement. They are available from a wide range of legal form providers, or from service providers who also offer the service of filing paper forms, or filing electronically, where available. UCC-1 forms identify debtor/lessee, secured party/lessor, and the subject equipment.

- **UCC-3 Amendment/Termination Form:** A UCC-3 should be filed in the event of a change in leased equipment or at the termination of the lease (once the lessee has fulfilled all obligations including the obligation to return equipment). In some jurisdictions[23], the lessor must file UCC-3 terminations after all requirements of the lease have been met; otherwise, the lessor faces financial penalties; in others, the obligation to file a termination statement only arises if the debtor requests a release be filed.

Keep the following filing requirements in mind when preparing UCC filing statements:

- **Location**: These need to be filed at the lessee's "location," which is usually the state of residence for individuals and the state of formation for other entities (corporations, LLCs).

- **Timeliness**: To attain Purchase Money Security Interest status and take priority over existing liens, proceeds must be used to acquire the equipment with financing statements filed within twenty days of delivery in most jurisdictions (pay attention to requirements by location). However, there is nothing wrong with filing before delivery.

---

[23] Note: This is a requirement for consumer lending, but commercial lending you do not need to file a termination unless requested, then the lender has 20 days (a few exceptions for longer time frames- ND, GA) to terminate the UCC. See UCC law 9-513(c) (Clarification provided by CLFP Handbook Contributor Barry Marks, Esq., CLFP)

- **Continuation:** In most states, financing statements are valid for five years. If the obligation or lease extends beyond that, a "Continuation Statement" should be filed before the expiration of the first financing statement. Continuations may be filed up to six months prior to expiration.

- **Fees**: Publications are available which identify, by state, the costs for various filings. These should accompany filings to ensure that the correct fee is submitted. A filing could be rejected without it, which may potentially miss the critical time frame referred to above.

- **Signatures**: The old law required the signature of the debtor; however, this is not necessary under Revised Article 9. The lessee must authorize the filing without a signature, either by entering into the transaction (if a secured transaction), or by a lease provision giving permission (if a true lease). Lessors should consider including a provision authorizing such filing in all lease contracts and even in the application process.

Precautionary Filings: As described in Chapter 3 – Leasing Law, although technically a true lease does not require a filing, it is still a good idea to file. Thus, preserving the lien position in the equipment should the agreement be subsequently re-characterized as a secured transaction. This is because the lessor has satisfied requirements of purchase money security interest and by doing so, has first priority in the equipment even though the court determined they didn't own it. Additionally, if the filing is not required, filing still provides notice to third parties of the lessor's interest. It is allowable on financing statements to identify the secured party as "lessor" and debtor as "lessee" if seeking to file for precautionary purposes only.

Purchase Order

A purchase order is issued by some lessors to the supplier and specifies the lessor's order for the equipment. It states that if the supplier complies with all terms and conditions and then appropriately delivers all equipment, the lessor agrees to make payment. It is important that any purchase order make it clear that the lessor or lender is not obligated to fund the transaction, at least until all documents are signed and the lessee accepts the equipment in accordance with the financing documentation.

The document defines the terms of purchase of the equipment by the lessor from the supplier, including terms of payment and any conditions the lessor requires to be fulfilled by the supplier. As previously discussed, this means that under Article 2A, the lessor has, in essence, "fully performed."

The purchase order may or may not include an acknowledgment section for the supplier to sign. More often, it consists of a section stating that the supplier's delivery of the equipment, rendering of invoice, or acceptance of payment is deemed an acceptance by the supplier of the terms of the purchase.

The following content is typically included in a purchase order document.

Representations by Supplier: This usually requires the supplier to warrant that

- All equipment is delivered to the lessee;
- The vendor is the owner of the equipment;
- Title is now vested in the lessor with no liens of any kind; and
- The supplier indemnifies the lessor against any claims having anything to do with the equipment, or if the lessee fails to accept the equipment or makes a claim relating to the conduct of the supplier.

Disclaimers and Conditions by Lessor: These require that:

- The supplier takes full responsibility for any and all issues arising concerning the equipment;
- The supplier conveys full and unencumbered title to the equipment to the lessor; and
- By invoicing the lessor, the supplier is affirmatively representing to the lessor that all equipment described is entirely delivered and accepted, not subject to any claim by the lessee, and agreeing that any warranties may be enforced by the lessee if the lessor so consents.

The use of a purchase order by the lessor ensures that the terms of the purchase meet the lessor's requirements and attempts to eliminate any unacceptable terms, which might be proposed by a supplier by way of, for instance, the vendor's invoice.

Invoice

The invoice shows the sale of the equipment from the supplier directly to the lessor (or, in an EFA or lease intended as security, to the borrower/lessee) and describes terms, if any, of the purchase. An invoice directed to a party other than the lessor may trigger issues concerning the passage of title, for example, whether liens against third parties may have attached and the potential additional tax liability. The parties and the equipment description should be clear, and the date should be correct.

Timing of Title Transfer

In some states, there is a very short window of time for transfer of titles and avoiding fines to the customer (as an example, in California there is a 10-day window for transfer of title).

For instance, imagine an invoice for a titled piece of equipment, such as a truck. The sold date on the invoice is listed as November 10 but the lessor is not funding the transaction until December 1. It would be crucial for the lessor to have the current date indicated on the invoice, otherwise, the customer will incur fines and penalties due to timing requirements for title transfer.

Advanced Funding/Prefunding Agreement

The purpose of an advanced funding document is to accommodate vendors that require payment before delivery. These may be vendors who need progress payments as multi-stage equipment is assembled and/or delivered; or vendors whose standard terms require payments in some amount before the time the equipment is 100 percent delivered and accepted, as would be the norm with an equipment lease.

Parties to an advanced funding agreement (so-called "prefunding" agreements) commonly include the lessee and lessor and, in some cases, the supplier.

The advance funding agreement defines what portions of the payment from the lessor to the supplier are due at what points in time. This payment amount typically is a set percentage upon all or some of the following factors: receipt of order; acceptance of the order; shipment; delivery; acceptance; or other events. The document prepared also should be used to define what happens in the event of no delivery, partial delivery, and different sets of circumstances.

There are two basic approaches to this type of agreement and a multitude of different styles within those approaches.

- **Lease Commencement:** Many agreements simply state that the lease is to commence immediately, and the lessee acknowledges it must pay no matter what happens concerning the equipment or its delivery. The lease commences when the lessor receives the document, and the lessee is obligated to make all payments regardless of whether the equipment is ever delivered.
- **Interim Funding:** This agreement provides for some sort of loan in the amount of advances required, to culminate in an equipment lease once the equipment has been fully assembled, installed, and accepted. If such acceptance has not occurred within a set period (e.g., ninety days), the lessee may be obligated to fully repay the interim funding. Additionally, the supplier may be made a party to this type agreement and may be required to repay funds to the lessor in such event.

Lessors should exercise caution when entering into prefunding/advanced funding agreements for a number of reasons, including the following:

- The lessor may be giving up or delaying the best protection it has against defaults relating to the equipment since the lessor has not yet received the "unconditional acceptance" (Article 2A) to attain statutory finance lease treatment.
- The lessor is essentially putting its cash in the hands of a third party (the vendor), which it may or may not have determined to be creditworthy.
- The lessor is giving up some or all of the leverage it might otherwise use to ensure complete performance and delivery by the supplier since the supplier has already received some or all of the consideration due to them.
- Vendors who insist on "upfront" payment may, in fact, be using the progress payment to acquire the equipment from the manufacturer so

that the lessor is unintentionally doing inventory financing for the supplier.

These concerns are typically addressed by using the prefunding agreement document or including progress payment language in the lease documentation.

Purchase and Renewal Options

Purchase and renewal options (also called end-of-term options) are sometimes included as part of the lease document or in a separate agreement. This document describes whether and how a lessee may be able to acquire ownership of the equipment at the end of the lease term. The details of the purchase option may significantly impact whether or not the lease is characterized as a true lease or a lease intended as security.

The parties are typically the lessor and the lessee with the lessee given the right, at some point (ordinarily following the conclusion of the lease), to exercise their rights under that option.

Although it is typical to encounter a variety of creative purchase option scenarios across the industry, the following types of purchase options are most commonly used in equipment finance.

- **Nominal Option:** This option allows the lessee to purchase the equipment at the end of the lease for $1, or some other minimal payment such that they are extremely likely to exercise the option and the lessor is unlikely to have a "meaningful residual interest." The fact that the lessor has no residual interest in the asset at the end of the term is enough to "re-characterize" it as a secured sale or financing transaction rather than a true lease.

- **Fair Market Value Option (FMV):** An FMV option provides that at the end of lease, a determination is made for the then-value of the equipment, at which point the lessee has an opportunity to acquire it for that amount. Usually, a pure FMV is indicative of a true lease, but the presence of the option does not necessarily ensure a finding that it is a true lease. For more information on how this value is determined, see Chapter 9 – Portfolio Management.

- **Purchase Upon Termination (PUT) Option:** This gives the lessor the ability to require the lessee to purchase the equipment for an agreed price following the conclusion of the lease. Usually, a lease with a "PUT" will not be found to be a true lease, since the lessor has no meaningful residual position but rather knows it can receive a specific amount at the end of the lease.

- **Renewal Option:** This provides that if the lessee wishes (or if it doesn't indicate otherwise), the lease may, or will automatically, renew from period to period. Renewal continues until the lessee indicates it wishes to terminate the renewal or until the equipment is returned to the lessor. A renewal option is a standard tool used by lessors to ensure the timely return of equipment, or if it is not timely returned, the lessee compensates the lessor for the decrease in value during the time the equipment remains at the lessee's location. Considerations as to whether such options affect characterization as a true lease or as a loan are similar to those for purchase options. These have to do with the relation between the rental value of the equipment and amount charged.

- **Early Pay Off (aka Early Buyout) Addendums:** Although the lease agreement is "non-cancelable" in nature, in this type of option, a customer agrees upfront to an option to pay off the lease and buy the equipment for a premium at a specified point during the contract term.

Additional Collateral as Security

Additional collateral is typically used to enhance the credit of an applicant that might not otherwise qualify, and make the lessor feel more secure, by taking an interest in additional assets. It may also be used in cases where the equipment is closely related to the additional collateral (e.g., a building to a parcel of real property, a refuse compactor on a truck) such that for practical reasons, the lessor wishes to have an interest in both. There are a variety of reasons for taking additional collateral as described in Chapter 6 – Credit.

Parties to the agreement are the lessor (the secured party) and all parties with interest in the collateral that would otherwise be prior to the lessor as a secured party (e.g., owner of the property and existing lien holders). As with guarantors, ensure that consideration has passed to the party providing the additional collateral.

Documentation should be prepared with a "standard" security agreement, providing that the secured party (the lessor) is granted a security interest in the additional collateral (the property not subject to the lease itself). This document secures the obligations of the debtor (the lessee) under the lease.

To ensure a first priority security interest in the additional collateral, the lessor should follow the same procedures concerning leased equipment. More significant attention, however, should be directed to obtaining appropriate waivers or subordination agreements from other lienholders. Some procedures to keep in mind include:

- The additional collateral is documented as a secured transaction (be it personal or real property), so it is almost surely subject to Article 9.
- The additional collateral is not usually being directly or indirectly acquired with funds provided by the lessor. It, therefore, is unlikely to qualify for "Purchase Money Security Interest" (PMSI) treatment, so there is no mechanism to jump ahead of existing secured parties. Instead, it is necessary to obtain consent from all interested parties in one form or another (See Chapter 3 – Leasing Law for more detail on PMSI).

Real Estate as Additional Collateral

Following are considerations for taking real estate as additional collateral:

- **Forms of Security:** There are several methods for taking an interest in real property, including traditional mortgages or deeds of trust. Requirements for formation and rules of enforcement vary widely from state to state, as does the preference of practitioners for the particular type of real estate hypothecation[24] (to pledge as security without delivery of title or possession) form they prefer.

- **Requirements for Filing and Perfection:** Generally, the rules for real estate filings are similar to those described above regarding property waivers. Signatures of parties against whom the interest will be asserted need to be obtained and likely notarized. The document needs to be filed in the office of the county recorder of the real property's location, whether or not that is the equipment location's county.

- **Anti-Deficiency Laws:** These laws prescribe practices for particular states concerning situations in which a lessor or secured party has an interest both in personal property and in real property. Under some circumstances, by pursuing a remedy such as foreclosing on real property, a lessor may lose the right to further pursue a deficiency under the equipment lease (or vice versa). These laws are very state specific, and, in all cases, where a lessor is considering obtaining real property as additional collateral, local counsel should be consulted.

- **Regulations:** It is becoming increasingly difficult to take real estate to support an equipment lease or loan transaction due to federal regulations on Flood Insurance, FDICIA, etc.

Equipment Finance Agreements (EFAs)

An EFA is a contract used as an alternative means to finance equipment. An EFA is a loan document that creates indebtedness on the part of the customer (a borrower, rather than a lessee) and a security interest in favor of the creditor (a lender, rather than a lessor). The economics of an EFA are very similar to those in a lease intended as security: Each payment consists of a principal repayment (amount for the purchase price of the financed equipment) and an interest component. These components may or may not be identified in the document.

EFAs may be viewed as a combination note, loan agreement, and security agreement. This is in part because they are simple in comparison to traditional bank leasing documents. EFAs are becoming increasingly popular because they avoid several problems inherent in leases intended as security. One

---

[24] source: "Hypothecate." Merriam-Webster.com. Merriam-Webster, n.d. Web. 24 Apr. 2018.

principal advantage of an EFA over a lease is that an EFA lender is unlikely to face liability to third parties injured by the financed equipment because the lender does not own the equipment nor are there tax implications related to the purchase of the equipment or filing of property taxes.

Most of the documentation used in connection with a lease can and should be used with an EFA. For example, guaranties, corporate resolutions, real estate waivers, invoices (which should be made out to the borrower), and documents regarding security deposits can, with minor modification, work equally well for an EFA transaction. Some EFAs do not provide for acceptance certificates, but the decision not to have some indication of equipment delivery and acceptance can add risks that should be discussed with qualified counsel. As the EFA is a debt instrument, it is imperative for UCC filings to be handled correctly.

There are several notable differences between EFAs and leases as illustrated in Table 24. Failure to take these into account may result in problems enforcing the EFA and in confusion between the lender and borrower. One of the most frequent problems is that conversion of a lease agreement into an EFA misses one or more of these key differences.

First, the parties may be designated "lender" and "borrower" or any of several other names, but "lessor" and "lessee" is inappropriate. More serious issues can arise with the inclusion of the remedies language of a lease in an EFA. The EFA remedies should look more like those of a secured loan governed by UCC Article 9.

Purchase options and return provisions are inappropriate for EFAs. However, deleting the return provision can require an examination of the maintenance language to preserve the value of the lender's collateral. The EFA should grant a security interest in the equipment to the lender.

Some lenders do not require liability insurance in EFA transactions because the potential for liability for damage caused by collateral is less than when the lessor owns the equipment. Consider also the calculations of casualty values and whether a Hell or High-Water clause is necessary.

The question of interest is perhaps the most perplexing issue when entering into EFA transactions. Since interest is charged under an EFA, whether as an imputed portion of the periodic payment or as separately stated, EFA transactions are very likely subject to usury law and other legal interest rate limitations.

Table 24 EFA vs. Lease

Elements	EFA	Lease (True Lease)
Owner of Equipment	Borrower	Lessor
Complexity of Documents	Lower	Higher
Parties	Lender and Borrower	Lessor and Lessee
Lease Remedies Language	Lease remedies are inappropriate for the EFA, the remedies should look more like those of a secured loan (UCC Article 9)	Appropriate
Loan Remedies Language	Appropriate	Inappropriate
Purchase Options	Inappropriate	Appropriate
Return Provisions	Inappropriate	Appropriate
Security Interest	Granted to the lender	Only granted as precaution and only if lease is determined to be a loan
Liability Insurance Requirement	May not be required	Required
Hell-or-High Water Clause	Still common but may not be necessary	Required
Interest	Appropriate	Not appropriate
Interim Rent	Although not called "interim rent," since there is not a "rental" component, some lessors/lenders do still bill a pro-rated amount for the days between when funds are released and when the contract "commences"	Appropriate
Guaranties	Appropriate	Appropriate
Corporate Resolutions	Appropriate	Appropriate
Real Estate Waivers	Appropriate	Appropriate
Invoices	Should be made out to the borrower	Should be made out to the lessor
Security Deposits	May be included as a separate document or as a clause	May be included in leases
D&A	Appropriate but not always required	Appropriate
UCC Filing	Must be handled accurately	Must be handled accurately
Sales and Property Taxes	Customer is responsible	Lessor is responsible

Municipal Leasing Documentation

This section covers the municipal aspect of government leasing documentation, for additional information on documentation for leasing to Federal Government or Native American Tribes, see Appendix 1 Government Leasing.

Typical examples of municipal leases include financings for firetrucks, ambulances and police cars, and for copiers or computer equipment by a city, county or other municipality.

Before discussing specific documentation, it is necessary to consider and understand the "non-appropriation" clause, also known as a "fiscal-funding" or "annual-out" clause.

It is unlawful for a currently serving government to obligate funds to be expended after the end of the current fiscal year for which such funds have been budgeted or "appropriated." Such an obligation may be "debt" prohibited by applicable state law without voter approval. That is why long-term bonds are issued only after approval by the citizenry in an election (or referendum) held for that specific purpose. Such a costly, time-consuming step would be impractical given that one of the advantages of municipal leasing is its low cost and flexibility, as well as the fact that it is not counted as debt against the municipality's borrowing limit.

Given the above, a standard feature of a municipal lease is a provision that the contract may be terminated without penalty if funds are not appropriated for a particular fiscal period during its term. To help mitigate the risk, this right of termination is limited in specific ways:

- It usually applies to a whole fiscal year and all remaining fiscal years.
- It provides an honest, best efforts attempt to secure budget funds.
- Usually, the title to equipment is held in the municipality's name, but if needed by the customer, an important feature of a municipal lease is the option to purchase at the end of the lease term, which is typically for one dollar. Under this option, the Internal Revenue Code provides that "to be tax-exempt," the agreement must provide for the passing of title for a nominal amount. Options of as little as 10 percent have been held to disqualify interest as being non-taxable.

There is, therefore, an interesting paradox: a tax-exempt municipal lease is not a lease, but a lease intended as security. At the same time, the "lease" must not be considered actual "debt" under state law.

The Public Finance Equipment Lease Application is specific to municipal leases and outlines the following:

- The payment terms
- Authorized signors
- Whether competitive bidding is allowed for awarding the transaction
- Whether the relevant governing body has formally approved the acquisition
- Ordinance or resolution

Due to SEC and IRS oversight, municipal leasing documentation is very structured and standardized, but typically consisting of the following core documentation:

- Lease-Purchase Agreement
- Authority/Purchase Order, Council Resolution, board resolution minutes, etc.
- Evidence of Insurance, or statement relating to self-insurance
- Schedule of Equipment (this may also be an invoice referred to throughout the documentation set as the description of equipment)
- Loan amortization schedule (details running outstanding payoff balance after each payment ending with a zero balance on full payment of the obligation)
- Certificate of Incumbency or Authority to Sign the Lease
- For vehicles, Certificates of Title or Origin
- UCC-1 (See section below)
- Opinion of lessee's legal counsel, as to legality, enforceability, tax-exempt status
- Bank Qualification Statement
- Information Return Form 8038. (Form 8038-GC for transactions smaller than $100,000 and Form 8038-G for larger leases)
- Credit information, credit reports, audited financial statements, budget
- Certificate of Essential Use of Equipment
- Certificate that current-year funding is in place

In actual usage, it is unlikely to include all of these documents in a package. For small-ticket leases (typically under $25,000), although not considered a best practice by some lessors, it is not uncommon for funding to take place with only the lease, purchase order, and invoice.

Escrow Agreements
One variation that comes into play in municipal lease documentation is the need for an Escrow Agreement when funding needs to be released while the equipment is under construction. For example, let's say a city wishes to lease a fire truck, the funding goes into escrow allowing the municipality to release funds during equipment construction.

Each state has statutes on how escrow funds are to be invested. The municipal entity should select the investment. There are also arbitrage rules that must be followed.

According to AGLF[25]: A Government Body acting as a lessee under a tax-exempt municipal lease must comply with the applicable requirements under the Internal

---

[25] Source: An Introduction to Tax-Exempt Municipal Leasing: Answers to Frequently Asked Questions http://www.aglf.org/faq

Revenue Code to assure that the lease will not be treated as an "arbitrage bond," including compliance with arbitrage rebate where necessary. Whether a particular transaction is subject to arbitrage rebate and other federal tax law requirements depends largely upon the type of transaction.

There are a handful of documents that are unique to municipal leasing that a lessor not usually involved in this aspect of the industry may find unusual:

- **Certificate of Incumbency, or Authority to Sign Lease:** This serves the same purpose as a Corporate Secretary's Certificate or Corporate Resolution to Lease. For example, a county clerk might certify that the county board has given the director of public works authority to sign agreements on behalf of the county.
- **UCC-1:** The latest version of UCC provides that the filing of Form UCC-1 does not apply to governmental entities as a means of recording security interests. More than forty states adopted this version. In most states, therefore, it should be recognized that a filed UCC-1 would add nothing to the quality of the obligation, even though there is nothing that prevents such filing. (When in doubt, local law or a good UCC manual, should be consulted).
- **Certificate of Essential Use:** Given the contractual right to terminate under certain carefully defined conditions, it is vital to the lessor that the equipment is essential to the lessee. Municipal leases usually speak to this point. To emphasize the importance of this, it is not unusual to also request a separate certificate to this effect. Similar to commercial leasing, there are many variations in practice.

Bank Qualification Statement: The Tax Reform Act of 1986 (TRA '86) provided that municipal interest would continue to be exempt from federal income tax except for interest received from a large issuer by a commercial bank (For more information see Chapter 1 – History and Overview).

- TRA '86 then went on to define a "large issuer" as one that issues more than $10 million in tax-exempt obligations in the current calendar year.
  It is crucial, therefore, to obtain such a statement whenever originating a lease that may be destined for bank funding. Briefly, it states that the lessee does not "reasonably expect" to issue $10 million or more of tax-exempt obligations in the current calendar year and promises that if it does issue more than that amount, it will designate the subject lease as being within the "allowable" amount of tax-exempt debt. It is also possible to include the appropriate wording in the lease. In fact, this may be tactically desirable for all but the very largest transactions.
- **Form 8038:** TRA '86 provided that municipalities that lease equipment under tax-exempt leases should file information returns with the U.S. Treasury Department on Form 8038. The penalty for non-filing is the loss of the tax-exempt status of the underlying lease. Lessors commonly request the inclusion of a signed form with the lease document (Form 8038-G is for every transaction over $100,000 and

Form 8038-GC is for the aggregate of leases under $100,000 each, entered into by the lessee).

- **True Leases:** While not qualified for tax exempt treatment in most cases, leases with fair market value or no purchase options with municipalities are not uncommon. These still usually require non-appropriation clauses but are otherwise similar to commercial leases.

Federal Leasing Documentation

There is one point which invariably surprises commercial leasing professionals: there is no official lease form prepared as a specific lease document in federal transactions.

Given the many possible lease variations, the federal government recognizes none of them. Instead, it puts the relevant information right on the purchase order. It is normal for funders to ask for the inclusion of additional binding language on the purchase order. Federal government contracting officers, of course, vary widely as to their degrees of receptivity to the inclusion of such language, which often leads to conference calls, negotiations, and compromises.

Lessors should seek outside counsel for federal leases.

For more information see Appendix 1 Government Leasing.

Agricultural Leasing Documentation

For more information on Agricultural Leasing see Appendix 2.

Documentation for agricultural leasing is similar to standard leases. However, there are typically more fixed assets and various other nuances to consider. As an example, a grain dryer attached to the grain bin requires a fixture filing and severance agreement to be filed with the county recorder. Due to situations like these, fixture filings and severance agreements are often necessary for agricultural transactions.

Documentation specific to agricultural leasing includes added levels of due diligence pertaining to sales tax. In the majority of cases, an exemption form is part of the document package. Each state has different tax exemption rules for agriculture.

Examples of Tax Exemption Variations for Agricultural Equipment

The storage of grain in one state may be exempt, while in another state it is not. Or, in the case of customers who are treating seeds or providing another service that is not directly related to agricultural production, the usage of the equipment may not be tax-exempt according to the state tax regulations. Still another example, an all-terrain vehicle (ATV) used to get around on the farm, in some states may be considered tax-exempt yet in some states it is not.

Because of the variety of customer scenarios and differences in tax law from state to state, the due diligence for sales tax treatment may be a bit more in depth for these transactions. Often the transaction may be exempt, but it is essential to understand the purpose of the equipment acquisition and use along with state tax resources (such as state websites) to determine the tax requirements for each situation.

Additional considerations for due diligence in preparing documents for agriculture transactions are:

- Is the transaction tax-exempt or not?
- How is the equipment being used?
- Who are the parties to include in the documentation?
- If there is additional collateral, who is the owner?
- Are there any non-standard payment structures?
- What are the requirements for a UCC search or fixture filings?

Standard Agricultural Leasing documentation set.

- **Sales Tax Exemptions:** Sales tax exemption forms are more often necessary in agricultural transactions.
- **Fixed Assets:** Severance agreements and fixture filings are more often necessary for these transactions.
- **Additional Collateral:** With the increase in the use of agriculture technology, it is common for new equipment to be attached to existing equipment. For example, a farmer may want to connect a new GPS unit to a tractor they already own. In this case, the credit approval may include a requirement to take the tractor as collateral. Thus, making it necessary to perform a UCC search, identify the owner of the equipment, and prepare a security agreement.
- **Organization Structures:** Because of the variation in operating structures for farms, it may be necessary to perform UCC searches on multiple people or entities. It is important to understand the customer's operating structure and who is involved in running a farm so that you identify the right parties for documentation.

Payment Schedules: The payment schedule is another common variation for agricultural documentation. These transactions are typically not monthly payment schedules and are more often set up with annual or semi-annual payments (see Chapter 4 – Lease Pricing) for more information on these types of payment structures).

Summary

There are a wide variety of lease contract document types, elements, and provisions and it may seem a bit overwhelming, but becoming knowledgeable of the foundational lease documentation concepts presented here goes a long way toward expanding your knowledge of equipment finance. Although the exact language and approach to documentation may vary from company to company and by transaction type, the fundamentals are applicable across the industry. The proper documentation of lease contracts has a widespread impact on the rest of the transaction lifecycle.

Chapter 8 - Funding and Operations

- Understand the different sources of financing and the purpose of each.
- Develop a broad understanding of why and how major state and federal regulatory requirements are applicable to equipment finance as well as the key state licensing requirements for a leasing company.
- Describe the purpose of the funding package audit and typical major components of both standard and titled funding packages.
- Understand the major types of technology typically used to operate an equipment finance company.
- Describe the major components of standard and titled transaction funding packages and the purpose and use of each.
- Understand at a high level the typical roles in a leasing organization and some of the various ways that operation teams are structured across the industry.

Each equipment finance company structures its "Operations" function differently. For the purpose of this text, the term "operations" refers to the functions involved in funding, customer service, insurance administration, title administration, and technology specific to equipment finance. You will see that there are overlaps in many functions and roles. The key is understanding what is required and why it is required regardless of who performs the responsibility or how exactly it is performed.

As the final stage of the origination process, funding is often the point at which customer interaction formally transitions to customer service professionals. While each equipment finance company may structure its funding, operations, and customer service functions differently, the fundamental roles, responsibilities, tasks, and considerations are universal.

This chapter spans origination and servicing concepts and covers the topics shared in the following BOK framework diagram.

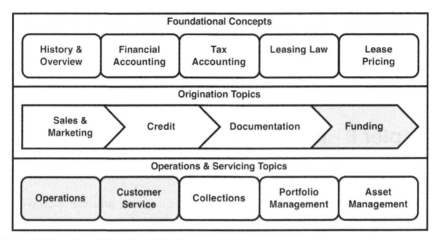

Figure 38 Operations & Funding BOK Framework Coverage

Sources of Capital

The most basic resource that all equipment finance companies need is capital. Without internal capital or access to a capital source, the company is unable to operate. Because of the paramount importance of capital, management of the company must devote significant attention and resources to attracting an adequate and stable supply of capital. Cultivating and protecting sources of capital should be one of the primary tenants of its mission.

There are a variety of methods used to fund an equipment finance company. A combination of internal and external factors may be used to determine the funding approach.

Internal Factors	External Factors
• financial strength of the company and its principals • company infrastructure • management capabilities • risk tolerance • strategic goals	• conditions in the equity and debt markets • market perceptions of the leasing industry in general

There are various sources of capital. Capital may be:

- contributed directly by owners as paid-in capital
- grown organically in the form of retained earnings
- borrowed from conventional lenders, such as banks or other financial institutions or commercial finance companies
- invested by/borrowed from less traditional, sources, such as pension funds, insurance companies, and other private or public investors — or even other leasing companies

The most common methods of funding in the industry today are:

- internal funding
- brokering
- discounting
- equity and debt
- asset securitization

The simplest form of external funding is brokering a lease transaction to a funding source on a one-off basis. The most complex is asset-backed facilities such as lease securitizations. Between these two extremes are a variety of alternatives and combinations, each with their advantages and disadvantages. The following sections summarize these methods and discuss the associated benefits and risks.

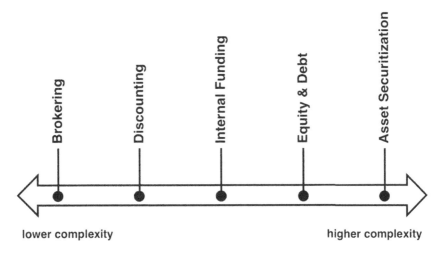

Figure 39 Complexity Spectrum - Sources of Capital

Management Considerations

In deciding what combination of debt best meets company goals, management must consider all of the factors being considered by its lenders. If those elements are positive relative to the amount and type of debt desired, management must then decide what mix of the various debt facilities best meets the overall needs of the equipment finance company. In determining the desired debt structure, management strives to achieve short- and long-term positive cash flow, flexibility to fund the amount and type of leases originated, the lowest overall cost of funds, acceptable interest rate exposure, manageable credit and financial risk, and a satisfactory debt-to-equity ratio.

- **Cash flow** is a constant concern for virtually all lessors. A lessor incurs the majority of the expenses in originating, underwriting, and funding a lease, while the income and cash flow are received over the lease term. Though reasonable debt may be available, a company may have to broker, assign, or discount some or all of its leases to meet cash flow needs.

- **Flexibility to fund the amount and type of contracts originated** is often a luxury. Management frequently must make decisions to reduce originations in a specific business segment or charge a premium to offset the higher cost of obtaining debt to avoid building segments of the portfolio for which no appropriate debt is available.
- **Achieving the lowest overall cost of funds** is the goal of a company treasury group. The "average cost of debt" measures the total interest cost related to financing the lease portfolio. It usually is shown as an interest rate percentage and is calculated by dividing the total interest expense of all company debt by the weighted average net portfolio balance for the period. The difference between the weighted average interest yield of the portfolio and the weighted average interest cost is the interest margin. The amount of interest margin is the gross profit of a leasing company from which all operating expenses, losses, and other costs are deducted to establish the net profit.
- **Interest rate exposure** relates to the potential rise in interest expense due to market rate fluctuations. Since most contracts have fixed payments, if the underlying debt has a floating rate of interest, then the equipment finance company could have a lower margin if interest rates rise over the life of the debt. This is generally known as margin compression.
- **Manageable credit and financial risk** are paramount to management's planning and execution. By carefully and continuously monitoring the portfolio and market conditions, management can appropriately balance the mix of floating and fixed-rate debt.
- **The debt-to-equity ratio** is a key performance indicator for any company. It measures the amount of debt compared to equity used in financing, and the related recourse exposure to its lenders. The use of partial recourse or non-recourse debt can reduce a lessor's financial exposure and can make it more attractive to lenders, and more likely to gain the various types of debt desired.

Determining the Desired Debt Structure

Management should continuously review its lenders' strength and preference for the equipment finance industry, the economic conditions, the interest rate environment, its originating capabilities, and portfolio performance. The best funding strategy is likely a combination of several types of debt. Some leases may be brokered, or discounted without recourse, immediately upon origination to meet cash flow needs and reduce risk. Others may initially fund on short-term revolving lines to increase the company's ability to take deals "off the street" rapidly in support of its sales efforts to serve its vendors promptly. Later those leases may be discounted or moved efficiently in bulk to partial recourse or non-recourse permanent financing sources. By doing so, the company reduces interest rate exposure and credit risk while taking advantage of possible economies of scale. Management may extend the time leases are held on floating rate lines of credit in times of falling interest rates.

Management is wise to maintain good relationships with every debt provider regardless of the funding strategy.

The most critical resource to the industry, however, is the availability of funding. Due to the industry's creative and entrepreneurial nature, current methods of funding continue to change and evolve, and new techniques emerge. With such complexity and variety of funding, it is essential that professionals within the industry stay abreast of these changes so they can take advantage of new opportunities.

Funding Methods

Internal Funding

Many banks and other large financial institutions have either purchased or started equipment finance companies. In many instances, these subsidiaries are funded entirely by the parent financial institution, thereby eliminating the need for external sources of funding. If the parent is a bank, then a significant portion of the funds comes from relatively low-cost deposits. If the parent is an industrial company or a diversified financial services company, funds most likely are generated in the public debt market. Either way, the parent typically charges the leasing subsidiary a premium and the leasing subsidiary pays the parent interest, which can be either fixed, variable or a combination of both; considered their cost of borrowing, better known as the cost of funds (COF) or funds transfer pricing (FTP).

Brokering

As described in Chapter 5 – Sales and Marketing, brokering a lease transaction to a funding source is a form of funding where a broker serves as an intermediary between the end-user (lessee) and the funding source.

Establishing a relationship with a funding source usually starts with an application initiated by the broker. Funding sources traditionally look at the broker's origination model (vendor, end-user, third party), length of time in business, management knowledge, reputation in the industry, portfolio performance directly or with other lenders, and the creditworthiness of the company and its owners. Once a broker is approved, an agreement is required, which establishes the nature of the relationship. The agreement usually includes representations and warranties related to accuracy, the full disclosure of all credit, vendor, and equipment information being provided by the broker, and enforceability of the contract against the lessee and guarantors except as to the credit strength of the obligors (those bound to the contract).

In many cases, the funding source publishes a rate chart of lease rate factors for use by the broker. The broker marks up the lease rate factor by the desired commission rate, and the resulting factor is multiplied by the equipment cost to determine the lessee's lease payment. More often than not, the funding source places limits on the amount of commission or points that will be allowed on a transaction. Rate charts typically take into consideration the size, term, residual assumption, and number of prepayments of the lease transactions.

The advantage of these types of relationships is that there is little or no economic risk on the part of the broker relative to the transaction and capital requirements. The funding source is taking all of the credit and equipment risk associated with the deal, and the broker's risk is limited to the representations and warranties included in the broker agreement. These often include the risk of unenforceability due to fraud.

On the other hand, the broker's profit under this structure is limited to the upfront commission paid on the transactions. The funding source is entitled to the income on the transaction, including late charges, gains on early terminations, residual profits, and other miscellaneous income. Since the funding source is responsible for the administration, servicing, and collection of the transaction and the related costs, the broker is not required to have a servicing platform in place under this structure.

Because of the minimum financial requirements, infrastructure requirements, and lessened risk, this form of funding is widespread in the industry.

Discounting

The term discounting is used to describe a method to fund transactions whereby the equipment finance company is the lessor, but it sells off the remaining rents of a lease to a funding source while retaining ownership of the leased equipment. Discounting the future rents to their present value is the method for determining the value of the rents sold. This is done through a series of calculations. For a company to avail itself of this funding method, it must possess specific financial and operational capabilities.

Discounting transactions may be structured as a sale of the lease rental stream to the funding source or as a loan to the borrower by the funding source secured by an assignment of the rental stream. In the case of a loan-type discounting, payments of principal and interest amortizing the loan are matched to rental payments under the lease. In either event, the funder generally takes a security interest or "collateral assignment" of the lease and a security interest in the equipment (which the lessor continues to own).

Initially, when establishing a discounting relationship with a funding source, the parties execute an agreement describing the relationship and each party's rights and responsibilities. These arrangements can vary in structure to suit the relationship requirements.

Discounting and Recourse Arrangements

Discount without Recourse: The purchaser of the rental stream does not have recourse against the lessor should the lessee default, except in the case of the lessor's breach of its representations or agreements in the sales or loan contract with the funding source. The lessor often does not service the transaction, unless it is appointed agent for that purpose by the funding source.

Discount with Recourse: The purchaser of the rental stream has full or partial recourse against the lessor should the lessee default. In recourse discounting, it is possible for the lessor to retain servicing rights to the transaction. Often the purchaser may request that the lessor utilize a lockbox for lease payments. This arrangement gives the purchaser the rights to control the cash from the leases should the lessor default under their servicing agreement.

The graphic below depicts the typical flow for a transaction originated under this funding method.

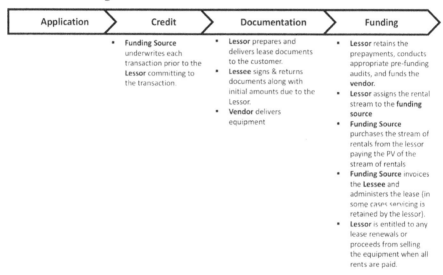

Figure 40 Typical Origination Flow - Discounting

Benefits of Discounting

Discounting gives the equipment finance company a lower cost of funds, greater flexibility, and more control compared to brokering transactions. Since the company is the lessor, its brand identity is enhanced. The lessor may achieve an improvement in service levels because they control the funding of a transaction. The lessor can also earn increased revenue related to servicing fees, late charges, early termination fees, and the sale of the equipment either at lease termination or earlier if the lessee chooses to terminate the lease before the scheduled term. Any lease renewals benefit the lessor. The lessor retains more control over the relationship with the lessee.

Risks and Responsibilities of Discounting

Along with the advantages of discounting comes more risk and responsibility. In many discounting agreements, significant representation and warranty clauses affect the lessor. The originator in a discounted transaction retains some if not all of the risks that may otherwise be transferred when brokering a transaction. A few of the typical representation and warranty issues include enforceability of the lease documents, valid and binding lessee and guarantor signatures, equipment delivery representations, and representations regarding clear title to the equipment. If the lessee defaults, the credit risk is being born by the lessor up to the level of recourse established in the discounting agreement. This includes risk resulting from a lessee default and a breach by the lessor of its representations or agreements in its contract with its funding source.

The lessor also retains equipment risk. Should the equipment become obsolete or undesirable to the lessee, this hurts the lessor's revenue expectations regarding the residual value or renewals. In rare circumstances, a lease may default before the transaction has been discounted to a funding source. In these situations, the lessor is left with a non-performing contract and possibly no way to recover the investment. Careful consideration must be given to all aspects of this type of funding because essentially a lessor is taking on a higher degree of risk than in a traditional broker relationship.

Financial Considerations

Given that the lessor is funding the transaction immediately, the proceeds from the sale of the rents do not usually happen simultaneously. Adequate working capital must be available, and the amount required is primarily affected by the volume of transactions, and the amount of time between funding the vendor and receipt of the proceeds from the sale of the rental stream.

As a rule, the unguaranteed residual positions are not discounted in this type of transaction. The upfront profit realized is commonly less than a brokered transaction. The income on the residual can be earned over the remaining life of the lease, despite the fact that there is typically no cash flow generated until the sale of equipment or renewal of the lease.

Tax and Operational Considerations

In a simple broker relationship, the funding source is responsible for sales, use, and personal property taxes. In the case of a discounted transaction, it is typical for the party servicing the lease to collect and then report sales and use taxes to the proper jurisdiction(s); requiring the servicing party to be licensed and registered in those jurisdictions it intends to conduct business. Furthermore, they must be versed in the proper application of tax law in each of the jurisdictions.

The lessor (as the owner of the equipment) is legally responsible for reporting all equipment it owns in a state or county to the local assessor on an annual basis for personal property tax purposes. In the case of an EFA, the borrower has this responsibility. The assessor then assesses the equipment and applies its tax rate to the assessed value. The lessor or borrower is then responsible to remit the tax. Most leases require the lessee to reimburse the lessor for any taxes assessed on the equipment, but the lessor must have (or outsource) the administrative capabilities to handle this process. In some leases and most EFAs, the lessee or borrower reports and remits directly to the state or county and furnishes the lessor or lender with proof of compliance with the law. Sometimes, the funding source will manage this process to protect its position and because it probably has the required knowledge, systems, and staff.

For federal income tax purposes, the owner of equipment is required to capitalize and depreciate the equipment according to the IRS code. Lessors must have the capability to create the proper depreciation schedules for each item of equipment to report accurate depreciation expense on their tax return. Once again, the lessor must possess the required knowledge, systems, and staff to meet these requirements or outsource these functions.

Summary of Discounting

Discounting is an excellent method of funding for an equipment finance company transitioning from being a broker to a traditional lessor. When risks are correctly understood, profitability is improved, and the lessor has more control of the lessee relationship. Credit risk may be transferred as well as servicing if capital requirements are less than adequate, and operational requirements and capabilities are limited. The gradual increase in taking on risk and responsibility paves the way for more sophisticated funding methods.

Equity and Debt

The long-term economic benefits of holding leases can be an attractive business model, assuming the lessor has the necessary financial and operational capabilities as well as a thorough understanding of the legal, tax, and accounting issues relating to equipment financing. Furthermore, having a long-term perspective, sound credit and pricing policies, in addition to robust risk management capabilities, are critical to attracting capital through a combination of equity, debt, and the more complex asset-backed methods, such as securitizations.

Treasury Terminology

Leverage: In the simplest form, *leverage* is the ratio of debt to equity. In other words, if an organization has $3MM in debt and $1MM in equity, it is leveraged 3 to 1.

Weighted Average Cost of Capital: The cost of capital when multiple capital costs are used together to provide funding. For example, if a funding source has sub-debt at a cost of 10% for 25% of its funding and lender debt at 5% for 75% of its funding, the funding sources *weighted average cost of capital* is the mathematical average of these borrowing rates when including the volume of each in the calculation.

Equity

First and foremost, a viable equipment finance company wishing to build and hold its own portfolio must have an appropriate amount of equity. A variety of factors dictate what is appropriate. The primary considerations are advance rate and leverage requirements of the debt, the size of the portfolio, type and source of debt, attributes of the portfolio (e.g., transaction size, equipment, and geographic concentrations), credit risk, and loss expectations, longevity, and experience within the industry.

Equity, either in the form of paid-in capital or retained earnings, is used to provide leverage to the company in acquiring additional funding. Lenders are not only focused on the amount but also the quality of equity. To establish the tangible equity of the company, it is not unusual to reduce intangible assets such as goodwill from total equity.

Quality of earnings also impacts the perceived value of a company's equity. Aggressive income recognition or inadequate provisions for bad debt are typical examples. Lenders are looking at equity as a cushion to absorb any unexpected losses between the value of the assets and the finance amount. High leverage ratios (typically greater than 5 to 1) are perceived as higher risk, and therefore impact the pricing of the debt as well as the availability. The bottom line—without the appropriate amount of equity, it is difficult, if not impossible, to attract lenders.

Debt

Lessors use debt to finance the earning assets (leases). Effective liability management is a crucial factor in ensuring both short-term cash flow and long-term profitability. Management must determine what type of debt is currently and likely to be available, given the circumstances and the time frame under which the company is expected to operate. Also, management must ensure that the marketing, underwriting, and servicing functions produce portfolio performance commensurate with the desired debt terms and cost. Factors that lenders consider, which impact the availability of the type, structure, and cost of debt, include:

- Experience and reputation of owners and management
- Amount of capital (equity) now and in the future
- Historical portfolio performance
- History and stability of company operations
- Availability/integrity of financial reports and portfolio performance indicators
- Cash flow needs now and, in the future,
- Type of leases (capital and operating)
- Projected volume of new originations
- Size of portfolio to be financed
- Servicing, collection, recovery, and remarketing capabilities
- Company income tax considerations
- Credit risk performance indicators

- Financial risk performance indicators
- Business risk performance indicators

Based on the factors and circumstances listed above, some or all of the various types of financing may be available to finance lease originations. Variations of debt include the following areas.

Subordinated Debt

One level up from equity is a form of debt that is close to equity in the eyes of a lender. This type of debt is either unsecured or expressly made subordinate to other, "senior," debt. In a liquidation or bankruptcy, unsecured debt holders are paid after secured debt holders and subordinated debt holders are paid after senior debt holders, whether or not the senior debt is secured; therefore, a lender usually values this debt similar to equity.

For the closely held company, subordinated debt may be supplied by its stockholders or provided by some other related party. For well-established, larger companies, the sources may be private equity firms, commercial finance companies, insurance companies, and pension funds. Due to the higher risk associated with this type of debt, rates are significantly higher than senior debt. Often stock warrants or some other form of equity or right to acquire equity further enhances the subordinated debt holder's return.

Warehouse Lines of Credit

Combining the equipment finance company's working capital with a revolving line of credit (commonly referred to as warehouse lines) further enhances the company's ability to fund transactions. Revolving lines are used to manage the funding and liquidity requirements of a company conveniently. They are typically recourse obligations. Revolving lines of credit are used to temporarily fund leases, or "warehouse" them until a permanent source of funding takes place. A commercial bank usually supplies these lines and ties the interest rate to an index such as the prime rate or LIBOR plus a spread. Typically, the facility is committed for a one-year period. Therefore, if the lender chooses not to renew the line, then the borrower must pay off any amounts owed at the expiration of the note.

The lender does not usually underwrite, fund, or take a security interest in individual transactions. The lender secures the note by taking a general pledge of the company's assets, including the leases and the underlying equipment. Availability of credit is typically based on a monthly borrowing base certificate to establish the amount of collateral available. The borrowing base is usually the net investment or principal value of those leases not explicitly pledged or sold to others.

The lender often requires some over-collateralization, so an advance rate is established. This advance rate is applied against the collateral value to establish the maximum amount available under the line. Typical advance rates range from 70 percent to 90 percent of the collateral value or underlying equipment cost. The borrower (lessor) makes advances and pay-downs as needed. The lender is commonly paid interest on a monthly basis.

Due to the temporary nature of this type of debt, the lender often requires that permanent facilities be available to the borrower. As leases are financed or sold, the proceeds are used to pay down the revolving line. Without the availability of permanent or "take-out" financing, facilities of this type are usually not available.

Permanent or Term Debt

Typically, permanent debt facilities are provided by commercial banks and used to fund leases on a long-term basis. The interest rate for all future loans under the program may be fixed or structured on a floating rate basis and locked in at a fixed rate at the time of funding.

In the purest form, the collateral for a note is a single lease with the term of the note tied to the remaining term of the lease. "Note payments" can be structured with a level total payment similar to an auto loan or mortgage. It may even be possible to have a balloon payment on the note, which coincides with the residual assumption on the lease—the optimal structure for matching the incoming and outgoing cash flows. In some instances, the lender may require constant principal reductions plus interest, which results in a more substantial total payment in the early life of the note. Therefore, this structure most likely creates negative cash flows early in the life of the note.

In more complex structures, multiple leases are bundled together and are tied to one note. In this case, determining the term and amortization schedule can be problematic because of the variety of lease payments and terms contained within the portfolio. The simplest method is to negotiate a term that roughly matches the term remaining in the portfolio of leases being used as collateral. This method does not match cash flows exactly but may be the most natural solution. An optional method is to match the cash flows of the leases with the note payment. The scheduled lease payments are totaled month-by-month, and this total is used to apportion principal payments on the note. The result is a variable payment schedule with a larger principal payment early in the life of the note.

The amount, which can be financed, is another variable to be considered. Most facilities limit the advance amount to less than the net investment, or the principal amount of the lease. This creates some over-collateralization. The amount of the advance rate is determined by the overall strength of the lessor, expected default rates, and other covenants and conditions contained in the loan agreements. Some of the major covenants include minimum tangible net worth, minimum profitability, interest coverage ratios, and debt-to-worth relationships. Some other common covenants and loan restrictions are limits on the number of dividends or distributions to stockholders, change in ownership restrictions, and capital expenditure restrictions.

Should a lessee default under the lease, then the lessor's note to the funding source must be paid off. More often than not, note default is defined as any lease default that remains uncured greater than sixty or ninety days, as agreed by lessor and funding source in the funding documents.

If the note is a non-recourse obligation, the funding source will generally foreclose on the equipment and lease and take over active management of the relationship with the lessee, excluding the lessor. This means that the lessor will most likely lose any residual interest in the equipment or other rights it had retained.

If the note is a recourse obligation, the funding source will have the right to recover its investment from the lessor. Having adequate financial capacity and liquidity to pay off the note is critical. Should the lessor fail to meet this requirement, not only would they be in default under this facility, but they also would likely trigger other covenants under other loan agreements.

Avoiding this situation is critical to the continued operation of the lessor. As mentioned previously, a lessor should have adequate cash reserves or borrowing capacity under other debt facilities to mitigate this risk. Management should have a keen understanding of how various levels of defaults affect their borrowing relationships.

In nearly all cases, the lessor is responsible for servicing the portfolio which they accomplish through internal systems, bank mandated lock-box arrangements, and the utilization of third-party servicing organizations.

Asset Securitization

As the equipment finance industry has matured, more sophisticated methods of financing have become available to a limited number of well-capitalized, high-volume lessors. Commercial paper conduits and lease securitizations are the most common facilities available. They are not unlike revolving lines of credit or term facilities. The primary differences relate to 1) who the ultimate lenders are, and 2) the sheer complexity of the facilities. The benefits to lessors are access to the capital markets, potentially a lower cost of funds, and the possibility of treating this type of debt as "off-balance sheet financing."

Commercial Paper Conduits

Commercial paper conduits are facilities whereby lessors can participate in the issuance of commercial paper. Commercial paper is the term given for short-term debt issued by commercial entities. These typically are large corporate borrowers and financial institutions. We use the word "conduit" because even though there is only one issuer, multiple participants are originating into the issuer. Investors (usually insurance companies or money managers) require that an issuer have their debt rated with a debt-rating agency. The conduit aggregates a variety of assets from the originators and issues commercial paper. Often the rating agencies require a surety company to guarantee an originators portion of the debt. Due to the complex nature of these facilities, there are significant upfront legal fees and costs; one of the reasons why transactions of this type on average are higher than $100 million.

Securitizations

The term securitization is used to describe the aggregation of similar types of assets (in this case, equipment leases) into a legal structure whereby the assets are used as collateral to support a bond or note. Securitizations may be brought to market either through private placements or public offerings. The appropriate method selected is determined by the size of the transaction and the status of the issuer. Publicly offered transactions are rare, and only the largest diversified commercial finance entities can access the public debt market. The significant benefits to a lessor of a securitization are:

- low cost of funds
- potential off-balance sheet treatment of debt
- access to the capital markets
- scale

More often than not, the leases to be securitized are sold or transferred to a wholly owned, bankruptcy-remote subsidiary of a leasing company. The reasons for the transfer are sound. If the originator/servicer fails and files bankruptcy, the transferred leases are not considered assets of the bankrupt lessor. Legal counsel crafts the transfer agreements in such a way that there can be no claim made by the lessor's creditors against the transferred leases.

Each securitization is uniquely structured, but it is typical to have a series of "tranches" (a specific class of bonds) with different risk levels and corresponding interest rates. The "A" tranche is superior to claims of others, and it carries the lowest interest rate since it is of lowest risk. "B" and "C" tranches are each higher in risk, and accordingly a higher rate of interest is paid. It is very common for the lessor to retain the lowest grade tranche. Insurance companies or other financial institutions investing in bonds usually purchase the higher-grade tranches.

Alternative Sources of Funding

The commercial equipment finance industry has a strong track record of performance. This predictable income stream and scale are attractive to many insurance companies, pension funds, income funds, private equity, and hedge funds. Each of these types of organizations has its criteria for investment in the commercial equipment finance market. Some are very long term in nature, such as insurance companies. Others generally have a window that may be 3-5 years to earn their return. In most cases, a large scale is necessary to access these sources of funding as the investment must be impactful to their overall investment strategy.

Regulatory Compliance

Please Note: Nothing in this or any other section of this book is intended as legal advice. Regulatory requirements change from time to time and their application is highly dependent on facts and circumstances that are difficult to generalize. Consult qualified counsel as to your specific exposure and needs.

The equipment finance industry is subject to a variety of regulations. Institutions are subject to varying degrees of regulation based on the type of institution (i.e., bank or non-bank), the size of the corporate entity, the type and size of transactions (i.e., consumer vs. commercial transactions), yields, and the nature of transactions (i.e., leases or loans).

Localities, states or the federal government can create regulations. Generally speaking, federal law always takes precedence over local laws. Pursuant to the Supremacy Clause (Article VI, clause 2) of the United States Constitution,

"This Constitution, and the laws of the United States which shall be made in pursuance thereof; and all treaties made, or which shall be made, under the authority of the United States, shall be the supreme law of the land; and the judges in every state shall be bound thereby, anything in the Constitution or laws of any State to the contrary notwithstanding."

The vast majority of regulations encountered in the equipment finance industry are federally mandated, although the states are beginning to impose more reach in the industry.

State Regulations

State regulations are applicable in several areas, including data security, electronic recycling, licensing of lenders, and regarding automatic renewal clauses.

State Electronic Recycling Regulations

Approximately half of the states have passed electronic recycling legislation. California remains the only state to adopt an Advanced Recovery Fee (ARF) to finance electronic recycling by imposing a fee on the purchase or lease of new electronic devices. Electronic recycling laws tend to cover televisions, computer monitors, computers, computer peripherals, or some combination of the four[26].

State Security Breach Regulations

Forty-seven states, the District of Columbia, Guam, Puerto Rico, and the Virgin Islands have enacted legislation requiring private, governmental, or educational entities to notify individuals of security breaches of information involving personally identifiable information.

Security breach laws typically have the following provisions:

- who must comply with the law (e.g., businesses, data/information brokers, government entities, etc.)
- definitions of "personal information" (e.g., name combined with SSN, driver's license or state ID, account numbers, etc.)
- what constitutes a breach (e.g., unauthorized acquisition of data)
- requirements for notice (e.g., timing or method of notification, who must be notified)
- exemptions (e.g., for encrypted information)

---

[26] Source: https://www.elfaonline.org/advocacy/state-issues/electronic-recycling-and-elfa Website Title: Electronic Recycling and ELFA Date Accessed: January 05, 2018

Automatic Renewal

Because of unscrupulous business practices whereby consumers and businesses are charged for amounts above and beyond the expected contractual rates due to the borrower not paying close attention to the number of payments they have made, or the fact that the contract is past its termination date, or similar situations, a few states regulate the renewal of financing contracts for equipment between a commercial entity and a lender or lessor. Louisiana, New York, and Rhode Island have regulations limiting the ability of a provider of services or goods to automatically renew any contract regardless of whether it is a consumer or commercial in nature. Thus, automatic renewal of equipment finance transactions in these states is restricted. Wisconsin regulates business contracts only, and California, Connecticut, Hawaii, Illinois, North Carolina, and Oregon regulate the automatic renewal of consumer contracts only.

California Finance Lenders Law Requirements

The California Finance Lenders Law requires licensing and regulation of finance lenders and brokers making and brokering consumer and commercial loans, except as specified; prohibits misrepresentations, fraudulent and deceptive acts in connection with making and brokering of loans; and provides administrative, civil, and criminal remedies for violations of the law.

The law defines a finance lender as "any person who is engaged in the business of making consumer loans or making commercial loans." There are many "non-loan" transactions, such as bona fide leases, automobile sales finance contracts, and retail installment sales that are not subject to the provisions of the California Finance Lenders Law.

In addition to the lending authority provided by the law, the California Finance Lenders Law provides limited brokering authority. The law defines a "broker" as "any person engaged in the business of negotiating or performing any act as broker in connection with loans made by a finance lender." Brokers licensed under this law may only broker loans to lenders that hold a California Finance Lenders license.

Section 22100 of the California Financial Code outlines the requirements for a license. The law requires applicants to have and maintain a minimum net worth of at least $25,000 and to obtain and maintain a $25,000 surety bond. In general, principals of the company may not have a criminal history or a history of non-compliance with regulatory requirements.

Finance companies located in California, whether brokers or funders or both, are required to apply for a California Finance Lenders license. Companies engaged in business with California borrowers are also highly encouraged to apply for licenses and run a risk of invalidating the contract by not being a licensed lender or broker.

If a lender obtains a transaction through an unlicensed broker, the lender must provide the borrower with a written statement detailing the referral arrangement in 10-point font or larger, at the time the licensee receives an application for a commercial loan, and require the borrower to acknowledge receipt of the following statement in writing:

"You have been referred to us by [Name of Unlicensed Person]. If you are approved for the loan, we may pay a fee to [Name of Unlicensed Person] for the successful referral. [Name of Lender], and not [Name of Unlicensed Person] is the sole party authorized to offer a loan to you. You should ensure that you understand any loan offer we may extend to you before agreeing to the loan terms. If you wish to report a complaint about this loan transaction, you may contact the Department of Business Oversight at 1-866-275-2677) or file your complaint online at www.dbo.ca.gov."

Usury

Usury is the practice of lending money at higher interest rates than the maximum, if any, permitted by applicable state law. In general, commercial transactions are not subject to usury laws, but several states have usury laws applicable to commercial loans as well. Some states, such as Florida and Texas, have usury laws that may apply to equipment finance transactions. Usury laws apply to EFAs and probably leases intended as security, such as dollar purchase option leases. As a general rule, usury laws do not limit the implicit rate used to calculate rent in true leases. To ensure compliance with the laws, many lenders make sure all loans are within the usury law limits of the state where the borrower is located, structure transactions as leases rather than loans, or stay away from states with onerous usury laws.

Licensing and Being in "Good Standing"

There are many ways states regulate and license commerce, from organizational documents and city licenses to permits and tax registration. In addition to maintaining good standing and active status in the state of incorporation by paying annual franchise taxes and filing annual reports, all states require that foreign corporations and limited liability companies (those formed outside the state) "qualify to do business" by obtaining a certificate of authority if the corporation is "doing business" within the state. (For purposes of the following discussion, we will address corporations, but similar laws apply to LLCs).

"Doing business" is defined differently in each state. In most, having an office or an agent that regularly transacts business in the state is required. In some, merely having a significant number of leases or other business, or obtaining a sales tax or other registration, may be enough to require the corporation to "qualify to do business." The good news is that in every state, the corporation can retroactively cure the failure to qualify if it is found to be necessary. This means that a corporation transacting business in a state without qualifying can cure the legal effect of the failure by paying a fine and qualifying. What is more, failure to qualify, if actually required to do a corporation's business in a state, does not affect the validity or enforceability of contracts or otherwise adversely impact leases or loans made by or to the corporation.

Most businesses are likely familiar with how states are permitted to regulate licensing requirements for occupations and trades, for example, as it may apply to insurance agents, mortgage brokers, real estate agents, various contractors, and engineers. For many years, only certain micro-ticket lessors and automobile lessors were required to be licensed, in addition to qualifying to do business (if necessary, under state law) and obtaining tax registrations.

Recently some states have begun to set forth licensing requirements for finance lenders that are engaged in the types of transactions that may include commercial loans, credit cards, and lines of credit, and that manage deposits, advance rents, or advance fees. Examples include the California Finance Lenders Law mentioned earlier, and licensing laws in Nevada, North Dakota, and South Dakota.

In addition to laws applicable to lenders generally, several states require licenses for motor vehicle leasing or finance, high rate or very small-ticket leasing, and/or for sales of off-lease motor vehicles to lessees or third parties. Some of these laws can be quite onerous.

Other states may also set forth requirements pertaining to loan brokers and advance fees. Providers of vehicle finance must understand the licensing requirements from state to state. It is always worthwhile to look into the laws and rules applicable to the states where conducting business.

This is a very brief introduction addressing state licensing requirements for lessors and lenders. Consult an attorney for advice on the advantages and disadvantages of meeting the criteria to invest in and transact business in specific states.

Federal Regulations

Consumer Financial Protection Bureau (CFPB)

Although the CFPB was created to protect individual consumers, many of the laws are written in such a way as to apply to smaller equipment financing transactions and sometimes extend to larger ticket transactions as well.

"In June 2009, President Obama proposed to address failures of consumer protection by establishing a new financial agency to focus directly on consumers, rather than on bank safety and soundness or on monetary policy. This new agency would heighten government accountability by consolidating in one place responsibilities that had been scattered across government. The agency would also have responsibility for supervision and enforcement with respect to the laws over providers of consumer financial products and services that escaped regular Federal oversight. This agency would protect families from unfair, deceptive, and abusive financial practices.

In July 2010, Congress passed, and President Obama signed the Dodd-Frank Wall Street Reform and Consumer Protection Act. The Act created the Consumer Financial Protection Bureau (CFPB). The CFPB consolidates most Federal consumer financial protection authority in one place."[27]

Equal Credit Opportunity Act – "ECOA" (Regulation B)

"The statute provides that its purpose is to require financial institutions and other firms engaged in the extension of credit to "make credit equally available to all creditworthy customers without regard to sex or marital status." Moreover, the statute makes it unlawful for "any creditor to discriminate against any applicant with respect to any aspect of a credit transaction (1) on the basis of race, color, religion, national origin, sex or marital status, or age (provided the applicant has the capacity to contract); (2) because all or part of the applicant's income derives from any public assistance program; or (3) because the applicant has in good faith exercised any right under the Consumer Credit Protection Act." The ECOA has two principal theories of liability: disparate treatment and disparate impact. Disparate treatment occurs when a creditor treats an applicant differently based on a prohibited basis such as race or national origin. Disparate impact occurs when a creditor employs facially neutral policies or practices that have an adverse effect or impact on a member of a protected class unless it meets a legitimate business need that cannot reasonably be achieved by means that are less disparate in their impact."[28]

Also, Regulation B covers the ability of a financial institution to require spousal guarantees. A creditor may not request information about an applicant's spouse or former spouse except under the following circumstances:

- the non-applicant spouse will be a permitted user of or joint obligor on the account.
- the non-applicant spouse will be contractually liable on the account lease or loan.
- the applicant is relying on the spouse's income, at least in part, as a source of repayment.
- the applicant resides in a community property state, or the property upon which the applicant is relying as a basis for repayment of the credit requested is located in such a state.
- the applicant is relying on alimony, child support, or separate maintenance income as a basis for obtaining the credit.

A credit applicant must receive a notice of "adverse action" (the transaction has been "declined") stating the reason for denial of credit within thirty days of the application. The lender must respond in writing to any

---

[27] Source: https://www.consumerfinance.gov/about-us/the-bureau/creatingthebureau/ Website Title: Creating the Bureau | Consumer Financial Protection Bureau Date Accessed: January 05, 2018

[28] Source: http://files.consumerfinance.gov/f/201306_cfpb_laws-and-regulations_ecoa-combined-june-2013.pdf Website Title: CFPB Consumer Laws and Regulations ECOA Date Accessed: January 05, 2018

request for the specific reason (s) for the decline. Lender or lessor must maintain records for seven years. Most of these requirements can be covered in the lease or loan application in the case of smaller lessors or lenders.

BSA / AML / USA PATRIOT Act

"The Currency and Foreign Transactions Reporting Act of 1970 (which legislative framework is commonly referred to as the "Bank Secrecy Act" or "BSA") requires U.S. financial institutions to assist U.S. government agencies in the detection and prevention of money laundering."

As a result of the events of 9/11, BSA was revised by the USA PATRIOT Act (Uniting and Strengthening America by Providing Appropriate Tools Required to Intercept and Obstruct Terrorism) and other regulations to help detect and prevent terrorist financing. Over the past several years, the financial services industry has made significant strides in money laundering detection and prevention. However, the industry continues to be vulnerable to the criminal element intent on using the system to launder illegally obtained funds.

The BSA requires financial institutions to:

- keep records of cash purchases of large monetary instruments
- file a Currency Transaction Report (CTR) for cash transactions (deposit, withdrawal, purchase, or other transfer) exceeding $10,000 (daily aggregate amount)
- report suspicious activity that might signify money laundering, tax evasion, or other criminal activities
- financial institutions must also maintain records of significant wire transfers and due diligence performed on foreign account relationships. The BSA is sometimes referred to as an "anti-money laundering" law ("AML") or jointly as "BSA/AML."

The USA PATRIOT Act enhanced the BSA by establishing requirements for financial institutions which include implementation of a Customer Identification Program (CIP), customer due diligence commonly referred to as Know Your Customer (KYC), training, and, in some cases, enhanced due diligence for clients identified as posing a higher risk.

The USA PATRIOT Act amended the BSA to increase civil and criminal penalties. Non-compliance or violations of BSA may lead to penalties assessed against the financial institution or its employees. Penalties include memorandums of understanding documenting required improvements, cease and desist orders, or denials of mergers, acquisitions, or expansions. Criminal penalties include fines up to $1 million per violation for financial institutions and up to $500,000 per violation and/or up to ten years in jail for individuals.

In 2014, the Federal Financial Institutions Examination Council (FFIEC) released a revised Bank Secrecy Act Anti-Money Laundering (BSA/AML) Examination Manual.

OFAC and FinCEN

Both OFAC and FinCEN[29] are bureaus of the U.S. Treasury Department; however, FinCEN requires searches for suspected criminals and OFAC queries identify known criminals.

FinCEN is the delegated administrator of the BSA. Among its many responsibilities, FinCEN issues 314(a) requests approximately every two weeks. When these notices, which identify individuals and entities suspected of illegal activities, are received, banks or other financial institutions are required to access the secure website at https://www.fincen.gov/314a/, log-in, and review the lists of businesses and individuals to determine if there is a relationship with any party identified on the system.

Institutions required to file FinCEN reports include banks, casinos, money services businesses (wire transfer), insurance businesses, securities businesses, and precious metals businesses.

OFAC administers and enforces economic and trade sanctions based on U.S. foreign policy and national security goals. Each financial institution is required to do an OFAC search for each potential customer, including vendors, and employee to verify they are not on the government's watch list and maintain evidence regarding the results of the search.

OFAC requirements often extend to lessees, signatories, and guarantors on equipment finance transactions.

Various reporting agencies sell reports that check for OFAC violations and comply with OFAC requirements.

Office of the Comptroller of the Currency (OCC), a division of the U.S. Treasury Department, examines banks regarding their compliance with FinCEN and OFAC requirements.

OFAC Regulations[30]

OFAC administers and enforces economic sanctions programs primarily against countries and groups of individuals, such as terrorists and narcotics traffickers. The sanctions can be either comprehensive or selective, using the blocking of assets and trade restrictions to accomplish foreign policy and national security goals.

OFAC's regulations are broader than the specific laws that deal with the terrorists and persons who support them. All individuals and entities that fall under U.S. jurisdiction should use OFAC's list of Specially Designated Nationals and Blocked Persons ("SDN List"). This list includes designated terrorists and is available on OFAC's website. It is important to note that some OFAC sanctions, such as those pertaining to Iran, Sudan, and Cuba, apply to

---

[29] Source: http://www.regulatorycompliance.com/newsletter/2007/June/fincen_ofac.htm
Website Title: Fincen, OFAC, Regulatory Compliance, Broker Dealers Date Accessed: January 05, 2018

[30] https://www.treasury.gov/resource-center/faqs/Sanctions/Pages/faq_general.aspx
Website Title: OFAC FAQs: General Questions Date Accessed: January 05, 2018

persons acting on behalf of those targeted governments even if those persons do not appear on the SDN list. It is also important to note that OFAC's Cuba sanctions prohibit most transactions with Cuban nationals, wherever located. U.S. persons are expected to exercise due diligence in determining whether any such persons are involved in a proposed transaction.

There is no single compliance program suitable for every financial institution. OFAC is not itself a bank regulator; its basic requirement is that financial institutions not violate the laws that it administers. Financial institutions should check with their regulators regarding the suitability of specific programs to their unique situations.

Beneficial Ownership Interest

FinCEN's customer due diligence (CDD)[31] rule, is intended to thwart terrorism, hinder illicit money laundering activities of criminals, and help financial institutions avoid illegal transactions by providing greater insight into their customers' identities and business relationships. In effect since May 2018, the rule contains the first prescriptive regulatory obligation to identify and verify ownership information of legal entity customers.

CDD requires covered financial institutions such as commercial banks to collect beneficial ownership information prior to funding or when there is a triggering event (anything that creates a material change in the customer relationship or ownership structure such as a business name change or contract assumption) for individuals meeting either of the following criteria: (a) at least a 25% equity interest in the legal entity; (b) significant responsibility to control or manage the legal entity. Additionally, financial institutions are required to understand the nature and purpose of the customer relationship and conduct ongoing monitoring for suspicious activity.

While the application of the CDD rule has a prescriptive 25% beneficial ownership threshold, the use of a lower threshold may be warranted based on the financial institution's assessment of customer risk. Because both the Bank Secrecy Act (BSA) and Federal Financial Institutions Examination Council (FFIEC) guidance calls for a risk-based approach to applying CDD, strictly applying the 25% threshold to all customers regardless of risk could conflict with regulatory expectations. As a result, firms should consider incorporating a methodology for determining whether or when to drill down past the 25% threshold for higher-risk customers considering their customer's risk rating, industry, activity, and client onboarding processes. A recent study shows that over half of surveyed financial institutions apply a 10% threshold for higher-risk customers, utilizing an Enhanced Due Diligence (EDD) process.

---

[31] source:
https://www.ffiec.gov/press/pdf/Beneficial%20Ownership%20Requirements%20for%20Legal%20Entity%20CustomersOverview-FINAL.pdf and https://www.pwc.com/us/en/industries/financial-services/financial-crimes/library/pwc-cdd-faqs.html

Equipment Finance and Lease Exemption: Definition of Equipment

What kind of businesses and equipment are covered under the equipment finance exemption?

The exemption from the CDD rule reflects FinCEN's understanding that businesses require financing to obtain equipment to conduct ongoing business operations. Many such businesses, including both large and small businesses, open accounts solely to finance the purchase or lease of equipment. Subject to certain limitations, the rule provides an exemption from the requirement to identify and verify the identity of a legal entity customer's beneficial owners for equipment finance and lease accounts because of the low risk for money laundering posed by these accounts. The exemption intention is to cover business equipment such as farm equipment, construction machinery, aircraft, computers, printers, photocopiers, and automobiles that a business may purchase or lease. Regardless of the application of the exemption, a financial institution must still comply with all other applicable BSA/AML obligations, which may include the obligation to file Suspicious Activity Report (SARs) where there is a suspicion that the equipment may be used to facilitate criminal activity.

Under the advocacy of the ELFA, the equipment loan/lease exemption is helpful to Lessors. The key attribute of the exemption is that cash not be remitted to the Lessee and that payments are directed to the third-party dealer (seller), manufacturer, or vendor for the acquisition of the underlying asset. Caution should be exercised in any cases where cash is paid to the customer such as sale lease back or working capital.

Service Organization Controls (SOC) Framework[32]

Bank regulators are also generally charged with making sure third parties that banks use to process payments or administer transactions, are governed correctly. As a result, many independent finance companies that service transactions on behalf of banks are required to submit third-party attestation reports for both controls over financial reporting and other subject matters. In response, the American Institute of Certified Public Accountants (AICPA) has developed the Service Organization Controls (SOC) reporting framework. The new Statement on Standards for Attestation Engagements 16 (SSAE 16) standard, used to create a SOC 1 report, focuses solely on a service organization's relevant internal controls over financial reporting. SOC 2 and 3 reports are not defined by SSAE 16 and focus on the organization's controls over its system's security, availability, processing integrity, confidentiality, and privacy. Most accounting and payments software providers to the equipment finance industry and companies servicing payments are required by banks to have a SOC 1 audit at a minimum. The SOC audits require companies to have adequate controls and systems in place regarding security,

---

[32] http://www.bakertilly.com/SOC-reporting-what-service-organizations-need-to-know
Website Title: SOC reporting: What service organizations need to know Date Accessed: January 05, 2018

system security, payments, billing, customer service and other related functions.

Funding

The last phase of the origination process, the funding audit is a critical step in the final examination of the executed document package prior to sending money out the door.

Each company performs processes during the funding stage of the lifecycle slightly different depending on the way the company is structured, the origination model(s), and market, regardless the following fundamental processes are performed in some way during the funding process.

As an example, a common process scenario for third-party originated transactions is pictured below. At a high level, this process can be extrapolated to other origination methods.

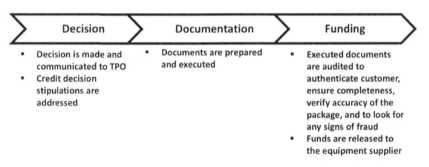

Figure 41 High Level Origination Flow - TPO

In this example, a decision is made and communicated to the third-party originator who will address any credit stipulations such as time in business, equipment approval, etc.

The documents are prepared and sent to the customer who signs and returns the document package.

The funding specialist receives the executed document package and performs specific due diligence and document examination steps to authenticate the customer (perform KYC checks such as OFAC, CIP process, secretary of state verification, and more depending on company policy), validate completeness and accuracy of documents, and look for any signs of fraud as one last loss mitigation check before releasing funds to the equipment supplier.

"The ultimate goal of this function is to put quality assets on the books."
~Operations Leader and CLFP

Funding Package Audit

While the process for collecting this information may vary depending on origination model, the standard content for the package and fundamental reasons for the audit are the same. Reviewing a standard funding package for a small-ticket transaction that is non-titled equipment typically consists of the following contents.

- Verification of Executed Documents & eSignature
- Invoice
- Insurance
- D&A
- UCC
- Verbal Verification
- Tax Treatment
- Equipment Inspection
- Driver's License

For each item, the funding professional verifies and validates that the information is correct and complete. The following sections describe common approaches to verification for each of the elements of a funding package.

Standard Funding Package

Verification of Executed Documents

Many lessors and lenders still require wet signatures; however, eSignatures are gaining adoption across the industry. Regardless of signing method, funding professionals examine executed document packages to verify:

- that the executed documents are original copies.
- that each document is properly signed by the appropriate authority.
- resolution documents are included and properly signed if required for the customer entity type and transaction size.
- document language is not crossed out, erased, or modified.

Wet Signatures

When verifying the paper document and ink signature, a driver's license is required to verify signature and identity of the signor. Collateral pledged is typically a wet signature. Many lessors are working with their sources of funding to allow acceptance of electronically signed documents.

eSignature
Electronic Signature (eSignature) allows for documents to be signed (executed) digitally via multiple platforms. In the equipment finance industry, electronic signatures are employed in a variety of document situations such as vendor program agreements and contract documentation.   See the technology section in this chapter for the fundamental components needed for eSignature capability.

Verifying eSignatures

There are a variety of electronic document solutions used by the leasing and equipment finance industry. Regardless of the provider used, the key to verifying electronically signed documents is how the signor is authenticated (how the customer proves they are who they say they are). Many different methods are used for authentication of signors:

- email authentication
- passcode: for example, the customer will receive a text with a code
- knowledge-based authentication: questions that the signor answers to prove their identity ("out of wallet questions")

For electronically signed transactions, the funding professional will look for a certificate outlining the history of document signing interactions that confirms signor authentication and when it happened.

Vaulting has to do with transfer of custody and the proof of ownership of chattel paper. Vaulting technology is a method for ensuring that you are transferring the "authoritative copy" or the true original stored in a tamper proof way to remain the one true original. Printed copies for example, would have watermark "copy."

Due to comprehensive federal legislation and changes to the UCC, most lessors, lenders, and funding sources are comfortable with the enforceability of electronic and electronically signed documents. After some initial hesitation, most funding sources accept these documents and are satisfied that the vaulting process allows them to perfect their security interest in, or take clean assignments of, leases and EFAs.

The technology requirements for eSignatures is discussed in more detail in the technology section of this chapter.

Examining the Invoice

While each lessor likely has different requirements for invoice formats, for example, "no hand-written carbon invoices," the following basic elements are typically verified for all invoices to accurately reflect who owns the equipment and makes sure that information matches the contract documentation:

- verify that the sold to and shipped to addresses are accurate according to the type of document package.
- for a lease, the leasing company is owner and should be listed as "Sold to" and "Shipped to" should list the customer address.
- for a lease intended as security, EFA for example, the customer is equipment owner and the lessor is secured party, therefore, the "Sold to" and "Shipped to" address should list the customer.
- verify the equipment description make, model, and serial number matches what is listed in the contract documentation.

Verify tax information: if the contract is a lease, then depending on the state, sales tax may or may not be reflected on the invoice and the lessor is responsible for sales tax. For a lease intended as security, the customer is responsible for the sales tax.

Validating Insurance Requirements are Met

The funding professional reviews the insurance certificate and verifies the following elements:

- proof of insurance
- property coverage listing the equipment description and lessor as "Loss Payee" or if available "Lender's Loss Payee." Liability coverage listing lessor as "Additional Insured," due to vicarious liability implications as required by lender (See insurance section for more detail).
- Correct amount of liability: limits of liability are a lessor business decision depending on level of acceptable risk and for some equipment types, requirements by state of equipment location. The industry standard is $1 million. Liability is not required for EFA contracts.

Note: Some Lessors outsource insurance placement and tracking.

UCC

If the transaction is assigned and the broker has already filed a UCC, request an assignment of the UCC.

Use invoice date or ship date on the invoice and file the UCC within 20 days of this date (or the requirements for timing for the specific state). For corporate customers, use secretary of state information or formation docs to ensure the legal name is correct for filing the UCC. For a sole proprietor, the customer name must match the unexpired driver's license for the state of the customer's principal residence.

Verbal Verification

Many lessors handle verbal verification in combination with the D&A. The funding professional will verify that the customer has signed the authorization to pay the vendor. In this authorization, they are stating "I have received and inspected the equipment, it's good, go ahead, and pay."

Prior to releasing funds, it is a good practice to call the customer to verify the customer's identity. Final questions are used as a last line of defense to ensure a valid transaction.

Validate Tax Treatment

To ensure accurate booking of the contract, the funding professional will verify that the tax treatment is accurate for the equipment location state, transaction type, and equipment type and usage. For example, is the tax upfront or on the stream of payments? If applicable, ensure that the appropriate tax exemption forms are included. Many lessors verify this data prior to preparing documentation to streamline processing.

Equipment Inspection

Depending on the credit conditions, transaction type, the equipment situation (new/used), or for a private party sale, a site inspection may be required in which case a third-party or staff member will physically view the equipment, take photos, note the serial number, and verify that the equipment matches the transaction. The funding professional will review the report from that site inspection and make sure it fits the transaction.

Driver's License

The driver's license is key not only for verifying signatures, it is especially important in sole proprietor transactions to accurately file the UCC. Most states require that the UCC filing name match exactly the name on the non-expired driver's license[33]. Even something as simple as entering the full middle name on UCC when only the middle initial is on the driver license could be considered seriously misleading in the UCC filing.

Titled Transactions

Some lessors/lenders may have entire departments dedicated to the management of titles. While exact practices and staffing models will vary from company to company, the following fundamental practices are commonly included in the audit of titled transaction document packages prior to funding.

- Verification of Executed Documents & eSignature
- Invoice/Notarized Bill of Sale
- Power of Attorney (POA)
- Title/Manufacturer Statement of Origin (MSO)
- Notary
- Driver's License
- Lease/EFA differences from a lien perfection standpoint
- Electronic titles (when auditing and when perfecting)
- Tax treatment variables

Power of Attorney ("POA")

It is a good practice to get power of attorney for the owner or seller of titled equipment (such as motor vehicles or some vessels). In the event that a title comes in incorrectly, with power of attorney, the lessor can correct titling issues without customer intervention. When doing a third-party transaction, it is a good practice to require a POA so that the lessor can handle title work on behalf of the lessee without going through the third-party. It is also a good practice to obtain POA when taking titled equipment as additional collateral or from a seller on private party transactions. When the customer sells or pledges the additional collateral, it is important to examine both the front and back of the title before documenting the transaction. Using the POA, the title professional may correct any deficiencies in the certificate in accordance with approved state procedures, including showing the lessor as owner or lender

---

[33] for additional information pertaining to driver's license and UCC.
https://www.cscglobal.com/service/campaigns/debtor-name-white-paper
https://www.cscglobal.com/blog/wp-content/uploads/2017/11/DL_Checklist_092017.pdf
last accessed January 30, 2018

as lienholder. There may be legal issues involved in the choice of being shown as owner or lienholder and counsel should be consulted.

Title/MSO

Manufacturer Statement of Origin (MSO) is like the birth certificate of a vehicle or trailer. It is the document produced before a title is created. For the current title or MSO of the unit you are financing, examine the front and back to look for proper chain of ownership.

- Does the party selling the equipment have the right to do it?
- The vendor will sign the title over to the lessor when paid.
- For a lease, the title should be in the lessor's name and the lessor should be listed as lienholder in most states, so the title is mailed to the lessor and not the customer. Verify that the registration address is the address of the customer to ensure that the annual registration renewal is mailed to the customer.
- For a lease intended as security (e.g., EFA), the lessor should be listed as lienholder.

Notary

For all documents that require notarization, ensure that they are notarized. For example, changes of ownership on a title may require that signatures be notarized (requirements may differ by state). Bill of Sale, POA may also require notarization with specific requirements varying from state to state.

Driver's License

Practices are generally the same as for the standard funding package. For commercial vehicles, ensure that the driver's license has appropriate and valid endorsements. Some states require that sole proprietor titles be listed with the name exactly as it appears on the driver's license.

Lien Perfection for a Lease vs. EFA

Lien perfection is needed for both lease and lease intended as security (such as EFA). For an EFA, the lessor is listed as lienholder. If the contract is a lease, the lessor is also the owner. The lessor in most states is allowed to be listed as the lienholder as well to ensure that titles are mailed to the lessor rather than to the customer.

Electronic Titles

Auditing

When auditing an electronic title, you must look for the print screen from the mainstream e-title database (like eSignature, you see similar providers often and can tell which provider it is from or whether from the state), and examine the e-title looking for the following vital information:

- Who does the title list as the owner?
- Is there a lien present?

- Does the sole proprietor name match the driver's license?

It is also important to confirm and verify the VIN, year, make, model, state of issuance, issue date, and title number match your transaction to ensure it the e-title is generated correctly.

During an audit of an e-title, in some cases, it may be necessary to "drop to paper." **"Drop to Paper"** in the context of e-titles is a process similar to the **"paper out"** process used for electronic documents. In either case, the process converts the electronic document to a paper document for purposes of transfer. As an example, let's say the seller of a vehicle is in Florida, they may have to drop the title to paper for the e-title to transfer to Georgia.

For a lease, if it is titled in the lessor's name and the customer tries to title in a state different from the equipment location, there may be sales tax implications. For example, customers may want to title in Oklahoma and Maine because the tax is lower and there is no requirement that they must have a residence in the state. The problem is that if the equipment location is a different address from the titling location, there are tax implications and it could lead to problems during a sales tax audit. A best practice is to require the customer to title in the state of the equipment location or have a process in place for submitting the necessary taxes to the correct jurisdiction.

Perfecting

When perfecting the title, you should look at whether it is staying in the same state. If it is staying in the same state, update the DMV database. If it is changing states, look for a paper title prior to transfer.

There are certain organizations approved to do e-titling and a variety of these are used in the equipment finance industry, for example, Decision Dynamics, Inc. (eTitleLien™), DealerTrack, as well as many more sources which may be found by referring to specific state departments of motor vehicles. It is important to pay close attention to state level requirements for filing as well as storage of electronic title data.

Tax Treatment Variables

It is essential to verify that the tax treatment is accurate for the transaction before funding. To streamline processing, many lessors will verify this data before preparing documentation. Depending on the state, sales tax may be required by the DMV at the time of title transfer. Some states require upfront tax payment and some through tax returns.

Many lessors will develop a matrix internally to assist in determining the sales tax treatment for different types of transactions from state to state. There are many tools to which a lessor might subscribe to in order to automate the determination of tax treatment using rules. These resources help in determining whether the tax is paid upfront, on the stream, and for different asset and transaction types.

Technology

In the past, technology was looked at as an expense necessary to keep equipment finance operations running. Now, technology capabilities are a critical factor in running businesses of all sizes. With the emergence of new technology companies focused on financial services (fintechs), exponentially advancing technology, and changing customer expectations, technology has become not only a strategic component, but in some cases a key driver for the business.

The purpose of this section is to provide an overview of the software applications generally used in a leasing business. Software is a very broad category and an entire book could be dedicated to just this topic. To limit the scope, we will focus two main areas:

1.   software selection, implementation, and maintenance
2.   solutions specific to running an equipment finance business.

Software Selection, Implementation, and Maintenance

With the rapid pace of technological change, it may seem a daunting challenge to select and invest in new technology knowing that it will not last forever, but it is important to understand that most technology reaches a point of obsolescence. The following list is a simplified framework for thinking about the lifecycle of software applications:

- **Analysis**: Assess the current state and understand the right problems to solve before investing in technology. What is the current state of systems in the organization? Where are the pain points? Is there an understanding of the current processes?

- **Prioritization**: Trying to execute on solving every business problem and technology gap simultaneously is challenging from both a time and budget standpoint. The method used to prioritize is not as important as the discipline of collaboratively prioritizing. Key elements to consider when prioritizing technology efforts are budget, current and future needs, minimum requirements, framework, internal and external resources, and competing projects.

- **Selection:** Consider both functional (what you need to be able to do in the software to process business) and non-functional requirements (such as performance, speed, uptime, etc.) and match the software selection to the business needs. Remember, there is "NO single silver bullet solution."

- **Implementation:** When implementing a core technology solution, there are key considerations to help ensure a successful implementation such as: appropriate staffing and roles, resource availability, and maintenance.

- **Maintenance**: When you are considering adding new technology capabilities to your business, consider not only the cost of implementing the technology, also take into account the cost of ongoing maintenance such as patches, optimization, enhancements, upgrades. Upgrades and patches are necessary to keep pace with change and ensure that your system remains secure and supportable.

- **Decommission:** Understanding which applications are nearing end of life enables you to think ahead to impacts of removing or replacing components of your architecture.

Software Solutions Specific to Equipment Finance

The EF Technology Solutions Framework (Figure 42) is a conceptual diagram for visualizing the types of capabilities typically needed in a leasing company. Each company will have a different mix of core technology components based on size, operating model, structure, parent company, or geography.

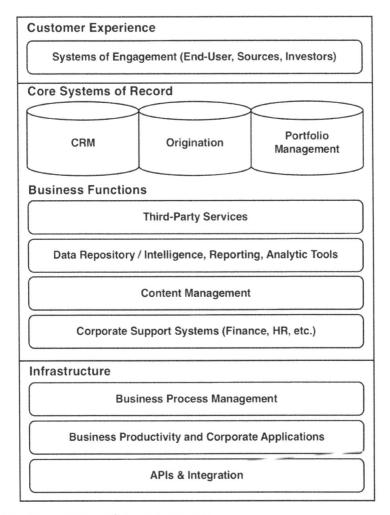

Figure 42 EF Technology Solutions Framework

Source: Framework for Understanding Equipment Finance Software © 2017 Kristian Dolan, CLFP & Deborah Reuben, CLFP – used with permission.

Customer Experience

Systems of engagement enable digital interactions between your company and your customers, vendor partners, sources of business, and investors. It is important to provide a cohesive experience regardless of how they interact with your company. Some examples of the digital touchpoints may include web portals, mobile applications, interactive chat bots, and more. Rapid advances in technology and related changes in customer expectations are continually driving changes in the possibilities of the engagement layer to enable differentiating customer experience.

Core Systems of Record

A core system of record serves as the "Source of Truth" for a particular set of information. There are a variety of combinations of systems used in equipment finance, the following three core systems are most often used across the industry:

- **Customer Relationship Management (CRM)** is a system of record for tracking interactions and activities with contacts, prospects, leads, and accounts. This data allows you to track your sales pipeline.
- **Origination systems** serve as a system of record for lease and loan origination data from quoting, to credit application, all the way through documentation and funding. This data allows you to track the progress of your origination pipeline across all stages of the origination lifecycle.
- **Portfolio Management (Accounting and Servicing)** is the system of record for funded and booked leases and loans. It tracks the transaction, asset, and customer account data for the life of the transaction. This data serves as a key input for portfolio monitoring, billing, collecting, customer service, asset, and end of lease management.

Electronic Signature Technology

Three fundamental components make up eSignature capability.

1. **Authentication.** Most solutions allow you to send an email for signature and the recipient of that email can simply open the document and sign. There are some "add-on" authentication solutions that can provide an additional level of security. They might ask the signer questions such as: Choose your address in 2012. What type of car did you own in 2008? By asking these questions, the eSignature solution can add an additional level of security.
2. **Signature.** This is the component that allows for the signer to receive and electronically sign a document. Typically, these solutions will allow you to use templates or upload documents that can be "tagged" with the signers' information. These solutions manage providing the means to deliver the eSignature request (typically email) and then the platform for the signer to sign. Keep in mind most of these solutions allow for some of the signers to continue to manually sign and then receive the signed version via scan or fax.
3. **Vaulting.** This is used after the document has been signed, i.e., fully executed. This portion of the solution is used for maintaining the "Original" version. Any downloaded copy of the executed document might have a watermark indicating it's not the original. It will also keep a detailed ledger of who/what/when any action occurred on this digital original. Normally, these solutions also allow for a secure transfer of documents between institutions.

Business Functions

Third-Party Services: Third-party services are all the external services that are used to conduct business. Examples include services to calculate sales tax, perform UCC lien searches, and pull consumer credit bureaus. These services can be accessed directly via their online access or you might have these services tied-in directly to your internal systems.

Data Repository/Intelligence, Reporting, Analytic Tools: Easy and intuitive access to your data is necessary to operate and grow your business. Data analytics can help answer a variety of questions including:

- which partner is referring the most qualified prospects?
- where can I improve my "time to funding"?
- what leases are coming to the end of term?
- are there red flags that can be identified before borrowers go into default?
- how is my portfolio performing based on industry standards?

While many of the core systems of record include reporting and analytics capabilities, often you can gain greater insight by combining data across multiple systems of record. For example, you might need to combine your new business pipeline with your renewal pipelines. To do this effectively, you may want to utilize business intelligence analytics tools outside of the core system.

Content Management: Traditionally, documents related to the borrower or transaction were physically stored both on- and off-site. Online content management systems are replacing this and providing faster, more manageable systems for accessing documents. Some important things to consider when looking for a system are:

- security: control who can create, edit, or delete files
- redundancy: backups of files
- audit tracking: who, what, and when documents change
- findability: search or navigate to find needed files
- corporate support systems: (Finance, HR, etc.)

This chapter focuses on systems specific to running an equipment finance company. Accordingly, there are other systems critical to running a business. One of the most important will be your accounting or general ledger system. Other business systems to consider are human resource management, inventory, ERP, procurement, and facility systems.

Understanding these in the context of your current system landscape is important so that you can factor in requirements for your equipment finance system to interact with these additional systems.

Infrastructure

This area reflects the software components to run your business.

Business Process Management: Many equipment finance specific, core system solutions include a business process or workflow component embedded in the tool. However, since many processes are cross-functional, it is also beneficial, depending on the structure of your application landscape, to include a business process layer that ties your process together across multiple core systems.

Business Productivity and Corporate Applications: Like most businesses, equipment finance companies benefit from the efficient application of common business productivity tools such as spreadsheets, word processing, presentation, project management, collaboration, communication, and more. While we do not cover these types of tools in detail in this guide, it is important to consider these applications as part of the holistic picture when considering potential integrations, specific to equipment finance.

APIs and Integration: Stop, do not skip this section. This acronym should not scare you. In fact, this might be one of the most powerful elements of your technology ecosystem. Application Programmable Interfaces (APIs) are the means to which different disparate systems can integrate with each other. They allow your systems of record to talk to services such as credit bureaus, UCC providers, tax rate services, eSignatures, and more.

Examples of common APIs used in an equipment finance business include the following:

- business and consumer credit bureau reports and scores
- tax rates
- UCC search and filing services
- titling services
- asset valuation data
- insurance
- background checks
- importing bank statements
- receiving financials
- acquiring customer demographic information

Using APIs also allows different parties within the lifecycle to share data with each other. For example, many funding sources offer APIs to allow originators to automatically submit their transactions.

Future of Equipment Finance Technology

The framework we present here is a simplified approach to thinking about technology as it specifically relates to leasing and equipment finance based on the solutions commonly available today. This framework is anticipated to evolve as new technology evolves within the industry. As we have previously mentioned, technology is constantly changing, and the pace of change is increasing. With the rapid advances in artificial intelligence (AI), machine learning, bots, cloud, mobile, connectivity, internet of things (IoT), verbal commerce, micro-services, distributed ledger technology (blockchain), and more, we can be certain that the development of more powerful leasing technology applications will continue.

As the pace of technology changes and increasing capabilities continue to influence customer expectations and behaviors, it is imperative to keep apprised of emerging trends. Future-proof your technology choices by choosing technology solutions that will continue to be upgraded and improved as technology advances. Your solutions should grow with you. Choose vendors who are committed to keeping you current as technology evolves. Building a strong digital leasing foundation will enable you to continue to evolve your business processes and products to respond to market changes, regulatory requirements, and meet evolving customer expectations.

Customer Service

While customer service may often be thought of as a back-office or booked transaction consideration, in today's highly competitive marketplace, customer experience is key throughout the entire lifecycle. Each touch point with a customer is another opportunity to provide a positive experience.

What do you think of when you hear the phrase, "Customer Service?" Some may feel that it is a role in a company; others may think it is a specific company department; still, others view it as an activity, and many companies today see customer service as a significant corporate value, element of organizational culture, and differentiator in a highly competitive marketplace. Customer service is not only a back-office consideration. Customer service, providing an excellent experience for the client, begins during the sales and origination process for a leasing and equipment finance transactions and continues throughout the entire lifecycle of the customer relationship. While the quantity and types of customer touch points vary by transaction type, origination model, and company structure, the universal concept is that customer service is a fundamental necessity for any successful equipment finance or leasing organization. As one operations leader stated,

"From the very top to the bottom, everyone in an organization is the customer service department."

In addition to how you interact with customers, a key consideration for leasing and equipment finance companies is, "Who is the customer in this situation?" As you learned earlier in this handbook, there are many different participants in the equipment finance industry. Depending on the origination source, in a given scenario, the customer could be the end-user of the equipment, the vendor or source of business, or if selling transactions, you could even think of investors as your customer. Industry service provider customers are the users, consumers of services and software. Regardless of who your customer is, providing excellent service is key for a successful business.

Customer Service Pre-Booking

Depending on the lessor or lender, different aspects of customer service pre-booking may be handled by different functions other than a formal customer service function. For example, in cases of prefunding or progress funding, the customer service interactions may be handled by documentation staff.

Customer service begins with matching the lessee or borrower with the right equipment and financing solution for their business. During underwriting, credit develops an understanding of the customer situation, collateral, industry, and more, so that they can provide useful service in credit analysis and decision. Understanding the customer and becoming a trusted advisor can help a finance company professional stand apart. In addition to providing exceptional service to end-users of equipment, it is crucial to provide excellent customer service to partners and vendors. Some companies even view internal collaboration as providing customer service to team members.

Customer experience also comes into play during the documentation phase of transaction origination, whether negotiating contracts for a complicated large-ticket transaction or helping a customer through the execution of documents to ensure that all contracts are correctly signed. Depending on the nature of the transaction and parties involved, there can be many opportunities to provide excellent customer experience during this phase of origination.

A key consideration for customer service during the documentation phase in this modern age is leveraging technology to help customers get what they need faster with less error, thus accelerating time to funding. With electronic signatures, it is imperative to assist customers in overcoming hesitancy to adopting eSignature. Guiding and walking a customer through the process for the first time so that they can become comfortable with executing the transactions in a new manner, is a vital customer service touch point.

Documentation and funding personnel play a key role in closing the transaction by tying up loose ends and interfacing with the customer.

A key to customer service is developing the customer relationship and providing a consistent experience so that the customer knows what to expect in all of their interactions with your company. This is especially important to consider during origination since in many companies a variety of people may collaborate on various aspects of a transaction as it progresses toward funding and booking.

In the case of advance funding or progress funding scenarios (may also be referred to as prefunding or progress pay), operations staff may follow up with customers or vendors to execute documents, verify equipment delivery dates, and ensure timely UCC filing.

In the funding phase of origination, keep in mind that your customer could be the end-user, the source of business, the vendor/equipment supplier, or all of them. Timely and accurate funding is a crucial customer touch point and an opportunity to provide a consistent experience and drive return business.

Everyday customer service interactions at the end of the origination process may include ensuring the customer has all they need, sending a welcome packet, conducting a final verbal audit, and an explicit handoff to servicing staff.

Customer Service Post-Booking

Many equipment finance organizations have a formal customer service department or team that focuses on customer interactions post-booking. Customer service staff responsible for fielding customer questions after booking need to have a working knowledge of the full transaction lifecycle so that they can address customer concerns and explain various aspects of leasing. Customer service representatives must be able to deal with initial customer inquiries about the first invoice, insurance premiums, explanation of contract documents, description of interim rent (or pro-rata payments), and more.

Customer service professionals may encounter a variety of customer inquiry scenarios most often interacting with the end-user of the equipment. Although not exhaustive, some of the more common cases that an equipment finance customer service professional may encounter after booking are listed here.

Payoff Scenarios

Payoff requests are a typical scenario and may take several different paths. The complexity of these situations varies depending on the lease accounting system used, the structure of the equipment finance portfolio, company policies, and industries served.

- **Payoff Request**: Although leases are non-cancelable, customers will sometimes call to request a payoff quote. The quote to payoff ratio is an essential consideration in these cases. Often, the customer does not desire to pay off the equipment lease; they may just want to understand where they are in the transaction. Asking questions and listening to the customer can help the customer service professional to understand what the customer needs and provide the right service and saves time by avoiding the creation of unnecessary payoff quotes. Ask a clarifying question such as, "Are you prepared to pay off this transaction, or do you want to know where you are at on the deal?"
- **Early Termination Payoffs**: Early termination is typically an upfront agreement included in the contract documentation. As an example, a guaranty of net present value after a specified number of payments. In these cases, when the customer chooses to exercise an early payoff option, it is important to calculate and collect appropriate sales tax and property tax according to the state guidelines for filing and rendition specific to that transaction. If upfront documentation is not obtained, payoffs usually are handled based on the lender's internal guidelines, which may or may not include a discount of some sort.

There is sometimes an expectation of a present value payoff on EFAs, where the customer is the owner.

- **End of Lease Term:** Especially in the case of FMV transactions, it is important to factor the FMV residual, sales, and property tax into the purchase price of equipment at the end of the term.

Too often, a payoff quote omits amounts owed by the lessee or borrower, therefore, the following elements should be considered when calculating the payoff quote:

- unassessed property taxes for the last year of the lease
- amounts advanced by the lessor for insurance or taxes
- penalties for traffic violations unknown to the lessor
- other unexpected costs that come to the lessor's attention after the lessee has received a quote or even a full release of all obligations under the lease.

Renewal Scenarios

The key to processing renewals is understanding the renewal structure in the contract and requirements for communication to the customer. In some states, Vermont as an example, no longer allows the practice of automatic renewal and billing for an indefinite time (also referred to as an "Evergreen Renewal"). There are time limits for renewal and notification about renewals. For example, the leasing company is required to notify the customer of the renewal a certain number of days (e.g., 120 days), in advance of the term end. The customer is required to provide notice to the lessor within a specific timeframe. For example, the customer must notify lessor of their intent 90 days before the end of the term. Customers may not remember that they have a renewal clause in their agreement and customer service professionals frequently field questions about this aspect of lease contracts, especially when customers receive a renewal reminder notice.

Equipment Liquidation Scenarios

If the contract does not require equipment purchase at the end of the lease term, the lessor has to deal with returned equipment and properly dispose of it or remarket it. Equipment finance and leasing companies may outsource this process to a third-party or have entire departments internally to handle returned assets (often connected to the collections department) and asset remarketing.

Sales Tax Inquiries

Customer service professionals frequently address customer inquiries about sales tax. Customers may have questions about lease payment amounts in states that require sales tax on each lease payment. In this case, the customer service professional educates the customer on the requirement for payments on the stream in the state of equipment location.

Property Tax Inquiries

Some lenders estimate taxes and build taxes into the contract; some let the customer claim equipment and pay taxes directly themselves. Still, others file the property tax themselves and bill the customer for reimbursement. A customer may have multiple lenders. Therefore, education on property tax and leasing as well as the variation in approach from lender to lender is necessary for adequately addressing customer property tax inquiries. As an example, in the case of an EFA type contract, the customer is considered the owner of the equipment, so there may be less confusion on the part of the customer who would typically include the property tax on their tax return.

Year-End Tax Inquiries

The end of the year and the first quarter of the year may be a busy time for customer service representatives in this industry. Often customers will call to ask end-of-year tax questions and may need help understanding the difference between their lease and a simple interest loan. It is important in these situations to continue to educate customers on the product, especially when they ask for amortization schedules.

General Customer Account Inquiries

From time to time the customer may call and ask questions about their lease or loan, such as:

- what is my balance?
- when is my next due date?
- how may I obtain a copy of the contract documents?
- how can I make a payment?
- how might I add a signor?
- can we extend the term of this contract?
- how might I obtain a copy of an invoice?
- how much interest has been paid?
- what is your motor vehicle titling process?

Many of these types of questions can be candidates for self-service. With continuing advances in technology and changing customer expectations and technology comfort levels, many lessors are now providing online capabilities to enable customers to answer many of these questions for themselves ("Self-service"). However, even with ongoing technology advances, there are still many customer service scenarios where technology cannot take the place of the human touch of a knowledgeable and experienced customer service professional.

Contract Adjustments

Customer service professionals serve as solution providers helping the customer with a variety of situations. One area where creative solutions come into play is requests for contract adjustments which happen in a variety of customer scenarios.

In the case of a hurricane, severe weather events, market downturns, or equipment repair needs, a customer may request payment relief. While the approach to payment relief requests varies, a conventional method is "Skip Payments" or "Skipped Payments" which significantly minimize the contract payment for a specified period. While not reducing it to zero, the amount is minimal enough that the customer can pay it during this period and remain in the habit of receiving and paying invoices for the contract. This is an example of contact payments (also called touch payments), mentioned in chapter 4 – Lease Pricing. In some cases, a more significant restructure is needed to help the customer. For example, a business may have agreed to an initial transaction with a monthly payment schedule, and later determines that a change to an annual structure would better meet the customer needs.

When these cases come up, the path for processing will vary by complexity and company policy. While a simple skip payment request may be handled directly within customer service, other cases may require the involvement of additional team members to take a look at credit, perform due diligence, and document the change in contract structure. Depending on the scenario and exposure implications, it may be necessary to pull new credit reports and take a look at the current credit situation. For example, if there are only a few payments left and a low remaining balance, the situation may not warrant another look at credit. In addition to credit considerations, there are also documentation considerations. Typically, there is some degree of documentation required to outline the new payment schedule. This documentation may take the form of a contract addendum or other document depending on complexity. Once the customer executes the contract, the transaction must be updated in the lease and loan servicing system to restructure and reflect the new payment schedule.

Contract Assumption Scenarios

Another frequent customer service scenario is an assumption where the lease contract is to be taken over by another customer. This can occur for a variety of reasons, for example, a farmer who has been operating as a sole proprietor decides to form an LLC. Or, a customer may be selling their business, and as the ownership of the business transfers to the new party, the equipment lease also transfers. In some ways, an assumption is similar to processing a new origination and could involve multiple team members depending on how the equipment finance company is set up. An example of a typical assumption processing approach follows.

- The new customer assuming the contract completes a credit application.
- The credit analyst reviews the new customer and performs underwriting similar to a new contract origination.
- The documentation specialist prepares a set of assumption-specific documentation (less than a full set of new contract documents).
- The customer executes the documents.
- Changes are made in the lease and loan servicing system to reflect the contract assumption and ensure accurate billing.

Proactive Payment Relief Scenarios

From time to time, an equipment finance company may choose to proactively offer payment relief options to its customers, for example, payment relief for customers in a flood-affected area. In these cases, customer service works with the customer to restructure the contract utilizing skip payments as described above, step payments, or some other type of restructure to help the customer through recovery from a natural disaster.

Contract restructuring may serve as a mechanism to keep the customer business going. Mutually beneficial modification and adjustment of a contract is a way to meet the current needs of the customer. The drivers for the approach to contract adjustment are company policy, philosophy, and culture. Key considerations in approach to contract adjustments are reputation, brand, company policy and guidelines, relationship, and regulatory requirements. Due to the variety of scenarios encountered in customer service interactions, ongoing training in policy, procedure, use of technology, and effective communication is vital for all aspects of equipment finance operations.

Servicemembers Civil Relief Act ("SCRA") The SCRA's benefits and protections include a six percent interest rate cap on financial obligations that were incurred prior to military service.[34] For proactive payment relief scenarios, it is ultimately a restructure, dictated by the government, based on active duty status. It impacts lenders in that accommodations are required to be given based on active duty status. This may manifest in a reduction in rate down to 6% for the term of the customer's deployment. Once the deployment has ended, the rate resets to the original rate.

Customer Service Considerations in Billing and Collecting

Billing (also referred to as invoicing) and collecting is an ongoing customer touch point and a key to the customer's impression of the equipment finance company. There are several considerations for managing billing processes. Many equipment finance companies have internal departments responsible for billing customers, and others choose to outsource billing to a third-party service provider.

However you choose to handle billing, you must understand the implications of billing and the impression it makes on the customer experience and the potential impact on the company's reputation should things not go as expected.

Outsourcing Considerations

Outsourcing of billing can provide flexibility from a marketing perspective. As an example, outsourcing may enable you to have more dynamic invoices or ability to include promotions in billing cycles. Internal

---

[34] source: https://www.justice.gov/servicemembers/servicemembers-civil-relief-act-scra

billing capacities may be more restricted compared to the capabilities of a company that focuses on billing as a core competency.

When choosing to outsource billing, consider the implications of data transfer, security, risk of breakdown in process, and possible impact on your business. As a lessor or lender, you must have some degree of control over the look and content of the invoice. Process and performance are an important consideration as issues may arise when the billing process does not execute as expected.

Considerations for Billing and Payment Processing

There are many considerations for setting up billing and payment processing for a leasing and equipment finance company.

- **Due Dates:** How many due dates will you manage for customers? Will you have specific due dates or variations in due dates?
- **Payments**: How will you account for payments? How will you staff billing and payment processing?
- **Invoice Formats**: Will you provide paper invoices? Will you provide electronic invoices?
- **Invoice Processing**: Will processing be outsourced, internal, or some form of hybrid? How will invoices be delivered to customers?
- **Payment Methods**: What payment methods will you accept: customer portal, pay by phone, ACH, checks, lockbox?
- **Automation and Self-service Capabilities**: What level of self-service capability will you provide to customers for invoices and payments? What level of automation will you include in your billing and payment processes?

Technology capabilities are a significant consideration when answering these questions for your company.

Timing Considerations

To adequately address customer concerns around billing and payments, customer service professionals must understand their company's internal late fee process, policies, and timing.

- When are late fees assessed?
- When does the invoice go out?
- What is the timing of opening invoices?
- What is the timing of mailing invoices?
- What is the timing of posting payments?

Understanding these processes and policies will help the customer service professional to field questions especially when the answers come down to tricky timing issues.

Insurance Administration

For lessors, there are many different aspects of insurance that must be considered to protect the assets of the company, the employees, and shareholders, in addition to the equipment or vehicles leased to their clients.

Definition of Insurance: Insurance is a contract, represented by a policy, in which an individual or entity receives financial protection or reimbursement against losses from an insurance company.
Insurance policies are used to hedge against the risk of financial losses, both big and small, that may result from damage to the insured or her property, or from liability for damage or injury caused to a third party.[35]

There are five important details to note about insurance:

1. insurance provides a means of shifting one's financial responsibility for a loss to another party.
2. payment will be made only in the event of the happening of a certain risk or peril.
3. the amount of the payment is restricted to the amount required to indemnify the policyholder.
4. insurance covers losses to which the object of insurance may be exposed.
5. the indemnity provided may be in the form of a sum of money or other thing of value.

Insurance Considerations for Equipment Finance

In the context of equipment finance, insurance can be a complex topic and the requirements vary depending on the type of transaction. In the case of leases, for the lessor (i.e., the owner of the equipment), the concept of vicarious liability enters the picture.

It is important to verify that the customer has adequate coverage for property and liability depending on the nature of the transaction and type of equipment. For example, property insurance is needed to cover repairing or replacing the equipment and the lessor should be listed as "additional insured" under the customer's liability policy.

Property Insurance

Lessees are typically required to carry property insurance (comprehensive all-risk). The policy should name the lessor as the loss payee so the insurance company may deal separately with lessor to adjust their interest in an amount sufficient to compensate lessor for loss of its equipment. With property coverage, ensuring sufficient coverage can be a challenge. Some types of property damage are not covered in a standard policy (e.g., theft, flood,

---

[35] URL:https://www.investopedia.com/terms/i/insurance.asp Website Title: Insurance - Investopedia - Sharper Insight. Smarter Investing. Date Accessed: April 25, 2018

terrorism, etc.) so the lessor has to understand what coverage the customer has and make sure they obtain what is required for a specific lease.

For non-titled equipment, automatic (AKA force-placed) insurance is a popular choice in the market. The customer may provide a certificate of insurance outlining their coverage, but if they do not, the lessor has the ability to enroll them in an automatic insurance program to cover the equipment. Due to the liability requirements, titled equipment is typically not covered with an automated approach.

Some lenders may also sell property coverage up front as a proactive offer and service.

Automatic/Force Placed Insurance

Many lessors reserve the right to "force place" insurance (may also be referred to as "automatic insurance" especially in the case of bank lessors), that is, buy insurance coverage and charge the lessee if the lessee fails to provide or maintain required coverage. This requires additional disclosures in the lease (see documentation chapter). Among other things, over the years, class actions have focused on lack of adequate disclosure of the added cost of the insurance, profit to lessors, and requirements that ensure coverage provided does not benefit lessees.

Liability Insurance

For rolling stock and other equipment that has the potential to cause physical injury, lessors should always require the lessee to carry liability insurance, naming the lessor as additional insured. Although in the case of a mishap involving the leased equipment, lessors are not usually the primary cause of injury. Still, it is not uncommon for lessors to be named as defendants in actions arising out of such injuries.

These claims may include liability as the owner of the equipment because of the lessee's negligence, which is referred to as vicarious liability. A lessor might also be liable under state law if it (or the lessee) was negligent because of a "strict liability" or "dangerous instrumentality" rule making the owners responsible for any damage caused by their dangerous property. In the case of titled motor vehicles, these two types of claims have been preempted by federal laws designed to protect lessors. Federal law does not, however, shield motor vehicle lessors from liability for their own negligence, if the plaintiff's lawyer can establish such negligence to exist.

The additional insured endorsement ensures that not only eventual losses will be covered by insurance, but also the costs of defense, which may be very costly. In addition to protecting the lessor, the lessee's insurance may serve to maintain the lessee's creditworthiness.

It is important to understand the insurance-related requirements within your own company. It is possible to encounter complexity with requirements for liability limits since adding additional insured or increasing liability limits may increase costs for the customer.

EFA as an example is less complex for insurance requirements because liability is not as critical. Some insurance companies will not list the lessor as "additional insured" for EFA transactions because the lessor does not own the equipment, they merely have a security interest. Generally speaking, a lender with a security in its borrower's equipment does not face any form of vicarious liability or strict liability and cannot usually be shown to be negligent.

Insurance Binders

Lessees must provide adequate proof of insurance during the term of the lease. In the case of liability insurance, the lessor may want to consider declaring a default if the lessee fails to provide adequate proof of insurance. An insurance binder is a temporary document used as proof of insurance and confirmation that the customer has applied to purchase an insurance policy.

Insurance Certificates

Most lessors and lenders require their lessees and borrowers to provide proof of insurance meeting the requirements of the lease or EFA. This proof is usually in the form of an insurance certificate issued by the insurance agent of the company confirming that the lessee or borrower has the necessary coverage. The lessor or lender must carefully inspect all insurance certificates to ensure that they properly name the lessor or borrower as a loss payee on casualty insurance policies and additional insured in the case of liability coverage. An insurance certificate cannot create coverage, it can only confirm that the policy provides it. If the certificate is improperly issued and the policy does not actually provide the retired coverage, the lessor or lender will not be protected. For this reason, some lessors and lenders require certified copies of the policies or formal endorsements.

Insurance Claims

Insurance claims or potential claims should be reported to the insurance agent/broker or insurer immediately; otherwise, the claim may be denied due to the insurer's position being prejudiced.

Customer Service and Insurance Administration

While the task of insurance administration may be part of a customer service department's responsibilities, some companies have entire departments dedicated to managing insurance; other companies outsource insurance administration. Regardless of approach, there are fundamental aspects of insurance administration that must be understood by equipment finance professionals.

For any transaction type, the verification of adequate insurance coverage and tracking of expirations is similar in process. An important consideration for insurance administration is knowing how you will track that the customer has appropriate coverage and that it is not expired. This is handled in a variety of ways from lender to lender. A benefit of automatic insurance enrollment is the tracking that comes along with the service.

Great American Insurance, American Lease Insurance, and Assurant are examples of insurance service providers in the equipment finance industry.

Considerations for Insurance Administration

The following are key considerations for insurance administration:

- **Tracking**: How will you track insurance coverage, expiration, renewal, and certificates?
- **Systems**: What systems are involved in insurance administration?
- **Integration:** How will you integrate with the lease and loan accounting system or with the outsourced insurance service provider?
- **Staffing**: How will you staff insurance administration?
- **Billing:** How will you bill for insurance and how will it impact the process?
- **Training:** How will you train customer service professionals on insurance requirements?
- **Outsourcing**: What level of control of the customer experience might you lose if outsourcing?

Title Management

Managing the perfection of titles is another aspect of contract servicing. Often managed by customer service professionals, some leasing companies have entire departments dedicated to managing title processes. Like insurance administration, there are many variables and title management can benefit from automation.

Some key considerations for managing titles:

- requirements vary from state to state.
- requirements vary for equipment that is used vs. new.
- consider in your policy whether you should finance tax and registration fees for vehicles.
- who controls the titling package? Is the package sent to the customer or directly to the DMV?
- understand the nuances of titling requirements.

Side note: many references are available for vehicle title administration, one example of a reference commonly used by industry professionals to understand the nuances of titling requirements by state is Peck's Title Book.[36]

Account Reconciliation

Account reconciliation is the process of making sure that you have paid everyone you should. It is an internal verification and external audit. This process may be managed internally or outsourced depending on the equipment finance company.

---

[36] http://www.peckstitlebook.com

Summary

This chapter covers a lot of material across a broad range of topics; the common thread tying them all together is that an understanding of these topics is necessary to the operation of an equipment leasing and finance company.

Compliance with applicable regulations is critical for staying in business and a key input to the design of business processes end-to-end.

The most necessary resource in an equipment finance company is capital. Without sources of capital, an equipment finance company cannot fund deals.

As the final stage in the origination process, the funding audit is an essential process of final due diligence to ensure documents are complete and accurate before releasing funds to pay for equipment.

Often considered more of a back-office function, in today's highly competitive environment, customer service has implications throughout the equipment finance lifecycle. More than a department, role, or activity, customer service is becoming a significant part of corporate culture and values.

Technology is more than just keeping operations running, today it has become a critical strategic differentiator for many companies in this industry. With the rapid pace of change in technology today, frameworks for thinking about technology can go a long way toward developing an understanding of how specific solutions fit into your business environment

Chapter 9 - Portfolio Management

The learning goals for this chapter:

- Understand the purpose of concentration and segmentation reporting related to Portfolio Management.
- Describe fundamental types of portfolio reporting for a leasing company.
- Understand the core purpose and responsibilities for the Collections function of an equipment finance company.
- Distinguish between the approaches for various types of collection scenarios.
- Understand the purpose and responsibilities of the equipment management function in an equipment finance company across the entire lifecycle of an asset.
- Understand the various valuation types and their applicability to equipment finance transactions.

Within the context of the CLFP Body of Knowledge framework, this chapter covers the highlighted topics as shown in Figure 43.

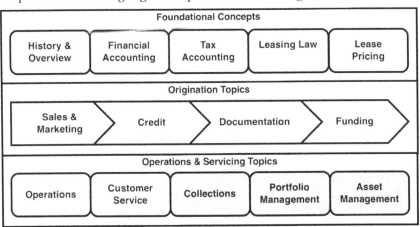

Figure 43 BOK Framework

All of the material covered so far leads into the topic of portfolio management, an important consideration for sales and market segmentation, origination, and setting credit policy. It also plays a key role in the managing and mitigating of concentration risk, as well as measuring the performance of the transactions on the books.

Whether a credit-based lender, broker, lessor, or service provider, broadening your awareness of the fundamentals of portfolio management will expand your understanding of the full lease/loan transaction lifecycle.

Portfolio management is important because:

- managing the performance of the portfolio helps lessors to maintain existing funding source relationships and access additional funding sources.
- the data helps lessors understand the impact of changes to its credit window, which also helps to manage the credit policy and validate the effectiveness of it over time.
- using portfolio metrics to look at segmentation and concentration helps lessors remain aware of exposure in any certain industry, region, state, etc.

Example
As you watch the economy, you can look at your portfolio by industry segment and assess potential risk given a downturn. Leases and loans to hair salons, for instance, may be a more recession-proof industry than other industries which are more susceptible to economic slowdowns, such as construction, transportation, high-end restaurants, or recreational vehicles.

Portfolio management is more than just reporting; it is about strategic management as well as operations. It is about managing the repayment and workout of the leases and loans written, as well as maximizing returns while identifying and minimizing losses. The portfolio management professional typically collaborates closely with sales, credit, and other aspects of management to strategize and plan for the future based on a variety of data-driven indicators.

As we touched on in Chapter 5 – Sales and Marketing, the types of equipment financed by a company are determined by a multitude of reasons, and an equipment finance company must ensure that the resulting portfolio is profitable; that it is financeable through available means; and that the overall operation is sustainable over the long run. Simply put, management should originate only those leases that contribute to the company goals.

Portfolio management is the continuous process of evaluating the nature and performance of the portfolio of leases to allow management to determine future underwriting adjustments, current loss reserves, and strategic planning.

Perhaps the most significant benefit of practical portfolio management is a thorough understanding of the existing portfolio segments. This allows company leadership to determine which new marketing opportunities closely align with company goals, which existing market segments are most profitable, which markets segments to expand, and which market segments to reduce or eliminate due to performance or exposure.

Cross-Functional Considerations for Portfolio Success

While one may view portfolio management as merely a back-office consideration, the concepts are a consideration throughout the entire equipment finance lifecycle. Policy and process, performance, and compliance, as well as cross-functional collaboration, all have an impact on the ultimate performance of the portfolio and impact the collections function.

Every lessor establishes collection policies and procedures. The policy should explicitly detail the authority from which the policy originates, that is, include citations of regulations and laws. In a broader sense, a policy should define "what" an organization does, and each procedure should detail "how" the organization accomplishes these tasks and standards.

Lessors achieve better portfolio performance by incorporating policies and procedures that take into consideration relevant factors from the following areas:

Cross-Functional Accountabilities

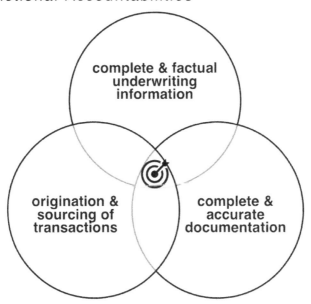

Figure 44 Cross-Functional Portfolio Management

The three basic functions in the diagram above are the cornerstone of successful portfolio management. If the sourcing of transactions and credit underwriting is flawed or lacks sufficient controls and audit points, collection activity becomes difficult, and, in many cases, unsuccessful. There are critical processes necessary to ensure a collectible contract which include:

- Origination process due diligence and data validation to ensure accuracy in sourcing of transactions.

- Credit information about the transaction must be complete and factual for in-house underwriting to analyze the risk and merits of the transaction properly.
- All documentation must be accurate and complete. Missing, incomplete, or inconsistent documents may materially impact collection ability (e.g., timely UCC filed, etc.).

Forthcoming CECL implementation may bring a strategic portfolio level impact for lessors who are doing longer-term transactions. See Appendix 5 Current Expected Credit Loss Model (CECL) for more information on the impact of the new standard.

Tracking Portfolio Performance

While each lessor may use slightly different terminology and approaches to portfolio management and reporting, the following terminology will be used in this chapter for discussion purposes.

Portfolio Segmentation: Segmentation is the division of the portfolio and market data into subsets or groupings consisting of specific characteristics and concentrations for further analysis. Each lessor approaches market and portfolio segmentation in a manner that fits their particular company strategy. There are numerous varieties in approach to segmentation, for example, a company may segment by industry, by company size, number of employees, revenue, or by number of assets on lease.

Portfolio Characteristics: Portfolio characteristics are the data elements used in portfolio segmentation and in calculation of performance indicators.

Portfolio Performance Indicators: Portfolio performance indicators are statistical measurements used to compare historical norms to business goals and identify trends in a portfolio.

Portfolio Management and Decision Making

Management should continuously review data for the overall portfolio to ensure that it is meeting goals and that there are no trends toward unacceptable performance. If problem areas begin to surface, specific attention is directed to more detailed data to ascertain the reason for the deterioration. Management should also periodically review each segment of the portfolio by comparing each of the segment's unique characteristics by each of its performance indicators. The volatility of the product, its size in relation to the portfolio, and any general danger signals of change determine the frequency of a segment's review. With regular segment reviews, management can make the best decisions regarding the mix of existing products, pricing considerations, and underwriting. They will gain a better understanding of how to evaluate the impact of prospective marketing programs and be able to tailor the best combination of capital and debt. In the following example of a segment review, you can see how a lessor may look at a portfolio and take all of this information into consideration when making policy decisions.

Example Segment Review

Segment Scenario: Imagine a lease financing source initiated an aggressive new marketing effort one year ago for one of its brokers to originate agricultural leases primarily in California. It created a program by establishing special rates, unique credit parameters, longer terms, and other characteristics different from the norm.

Segment Review Goal: The goal is to determine if the program is achieving its goals and if it should be continued as is, modified, or discontinued.

Review Approach: During the review, each of the product segment's performance indicators is reviewed and compared with those of the rest of the portfolio. For example, a lower gross yield might be tolerable if the cost to service and the charge-offs are less than average, or if longer terms may have exposed the company to higher net losses due to the unpredictable nature of the weather and also caused greater debt costs due to the interest rate risk. The losses may not be higher, but the cycle may have produced more past due contracts resulting in higher late fees.

Concentration: Imagine the data reveals that the broker did most of this business in California, the geographic concentration in the company portfolio now exceeds the limit, and management cannot borrow against approximately 5 percent of the portfolio under the terms of the company's debt structure without additional capital.

Managing an equipment finance company's portfolio is a dynamic and challenging responsibility. Rapid changes in the marketplace, economy, and other events demand that management make many decisions with limited information while trying to make decisions about future circumstances it cannot control.

If the company employs an efficient process of portfolio management based on the company's specific performance indicators, then many portfolio risks may be managed. This risk is managed by strategically focusing on business opportunities that fit the company's specific risk/return profile and avoiding further exposure to a business that is not performing.

Typical Portfolio Characteristics

Equipment finance companies can originate a great variety of transactions with widely differing characteristics, each of which can impact the profitability and availability of financing for the company. To effectively manage the company, management must determine which characteristics are most important and how those characteristics are best measured. By establishing a constant flow of information, management can determine what changes, if any, must be made to the marketing, underwriting, and reserve strategies. The characteristics most frequently used to segment the portfolio include the following:

Table 25 Typical Portfolio Characteristics

Customer:	Concentration in the amount outstanding per lessee or guarantor
Industry	Concentration in various industries
Equipment	Concentration in equipment types
Geographical	Concentration in lessee location
Source	Source of the origination (repeat customer, direct, vendor, broker)
Vintage	When the lease was originated (typically month and year)
Approval Type	Credit evaluation method (app-only or supported by financials)
Program Type	Specific credit program (medical, startups, etc.)
Contact Type	Type of lease (capital, TRAC, tax, operating, municipal)
Term Length	Length of the contract
Runoff	Used in conjunction with term to see how quickly the portfolio is paying off
Roll Rate	Measures the "roll" of accounts as delinquency increases or decreases

These indicators are not typically used in isolation, you need to look at multiple aspects of the portfolio on a monthly basis to see movements and trends, and to understand what is happening and where things are going.

Each lessor uses portfolio data in different ways. For example, term data is used for managing workload, understanding leases that are coming off the books, and projecting future earnings. Related to assessing portfolio by term, a lessor may also look at the roll rate pertaining to delinquency. This characteristic is helpful for understanding what is happening as transactions are becoming delinquent in the current, 1 to 30, 31 to 60, 61 to 90, and 91-plus buckets. By assessing what is happening in each bucket you can see high-level delinquency trends, predict potential losses, as well as identify the inflection point and where to direct portfolio resources to help ensure an account gets back to current vs. continuing to roll delinquent. This roll rate in combination with other segmentation characteristics helps to see trends and predict performance.

From a portfolio manager standpoint, in managing workload, it is helpful to understand which contracts are nearing end-of-term. From a sales perspective, a lessor needs to understand how many new leases need to be originated to maintain or continue to grow the portfolio as well as which customers may be looking to purchase new or replacement equipment as their leases are nearing the end of their term.

Another way to look at the portfolio is to assess performance by term. Are the 60-month transactions performing similarly to 24-month transactions? What does the portfolio look like 12, 24, and 48 months down the road?

Run rate is another key indicator. If the portfolio's average term is 48 months, then in four years of business one full year of business is running off the books. This helps the lessor to see how quickly the portfolio is paying off.

Typical Portfolio Reporting Performance Indicators

Equipment finance company management needs statistical information to determine the performance of a portfolio and identify any developing trends. Typically, these developing patterns are grouped into three general risk categories: credit risk, financial risk, and business risk. Each has several common measurements or "performance indicators," which are used to compare historical norms and business goals. For each indicator, management establishes both a goal and acceptable ranges.

Table 26 Typical Portfolio Performance Indicators

Credit Risk Indicators	• Frequency of delinquencies or defaults • 30-,60-, and 90-day receivables aging (number of days past due) • Amount of charge-offs of defaulted leases • Timing of defaults relative to origination date • Collection/recovery costs on defaulted contracts • Amount of recovery dollars net of costs
Financial Risk Indicators	• Gross interest yield (interest return on the assets) • Net interest yield (gross yield less IDC or the cost to originate) • Interest margin (difference between the gross yield and the cost of debt) • Interest rate risk (risk due to variable rates funding fixed-rate contracts) • Weighted average yields • Term (length of the lease) and rate of runoff • Residual value performance (actual compared to estimated) • Early payoffs or roll-ups to another lease • Servicing costs • Amount and type of fee income (e.g., late fees, service charges)
Business Risk Factors	• Market competition • Concentration by lessee industry, equipment, source, geography • Economic trends impacting origination volume or credit performance • Availability and cost of capital and debt • Availability and expertise of personnel to underwrite, fund, service, and collect leases • State-specific legal remedies • Documentation thoroughness • Application of Performance Indicators

Each of the credit and financial performance indicators is a calculated number normally derived from statistics readily available from most modern core portfolio management systems (See Chapter 8 – Funding and Operations). Lessors may represent these indicators in different ways: as a specific amount, a percentage, or as a ratio.

The overview of various performance indicators described above is not intended to be an exhaustive list of all potential portfolio indicators helpful to managers. These must be augmented by performance indicators, which are tailored to provide reliable, timely information about the performance and trends of each unique company.

Examples of Credit and Financial Performance Indicators

Each company establishes its own methods; the following are some examples to illustrate how some lessors calculate various credit and financial performance indicators.

$$\frac{30 - 60 - 90 - \textbf{Day Delinquencies}}{\textbf{Total Receivables}} = \textbf{Delinquency \%}$$

For example, delinquency rates are commonly stated as a percentage derived by dividing the total net receivable in the 30-60-90-day past due categories by the total receivables.

$$\frac{\textbf{total residual value collected}}{\textbf{estimated booked residual at inception}} = \textbf{residual value performance\%}$$

The residual value performance indicator is calculated by dividing the total residual value collected at the end of a group of leases by the amount of residual booked (estimated) at the inception of those leases.

These performance indicators are used in comparison with both recent and extended historical results of similar products and circumstances.

For example, a charge-off amount of $50,000 last month or an annualized 3 percent of a company's average portfolio might be excellent for a company that is accustomed to operating profitably with consistent 4 percent charge-offs; a calamity if the norm is 1 percent. On the other hand, a comparatively slight increase in the charge-off ratio during an economic recession may be evidence that the credit parameters were well set, and that the portfolio is expected to hold up well.

A relatively new company or a company having experienced a recent significant change in management policy (especially in credit procedures) has little historical data. It may need to determine its trends by comparing ratios with leasing industry peers using industry data such as the ELFA Monthly Leasing and Finance Index ("MLFI") or by merely estimating the results based on management's prior experiences.

The lack of historical data for comparison can create challenges for management in securing capital or funding. Absent evidence of consistent performance, investors and lenders may require higher interest rates, significant loss reserves, third-party guarantors, and/or over-collateralization.

Ongoing Credit Review

An ongoing credit review process is another important portfolio management activity for monitoring performance of booked contracts. Approaches vary ranging from complex and manual reviews to highly automated behavioral scoring and analytics.

The process of ongoing credit review for small-ticket portfolios is typically a data-driven exercise to monitor customer payment behavior patterns. Similar to credit scoring, behavioral scoring is designed to look at contracts already on the books rather than predicting how a potential new deal might perform. While customer payment history is a primary data point for behavioral scoring, it may also include external data sources such as credit bureaus to bring in payment performance data from other transactions. Portfolios are often scored by segments such as credit quality, collateral types, and transaction size. A typical approach is to run scores on the group of transactions and then focus the analysis on exception results depending on exposure size.

There are a variety of approaches to developing behavioral scoring. Some companies create models internally, while others may use off-the-shelf scoring products, and still others may use a hybrid of the two. Whatever the approach, when it comes to monitoring a high-volume, small-ticket portfolio, automation is ideal because it is not cost effective to spend time reviewing small transactions individually.

As the transaction size increases, in addition to payment performance, the individual financial performance of the company is taken into consideration and plays a more significant role in monitoring and ongoing credit review. Although the ticket size for behavioral scoring continues to increase with the accumulation of transaction data, for large deals, credit review is mostly a manual process requiring a transactional and relational perspective. To focus their efforts on deals with the most risk, some lessors may use scoring to determine which exposures require a full review. Manual credit reviews usually involve the gathering of financial statements, financial statement spreading and may include an analysis of the residual asset values. For some large exposures, the credit review process may also involve customer site visits.

Considerations for companies implementing behavioral scoring include access to key data points such as transaction size, the volume of historical transaction data, and the availability of external scores. Regulatory compliance requirements may also come into play, for instance, banks may face additional complexity when implementing internally developed models due to the need for independent validation of models.

Behavioral scoring and portfolio monitoring automation are continually evolving, and in the future, it expected that more companies will adopt automation and we may see an expansion of the dollar amounts of transactions included in scoring and automation.

Large-Ticket Credit Review
Throughout the life of a large-ticket lease, equipment finance companies monitor credit quality through periodic credit reviews which provide an opportunity to re-grade the transaction. The performance of comprehensive credit reviews may occur annually, semi-annually, or quarterly depending on the level of risk. A mostly manual process, this review typically includes full financial statement spreading and analysis, calculation and adjustment of PD and LGD based on updated financials, as well as an asset management review of collateral value assumptions. This extensive performance monitoring enables the lessor to manage large-ticket portfolios proactively.

Collections

Overview of Purpose and Responsibilities

An active and knowledgeable collections function in an equipment finance organization leads to more recoveries and, most likely, fewer legal fees and write-offs down the road.

Successful collection teams are solution providers who approach problem-solving in a way that benefits all parties to a transaction while providing a basis for avoiding future problems. In addition to the primary functions listed above, effective collection departments:

- Provide a crucial link between the lessor and the lessee.
- Establish and nurture open communication and information sharing between the lessor and lessee.
- Communicate with other departments (credit, marketing, funding, etc.) alerting them of adverse trends that may affect future credit decision-making.
- Contribute to the ultimate success of the entire company.

Delinquency and Charge-off Thresholds
Establishing and maintaining portfolio delinquency and charge-off thresholds is necessary to support and maintain a lessor's success. To accomplish this, collection departments:
- act proactively to collect past due payments
- manage delinquency to the established standard within the organization
- provide appropriate assistance to lessees

Importance of Industry Knowledge

The type of equipment, industry, and how they interact are basic factors in collections. Many industries are seasonal and require special handling, such as skipped payments, short-term extensions, etc. Certain types of equipment have significant value to the lessee, and, in some cases, hold sufficient value to pay off a lease. An understanding of this relationship allows the collector to use proper judgment when adjusting these types of accounts. Problem accounts are inevitable. A collection department that follows standardized procedures and is familiar with relevant collection and bankruptcy laws is in a much better position to handle such accounts.

Knowing Which Collection Practices are Lawful and Efficient

Adherence to the laws and regulations applicable to the collections activity of the lease contract is a requirement that protects the lessor. Collectors need to remain within the legal limits. They should have a working knowledge of applicable laws and exercise solid business practices while they collect monies due.

The Fair Debt Collections Practices Act (FDCPA) governs the debt collection practices for personal / consumer debt. The FDCPA sets forth a myriad of restrictions regarding the practices that debt collectors may use in their efforts.

While there are no federal laws governing commercial debt collections, most states have enacted statutes that govern commercial/business debt collections. Aggressive and unethical tactics are still prohibited, but the options available to commercial collectors are often more flexible than those available to consumer collectors. For this reason, a conservative approach to debt collection is advisable.

Collectors are prohibited from engaging in any conduct that one could interpret as an intention to harass, oppress, or abuse any person in connection with the collection of a debt. This type of behavior includes the following:

- The use or threat of use of violence or other criminal means to harm the lessee, reputation of the lessee, or property of a lessee.
- The use of obscene or profane language or language that one could interpret as an intention to abuse the listener or reader.
- Any false or misleading representations in connection with the collection of a debt.

Key regulatory considerations for collectors.
- **FDCPA** stands for Fair Debt Collection Practices Act
- **NACHA** stands for National Automated Clearing House Association

At a high-level, collectors need to understand their company's regulatory compliance policies.

Maintaining Customer Goodwill While Accomplishing the Job

The collection department's conduct is a direct reflection of the lessor's commitment to its lessee. Lessees may experience various circumstances that prevent timely payment. Maintaining goodwill with those lessees not only minimizes delinquency and potential losses but also positions the lessor to solicit future business with the lessee.

Proactively identifying problems and addressing them in their earliest stages is much more advantageous than reacting after a problem has escalated. It is necessary that a collection department identifies common challenges such as business seasonality, natural disasters, general geographic conditions and economic conditions, and maintains policies and procedures to address potential issues.

Primary Responsibilities of the Collections Function

Collection of Lease Contracts

The collection of a lease contract occurs when the following events occur:

- A regularly scheduled payment is not received in a "timely manner" by the lessor
- On notification of the failure of an attempted payment due to non-sufficient **funds** (NSF) activity or account closure
- On notification of some other breach of contract terms (failure to maintain insurance, etc.)

Initial delinquency resolution strategies include attempts to contact the lessee by phone, mail, or other authorized means. Communication with the lessee should be respectful and assume the lessee's intent to cure the delinquency. When electing to attempt contact by email, collectors should use only known email addresses and limit their message to their name, business, and a request for contact. All communications should be memorialized and saved in the lessor's collections system and should detail:

- All parties of the communication (lessee name, collector name, and names of any third parties participating in the communication),
- The date and time of the communication, and
- The outcome of the communication (promise to pay, follow up, etc.).

A successful collection department works to identify the root cause of the delinquency and collaborates with the lessee to resolve it professionally and courteously.

A lessee's failure to respond to contact attempts may result in an escalation of collection efforts. The collections department is responsible for additional collection activities, which may include:

- Notice to the lessee of the failure to pay or meet other contractual requirements sent by certified mail.
- A site visit by a representative or contracted agent of the lessor.
- Repossession as outlined in the "self-help remedies" of the lease contract and conducted by a contracted, bonded, and licensed agent.
- Litigation to recover the subject collateral, the monetary loss, or both.

Effective actions by the collections department may minimize delinquency and mitigate losses by identifying and addressing problems early. Efficiencies should contribute to reduced departmental costs (overhead personnel, space, outside activities, etc.).

General Collections

- **Collection of Residuals:** On expiration or earlier termination of a lease contract term, collectors may be responsible for the collection of the residual. Purchase agreements entered into at the origination of a lease may determine the amount of the residual; however, when the residual value is not pre-determined, the collector may be required to determine the fair market value of the leased asset and negotiate the residual with the lessee. The cost of repossession may diminish an asset's fair market value; therefore, this cost must be considered when negotiating the sale of an asset.
- **Collection of Taxes:** Depending on the language in the lease contract, a lessee could be responsible for paying any and all taxes due by local or federal governments. If the lessor declares the equipment to the taxing jurisdiction where it is located and is forced to pay taxes, then the collections department is responsible for contacting the lessee. When doing so, the department makes them aware of the amount, provides proof of the amount paid by the lessor, and then makes arrangements for the repayment of those amounts due to the lessor

by the lessee. In some circumstances, the collections department notifies the lessee directly of the amount due, and the lessee must pay this amount directly to the governing authority.

- **Collection of Insurance Premiums**: Lessees are required to maintain insurance and provide proof of insurance to the lessor for leased or financed assets. Failure to maintain insurance may result in the lessor using force-placed/automatic insurance to provide the insurance protection (see Chapter 8 – Funding and Operations for more detail on insurance). When this occurs, premiums are billed to the lessee in addition to the term payment until the lessee provides sufficient proof of other coverage. Cancellation of insurance or failure to maintain insurance may cause a lease to default. The lessor may then choose to exercise remedies detailed in the lease contract.

- **Collection of Late Charges:** A lessor assesses late fees based on the terms of the lease contract. Often, the lease will provide a grace period beyond the rent due date and the expiration of that grace period triggers the assessment of late charges. A successful collections department should include all late fees assessed when making a demand for payments.

- **Collection of All Other Amounts Due:** The collections department must be familiar with the language of its contracts. Inside the clauses of each contract are details about fees that may be due, given different circumstances. The collections department needs to know when each fee is triggered and due as well as why payment is required. The ability to notify and explain a charge that is due is the quickest way to getting it paid.

Identifying Accounts at Risk

The Signals of Potential Delinquency and Red Flags Indicating Potential Non-Performing Accounts

A collections department should be aware of and take the time to monitor for red flags that may indicate the potential for adverse activity or delinquency leading to non-performing accounts. Some signals may include but are not limited to:

- Returned mail
- Cancelling of an ACH
- Consistently returned payments (NSF)
- Lapse in insurance coverage
- Lack of communication on the lessee's part and prolonged delinquency
- Sudden change in the point of contact
- Lessee citing equipment issues or general dissatisfaction with equipment
- Repeated delays in payment
- Sudden adverse shift in payment habits
- Change in ownership or management
- Failure to return telephone calls
- Adverse economic news impacting lessee's industry

- Receiving a new credit application showing significantly deteriorating credit (an example of the need for credit and collections to communicate)

- Pattern of broken promises
- Deterioration in financial strength

 Lessors should institute procedures for recognizing and acting on signals and red flags indicating the potential for delinquency or non-performance of accounts. Some lessors today use automation systems and predictive data analysis to proactively identify accounts a risk, trigger alerts, and determine appropriate actions.

Tracking Collection-Specific Portfolio Indicators

Sufficient reporting capabilities must be in place to measure collector and portfolio performance. Historical portfolio data also assists with establishing and periodically updating underwriting and accounting policies. Of the metrics described earlier in this chapter, the key metrics used by the collections department typically include:

- Static pool (measures the characteristics of a specific transaction or pool of transactions originated during a set time frame)
- Roll rate
- Annualized charge-off rates

Acceptable performance levels are set based on the individual lessor's expectations, portfolio capacities, and concentrations.

Document Collection Activities

Collection notes may be used as evidence in court. Today's automated collections systems support chronological tracking of detailed collection records. Dates and times of discussions, the agreements, the problems, as well as summaries of all conversations should be noted. Any collector or third party must be able to review the collection notes and become familiar with an account's history. Both collectors and their portfolio managers must continuously monitor the activity of the portfolio and determine when to take action on any specific account. Explicit notes with times and dates help protect against unfounded claims.

Secondary Collection Responsibilities (When to Escalate)

In addition to its primary responsibilities, a successful collections department performs additional tasks when delinquency escalates, and telephone contact alone does not lead to a resolution. These secondary collection responsibilities include the following:

- Interface with attorneys on litigation matters
- Repossession of equipment
- Remarketing repossessed equipment

Interfacing with Attorneys on Litigation Matters

Collections management should ensure that policies and procedures are in place to escalate an account to litigation as needed. Collectors are responsible for identifying accounts that may require litigation when all other means of resolution have been exhausted.

When placing a file with an attorney, the attorney representing the lessor must have a working knowledge of leasing law. Many industry sources can help identify counsel who is best qualified to represent the lessor. These sources include the CLFP Foundation itself as well as Lease Enforcement Attorney Network (LEAN, www.leasecollect.com). The National Equipment Finance Association (NEFA, www.nefassociation.org), the American Association of Commercial Finance Brokers (AACFB, www.aacfb.org), and the Equipment Leasing and Finance Association (ELFA, www.elfaonline.org), also count among their membership several reputable law firms that focus on the industry and creditor rights.

Repossession of Equipment

A lessor may choose repossession of leased equipment when:

- Other means to cure an account's delinquency have been exhausted.
- A lessee requests recovery of the leased equipment.
- Judgment is awarded to the lessor requiring the lessee to surrender the equipment.
- Allowed under the terms of a bankruptcy filing.
- At the end of a lease term, the lessee chooses not to purchase the leased equipment.

Before any repossession, the collections department should confirm that the lessor's security interest has been perfected appropriately to prevent counter-claims by the lessee or by any third party. Leased assets considered fixtures may be exempt from repossession if the lessor failed to submit a fixture filing at the time of the UCC filing.

All repossessions should be cost-effective to prevent the lessor from incurring costs that may not otherwise be recoverable. To ensure this, the collector should determine the fair market value of the leased asset against the cost of repossession as well as liquidation/ownership of the asset. There could be cases where liens have been filed that would have to be cured before the sale of the asset. It is permissible to negotiate a sale with the property owner (assuming it is not the lessee) for fixtures and leased assets where the repossession is otherwise cost prohibitive.

When an asset is repossessed, a Notice of Repossession or Right of Rescission notice must be mailed to the lessee and all guarantors, if applicable. This notice grants the lessee ten days from the date of repossession to redeem the collateral by providing the full satisfaction of the debt.

Repossession

Repossession refers to the physical recovery of possession of the leased equipment. Leased equipment may be repossessed by court order, with the lessee's consent, or through self-help.

Self-help: Refers to the repossessing of equipment by the lessor instead of using an attorney. While this is legal, it may result in liability to the lessor if it disturbs the peace, damages property or, in some states, if the lessee objects.

Commercially Reasonable Sale: Lessors must provide written notice to the lessee, guarantors, and junior secured creditors who have requested notice. The sale may be by public auction or private. If by public auction, there must be a notice providing date, time, and location published in a paper of general circulation in the county where the sale is held at least five days before the sale. If the sale is deemed by the courts not to have been sold in a commercially reasonable manner, a lessor forfeits the right to pursue the lessee for any deficiency balance. If a judgment has already been granted, it may be set aside. Lessors should document a comprehensive policy and procedure for all staff to follow.

Remarketing Repossessed Equipment

Lessors are required under Article 9 of the UCC to conduct a "commercially reasonable sale" of repossessed assets to mitigate losses and to reduce the lessee's exposure to the lessor. Failure to do so may jeopardize the lessor's rights to pursue a deficiency balance from the lessee.

Remarketers and lessors are required to maintain a record of the sale to include:

- Condition of the leased asset at sale
- Medium of the sale (auction, private sale, etc.)
- Any record of advertisement used to affect a sale
- Buyer information

Lessors and their agents should maintain a record of all bids if an auction is used to affect a sale. Sales to private parties should be well-documented to prevent any challenges to the "commercially reasonable sale" requirement.

Alternative Collection Processes (Remedies)

A well-run collections department is also versed in collection activities other than full payment, or repossession of the underlying assets either through voluntary means or bankruptcy. These other remedies include, but are not limited to, those listed in Table 27.

Table 27 Alternative Collection Processes and Remedies

Partial payments	In many situations, lessors prefer the collection of partial payment to the collection of no payment. Partial payment arrangements should be carefully managed to achieve the goal of bringing an account current.
Extension agreements	In conjunction with partial payments, "rewrites" of transactions may allow a lessee breathing room, and then a way to make up the missed payments at a later date.
Changes in due dates	Some lessees prefer a different due date. If the changing of a due date can improve the lessee's payment performance, this is a viable option. Some lessors may assess an interim rent fee for the period between the current due date and proposed due date.
Recovery agreements	An agreement between the lessor and other parties related to the lease, such as the equipment vendor, wherein the underlying leased asset can be remarketed for maximum recovery to the lessor.
Forbearance agreements	Similar to extensions, these agreements allow a lessee some breathing room. In many cases, the lessor may require a change to the terms of the lease (rate, collateral, additional guarantors, etc.) to agree to forbearance.
Transfer and assumption agreement	Whereby an alternative party takes over the obligations of the original lessee, in many cases requiring the continuing financial guarantee of the original lessee.

Bankruptcy

Chapter 3 – Leasing Law describes in detail bankruptcy law and what it means for the leasing and equipment finance industry.

Typical Collector Approach to Bankruptcy

Each equipment finance organization defines their policies and procedures concerning bankruptcy; however, the following list is a brief overview of some of the typical approaches used by collectors in these cases.

Table 28 Collector Approaches to Bankruptcy

Verbal Notice Received	• During the initial notification stage, a verbal notice is received while conducting a collection call with the lessee.
	• The collector must be careful in the approach because some lessees use this excuse as a strategy to avoid paying and have no intention of actually following through with filing of a bankruptcy petition.
	• The collector expresses concern and sympathizes with the lessee's predicament.
	• The lessor assures the lessee of their cooperation through this difficult situation and requests the name and telephone number of the attorney handling the bankruptcy.
	• An attempt should be made to identify what bankruptcy chapter is being filed and the lessee's intent regarding the leased equipment.
	• If possible, pinpoint docket numbers and the exact date of filing.
Attorney Contacted and Filing Verified	• The collector files a proof of claim after contact with the attorney and verification that the lessee has or will be filing.
	• After receipt of the official notice to creditors, the collector immediately puts all non-bankrupt parties on written notice of any default situations.
	• Collectors use the utmost caution in future contacts with the bankrupt party since any contact for any reason could be considered as an unlawful interference subjecting the individual collector to a substantial fine or imprisonment.

The key point to remember is that once a lessee or borrower becomes a debtor in bankruptcy ("Chapter 7") or reorganization ("Chapter 11"), no action may be taken to repossess the equipment, enforce the provisions of the lease, or collect back rent or damages from the debtor except through the bankruptcy court. The "automatic stay" protecting debtors in these proceedings goes into effect upon filing of the bankruptcy or reorganization action. Lessors and lenders may generally proceed against guarantors and co-obligors who are not also in similar proceedings, but referral of the matter to qualified counsel is advisable.

The lessor may expedite the assumption or rejection process by filing a motion for "relief of stay" or motion to compel the assumption or rejection. If the lessee rejects the lease, the lessor may recover and liquidate the equipment, establish its deficiency, and file an amended, unsecured claim in that amount.

If the lease is not a true lease, but one intended as security or an installment sale, the debtor may continue to use the equipment as long as it provides adequate protection to the creditor. If the lease document is classified as a security agreement, the debtor is not required to "cure" past defaults or provide adequate assurance of future performance; it merely has to "adequately protect" the secured party's interest in the property. In this situation, the secured party only has a security interest in the equipment and does not have a right to any residual. If the debtor has any equity in the equipment, it could then choose to dispose of the equipment, pay off the balance of the debt, and retain any surplus.

In both true lease and security interest transactions, the lessor/secured party would be subject to the automatic stay provisions and be required to obtain relief before it can recover the equipment/collateral. Non-bankrupt guarantors can be pursued without obtaining relief from the stay.

When reviewing bankrupt accounts, it is important to remember that the lessor and its collections department need to be proactive in determining account strategy. The Bankruptcy Code is designed to protect creditors and debtors alike, but its provisions are available only through petitioning the court.

Asset Management

The asset management function (also called equipment management by some lessors) serves a significant purpose in the equipment finance company. The asset managers collaborate cross-functionally throughout the end-to-end equipment finance lifecycle to ensure equipment values are understood, evaluate equipment values during the origination process, assist in equipment recovery scenarios, and remarket equipment.

Some types of lessors may not be directly involved in this type of activity, especially if it is a credit-based lender, not holding paper, or not receiving assets back at the end of the lease. Capital or finance lessors typically do not have specific asset managers. Even so, it is still advantageous as a CLFP to be aware of the functions of asset management, especially if your funding source is concerned with this aspect of the business.

The equipment type sometimes drives the implications for asset management involvement in transactions. For instance, imagine a large-ticket, long-term transaction for an aircraft. The asset manager may be involved up-front collaborating with the sales professional to provide equipment valuations, payment structuring, and advice on the appropriate term, return options, as well as FAA regulatory considerations. In cases such as these, they will often coordinate with professional appraisers in determining equipment valuation.

For mid-ticket transactions, on the other hand, the asset manager may be dealing with equipment such as over-the-road trucks, trailers, machine tools, and more. In these cases, depending on the size and sophistication of the lessor, the asset manager is evaluating the age of the equipment, manufacturer, and servicing requirements, and may refer to pre-established residual values set by company policy.

The legal responsibilities of the asset management function are to ensure equipment is recovered and sold as required by UCC Article 9 so that deficiency balances may be litigated and collected.

These responsibilities span the full lifecycle of an equipment finance transaction. It is useful to consider the influence of the asset manager within the following phases of the leasing lifecycle: prefunding, post-funding, and asset recovery.

The primary role of asset management is to help the equipment finance company understand the upfront value of the equipment investment and the value at the end of the lease. The asset manager may have additional expertise about the current and estimated future value of the equipment which is a crucial input for credit.

The typical responsibilities of an asset management department include equipment valuation and appraisal, residual valuation, equipment recovery, inventory management, as well as secondary remarketing and valuation. Table 29 Asset Management Role in the Leasing Lifecycle illustrates the various ways an asset manager's influence and expertise comes into play throughout each stage of the transaction lifecycle.

Table 29 Asset Management Role in the Leasing Lifecycle

Pre-Funding	• Ascertain and establish the FMV of equipment to ensure lease is appropriately secured. • Verify that there is a realistic equipment value established for the lease. • Determine the estimated residual value of the equipment at the end of the term. • Determine initial (upfront) residual value used in pricing the transaction. • Advise on lease payment structuring and return options. • Advise on regulatory considerations for specialized equipment types. • For large-ticket transactions, coordinate with professional appraisers. • Advise on whether the lease term makes sense for the asset's value and intended usage.
Post-Funding	• Portfolio management • Profitability • Residual value review • Inventory management • Remarketing of assets returned at the end of lease. • Asset disposal at the end of lease.

Default Scenarios	<ul><li>Asset repossession</li><li>Write-down</li><li>Determine liquidation values</li><li>Determine cost of asset recovery, recondition, and sale</li><li>Advise on whether recovery of the asset makes sense for the lessor.</li></ul>

Pre-Funding

Equipment Type Implications

Every piece of equipment has specific characteristics that determine the useful life and market value for resale. With the wide variety of commercial equipment that is leased and financed, the asset manager cannot be an expert in every equipment category. While they typically will have expertise in specific equipment categories, more importantly, they know how to acquire the right information to accurately establish residual values and determine liquidation values when necessary.

Lease Structure Implications

Early Pay-Off ("EPO") An "early pay off" or "early term payoff" occurs when the lessee desires to pay off the lease before the termination date. Many lessors use a matrix or formula with a predetermined discount rate that allows the lessee to pay off for less than the total amount owed while allowing the lessor to realize an acceptable return on their investment. This may also be called Buy Out or Pay Off.

Various lease structures have implications for the Asset Management function as illustrated in Table 30.

Table 30 Lease Structure Implications for Asset Management

Scenario	Asset Manager Responsibility
EPO	For an EPO the asset manager must make sure the payoff accounts for the correct residual value.
Extension	In the case of an extension, the asset manager provides information on whether or not an extension to the lease will affect the residual based on the useful life of the equipment.
Return	In the case of equipment return, first, there is a determination as to whether the contract allows for a "return" and under what circumstances. After that, there is a determination of equipment value.

Value Verification

Based on asset type and through a variety of methods (e.g., market data, market knowledge, experience, appraisers, a network of valuation sources) an asset manager verifies the current value of the equipment and assigns additional equipment values described in **Table 31** for use throughout the lifecycle of the lease.

Asset Value Verification Example
Let's say the equipment vendor might sell the equipment for $70,000, but the asset manager sees that the equipment is being sold closer to

$50,000 on the market. The asset manager's input can help to verify the real value of the equipment now and in the future.

Table 31 Equipment Valuation Types

Valuation Type	Description
Fair Market Value (FMV)	According to GAAP, the FMV of an asset is the amount for which the asset could be bought or sold, in a transaction between a willing buyer and a willing seller in an open market.
Orderly Liquidation Value (OLV)	The orderly liquidation value (OLV) is typically part of an appraisal of hard tangible assets (i.e., equipment). It is an estimate of the gross amount that the tangible assets would fetch in an auction-style liquidation with the seller needing to sell the assets on an "as-is-where-is" basis. The term orderly implies that the liquidation would allow for a reasonable time to identify all available buyers, and the seller would have control of the sale process.
Forced Liquidation Value (FLV)	FLV is the amount of money that a company will receive if it sold its assets in an auction immediately. The idea behind this forced liquidation value is to get an estimate of the financial position of the company in the worst possible situation and circumstance. The basis for FLV is the assumption that the business will sell its assets in the quickest time possible, which will usually lead to a low price.
Relative Value (RV)	RV is a method of determining an asset's value that takes into account the value of similar assets.
Absolute Value	In contrast to RV, Absolute Value looks only at the asset's intrinsic value and does not compare to other assets.
Repossession Value	Repossession value is a calculation using the FMV less repossession costs, storage costs and/or liquidation costs to determine if there is sufficient value in the equipment to warrant repossession.
Residual Value	Residual value is the value of equipment at the end of lease term, usually determined through an FMV analysis. Residual value can be assigned at lease commencement as a percentage of FMV which could be negotiated at the end of lease term depending on the contract language.

The asset manager typically assigns FMV, OLV, and FLV during the prefunding phase of a lease transaction with each value informing future actions that the lessor may take concerning the equipment.

Data Considered in Equipment Valuation

Regardless of the equipment type or ticket size, in determining the asset values, the asset manager considers a variety of data points including the following.

- Equipment type
- Age of the equipment
- Manufacturer, make, model
- Servicing requirements

- Intended utilization (how will it be used, where will it be used, who will operate it)
- Maintenance (who will perform maintenance?)
- Depreciable life of the asset (3-5-10-15-20 years)
- Leasing scenario: restructure, refinance, residual

In some cases, asset managers may also consider the following in setting residual values:

- Market conditions
- Some asset classes, such as aircraft, marine, and rail, have specific regulatory requirements that must be satisfied by their various regulatory bodies (e.g., FAA, Coast Guard) before financing.

Residual Value Review

During the prefunding stage, the first residual value review is the initial assignment of residual value for small- to medium-ticket transactions. Generally, the purpose of a residual value review later in the lease lifecycle is to ensure that the initial residual value remains valid. This typically occurs when the credit goes through its annual credit review.

For large-ticket transactions, a periodic residual review and appraisal may be planned into the transaction. This may be a type of covenant for some large-ticket transactions and, in some cases, originators will require residual value write-downs. These write-downs are necessary when collateral value changes such that the residual value exceeds the actual value, in which case the write-down is taken for the difference. The higher the value of the asset, the more stringent the residual value review requirements. Residual reviews are usually necessary when there is a high concentration of risk or when required for regulatory compliance.

Write-down[37]: A reduction in the value of an asset carried on a firm's financial statements. Unlike a write-off, a write-down does not result in the elimination of the asset.

Return and Maintenance Agreements

The asset manager will be asked to review contract language to determine if these agreements or fees are reasonable and customary and cost-effective. In some instances, the asset manager will be asked to determine if an inspection of the equipment, which is usually required, may be waived for various reasons or to recommend an inspection company to be utilized.

When reviewing residual values, it is essential to look at the return and maintenance agreements negotiated at the beginning of the transaction. For

---

[37] write-down. (n.d.) Wall Street Words: An A to Z Guide to Investment Terms for Today's Investor by David L. Scott. (2003). Retrieved March 26, 2018 from https://financial-dictionary.thefreedictionary.com/writedown

example: if you lease a vehicle with mileage utilization restrictions, you would want to ensure that the lessee follows guidelines for mileage. It is a matter of understanding commitments. Who pays for returning the equipment? Who is responsible for shipping? Who is responsible for storage?

The return condition agreement outlines the conditions to satisfy when the equipment is returned, such as maintenance requirements, mileage, and utilization (See Chapter 7 – Documentation to review more detail).

Fees

As described in Chapter 7 – Documentation, the lease may outline fees for restocking, usage in excess of the limitations, as well as maintenance requirements. Any piece of equipment with a meter in it for amount of use and with parts that need special maintenance, may have requirements outlined in the lease for what is required. For example, a vehicle lease may specify that brakes maintenance is a requirement. Typically, the higher the value of the equipment, the more complex the maintenance provisions.

Inspections

The inspection is another element of due diligence - especially for used or mobile equipment.

Pre-funding inspections may be required based on transaction amount at installation, for example, a third-party site inspection may be ordered for a small-ticket transaction. Following is a list of the types of information that may be verified through this activity:

- The equipment listed on the documentation and invoice matches (serial, VIN Numbers, etc.)
- That equipment is installed and operational
- Timing of delivery/installation
- That it is in the condition it was represented to be
- General information about the business and its location (i.e., does the location make sense for the type of business).

Medium- to large-ticket transactions more often will require inspections. Each lessor sets policy for the dollar thresholds that require equipment inspections.

Post-Funding

As previously discussed, the asset manager's role in the prefunding phase is to ensure that the lessor understands their equipment investment. Involvement in the post-funding phase is about monitoring and realizing the value of the equipment investment.

Credit Reviews & Equipment Inspections

Annual credit review and equipment inspection requirements are often determined by lender criteria, especially if there are credit issues. For bank lessors, the asset manager will be made aware of any annual credit review that indicates impairment on the lessee's part to service the debt. Annual equipment inspections are not typically required unless there is an indication of a business experiencing financial difficulty, which maybe evidenced by defaulted payments or through an annual financial review. In other cases, lease documentation will dictate the inspection schedule for a lease. When necessary, the asset manager will facilitate an equipment inspection to determine the condition and value of the equipment.

The Value of Residual Value Review Example
A lessor completed an annual credit review on a lease secured with various mining equipment with a residual value initially set at 15.43 percent. The lessee, under the terms of the lease agreement, notified the lessor that they would purchase the equipment at the end of the lease term.

The contract called for an FMV residual. The asset manager called for a "Desk Top Appraisal" of the equipment (which involves looking up historical, auction, and fair market values to understand the value of the asset if it is returned) through a certified appraiser, and the FMV was determined to be much higher than the original residual set at lease commencement. The contract language required this information, along with a buyout, to be provided to the lessee along with the company utilized to determine the FMV. The contract language specified a process where the lessor and lessee negotiated and agreed on the actual FMV.

Because the asset manager was familiar with the contract agreement, the original residual value, and the process to be followed in obtaining an FMV from a certified appraiser, an amount was agreed upon which resulted in the lessor realizing a substantially higher gain on the residual than previously anticipated.

Residual Value Adjustments as Required

Ordinarily, residual value adjustments occur only at the end of lease term or during lease term if there is a question regarding an early term buyout or the lease is in default. For example, if the residual value is decreasing from the initial booked residual, the lessee may have to reimburse the lender for the loss of value of the asset.

Default Scenarios

While practices and assignment of responsibilities may vary from lessor to lessor, asset valuation comes into play to support liquidation, asset recovery, and monetization in default scenarios.

In the case of repossession, the "repossession value" is determined as described in Table 6 above.

Residual value is the value of equipment at the end of lease term, usually determined through an FMV analysis. Residual value may be set at lease commencement as a percentage of the FMV, which may or may not be negotiated at the end of lease term depending on the contract language.

For bank lessors, in default scenarios it may be necessary for the asset manager to play a role in evaluating the equipment value at the time of default in collaboration with other areas of the bank.

It is necessary to look at reserves, another element of portfolio data, and review this periodically (quarterly as an example) to make sure you reserve enough and write off what should be written off. The goal is to keep good assets on the books and manage the portfolio for good company financial condition.

Establish Risk Parameters

Lessors must establish acceptable reserve/losses that a portfolio can handle for the company to remain profitable. Management needs to continually monitor the net bad debt to ensure that it is within the reserve/loss expectations.

Should there be a deficiency in the value of defaulted equipment vs. the outstanding receivable, a write-off should be made. The write-off will come from the allowance for bad debt account on the balance sheet, which is funded by bad debt expense on the income statement. A lender must attempt to predict and reserve for these losses accurately or risk going out of business should losses outpace reserves. Defaulted leases equate to less cash flow; unanticipated write-offs can lead to negative consequences for any type of lessor including:

- Loss of funding sources
- Loss in company's equity
- Causing the lender to be outside of financial covenants
- Shutting down the business unit

Active portfolio management is an art and science. The goal is to anticipate future losses and market conditions to reserve for bad debt as accurately as possible.

In-Place Value vs. Recovered Value

Before a default happens, the collections team monitors accounts, and when they see the warning signs described earlier in this chapter, they will collaborate with the asset manager to obtain current asset valuation information. The asset manager typically performs a desk top appraisal.

The term, "in-place value" refers to the value of the asset if sold where currently installed. The term, "recovered value" refers to the value of the asset if it is removed from the currently installed location. For some types of equipment, it is more valuable to leave the asset in place rather than try to remove it for sale. Moving these types of equipment may limit the market of potential buyers. Following is a list of examples where the in-place value of the asset is better than recovery value:

- Dry cleaning equipment
- Restaurant equipment

- Parts washers
- Equipment that is hooked up to water, power, or gas
- Equipment that is custom manufactured
- Equipment built into a location

Another form of valuation is formal valuation vs. in-house valuation. Formal valuation refers to utilizing an outside professional (auctioneer, appraiser, etc.) to establish the value of the asset. In contrast, the in-house valuation refers to using the internal resources or remarketing resources to determine the value of the asset.

In a default scenario, when you are determining the value, is where the FMV, OLV, and FLV numbers that you established during prefunding stage come into play. Now you are using these to determine the value of the asset and loss potential or recovery.

Legal impact

In default scenarios, the fundamental question is, "what is more advantageous to the leasing company? Is it better to recover the equipment or sue the customer?" In this process, other aspects of the situation are considered such as guarantors and whether the customer requires the equipment to stay in business (essential use).

Equipment recovery must follow a legal approach, and the legalities vary from state to state.

While it is not legal to breach the peace or use force to recover the equipment, there are situations where titled vehicles and other equipment may be repossessed without permission by the lessee.

A Replevin Action is a lawsuit seeking an order from a judge requiring the lessee to surrender the equipment at a certain date, time, and place or face additional legal action.

A vital role of the asset manager in this situation is to help the lessor understand whether it is worthwhile to recover the equipment and, if so, what are the legal requirements to get it.

Commercially Reasonable Sale vs. Straight Liquidation

Lessors must provide written notice to the lessee, guarantors, and junior secured creditors who have requested notice.

Commercially Reasonable Liquidation: This type of liquidation requires the involvement of an attorney to provide proper notices as described earlier in the collections section of this chapter as well as Chapter 3 – Leasing Law. In these cases, the asset manager may be involved in performing any of the following tasks related to asset liquidation: appraising the asset, advertising the sale to interested parties, and providing a required notice to sell.

"Returned assets are easier to sell today because of the power of the internet. Now you can take a snapshot of the asset and slap it on the web and put it for sale on

the web. This is a lot easier than in the past where we had to advertise in the newspaper and whatnot." ~CLFP and Asset Manager

Straight Liquidation: In a bankruptcy scenario or when the customer is unable to pay. The customer settles with the lessor and surrenders the asset. Once the lessor has the equipment, they use the method of their choice to sell the equipment without involvement of attorneys and formal notices.

Costs to Recover, Recondition, and Sell

Companies may outsource recovery, reconditioning, and sale of returned assets or do it themselves with internal resources. Calculating the cost of recovery includes these resources. Asset managers typically build up a network of experts who know what is required (or allowed) legally and can recover the asset. These types of resources have specialized expertise in dismantling as needed, securing, and recovering various types of assets.

For large-ticket equipment, a skilled appraiser is usually engaged in assigning valuations and advising on the condition as well as estimating the costs for reconditioning and repairs. Depending on the scenario, targets may be a 2:1 or 3:1 return on investment.

Lessors may also use internal remarketing resources or outsource the asset sales function as well. Depending on the equipment type, location, usage, or other factors, recovery may not be justified. For example, the equipment may be considered obsolete, inaccessible, or can't be moved. In these cases, the lessor may choose to abandon the equipment.

The key to asset management for lessors:

"You have to know the value of the asset going into the transaction to know what you will recover on the asset getting out of the transaction"

Summary

The portfolio management function is more than just reporting or a back-office consideration. Thorough understanding of portfolio segments enables company leadership to determine which markets to pursue, which to expand, and which to reduce or eliminate. Portfolio management concepts are an important consideration, and cross-functional process, performance, policy compliance, and collaboration have an impact on portfolio performance as well as collections activities.

Even the best-managed equipment leasing and finance companies will encounter collection problems periodically. Having a process in place to deal with such situations as soon as they arise is important. Lease collection activities are an ongoing, fluid process that requires daily attention by a dedicated, well-trained staff and the support of upper management. A properly run collections department, or an outside collections agency experienced in the industry, is imperative for the smooth operation of any lessor.

The asset management function serves a significant purpose with asset managers collaborating cross-functionally throughout the equipment finance lifecycle. Asset managers help to ensure equipment values are understood, evaluate equipment values during the origination process, and assist in equipment recovery scenarios and remarketing.

Appendix 1 Government Leasing

The following is for informational purposes only; in all government leasing, it is advised that lessors seek legal counsel. Please see Chapter 7 – Documentation for details on municipal leasing.

As one CLFP and Bank Executive stated,

"I see many banks and independents doing municipal leasing wrong, which is technically a violation of the law and could create problems for the lessee, most specifically loss of tax exemption"

Federal Government

Although federal leasing is surely "governmental" it differs enough from municipal leasing to be treated separately. Having an overview of these differences is important for fielding questions in addition to knowing when to ask for assistance in a particular topic.

Rates

Lease rates quoted for the federal government are often considerably higher than municipal transactions. There are a number of reasons:

- The interest portion of municipal lease payments is normally exempt from federal income tax on the investor, while interest received from the federal government is fully subject to income tax. To the layperson, this sounds strange, but the IRC is very specific on this point.
- There are interruptions and delays in the payment stream of a federal lease that do not exist in other forms of leasing. These arise from the federal government's sheer size and compartmentalization, as well as its peculiar system.

In most cases, the feds will pay in arrears, which means that if a lessor pays a bill on the exact last day of the month, a thirty-day counter begins because the beds are now required to pay interest on payments later than thirty days.

Renewal purchase orders are rarely issued, as required, exactly on October 1, which is the start of the new fiscal year. A lag of two months or more is more common. This poses a problem since the investor is not able to bill without the new purchase order.

The payments on federal leases can be paid *double in arrears*. That means that a lessor cannot even send a bill until the end of a month, and then they have thirty days plus a "grace period" of fifteen days to send the check. This is a worst-case scenario and limited to a few civilian agencies. Department of Defense payments are automated and most often paid in less than thirty days, especially with electronic payments.

Administrative dealings with the federal government can be quite cumbersome. While all federal agencies work from the same Federal Acquisition Regulations (FAR), they do not all read or sometimes understand them. There are many instances, for example, when the IRS gives erroneous income tax advice, or differing advice to various inquirers, even though it's all from the same code. It is often necessary to spend time on the phone in lengthy discussions with various government employees to clarify problems.

There are several different ways the federal government can terminate a lease. Many of them are manageable, or there would be no federal leasing. But this reality leads to added uncertainty, risk, and possible expense.

Most of the above are problems for the funder rather than the vendor, but they all combine to ensure that federal rates should be, and are, considerably higher than municipal ones. It also means that the rates are usually higher than commercial ones. Also, any funder would have some reluctance to accept lengthy lease terms without some protection by the vendor. Given the natural human reaction to these hazards, it should be no surprise that the lessor charges more to compensate.

On the other hand, federal procurement officials are relatively inured to the rates they are charged. Their major emphasis is on the ease with which a payment schedule fits into their budget scheme, not worrying about interest rates.

There are a few other areas wherein federal government leasing differs from other types:

Documentation

There is one point which invariably surprises commercial leasing professionals—there is no official lease form that is prepared as a specific lease document. Given the many possible lease variations, the federal government recognizes none of them. Instead, it puts the relevant information right on the purchase order. It is normal for funders to ask for the inclusion of additional binding language on the purchase order. Federal government contracting officers, of course, vary widely as to their degrees of receptivity to the inclusion of such language. This often leads to conference calls, negotiations, and compromises

Nature of the Lease Obligation

Unlike virtually every other kind of lease, there is no "Hell or High-Water" payment obligation in a federal government lease. If there is a failure of contract performance or a breach of warranty by the vendor, the lessee agency can stop making payments. In this way, the very underpinning of lease financing is absent from federal government leasing. The frequency of termination for default, however, is very low. In all cases, the feds establish a "show cause or repair" period where the vendor can resolve most issues. If the project has a mission critical element, the federal entity will not want to terminate and start over with a new vendor.

This ability is an integral part of the governing law for federal government leasing, referred to as the Assignment of Claims Act of 1941. Briefly, the act allows federal government contractors/vendors to assign their payments to secure financing, but specifically forbids them to assign away any of their performance obligations or warranties. This hurdle is overcome by having the vendor execute an Assignment Agreement in which it agrees to make the funder whole if the vendor breaches its contract with the federal government, thus causing the funder to lose payments. Naturally, this characteristic of federal government leasing places an added burden on the funder of making sure that the vendor has the ability to fulfill the obligation if called upon.

The Assignment of Claims Act refers only to assignments to "financial institutions." Interestingly, for the purposes of the act, several case precedents have affirmed that third-party leasing companies are "financial institutions." Although this point is a basic one, it is not uncommon to encounter federal government contracting officers and lawyers who dispute it.

From the vendor's perspective, a leasing program opens the door to the world's largest customer for a multitude of products, in a wide variety of dollar sizes. Despite speculation to the contrary, selling to the federal government often is not much different than selling to anyone else.

For the originator or syndicator, a federal government lease can be a relatively easy, lucrative transaction. The documentation requirements are minimal-to-zero. There is no need for credit review. Yet the rates are at a level high enough to allow the broker to add in quite generous compensation if permitted by the investor.

Leasing to Native American Tribes/Nations

Most American Native American tribes, nations, and bands are sovereign nations, both by treaty and by various Acts of Congress. They often have their own laws, which are effective on their reservations. For leasing purposes, they are accorded the same status as municipalities in that the interest they pay for a tribal public purpose is exempt from income tax. If the lease is for the benefit of a tribal profit-making entity, the interest paid is taxable to the investor.

When working on an Indian tribal lease, documentation is much like any municipal lease, with certain differences as follows:

- A non-appropriation clause is generally not necessary.
- The lease may have a firm term.
- A certified resolution of the Tribal Council should authorize the lease.

As part of the council resolution, or as a separate document, the tribe should provide a "Limited Waiver of Sovereign Immunity." Because the lessee is a sovereign nation, this waiver is needed to allow the lessor to enter the reservation, if necessary, to repossess the equipment and to grant permission to sue the tribe in a court of competent jurisdiction.

If the tribe is a bona fide entity, it should be listed on the IRS's list of Indian Tribal governments. Because many tribes have their own laws, careful attention needs to be paid to the law applicable to the lease. Most tribal law and court systems parallel those of the United States, including the UCC, and appeals may be filed in U.S. federal courts. Nonetheless, it is best that the lessor understands what is being signed and why. The foregoing is meant to be precautionary only. When working on an Indian lease, there is no substitute for knowledge. Lessors are advised to contact and work with a company with experience in this complex area.

Appendix 2 Agricultural Leasing

Agriculture is defined in the dictionary as "the science or art of cultivating land in the raising of crops, husbandry or farming."

The United States is the leading producer of agricultural commodities in the world. All of the many business segments related to the agricultural industry in the U.S. have one thing in common—they need equipment and the capital to acquire and finance equipment. Aside from the classic cash grain operator or dairy farmer, agriculture also includes:

- **Apiculture**: the raising of bees and the production of honey
- **Aquaculture**: the raising of fish and shellfish
- **Poultry**: the raising of fowl and the production of eggs
- **Forestry**: logging, the production of lumber and timber products
- **Livestock**: the raising of cattle and other animals
- **Viticulture**: the planting and harvesting of wine grapes and the production of wine
- **Floriculture**: the raising and production of flowers
- **Horticulture**: the raising, production, and sale of landscape plants, both wholesale and retail; the growing and sale of food crops, such as grains, fruits, and seeds.

There are also numerous other industries that support it. "Agribusiness" includes all of the above plus other industries such as:

- Suppliers of fertilizers, seeds, and chemicals
- Suppliers of equipment
- Manufacturers of moveable structures
- Service companies such as shippers, cold storage providers, and contract harvesters
- Retail and wholesale marketers
- Manufacturers of food products

Agricultural Entities & Company Structures

Agricultural entities are similar to other companies in structure in that they may be corporations, partnerships, limited liability companies, sole proprietorships, or any other type of legal structure. One structure that is common in agriculture and somewhat uncommon elsewhere is the cooperative or co-op.

Co-ops are attractive to the agricultural community because they offer the smaller farmers the opportunity to join with others and take advantage of larger economies of scale. Co-ops may be beneficial to farmers for other reasons as well, by offering such things as processing and marketing services and crop inputs, niche products to consumers, quality control, and education.

There are many categories of businesses associated with the broad term agriculture and all perform different functions. The following is a listing of the most common types of agricultural businesses and their activities:

- **Custom Farmers:** a service business that may or may not farm its own land. A custom farmer typically owns equipment and does work such as tilling, planting, spraying, or harvesting for a landowner farmer.
- **Growers:** companies that grow an agricultural commodity. Examples include row crop, orchard, greenhouses, fruit and vegetables, or vineyard farmers. They may own their land or lease it.
- **Animal Husbandry:** the area of agriculture involved with the raising and breeding of live animals, such as cows, sheep, hogs, horses, and others.
- **Dairy:** a category of animal husbandry that deals with the production of milk. Dairy farmers can produce milk from cows, goats, or sheep.

Equipment

Agriculture is an extremely capital-intensive business that generally requires a large amount of land as well as equipment to cultivate it. The equipment needs of a farmer are diverse depending on the type of commodity being cultivated or raised.

Consider the equipment needs of a farmer in the Midwest growing wheat on a section of land that has not been farmed before. In order to prepare the ground for farming, the land needs to be cleared, leveled, plowed, and disked, which requires all of the various equipment plus a tractor to pull it. After the ground is prepared, the seeds need to be planted, which requires a planting machine pulled behind the tractor. Once the ground is prepared and planted, it needs to be watered and fertilized, which require some type of irrigation system. Once the plants begin growing, there are insects that may cause damage. Pesticides need to be applied either with a sprayer or crop duster. After the plants have matured, they need to be harvested, which requires a combine harvester as well as a vehicle to transport it.

As illustrated in the paragraph above, a farmer growing something as simple as wheat requires numerous pieces of equipment in the process of growing and harvesting. The following is a listing of equipment commonly used in agriculture that may be financed:

- Irrigation equipment such as pumps, aluminum pipe, drip and pivot systems
- Tractors
- Harvesters

- Storage bins, plastic and wooden
- Automatic milking equipment for dairies
- Farm implements such as mowers, land levelers, disks, planters, and sprayers
- Tree shakers
- Transportation (trucks, trailers)
- Forklifts, backhoes, construction equipment
- Feed equipment, dairy parlor equipment
- Structures
- Processing/bagging lines

In addition, technology has become more important for farmers. Today laser devices are used for leveling fields. GPS devices are used for determining the exact size of areas for soil preparation and for the precise placement of fertilizers and pesticides and soil moisture is measured by electronic sensors.

Transaction Structures

Unlike most industries, agriculture has a unique cash flow cycle. Most farmers have one or possibly two harvests per year, leading to an irregular cash flow. For this reason, agricultural entities often require annual or semi-annual payments to coincide with the sale of their crops. There are some exceptions to this cycle, which may be found in the animal husbandry and dairy segments. These types of entities have a more even cash flow, conducive to monthly payments.

Seasonality in agriculture has several drivers. Greenhouses, for instance have two primary seasons, spring and the holidays. Often, they may require payment structures with certain months on and off.

Crop cycles are regionalized, and in warmer areas of the country, the growing season may be longer, even year-round. For example, in Midwestern regions, a typical crop cycle begins in the spring when the crops are planted and ends in the fall when crops are harvested. By the time the farmer receives payment from the harvest, it can be late in the year or early in the next. For this reason, it is common for lenders to offer a structure that is referred to as a "harvest plan." With a harvest plan, an entity borrows money for equipment early in the year and skips several months before making an annual payment. Typically, the borrower pays the lender an advance payment that is greater than or equal to the interest being accrued during the period between funding and when the first annual payment is due (referred to as the "skip period"). This advance payment keeps the loan from negatively amortizing prior to the first payment being made and mitigates some of the lender's initial risk.

When payments are only made once a year, some lenders require a monthly "contact" payment. This may consist of a small amount and is less than the regular payment. It allows the lender to keep in frequent contact with the borrower.

A lease to a dairy farmer may include an "Assignment of Milk Proceeds." Dairy farmers sell their milk to a dairy. The proceeds from the sale can be assigned to the lessor so that the lessor can collect the payments directly from the dairy in the event the farmer defaults.

Lending to Agricultural Businesses

As mentioned previously, due to the seasonality of the agricultural industry, lenders that deal with agricultural credits need to understand how the cash flow may be affected to be successful.

Many crop cycles begin in spring and this is when most farms are low on cash but need working capital to gear up for the coming season. For this reason, most farming operations have an "operating line" with their bank (not to be confused with a "harvest plan"). Bankers that understand the seasonality of agricultural credits are willing to loan farmers money early in the year to pay for land preparation, planting, irrigation, and other costs related to growing their crops. Operating lines are made with the understanding that the money will be paid back after the harvest is complete. Often the operating line includes funds to make the annual lease payment if the lease payment falls before the harvest.

Because operating lines are short-term facilities, they are not intended to be used for the financing of equipment. Other options exist for farmers to finance or lease their equipment, including bank term loans, vendor/captive financing, and third-party equipment lessors or brokers. There is also the Farm Credit System (FCS), a nationwide network of cooperative banks and associations in place to help facilitate all types of lending to agribusiness entities.

FCS was established by Congress in 1916 to provide a reliable source of credit for the nation's farmers and ranchers. It has a unique structure consisting of associations governed by stockholders and directors and owned cooperatively by those that borrow from them. The FCS provides funding to thousands of qualified member-borrowers nationwide.

Nuances

Agriculture leases and loans often require special documents in addition to the standard lease or loan forms. See Chapter 7 – Documentation for more information.

Agricultural leasing may sometimes involve special insurance requirements such as crop insurance, which insures the value of the crops in the ground against the loss of the crop due to a variety of disasters (not all crops are insurable). Farmers also typically carry insurance insuring the value of the crops in transit and in storage.

Summary

The equipment intensive nature of the agricultural industry, in addition to components such as harvest cycle and cash flow, make equipment leasing and financing a popular method for acquiring capital equipment. Successful lessors and equipment finance companies in this arena are comfortable providing flexible transactions that are structured to match the cash flow or seasonal business patterns unique in the agriculture community.

Appendix 3 Pricing Sample Problems

These sample problems are included to help you practice the concepts introduced in Chapter 4 – Lease Pricing

Chapter Topic	Problems
Solve for an unknown element in a transaction	1-8
Lease Rate Factors	9-18
Beginning of Period (BOP) vs. End of Period (EOP)	19-23
Down Payments, Advance Payments, and Residual Values/End of Term Payments	24-32
Determining Profit	33-39

Solve for an unknown element in a transaction

In each of the following scenarios, solve for the unknown variable.

1. Lease = $75,000
    $I\% = 10\%$
    N = 60
    PMT = _____

2. Lease = $82,000
    N = 50
    PMT = $2,275
    $I\% = $ _____

3. $I\% = 11.5\%$
    N = 72
    PMT = $35,480
    Lease = _____

4. Lease = $12,000
    $I\% = 7\%$
    N = 24
    PMT = _____

5. XYZ Company wants to finance a new server, computers and routers in three offices. The total cost of the system is $100,000 and the customer wants to know what their payments would be for a 3, 4, and 5-year transaction. Given that the current funding rate for this particular transaction is 14 percent, what are the payments?
   a. Three years: _____

   b. Four years: _____

   c. Five years: _____

6. ABC Machine Shop is acquiring a CNC laser cutter and the president of the company would like you to arrange financing for them. They tell you that the total cost will come to $104,600. They like you enough to tell you that they have been quoted a monthly payment of $2,354 for a sixty-month transaction by their bank and say that if you can match their interest rate, you've got the deal.
   a. What interest rate is the bank charging ABC Machine Shop?
      I% = _____

7. In talking to the purchasing agent for Ohio Machining Incorporated, you found out that their bank has approved them at 13.75 percent for the turning center, which they are buying from Tipton Machinery for $87,000. You managed to get them to tell you that their exact monthly payment is $2,340. Now that you're off the phone, however, you realize that you forgot to ask what term they are going to spread their payments over.
   a. What is the term (in months)? _____

8. You have decided to buy a new car. The jet-black Porsche 944 will set you back $44,000. The dealer offers you a three-year financing program, which will require nothing down and cost $1,492 per month. You know that you can finance the car at your bank for 13.9 percent.
   a. Which should you choose, the bank or the dealer financing?
      _____

   b. What is the dealer's interest rate? _____

Lease Rate Factors

9. PV = $100,000
   I% = 10%
   N = 60
   PMT = $2,017

L.R.F. = _____

10. PV = $82,000
    N = 36
    PMT = $2,696
    I% = 12%
    L.R.F. = _____

11. I% = 11.5%
    N = 24
    PMT = $3,680
    PV = $79,317
    L.R.F. = _____

12. PV = $12,000
    I% = 17%
    N = 18
    PMT = $749
    L.R.F. = _____

13. PV = $1,232,033
    I% = 11.25%
    N = 72
    PMT = _____
    L.R.F. = _____

14. PV = $142,200
    N = 48
    PMT = $3,769
    I% = _____
    L.R.F. = _____

15. L.R.F. = .02333
    N = 60
    PV = $136,880
    PMT = _____
    I% = _____

16. L.R.F. = .03353
    PMT = $4,999
    N = 36
    PV = _____
    I% = _____

17. An executive wants to lease a telephone system. They know that it will cost approximately $62,000 but will not know the exact cost until it is actually installed. They would like to arrange financing ahead of time.

    a.   What lease rate factor will you quote the executive if they want a 60-month transaction at 14 percent? _____

    b.   If the exact cost comes to $64,230, what will their exact monthly rent be at:
12 percent? _____ and at 14 percent? _____

18. A hotel owner needs to borrow money to purchase all the televisions and telephones for their new motel on Lake Erie. Another leasing company has quoted them .02520 on 60 months.

    a.   They tell you that the T.V.s and phones cost a grand total of $31,000. What is their monthly rent on the other leasing company's proposal? _____

    b.   What interest rate is the other leasing company charging? _____

    c.   If you want to undercut the other leasing company's interest rate by 1.5 percent, what monthly payment will you quote? _____

Beginning of Period (BOP) vs. End of Period (EOP)

19. Scenario 1
N = 60
PV = $100,000
PMT = $2,534
I% = _____ (BOP)
I% = _____ (EOP)

20. Scenario 2
N = 36
PV = $2,345,200
PMT = 75,893
I% = _____ (BOP)
1% = _____ (EOP)

21. Scenario 3
N = 48
PV = _____ (BOP)
PV = _____ (EOP)
PMT = $1,515
I% = 11.75%

22. Scenario 4
    N = 72
    PV = $45,454
    PMT = _____ (BOP)
    PMT = _____ (EOP)
    I% = 15.5%

23. The leasing sales person decides to try their new idea on a machine shop owner who is buying a $100,000 CNC machine with nothing down for five years.
    a. If the leasing sales person quotes 14 percent EOP, then what is the machine shop owner's payment? _____

    b. If the leasing sales person wins the transaction and prepares the paperwork with this payment, but prepares the paperwork with the payments due in advance, what is the machine shop owner's actual interest rate going to be?
    _____
    The leasing sales person finds out that they have not yet won the machine shop owner's business and that the machine shop owner has a quote from another leasing company for $2,320 on a five-year dollar buyout. From past experience, we know that the other leasing company bills in arrears.

    c. What interest rate is the other leasing company charging?
    _____

    d. If the other leasing company makes an exception and bills the machine shop owner in advance, then what interest rate are they getting? _____

Down Payments, Advance Payments, and Residual Values/End of Term Payments

24. A business owner is buying a brand new $30,000 piece of equipment. If they put 12 percent down, what number will you enter as the present value when figuring their payments? _____

25. A business owner is short on cash and in need of a green widget with a sticker price of $370. The widget sales person is pleased to inform the business owner that they can offer a special widget financing plan. If the business owner acts today, they can get the widget with no money down and will only owe 20 percent of the original sticker price at the end of the term. When figuring the payments, what number will you enter as the future value?
_____

26. Scenario 1
    Equipment Cost = $100,000
    Down Payment = $5,000
    Interest Rate = 10%
    Term = 60 months
    Monthly Payment = _____

27. Scenario 2
    Equipment Cost = $35,000
    Monthly Payment = $1,126
    Term = 36 months
    Interest Rate = 13.9%
    Balloon = _____

28. Scenario 3
    Equipment Cost = $3,000,000
    Monthly Payment = $54,439
    Term = 72 months
    Balloon = 10%
    Interest Rate = _____

29. Scenario 4
    Equipment Cost = $250,000
    Monthly Payment = $5,516
    Term = 48 months
    Interest Rate = 11.75%
    Down Payment = _____

30. A business owner is purchasing a $96,000 wire EDM machine. They were quoted a payment of $2,300 per month for a five-year financing program.
    a. What interest rate are they being charged? _____

    b. Under the same financing program (i.e. same interest rate), what would their payment be if they put 10 percent down? _____

    c. What would their payment be if, instead, they had a 10 percent balloon and put nothing down? _____

    d. What would their payment be if they put 5 percent down and had a 5 percent balloon? _____

31. A car buyer has their heart set on leasing a brand-new Yugo. The sticker price is only $2,657.95 The dealer tells them that at the end of a two-year lease they can buy the car for its blue book value, which will be $364.00 and that if they act today, the interest rate for financing the car will be only 18 percent!

    a. If the car buyer takes advantage of this incredible deal, what will their payment be? _____

    b. The car buyer decides to turn the car in at the end of the lease instead of buying it and leaves the Yugo with the dealer. Because the dealer misjudged the blue book value of the car after two years, they are unable to sell the car (they received zero instead of $364), what was the actual rate of return that the dealer received from this financing?

    _____

32. Metal Manufacturing Corporation is acquiring three new pieces of equipment: a Mori Seiki Vertical Machining Center for $141,210; a 40V-Package-lM Tooling Kit for $7,411.80; and a Fluid Recovery System for $9,500. They have agreed with their bank to put 10 percent down on a 60-month transaction with a total monthly payment of $3,262.58.

    a. What is the interest rate? _____

    b. When evaluating the transaction, the bank decides that Metal Manufacturing Corp. is not financially healthy enough to approve the transaction as it stands. The bank finally approves the transaction at the same interest rate, but with 15 percent down instead of 10 percent. What will the new payment be? _____

    c. If the customer decides not to purchase the Fluid Recovery System, what will the new payment be (with the 15 percent down)? _____

    d. If another leasing company approves Metal Manufacturing Corporation with 20 percent down, and a monthly payment (on all three pieces of equipment) of $2,913.75, then what is the interest rate that they are charging? _____

Determining Profit

33. Cost = $100,000
    I% = 11%
    Bill = BOP
    N = 48
    PMT = _____
    L.R.F. = _____
    Buy Rate % = 8%
    Profit = _____

34. Cost = $56,000
    N = 36

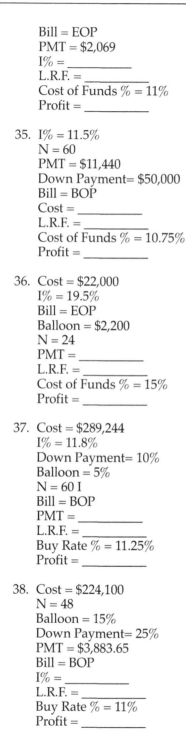

Bill = EOP
PMT = $2,069
I% = _____
L.R.F. = _____
Cost of Funds % = 11%
Profit = _____

35. I% = 11.5%
N = 60
PMT = $11,440
Down Payment= $50,000
Bill = BOP
Cost = _____
L.R.F. = _____
Cost of Funds % = 10.75%
Profit = _____

36. Cost = $22,000
I% = 19.5%
Bill = EOP
Balloon = $2,200
N = 24
PMT = _____
L.R.F. = _____
Cost of Funds % = 15%
Profit = _____

37. Cost = $289,244
I% = 11.8%
Down Payment= 10%
Balloon = 5%
N = 60 I
Bill = BOP
PMT = _____
L.R.F. = _____
Buy Rate % = 11.25%
Profit = _____

38. Cost = $224,100
N = 48
Balloon = 15%
Down Payment= 25%
PMT = $3,883.65
Bill = BOP
I% = _____
L.R.F. = _____
Buy Rate % = 11%
Profit = _____

39. You are bidding on your first transaction, and the customer has requested a dollar buyout. They want to finance a machine for sixty months and will put 10 percent down. The machine costs $325,000. You will be billing them on the first of every month. You are not sure what rate to quote, so you must determine profit to help you decide. You estimate that this customer's credit will merit a funding rate of 12.75 percent.

    a. If you quote 13.5 percent, what will the payment be?

    _____

    What will the profit be? _____

    b. If you quote 14 percent, what will the payment be?

    _____

    What will the profit be? _____

    c. If you quote 14.5 percent, what will the payment be?

    _____

    What will the profit be? _____

    Before you submit the quote, the customer tells you that their best quote so far is 13.75 percent, and that if you want their business, you must come in at 13.65 percent. However, you discover that the customer has figured the 13.75 percent rate with billing EOP; therefore, you need to quote 13.65 percent EOP to win their business.

    d. What is the payment for 13.65 percent EOP?

    _____

    e. What is the actual interest rate, billed BOP, for this payment?

    _____

    f. What will the profit be on this quote? _____

    g. If the bank approves this transaction, at 13 percent instead of 13.75 percent, then what will the profit be? _____

    h. If the bank approves this transaction, at 12.5 percent instead of 13.75 percent, then what will the profit be?

    _____

Answers
Solve for an unknown element in a transaction

	BOP	EOP
1.	$1,580.36	$1,593.53
2.	17.18%	16.41%
3.	$1,856,810.26	$1,839,184.74
4.	$534.16	$537.27
5.	a. $3,378.35	a. $3,417.76
	b. $2,701.13	b. $2,732.65
	c. $2,299.99	c. $2,326.83
6.	12.99%	12.51%
7.	47.99	48.73
8.	a. Go with bank	a. Go with dealer
	b. 14.28%	b. 13.45%

Lease Rate Factors

	BOP	EOP
9	.02017	.02017
10	.03288	.03288
11	.04640	.04640
12	.06242	.06242
13	PMT = $23,389.40	PMT = $23,608.67
	L.R.F. = .01898	L.R.F. = .01916
14	I% = 12.93%	I% = 12.35%
	L.R.F. = .02650	L.R.F. = .02650
15	PMT = $3,193.41	PMT = $3,193.41
	I% = 14.67%	I% = 14.12%
16	PV = $149,090.37	PV = $149,090.37
	I% = 13.44%	I% = 12.66%
17	a. .02300	a. .02327
	b. $1,414.61	b. $1,428.76
	c. $1,477.29	c. $1,494.52
18	a. $781.20	a. $781.20
	b. 18.35%	b. 17.64%
	c. $757.33	c. $756.23

Beginning of Period (BOP) vs. End of Period (EOP)

	BOP	EOP
19	18.62%	17.90%
20	10.82%	10.20%
21	$58,365.55	$57,799.60

	BOP	EOP
22	$961.10	$973.51
23	a. $2,326.83	
	b. 14.54%	
	c. 13.87%	
	d. 14.40%	

Down Payments, Advance Payments, and Residual Values/End of Term Payments

	BOP	EOP
24	$26,400	
25	$74	
26	$2,001.79	$2,018.47
27	$2,460.55	$3,039.06
28	11.50%	11.18%
29	$37,495.45	$39,556.05
30	a. 15.92%	a. 15.32%
	b. $2,069.95	b. $2,070.00
	c. $2,195.64	c. $2,192.55
	d. $2,132.79	d. $2,131.27
31	a. $118.21	$119.98
	b. 6.91%	7.81%
32	a. 13.85%	13.34%
	b. $3,081.33	$3,081.54
	c. $2,896.20	$2,896.40 (EOP)
	d. 14.07%	13.55%

Determining Profit

33 PMT = $2,561.08
L.R.F. = .02561
Profit = $5,606.11
34 I% = 19.57%
L.R.F. = .03695
Profit = $7,197.34
35 Cost = $575,159.80
L.R.F. = .01989
Profit = $8,770.63
36 PMT = $1,038.66
L.R.F. = .04721
Profit = $1,054.40
37 PMT = $5,531.96
L.R.F. = .01913
Profit = $3,292.59
38 I% = 12.5%

L.R.F. = .01733
Profit = $5,259.08

39   a. PMT = $6,655.51 / Profit = $4,787.56
b. PMT = $6,727.48 / Profit = $8,002.51
c. PMT = $6,799.86 / Profit = $11,235.45
d. $6,753.00
e. 14.18%
f. $9,142.65
g. $7,510.57
h. $10,787.74

Appendix 4 Financial Statement Review Sample Problems

These sample problems are included to help you practice the concepts introduced in the Financial Ratios section of Chapter 6 – Credit.

Calculating Financial Ratios

Learning goal: practice calculating financial ratios using these sample financial statements. Do you understand where to pull data to calculate each ratio?

Part 1

ABC Company has come to you to lease a $1,250,000 machine tool over a seven-year period. Review the following condensed financial information for ABC Company.

Income Statement		
Net Sales	$	18,000,000
(-) Cost of Goods Sold	$	15,000,000
Gross Profit	$	3,000,000
(-) Operating Expenses (G&A)	$	1,800,000
Operating Profit (EBIT)	$	1,200,000
Interest Expense	$	300,000
Earnings Before Tax	$	900,000
Tax Expense	$	100,000
Net Profit	$	800,000

Balance Sheet

Cash	$	1,000,000	Accounts Payable	$	1,500,000
Accounts Receivable	$	1,500,000	Notes Payable - Bank	$	1,000,000
Inventory	$	2,000,000	Current Portion LT Debt	$	500,000
Current Assets	$	4,500,000	Current Liabilities	$	3,000,000
Fixed Assets	$	6,000,000	Long Term Debt	$	4,000,000
Other	$	500,000	Total Liabilities	$	7,000,000
			Net Worth	$	4,000,000
Total Assets	$	11,000,000	Total Liabilities & Net Worth	$	11,000,000

Calculate each of the following financial ratios for ABC Company.

1. Gross Profit Margin

2. Current Ratio

3. Total Liabilities to Net Worth (Debt to Equity)

4. Return on Assets (ROA)

5. Return on Equity

6. Quick Ratio

7. Inventory Turn Over

8. Accounts Receivable Turn Over

9. Based on your analysis, what are the strengths and weaknesses of this transaction?

Part 2

Using the ratios you calculated in part 1, let's compare ABC Company's ratios to another firm in the same industry, XYZ Company. The two companies are located twenty-five miles away from each other and have nearly identical revenues and total asset bases. Assuming all other credit decision-making elements are identical, how would you interpret this information?

	ABC Company	**XYZ Company**
Gross Profit Margin		4%
Current Ratio		1.0
Debt to Equity		5.5:1
Return on Assets		6.5%
Return on Equity		10%
Quick Ratio		.7
Inventory Turn Over		90 days
Accounts Receivable Turnover		75 days

1. Inventory turns faster in which company?

2. Which company is converting inventory into cash faster?

3. Which company is selling more efficiently?

4. Which company is performing better?

Part 3

From a financial statement review perspective, there are some minor impacts to financial statements to consider. Note that cashflow does not change.

The following examples illustrate (in bold text) the impact of adopting the new ASC 842 accounting standard on financial statements and ratios using the ABC Company statements from Part 1.

In this scenario, under ASC 842:

- The income statement does not change, and net profit remains the same. Note that the Operating Expenses line item would include Lease Expense. Components of Lease Expense include "interest" and the amortization of the Right of Use Asset.

- The balance sheet changes with an increase in total assets and total liabilities, therefore, both the ROA and Total Liabilities to Net Worth (Debt to Equity) ratios will deteriorate.

See Chapter 2 – Financial & Tax Accounting for more information on the ASC 842 standard.

In conclusion, historically, the credit underwriter has already adjusted the financial statements for off-balance sheet obligations like operating leases. Accounting has now caught up with the credit underwriting practice. The financial statements will reflect an increase in total assets, an increase in total liabilities; however, there is no significant impact to income statement or cash flow. The impact on selected ratios like ROA, Debt to Worth (Debt to Equity), Current Ratio, and Quick Ratio is that all would deteriorate as illustrated above while all other ratios remain unchanged.

Income Statement

Net Sales	$	18,000,000
(-) Cost of Goods Sold	$	15,000,000
Gross Profit	$	3,000,000
(-) Operating Expenses (G&A)	**$**	**1,800,000** **
Operating Profit (EBIT)	$	1,200,000
Interest Expense	$	300,000
Earnings Before Tax	$	900,000
Tax Expense	$	100,000
Net Profit	$	800,000

** Under ASC 842, this line item would include Lease Expense. Components of Lease Expense include "interest" and the amortization of the Right of Use Asset.

Balance Sheet

Cash	$	1,000,000	Accounts Payable	$	1,500,000
Accounts Receivable	$	1,500,000	Notes Payable - Bank	$	1,000,000
Inventory	$	2,000,000	Current Portion LT Debt	$	500,000
Current Assets	$	4,500,000	**Current Portion - Lease Liability**	**$**	**250,000**
Fixed Assets	$	6,000,000	Current Liabilities	$	3,250,000
Right of Use Asset	**$**	**1,000,000**	**Lease Liability**	**$**	**750,000**
Other	$	500,000	Long Term Debt	$	4,000,000
			Total Liabilities	$	8,000,000
			Net Worth	$	4,000,000
Total Assets	$	12,000,000	Total Liabilities & Net Worth	$	12,000,000

Re-calculate each of the following financial ratios for ABC Company.

1. Gross Profit Margin

2. Current Ratio

3. Total Liabilities to Net Worth (Debt to Equity)

4. Return on Assets

5. Return on Equity

6. Quick Ratio

7. Inventory Turn Over

8. Accounts Receivable Turn Over

9. Compared to your answers in part 1, which of the ratios changed?

Answers

Part 1: Calculate Ratios for ABC Company

1   **Gross Profit Margin** calculated as:

$$\frac{Gross\ Profit\ on\ Sales}{Net\ Sales}$$

For this example:

$$\frac{\$3,000,000}{\$18,000,000} = \mathbf{16.7\%}$$

2   **Current Ratio** calculated as:

$$\frac{Current\ Assets}{Current\ Liabilities}$$

For this example:

$$\frac{\$4,500,000}{\$3,000,000} = \mathbf{1.5:1}$$

3   **Debt to Equity** calculated as:

$$\frac{Total\ Liabilities}{Net\ Worth}$$

For this example:

$$\frac{\$7,000,000}{\$4,000,000} = \mathbf{1.75:1}$$

4   **Return on Assets** calculated as:

$$\frac{Net\ Income\ After\ Tax}{Total\ Assets}$$

For this example:

$$\frac{\$800,000}{\$11,000,000} = \mathbf{7.27\%}$$

5   **Return on Equity** calculated as:

$$\frac{Net\ Income\ After\ Tax}{Net\ Worth}$$

For this example:

$$\frac{\$800,000}{\$4,000,000} = \mathbf{20\%}$$

6 **Quick Ratio** calculated as:
$$\frac{Current\ assets - Inventory}{Current\ liabilities}$$

For this example:
$$\frac{\$4,500,000 - \$2,000,000}{\$3,000,000} = .83$$

7 **Inventory Turn Over (in days)** calculated as:
$$\frac{Average\ Inventory}{Cost\ of\ Goods\ Sold} * 365$$

For this example:
$$\frac{\$2,000,000}{\$15,000,000} * 365 = 48.67\ days$$

8 **Accounts Receivable Turn Over (in days)** calculated as:
$$\frac{Average\ Accounts\ Receivable}{Net\ Sales} * 365$$

For this example:
$$\frac{\$1,500,000}{\$18,000,000} * 365 = 30.42\ days$$

9 **Strengths:** low leverage, attractive gross profit margin, adequate liquidity, acceptable ROE

Weaknesses: Inventory may be a little high, need to compare to industry averages

Part 2: Compare ABC Company and XYZ Company

Ratios	ABC Company	XYZ Company
Gross Profit Margin	16.67%	4%
Current Ratio	1.5	1
Debt to Equity	1.75	5.5
Return on Assets	7.27%	6.5%
Return on Equity	20%	10%
Quick Ratio	.83	.7
Inventory Turn Over (in days)	48.67 days	90 days

Accounts Receivable Turnover (in days)	30.42 days	75 days

1. Inventory turns faster in which company? ABC Company
2. Which company is converting inventory into cash faster? ABC Company
3. Which company is selling more efficiently? ABC Company
4. Which company is doing better? ABC Company

Part 3: Illustrating ASC 842 Impact

1   **Gross Profit Margin** calculated as:

$$\frac{Gross\ Profit\ on\ Sales}{Net\ Sales}$$

For this example:
$$\frac{\$3,000,000}{\$18,000,000} = \mathbf{16.7\%}$$

2   **Current Ratio** calculated as:

$$\frac{Current\ Assets}{Current\ Liabilities}$$

For this example:
$$\frac{\$4,500,000}{\$3,250,000} = \mathbf{1.38 : 1}$$

3   **Debt to Equity** calculated as:

$$\frac{Total\ Liabilities}{Net\ Worth}$$

For this example:
$$\frac{\$8,000,000}{\$4,000,000} = \mathbf{2 : 1}$$

4   **Return on Assets** calculated as:

$$\frac{Net\ Income\ After\ Tax}{Total\ Assets}$$

For this example:
$$\frac{\$800,000}{\$12,000,000} = \mathbf{6.67\%}$$

5   **Return on Equity** calculated as:

$$\frac{Net\ Income\ After\ Tax}{Net\ Worth}$$

For this example:

$$\frac{\$800,000}{\$4,000,000} = \mathbf{20\%}$$

6   **Quick Ratio** calculated as:

$$\frac{Current\ assets - Inventory}{Current\ liabilities}$$

For this example:

$$\frac{\$4,500,000 - \$2,000,000}{\$3,250,000} = .77$$

7   **Inventory Turn Over (in days)** calculated as:

$$\frac{Average\ Inventory}{Cost\ of\ Goods\ Sold} * 365$$

For this example:

$$\frac{\$2,000,000}{\$15,000,000} * 365 = \mathbf{48.67\ days}$$

8   **Accounts Receivable Turn Over (in days)** calculated as:

$$\frac{Average\ Accounts\ Receivable}{Net\ Sales} * 365$$

For this example:

$$\frac{\$1,500,000}{\$18,000,000} * 365 = \mathbf{30.42\ days}$$

9   Because the total assets and total liabilities increase, the following ratios will change in comparison to the previous calculations.
Current Ratio
Debt to Equity
Return on Assets
Quick Ratio

Appendix 5 Current Expected Credit Loss Model

Following the financial crisis of 2007-2008 in an effort to reduce the risk of a similar crisis, the FASB decided to revisit how banks estimate losses in their allowance for loan and lease losses (ALLL) calculations. On June 16, 2016, FASB issued Accounting Standards Update No. 2016-13 introducing the Current Expected Credit Loss (CECL) standard. In November 2018, FASB amended the standard which extended the implementation timing for nonpublic companies[38].

The basis for the current model is "incurred losses" whereby an investment is considered impaired when there is an assumption that future cash flows will no longer be collected in-full under original contract terms. This will be replaced by the new model, CECL.

Under the new model, all financial institutions that lend money or lease equipment will be required to utilize a combination of historical information, current conditions, and reasonable forecasts to estimate expected credit loss over the life of a loan; furthermore, they will need to maintain sufficient loss reserves to cover expected future credit losses.

It is important to note that this is an accounting rule applicable to any business that has financial statements, and not a government regulation.

Overview

ASC 326 provides new guidance on Current Expected Credit Losses (CECL). This FASB pronouncement establishes the process by which a lessor calculates the bad debt losses it expects to incur on the leases and loans it originates. The CECL on every new transaction must be shown as a loss on the income statement and an offset to the lessor's net investment in leases and loans on the balance sheet.

This offset, or contra-account, is known as the allowance for credit losses. The allowance, when netted against the net investment in a financial asset, results in what is referred to as the net carrying value of the asset. The net carrying value represents the amount the lessor expects to actually collect on its financial asset.

---

[38] FASB Accounting Standards Update No. 2018-19 https://www.fasb.org

Prior accounting guidance generally allowed delaying recognition of the full amount of credit losses until the loss was probable of occurring. The CECL rules eliminate the 'probable' approach to bad debt recognition, by requiring companies to currently recognize their estimate of all expected credit losses. The lessor generally only considered past events, such as historical loss experience, and current conditions when establishing the expected credit loss under prior rules. CECL expands the analysis greatly beyond historical loss experience.

In ASC 326, the measurement of expected credit losses is based on information about past events, including historical experience, current conditions, and reasonable and supportable forecasts of events that may affect the collectability of the receivables. Judgment must be used in determining the required information, along with estimation methods that are appropriate and relevant to the lessor's circumstances.

Implementation Timing

Implementation timing depends on company type.

Implementation was required for public business entities that meet the definition of a Securities and Exchange Commission (SEC) filer, for fiscal years beginning after December 15, 2019, including interim periods within those fiscal years.

Implementation Delay[39]

On November 15, 2019, the Financial Accounting Standards Board (FASB) issued Accounting Standard Update (ASU) 2019-10 delaying the effective date for the Current Expected Credit Losses (CECL) standard, Accounting Standard Update 2016-13. The ASU extends the effective dates of CECL for smaller public business entities and nonpublic business entities.

The FASB pushed back the effective date of CECL from January 2021 to January 2023 for smaller reporting companies as defined by the SEC and from January 2022 to January 2023 for nonpublic companies. The determination of smaller reporting companies shall be based on the entity's most recent determination as of November 15, 2019. The SEC defines a small reporting company as one with public float of less than $250 million or annual revenue of less than $100 million and either no public float or a public float of less than $700 million.

Cross-Functional Implications

Because of the change to forward-looking, as opposed to purely historical, performance data, lessors will now have to identify and capture a variety of inputs, some of which may be new. The CECL process, although involving

---

[39] Source: Delay for CECL Effective Date - Eide Bailly LLP.
https://www.eidebailly.com/insights/articles/2019/7/delay-proposed-for-cecl-effective-date

credit, asset management and other functions within the company, is primarily an accounting responsibility.

CECL implementation challenges reach beyond finance and accounting with potential impact for other functional disciplines, such as:

- finance and accounting
- credit/risk
- portfolio management
- information technology
- asset management
- analytics

Since the boundary lines for owning the implementation are somewhat blurred, implementing this standard will require a team approach.

The level of impact will vary by institution, credit type, and tenor. Transactions with worse rated credits and with longer-tenors will be impacted more than shorter-term ones. From a transactional standpoint, the scope of impact includes all financial instruments such as loans, leases, bonds, trade receivables, and off-balance sheet exposures such as letters of credit.

For accounting and finance, the new standard will, in most if not all cases, lead to increases in credit reserves and provisioning requirements. Due to historical data requirements, audit requirements may also increase as time goes on.

From a credit risk standpoint, CECL brings a strategic portfolio level impact. How are the expected losses going to impact the big picture? CECL is sometimes described as a "gold standard of credit risk" because it requires a significant shift in thinking from an incurred loss model perspective to expected loss over the life of a transaction. Note the Probability of Default is equally relevant.

From a portfolio management perspective, the anticipated increase in the cost of doing business as well as the added expense to comply with requirements, may discourage longer-term deals.

From a technology and data perspective, the transition to CECL is anticipated to require significantly more data as well as changes in the processes for calculating and accounting for expected losses. In addition to acquiring the technical capability to comply, the cost of tracking, extracting, and analyzing the data may also increase the costs of doing business.

Companies are likely to see an implementation impact on Day 1 with ongoing periodic adjustments and improvements to their methodology over time.

Calculation Method Considerations

FASB does not prescribe a specific implementation method and the unit of account may be the individual transaction level, or it may be pools of assets with similar risk characteristics. Loss forecasting methods may be top-down, a portfolio-level estimation or bottom-up, a transaction level loss estimation.

Regardless of approach selected, the change in methodology from incurred losses to expected losses will require historical loss data, preferably including a full economic cycle.

"While CECL will be something of a burden for everyone, there is a substantial silver lining in better understanding expected loss."

~Thomas E. Ware

CECL At-A-Glance[40]

Who? Applies to all lenders of all types, banks, independents, captives.

What? New accounting requirements to forecast all future losses on current portfolio.

When? Fiscal years starting 12/16/2019 for SEC filers; others implementation is delayed (see Implementation Delay section above)

Where? FASB's CECL applies in the United States. Abroad, IASB's IFRS-9 applies.

Why? Many lenders did not adequately reserve for losses going into the last recession.

How? A wide variety of methods are permitted.

Impact? FASB's chair expects CECL to increase loss reserves 15% to 50%. upon initial implementation

---

[40] Source: CECL: The New FASB Requirements for Loss Accounting by Thomas E. Ware, Equipment Leasing & Finance Magazine May/June 2018 and elay for CECL Effective Date - Eide Bailly LLP. https://www.eidebailly.com/insights/articles/2019/7/delay-proposed-for-cecl-effective-date

Appendix 6 Resources

The Certified Lease & Finance Professional Designation

The designation of Certified Lease & Finance Professional (CLFP™) sets the standard for professionalism in the commercial equipment leasing and finance industry. This prestigious and coveted designation is designed to identify and recognize those individuals within the profession who have demonstrated, through experience, testing and conduct, their competency in equipment leasing and financing. The letters "CLFP" behind their name represents a visible recognition of this professional achievement and status.

Certification Requirements and Eligibility

1. A minimum three years of verifiable equipment leasing and financing experience (one year may be substituted with acceptable financial experience not in the commercial equipment finance industry)

2. Completion of the required application to become a CLFP.

3. Pledge, in writing, to adhere to the Standards of Professional Conduct.

4. Acceptable character, ability and reputation.

5. Successfully complete the CLFP examination.

The Certified Lease & Finance Professional Associate Designation

While continuing to maintain the current high levels of competency, standards of professionalism and conduct required for CLFP designation, it is our goal to identify the younger professional who wants to attain the CLFP Associate designation, while still meeting our current 3-year time in the industry requirement for full certification. Toward that goal, we have identified the CLFP Associate Program for the individual who is motivated to participate in the education needed and sit for the exam prior to reaching the 3-year threshold.

As a candidate wishes to enter this early program they can do so under the following guidelines:

- Candidate must provide the name of an equipment finance industry professional referring the candidate.

- Candidate must meet the CLFP requirements and eligibility as stated above for the CLFP designation.

- Upon passing the required exam, the candidate will receive a designation as a CLFP Associate and will automatically qualify, subject to continued good standing as related to Standards and Ethics, renewals, and payment of annual dues, for their CLFP designation at their 3-year anniversary in the industry.

Standards of Professional Conduct

A CLFP and CLFP Associate will consent, in writing, to adhere to the Standards of Professional Conduct and the CLFP Pledge.

CLFP Standards of Professional Conduct

- A Certified Lease & Finance Professional will always strive to conduct all business dealings in an honest, ethical, and professional manner.

- A Certified Lease & Finance Professional will respect ownership of funds delivered as advanced fees or security deposits and will treat in a fiduciary capacity all funds received in that capacity.

- A Certified Lease & Finance Professional will strive to constantly gain additional education to improve his/her professional competency and will work to promote education and integrity within the leasing industry.

- A Certified Lease & Finance Professional will never knowingly make false or misleading statements to his/her employer, employees, customers, vendors, brokers or funding sources.

- A Certified Lease & Finance Professional will never be involved in fraudulent activities.

- A Certified Lease & Finance Professional will act in a leadership role in the industry and always be held to the highest standards of conduct applicable to the industry.

Upon achieving CLFP certification there are ongoing requirements to maintain the elite status as a CLFP in Good Standing. Attaining the CLFP accreditation is a lifetime achievement, however the designation is not perpetual; every year a CLFP is required to recertify. Recertification is a process in which CLFPs read about changes pertinent to the industry for the year and then complete a quiz regarding that material. Recertification can be completed online, and reexamination is not required.

Please visit www.CLFPFoundation.org for additional information.

Appendix 7 Industry Associations

AACFB
326 East Main Street
Louisville, KY 40202
P: 800-996-2352 • F: 877-875-4750
www.aacfb.org • info@aacfb.org

American Association of Commercial Finance Brokers

The American Association of Commercial Finance Brokers (AACFB) is the premier trade association empowering independent commercial finance professionals and their funding source partners. The AACFB represents the expanding interests of its growing membership by providing best practice education and funding partner networks, while promoting a culture of ethics.

Member benefits include:
- 24/7 Access to Funding Sources
- Members Only Online Community
- Annual Conferences & Expo
- Educational Programs & Resources
- Best Practices & Ethics Certifications
- Group Pricing for Discounted Credit Reports, Office Depot, UPS Shipping, and more
- Limited Free Legal Counsel
- Association Quarterly Newsletters and News Updates

Cindy Downs
President-Elect (2020-2021)
Heartland Capital Group, LLC
(701) 356-3002
cdowns@heartlandcg.net

Carrie Radloff, CLFP
President-Elect (2020-2021)
American Financial Partners
(507) 828-1039
carrie@FinanceWithAFP.com

Monica Harper
Executive Director
(800) 996-2352
mharper@hqtrs.com

Natasha Pitcock
Dir. of Membership &
Programs
(800) 996-2352
npitcock@hqtrs.com

Equipment Leasing and Finance
Association
1625 Eye Street NW, Suite 850
Washington, DC 20006
P: 202-238-3400 • F: 202-238-3401
www.elfaonline.org

Equipment Leasing and Finance Association

The Equipment Leasing and Finance Association (ELFA) is the trade association representing companies in the $900 billion equipment finance sector. Member companies include the nation's largest financial services companies and manufacturers, as well as small and medium independent finance companies and small and regional community banks throughout the country. Our mission is to provide member companies with a platform to promote and advocate for the industry, including attracting and developing new and diverse talent; a forum for professional development and training; and a resource that develops information about, and for, the industry.

ELFA is the only association with a wide range of benefits specialized for the equipment leasing and finance industry. Join today and:

- Grow and solidify relationships with other equipment leasing and financial services companies
- Exchange advice on best practices with industry experts
- Operate in a more favorable environment through ELFA's federal and state advocacy efforts
- Acquire information about changes to lease accounting and their impact on your business
- Participate in industry surveys and share feedback on the latest market statistics, trends and innovations
- Access ELFA Information Central, a member help desk for business and industry information
- Learn strategies for pursuing your business objectives at business and professional development events and learn best practices at in-person and online training courses and workshops
- Invest in the future of the industry by serving on governing, policy and business-sector committees
- Access diversity and inclusion resources through the Emerging Talent Advisory Council, Women's Council and Equality Committee
- Stay connected to industry news and colleagues through award-winning publications

To learn more about the value of ELFA membership, visit www.elfaonline.org/membership.

Questions? Email membership@elfaonline.org.

National Equipment Finance
Association
P.O. Box 69; Northbrook, IL 60065
P: 847-380-5050 • F: 847-380-5055
www.NEFAssociation.org

National Equipment Finance Association

The **National Equipment Finance Association (NEFA)** is a national association serving small- to mid-size independent equipment finance companies, bank-owned leasing companies, lessors, brokers and various service providers focused on the equipment finance industry. NEFA's history dates back over thirty years through its predecessor organizations, the United Association of Equipment Leasing (UAEL) and the Eastern Association of Equipment Lessors (EAEL). Today, NEFA is a strong and diverse association offering exceptional networking opportunities and various industry resources to members and the equipment finance industry.

The mission of NEFA is to provide a forum for members to pursue personal and professional growth, create an environment of ethical behavior, promote industry advocacy, provide premier networking opportunities and educational programs, and encourage association involvement. NEFA provides a range of benefits specifically structured to meet the needs of professionals in the equipment finance industry. Join NEFA today to take full advantage of the association's many valuable offerings including:

- Two multi-day conferences each year, the National Equipment Finance Summit and the Funding Symposium.
- Multiple regional networking events held throughout the U.S.
- Educational programs
- Monthly Virtual Exchange Webinar Series and Networking Events
- Increased brand visibility via the NEFA Partner Program
- Industry-focused website at www.NEFAssociation.org
- Bi-monthly association magazine, *Newsline* magazine
- Online membership directory
- Committee, volunteer and industry leadership opportunities

Chad Sluss
Executive Director / CEO
csluss@NEFAssociation.org

Blair Dawson
VP – Marketing & Programs
bdawson@NEFAssociation.org

Steve Elworth
Director of Membership & Sponsorship
selworth@NEFAssociation.org

Glossary

Absolute Value: In contrast to Relative Value, Absolute Value looks only at the asset's intrinsic value and does not compare to other assets.

Accelerated Cost Recovery System (ACRS): ACRS is a system of rapid depreciation of the costs of most assets for federal income taxation. The Economic Recovery Tax Act of 1981 created ACRS. ACRS was modified under the Tax Reform Act of 1986 establishing depreciation methods for each ACRS class, depending on the Asset Depreciation Range (ADR) class life.

Accelerated Depreciation: A depreciation method, usually for tax purposes, in which an asset's cost can be deducted in a faster manner than straight-line depreciation, allowing the owner of the asset to take more depreciation in the earlier years of an asset's life and less depreciation in the later years.

Acceleration Clause: A provision in a financial instrument, which provides that the occurrence of a default by one party makes that party's outstanding balance to the other party immediately due and payable.

Accounts Payable: Amounts owed by a business to its creditors.

Accounts Receivable: Amounts owed a business by its debtors. The term is usually used in reference to amounts owed by customers.

Accrual Basis: A method of accounting that shows expenses as incurred and income as earned even though such expenses and income have yet to be actually paid or received.

Accrual Basis Accounting: A method of accounting that recognizes revenues and expenses when the transaction is incurred. Thus, income is recognized when earned (a good is delivered or a service provided) and expenses are recorded when incurred. Accrual basis accounting employs the matching principal, where revenue is recorded in the same period (matched) as its related expenses.

Accrued Expenses: Expenses incurred but not yet paid.

Acid Test: The ratio between current assets (less inventory) and current liabilities as shown on a balance sheet. This test provides some indication of a party's liquidity. (Also, known as the "quick ratio").

Acknowledgment: A formal statement by a party before a notary public to the effect that they have executed a specific instrument or document.

Additional Insured: A party other than a party in whose name insurance is issued who is also protected against losses covered by such policy.

Advance Payments: One or more lease payments required to be paid to the lessor at the beginning of the lease term. A lease, commonly paid "in advance," requires the first payment up-front. The lessor can negotiate any number of additional rentals to be paid in advance with the first month's rent.

Advance Ruling: A request directed to the Internal Revenue Service, which seeks an advance ruling that a particular transaction will be recognized as a lease (or some other specific type of transaction). Such rulings have been requested in leveraged lease transactions.

After-Acquired Property Clause: A provision in a security agreement that gives the creditor a security interest in the property of the debtor acquired after the date of the security agreement. Normally found in addition to blanket lien language in a security agreement.

Agent: A person who has the legal authority to act for and represent another party in dealing with third parties.

Agreement: The bargain of the parties in fact as found in their language or by implication from other circumstances.

Allowance for Loan and Lease Losses (ALLL): ALLL is determined based on the incurred loss methodology and is an estimated loan and lease loss reserve for bad debt; it sets funds aside to cover future losses. It involves a degree of management judgment to estimate the uncollectible amounts used to reduce the book value of loans and leases to the amount that a bank expects to collect. ALLL is a credit loss reserve.[41]

Alternative Minimum Tax (AMT): A tax calculation which calls for the payment of the higher of the taxpayer's regular taxable income or an AMT liability, based on the taxpayer's preferences for the year. AMT is triggered by an event such as accelerated depreciation, thus preventing a taxpayer to

---

[41] Banking: Current Expected Credit Loss (CECL) - fas.org. https://fas.org/sgp/crs//misc/R45339.pdf

excessively reduce its tax liability. Such a taxpayer is known as an "AMT Taxpayer."

Amortization: Concerning a loan, the process of reducing a debt obligation through periodic payments. The payments usually include both an interest and principal component. In accounting terms, the spreading of the cost of an asset over its useful life for financial statement and/or tax purposes.

Appraisal: An evaluation of the value of a specific item of property, usually as conducted by a person with expertise concerning such property.

Appreciation: The increase in the value of an asset over time.

Artificial Intelligence (AI): A branch of computer science dealing with the ability of a machine to perform cognitive functions associated with human minds. Examples of AI technologies include robotics, autonomous vehicles, machine vision, language processing, virtual agents, machine learning, and deep learning.

ASC 840, 842 (Accounting Standards Codification): Formerly FASB 13 (See FASB 13)

Asset: An item of value

Asset Depreciation Range (ADR): A system for the depreciation of the costs of most assets for purposes of federal income taxation. The ADR system was substantially replaced by the ACRS system according to the Economic Recovery Tax Act of 1981 and replaced itself by MACRS in the 1986 Tax Reform Act.

Assign: To transfer or exchange future rights. In leasing, the right to receive future lease payments is usually transferred to a funding source in return for up-front cash. The up-front cash represents the loan proceeds from the funding source and is equal to the present value of the future lease payments discounted at the leasing company's cost of borrowing.

At-Risk Rules: Laws limiting the amount of losses a passive investor (usually a limited partner) can claim. Only the amount actually at risk can be deducted currently.

Attorney-in-Fact: One who has been given a power of attorney by another.

Bailment: The delivery of one's personal property to another with an obligation upon the recipient to return it. A lease is a type of bailment.

Balance Sheet: A list of one's assets and liabilities and their difference (net worth) on a precise date.

Balloon Payment: A payment on a loan that is unusually large in comparison to the other payments on the loan. A balloon payment is usually the final payment on a loan.

Bankruptcy: The financial condition of insolvency, particularly when such insolvency has resulted in the filing of a petition for reorganization or liquidation under Title 11 of the United States Code.

Bargain Purchase Option: A provision allowing the lessee, at their option, to purchase the leased property for a price sufficiently lower than the expected fair value of the property at the date the option becomes exercisable, so that exercise of the option is reasonably assured at the inception of the lease.

Bargain Renewal Option: A provision allowing the lessee, at their option, to renew the lease for a rental sufficiently lower than the fair rental of the property at the date the option becomes exercisable, so that exercise of the option is reasonably assured at the inception of the lease.

Basis: Also referred to as "Tax Basis." The original cost of an asset plus other capitalized acquisition costs such as installation charges and sales tax. Basis reflects the amount upon which depreciation charges are computed.

Basis Point: Units of 1 percent with each unit being 0.01 percent (1/100 percent (e.g., "50 basis points" is one-half of one percent).

Bill of Sale: A written document that evidences the transfer of ownership of property.

Blind Discount Program: Subsidized rate arrangements such as 0 percent financing for a customer.

Book to Tax Adjustment: The reconciliation of book and taxable income and deductions. Differences exist because of the differences between Generally Accepted Accounting Principles and tax law.

Book Value: Value according to accounting records, which may or may not be real market value.

Broker: The middleman who brings together lessors or funding sources, lessees, and vendors for the purpose of executing a transaction and who receives a commission for such service. The fee for service is known as the broker's fee.

Bundled Lease: A lease that includes many additional services such as maintenance, insurance, and property taxes that are paid for or performed by the lessor; the costs are included in the lease payments. Also referred to as a "full-service lease."

Call: The exercise of a call option.

Capital Lease: From a financial reporting perspective, a lease that has the characteristics of a purchase agreement and also meets certain criteria established by the Accounting Standards Codification (ASC 840). Such a lease is required to be shown as an asset and a related obligation on the balance sheet. Under ASC 842, it is referred to as finance lease.

Captive Lessor: A leasing company that has been set up by a manufacturer or dealer of equipment to finance the sale or lease of its own products to end-users or lessees.

Cash Basis: A method of accounting that shows expenses and income only when paid or received.

Cash Basis Accounting: A method of accounting that recognizes revenue and expenses only when the corresponding cash is received, or payments are made. Thus, you record revenue only when a customer pays for a billed product or service, and you record an expense only when it is paid by the company.

Cash Flow: Income inflows and expense outflows over a specified period.

Certificate of Insurance: A statement from an insurance company or its agent that a certain policy has been written. The certificate usually summarizes the policy's coverage.

Charge-Off: In the case of severe delinquency, a declaration by a creditor that an amount of debt is not likely to be collected.

Chattel: Personal property

Chattel Paper: A document that is a promise to pay and is either secured by personal property (such as equipment) or gives the person obligated to make payments the right to possess and use personal property.

Closing: The meeting at which all parties to a transaction sign and exchange all documents necessary to finalize the transaction.

Co-Lessee: An additional lessee to a lease. The lease will usually provide that the co-lessee is jointly and severally liable on the lease with the lessee.

Collateral: Security, usually property (real, personal, or intangible), pledged to secure the performance of an agreement.

Commercial Lease: (See Business Lease)

Commercial Term Loan: A loan agreement between a business and financial institution with a fixed maturity date and stipulated periodic payments.

Commitment Fee: A fee required by the lessor, at the time a proposal or commitment is accepted by the lessee, to lock in a specific lease rate and/or other lease term. A commitment letter is a document prepared by the lessor that details its commitment, including rate and term, to provide lease financing to the lessee. This document precedes final documentation and may or may not be subject to other conditions, such as lessor credit approval, guarantors, collateral, etc.

Common Law: The body of law developed through custom and usage as recognized and espoused by the courts.

Complaint: The plaintiff's initial, formal version of its lawsuit against a defendant.

Compound Interest: Interest computed on the sum of principal and accrued interest as of the date of computation.

Conditional Sales Contract: An arrangement in which a buyer takes possession of an item, but its title and right of repossession remains with the seller until the buyer pays the full purchase price (usually in installments). Sometimes called Conditional Sales Contract or CSC.

Consideration: The inducement to a contract; the value given for a contract. Consideration may be money, property, a promise, forbearance or any other thing, act, benefit, or value.

Contingent Rentals: The increases or decreases in lease payments that result from changes occurring subsequent to the inception of the lease in the factors (such as the amount of future use, percent of future sales) on which lease payments are based.

Continuation Statement: UCC-3 Continuation Statement is the amendment used to extend the effectiveness of a UCC-1 beyond the date which is five years after the date of its filing.

Contract: The total legal obligation, which results from an agreement.

Corporation: A company or group of people authorized to act as a single entity and recognized legally as a person. It has a continuity of existence without regard to transfers of interest in it.

Cost of Capital: The weighted-average cost of funds that a firm secures from both debt and equity sources to fund its assets.

Cost of Debt: The costs incurred by a firm to fund the acquisition of assets through the use of borrowings. The firm's cost of debt component is used in calculating the firm's overall weighted-average cost of capital.

Cost of Funds (COF): Cost of funds is the interest rate paid by financial institutions for the funds deployed in their business (the cost of borrowing).

Covenant: A promise to do something or that certain facts are true.

Cramdown: In the case of bankruptcy, the judge can often force the creditors to accept a reorganization plan in which the lender's recovery will be limited to the fair market value of the collateral – not the agreed loan repayment. This is only true for loans and leases intended as security, not true leases.

Credit: A tax incentive that allows taxpayers to subtract the amount of the credit they have accrued from the total tax they owe.

Credit Line: The total amount of credit a financial institution makes available to one of its debtors.

Cross-Border Leasing: The providing of leasing or financing by a funder in one country for a lessee or borrower in another country. Such transactions are subject to each country's applicable tariffs.

Current Assets: Assets, which are readily converted into cash.

Current Expected Credit Loss (CECL): The new accounting standard to forecast all future losses on the current portfolio.

Current Liabilities: Liabilities, which must be satisfied within one year.

Current Ratio: The ratio of current assets to current liabilities.

Customer Information Program (CIP): Customer due diligence process which may include various background checks and verification to comply with applicable regulations and internal company policies. Also referred to as Know Your Customer (KYC) or Know Your Client (KYC).

Customer Relationship Management System (CRM): A system of record for tracking interactions and activities with contacts, prospects, leads, and accounts. This data allows you to track your sales pipeline.

Debt: Money that is owed or due.

Deduction: An expense applied against income, primarily to arrive at taxable income. Deductions are generally limited to items that are ordinary and necessary to operating a business.

Defeased: A debt is considered defeased when a borrower deposits enough cash into a pledged or restricted account to service the borrower's debt.

Defendant: A party who must defend a lawsuit.

Delivery and Acceptance Certificate (D&A): A document that is signed by the lessee to acknowledge that the equipment to be leased has been delivered and is acceptable. Many lease agreements state that the actual lease term commences once the D&A is signed. (Also referred to as Certificate of Delivery and Acceptance).

Depreciation: A means for a firm to recover the cost of a purchased asset, over time, through periodic deductions or offsets in income. Depreciation is used in both a financial reporting and tax context and is considered a tax benefit because the depreciation deductions cause a reduction in taxable income, thereby lowering a firm's tax liability.

Direct Financing Lease: A lease classification per ASC 842 for a lessor. If a transaction meets the classification criteria for a sales-type lease and the 90% test is passed because there is a residual guarantee from an unrelated third-party, it is classified as a direct financing lease.

Discount Rate: A certain interest rate that is used to bring a series of future cash flows to their present value to state them in current, or today's dollars.

Discounted Lease: A lease in which the lessor assigns the payment stream to a funding source in return for the immediate payment of the present value of the stream of payments assigned.

Dividend: 1) The profits of a corporation as distributed to a shareholder. 2) A share of a fund.

Drop to Paper: In the context of e-titles, this is a process that converts the electronic document to a paper document for purposes of transfer.

Early Buyout Option (EBO): A lease containing an option for the lessee to pay off the lease and buy the equipment for a premium at a specified point during the contract term; sometimes called Early Payoff Option (EPO).

Early Termination: The termination of a lease before the end of its original term.

EFA: See Equipment Finance Agreement

EL: Expected Loss

End-of-Term Options: Options stated in the lease agreement that gives the lessee flexibility in its treatment of the leased equipment at the end of the lease term. Common options include purchasing the equipment, renewing the lease, or returning the equipment to the lessor. Options are sometimes given as an amendment to the lease documents and are not made part of the actual lease document. They may be a fixed dollar amount, a percentage of equipment cost, or fair market value.

Equal Credit Opportunity Act (ECOA): A law that applies to any person who, in the course of business, regularly participates in credit decisions and includes banks, finance companies, and credit unions.

Equipment Finance Agreement (EFA): An agreement, which resembles the structure of a finance lease, but provides for the lender/secured party to lend the obligor/borrower an amount for the purchase of specified equipment. Usually, the lender pays the obligor's vendor invoice for the equipment and establishes its security interest by filing a lien against the collateral.

Equipment Trust: A trust established for the purpose of purchasing and/or owning equipment for lease. Such trusts are utilized in the leasing of major capital assets such as aircraft, ships, and railcars.

Equity (Investor): An ownership interest in a business or property.

Estimated Economic Life of Leased Property: At the inception of the lease, the estimated remaining period during which the property is expected to be economically usable for its intended purpose by one or more users. The economic life is affected by such factors as technological changes, normal deterioration, and physical usage. Judgments regarding these matters are influenced by knowledge gained from previous experience. The estimated period is not limited by the lease term.

Executory Costs: Those costs such as insurance, maintenance, and taxes incurred for the leased property, whether paid by the lessor or lessee. Amounts paid by a lessee as consideration for a guarantee from an unrelated third party of the residual value are also executory costs. If the lessor pays executory costs, any lessor's profit on those costs is considered the same as executory costs.

Exemption Certificate: A document that certifies that a party to a transaction subject to sales tax is exempted from sales tax liability under certain specified circumstances. The most common exemption is for equipment being acquired for lease or resale.

Expected Loss: The calculation used by bank lessors as part of the collateral assessment of risk for large-ticket transactions. %PD * LGD * EAD = Expected Loss

Exposure at Default (EAD): Exposure at Default is part of the calculation to determine Expected Loss for large-ticket transactions. (Basel II requirement for bank lessors).

Factoring: The assignment by a lessee or debtor of accounts receivable to a lessor or creditor as collateral for a specified term and payment amount, resulting in liquidity, which can be used to improve cash flow or make capital equipment acquisitions.

Fair Market Value: The value of a piece of equipment if the equipment were to be sold in a transaction determined at arm's length, between a willing buyer and a willing seller, for equivalent property and under similar terms and conditions. Simply, the actual market value of the leased asset.

Fair Market Value Lease (FMV): A lease containing an option for the lessee to purchase leased property at the end of the lease term at its then fair market value.

Fair Value of Leased Property: The price the property could be sold for in an arm's length transaction between unrelated parties.

- Normal selling price, net of volume or trade discounts, for a lessor who is a manufacturer or dealer.

- Cost, net of volume or trade discounts for a lessor that is not a manufacturer or dealer (if the item has been held for a significant period, fair value is determined in light of prevailing market conditions). Thus, fair value may be greater or less than the cost or carrying amount of the property.

Farm Credit System: A cooperative network of agricultural borrowers that are governed by stockholders and directors. It was established by Congress in 1916 to provide a reliable source of credit for the nation's farmers and ranchers.

FASB 13: Statement of Financial Accounting Standards No. 13 issued by the Financial Accounting Standards Boards. This statement set forth the generally accepted accounting procedures for lessor and lessee accounting and financial statement reporting. The statement established criteria by which leases were classified as either a capital lease or an operating lease and is now replaced by ASC 842.

Finance Lease: Finance lease is a term used in many forms. As most frequently used, a net lease, which has as its purpose in the financing of the use of the property for a major portion of the property's useful life. The term is typically used in reference to leases written by third-party lessors. The term is often confusingly used to refer to a conditional sale in the form of a lease transaction. Finally, the term is a specified lease classification type under ASC 842

Financing Statement: Notice of security interest filed under the UCC. Under Revised Article 9 of the UCC, it is filed with the secretary of state in the state in which the lessee is incorporated.

FMV Lease Option: An FMV option provides that at the end of the lease, a determination is made as to the then-value of the equipment, at which point the lessee is given an opportunity to purchase it for that amount. Normally, a pure FMV is indicative of a true lease but the presence of the option does not necessarily ensure a finding that it is a true lease.

Forbearance: The action of refraining from exercising a legal right, especially enforcing the payment of a debt. "Forbearance." Merriam-Webster.com. Merriam-Webster, n.d. Web. 5 Mar. 2018.

Forbearance Agreements: Similar to extensions, used allow a lessee some "breathing room." In many cases, the lessor may require a change to the terms of the lease (rate, collateral, additional guarantors, etc.) to agree to forbearance.

Forced Liquidation Value (FLV): Forced Liquidation Value (FLV) is the amount of money that a company will receive if it sold its assets in an auction immediately. The idea behind this forced liquidation value is to get an estimate of the financial position of the company in the worst possible situation and circumstance. The basis for FLV is the assumption that the business will sell its assets in the quickest time possible, which will usually lead to a low price.

Foreign Sales Corporation (FSC): Under the U.S. Internal Revenue Code, a Foreign Sales Corporation (FSC) was a type of tax device that allowed companies to receive a reduction in U.S. federal income tax for profits derived from exports.

Full Payment Lease: (See Full Payout Lease)

Full Payout Lease: A lease in which the lessor recovers, through the lease payments, all costs incurred in the lease plus an acceptable rate of return, without any reliance upon the leased property's future residual value.

Full-Service Lease: (See Bundled Lease)

Funding Audit: A critical step in the final examination of the executed contract document package before funding an equipment lease or equipment finance transaction.

Funding Source: A party who provides financing for a lease transaction. Brokers frequently use the term in reference to lessors, but lessors can also use it in referring to those parties who provide lessors with the funds they use to purchase equipment.

Funds Transfer Pricing (FTP): Funds transfer pricing (FTP) is a method used to individually measure how much each source of funding is contributing to overall profitability. The FTP process is most often used in the banking industry as a means of outlining the areas of strength and weakness within the funding of the institution.

GAAP: Generally Accepted Accounting Principles: The accounting principles used in the preparation of financial statements as outlined in FASB.

Good Faith: Honest intention and action

Gross Investment: The aggregate of the minimum lease payments receivable by a lessor under a capital lease and any unguaranteed residual value accruing to the lessor.

Gross Lease: (See Service Lease)

Guarantor: One who is obligated on a guaranty agreement.

Guaranty: An agreement to answer for the debt or obligation of another if that other party fails to pay or perform.

Half Open-End Lease: (See Partial Open-End Lease)

Half-Year Convention: Half-year convention is a depreciation method that treats all property acquired during the year as being acquired exactly in the middle of the year meaning that only half of the full year of depreciation is allowed in the first year, with the remaining balance deducted in the final year of the schedule.

Half-Year Convention Taxpayer: A taxpayer who must use the half-year convention in computing its MACRS deductions because it does not place more than 40 percent of its property into service during the last quarter of its tax year.

Harvest Plan: In agricultural lending, this refers to a structure where an entity borrows money early in the year and skips several months before making an annual payment.

Hell-Or-High-Water Clause: Lessee must make rental payments for the equipment irrespective of any claim it may have against the lessor and without setoff.

Implicit Interest Rate: The discount rate that equates the present value of the minimum lease payments and any unguaranteed residual to the fair value of the leased property, minus any investment tax credit retained by the lessor.

Incremental Borrowing Rate: The rate that, at the inception of the lease, the lessee would have incurred to borrow, under like terms, the funds necessary to purchase the leased asset.

Indemnification: To indemnify (compensate for damage or loss) and hold lessor fully harmless from and against any such claim, including all costs of defense and attorney fees.

Indemnify: To reimburse another for a loss.

Indemnity: An agreement to reimburse another for a loss.

Independent Lessor: A type of leasing company that is independent of a vendor or manufacturer and, as such, purchases equipment from various unrelated manufacturers or dealers. The equipment is then leased to the end-user or lessee. This type of lessor may also be called a third-party lessor.

Initial Direct Costs (IDC): Only those costs incurred by the lessor that are 1) costs to originate a lease incurred in transactions with independent third parties that a) result directly from and are essential to acquiring that lease and b) would not have been incurred had that lease financing transaction not occurred; and 2) certain costs directly related to specified activities performed by the lessor for that lease.

Installment Credit: A type of credit that has a fixed number of payments, in contrast to revolving credit.

Installment Loan: Any loan, the terms of which call for regular or irregular periodic payments, the sum of which will repay the debt and interest.

Insurance Binder: A temporary document used as proof of insurance and confirmation that the customer has applied to purchase an insurance policy.

Interest: A charge for the use of money.

Interim Rent: A charge for the use of equipment from delivery date until the base term of the lease commences. The use of interim rent allows the lessor to have a common commencement date for its leases.

Internal Rate of Return (IRR): The unique discount rate that equates to the present value of cash flows (i.e., lease payments, purchase option) to the present value of the cash outflows (equipment or investment cost). The IRR is the most common method used to compute yields.

Internal Revenue Service (IRS): Applicable rulings to the leasing industry worth noting are IRS Revenue Ruling (RR) 55-540 (1955) and Revenue Procedure (RP) 75-21. Both relate to how the IRS treats a lease for tax purposes, that is, whether it is a lease summarized by the conditions described as necessary for a lease. RP 75-21 addresses the same issue, but from the lessor's viewpoint. This procedure, which came twenty years after RR 55-540, defines in detail the requirements which must be met with for a transaction to be construed a true tax lease. They are:

- The lessor must have 20 percent minimum at-risk investment in the property at the inception, during and at the end of the lease term.
- The exercise price of any lessee purchase option must not be less than the fair market value.
- The lessee may not make an investment in the lease, nor can it lend to the lessor any purchase money or guarantee any lessor loans.
- The value of the property's original cost and the useful life of the property at the end of the lease term must be equal to the greater of (a) one year or (b) 20 percent of the originally estimated useful life.
- The lessor must have positive cash flow and a profit from the transaction independent of tax benefits.

Investment Tax Credit (ITC): A credit against taxes otherwise due from a taxpayer under the Internal Revenue Code. The credit is generally computed as a percentage of the costs of certain types of assets. (See IRC Sections 38 and 46-50). The Tax Reform Act of 1986 effectively repealed the ITC for newly acquired property.

Invoice Factoring: This product is also called accounts receivable financing, invoice financing, or factoring. It doesn't involve any financing; instead, this solution accelerates the cash flow of the business in exchange for a slight discount on the face value of the invoice.

Joint and Several: Joint and several liability is defined: "A liability involving two or more parties in which each party is liable individually and independently as well as together."

Know Your Customer (KYC): Customer due diligence process which may include various background checks and verification to comply with applicable regulations and internal company policies. Also referred to as Know Your Client (KYC) or Customer Information Program (CIP).

Landlord Waiver: A document in which a landlord acknowledges that certain property on its tenant's premises is owned by a third-party (the lessor) and is leased to the tenant and in which a landlord agrees to recognize and not interfere with the lessor's rights respecting the lessor's property.

Lease: A transaction in which use and possession of, but not title to, tangible personal property is transferred for consideration.

Lease (Tax Definition): A transaction in which the lessor is the owner of the equipment and receives tax benefits of ownership, including depreciation and tax credits. The lessee may claim the lease payment as an operating expense deduction in exchange for its right to use the asset.

Lease Agreement: The contractual agreement between the lessor and the lessee that sets forth all the terms and conditions of the lease.

Lease Broker: An entity that provides one or more services in the lease transaction but does not retain the lease transaction for its own portfolio. Such services include finding the lessee, working with the equipment manufacturer or dealer, securing debt financing for the lessor to use in purchasing the equipment, and locating the ultimate lessor or equity participant in the lease transaction. The lease broker may also be referred to as a packager or syndicator.

Lease Intended as Security: A transaction in which the form is a lease, but the substance is a conditional sales contract or a loan with a security agreement on the property. (sometimes called Lease Intended for Security)

Lease Line: A committed amount by a funding source, which is used by a lessor to acquire equipment for lease to a lessee.

Lease Origination: The process of uncovering, developing, and consummating lease transactions. Steps in the process could include, but are not limited to, prospecting for new lease business, pricing potential transactions, performing credit reviews, and completing the necessary documentation.

Lease Payment: The periodic payment made during the lease term. Such payments are frequently a level amount paid periodically over the lease term, but it is not uncommon for a lease to have a skip payment, or to be otherwise contoured to fit, for example, the seasonal fluctuations of a lessee's income. (Generally, leasing may provide for more creativity in this regard than a loan).

Lease Term: The fixed, non-cancelable term of the lease plus:
- The period covered by bargain renewal options;
- The period covered by a renewal when a significant penalty for failure to renew exists;

- Ordinary renewal periods if they occur during a time when the lessee continues to guarantee the lessor's debt related to the property;
- Renewal periods that precede a bargain purchase option;
- Renewal periods that are at the option of the lessor
- The lease term does not extend beyond the date a bargain purchase option becomes exercisable or beyond the useful life of the leased asset.

Lessee: The user of the equipment that is the subject of a Lease Agreement.

Lessor: The owner of the equipment that is the subject of a Lease Agreement.

Leveraged Lease: Any of several specific types of leases involving, at a minimum, a lessee, a lessor and a funding source from whom the lessor borrows a significant portion of the cost of the equipment and takes an equity position in the remainder.

Liability: An obligation that one is legally bound to satisfy.

Lien: An encumbrance upon property.

LILO: LILO stands for Lease in Lease Out which was a specific type of leveraged lease transaction where defeasance was a distinguishing feature of the lease.

Limited Liability Company (LLC): A type of business entity that came into existence during the 1990s, which consists of one or more members which may be individuals, partnerships, limited partnerships, trusts, estates, associations, corporations, other limited liability companies, or other business entities. The members of a limited liability company are afforded limited liability similar to shareholders of a corporation and have pass-through taxes comparable to a partnership.

Limited Liability Partnership (LLP): A limited liability partnership (LLP) is a partnership in which some or all partners (varies by jurisdiction) have limited liabilities. Therefore, it exhibits elements of partnerships and corporations. In an LLP, each partner is not held responsible or liable for another partner's negligence or misconduct.

Line of Credit: A pre-approved amount of borrowing allowed a debtor by a creditor.

Loan Loss Reserve Fund: Valuation reserve against total leases or loans on the balance sheet, representing the amount thought to be adequate to cover estimated losses in the portfolio. This fund may consist of actual cash from the lessor or borrowed money. When a lease or loan is charged off, it is removed from the portfolio as an earning asset and its book value is deducted from the reserve account for loan losses. Recoveries from the liquidation of collateral repossessed from the lessee are credited to the reserve account. The Tax Reform Act of 1986 disallowed the tax deduction of loan loss reserves held by banks with assets over $500 million.

Loss Given Default (LGD): Loss given default refers to the amount of money a bank or other financial institution would lose should a borrower default on loan.

Loss Payee: A party entitled to receive proceeds from an insurance settlement arising in connection with a covered casualty or loss.

Loss Reserves: Valuation reserve against total leases or loans on the balance sheet, representing the amount thought to be adequate to cover estimated losses in the portfolio. This fund may consist of actual cash from the lessor or borrowed money. When a lease or loan is charged off, it is removed from the portfolio as an earning asset, and its book value is deducted from the reserve account for loan losses. Recoveries from the liquidation of collateral repossessed from the lessee are credited to the reserve account. The Tax Reform Act of 1986 disallowed the tax deduction of loan loss reserves held by banks with assets over $500 million.

Maintenance Lease: (See Service Lease)

Machine Learning: A branch of artificial intelligence, machine learning is a data analysis method that automates analytical model building based on the idea that systems can identify patterns, learn from data, and make decisions with minimal human intervention.

Managed Services (Contract Services): A service level agreement (SLA) between a Managed Service Provider (MSP) and its client that outlines both parties' responsibilities, including which services the MSP will provide, minimum response time, and liability protection for the MSP. The contract also specifies the payment structure. Many MSPs, although not all, offer their services on a flat-fee basis, charging a flat-fee per month for each desktop or server, for example.

A managed service rental/lease is a hardware rental program that matches the MSP's Managed IT Services selling process and incorporates a standard technology stack bundled with monthly services fees. The equipment and installation are funded to the MSP up-front, and the services are billed monthly, collected from the lessee and passed through to the MSP.

Manufacturer Certificate of Origin (MCO): (See Manufacturer Statement of Origin (MSO))

Manufacturer Statement of Origin (MSO): Manufacturers Certificate of Origin (MSO) is the official document of ownership produced by the Original Equipment Manufacturer (OEM), which contains vehicle specifications and vehicle identification number. Also called Manufacturer Certificate of Origin (MCO), it serves as proof of ownership before the creation of the title.

Master Lease: A lease document, not a lease classification, that allows a lessee to obtain additional leased equipment under the same basic lease terms and conditions originally agreed to, without having to renegotiate and execute a new lease contract with the lessor.

Merchant Cash Advance (MCA): An advance on future credit card receivables with payments calculated based on the total amount to repay. It is generally a percentage based on the borrower's or merchant's credit card volume. Once the merchant takes the advance, their total credit card receivables now cease to go to the merchant and are signed over to the advance company through a process called a lockbox. The MCA company takes its predetermined amount and forwards the remainder to the merchant's bank account.

Middle Market: A nebulous term that denotes the size of the transactions in which a market is generally involved. A common designation of the middle market is for transactions between $100,000 and $2 million

Minimum Lease Payments: All payments the lessee is obligated to make under the lease agreement, except any lessee guaranteed payments in support of lessor debt and executory costs (i.e., insurance, maintenance, and taxes). Amounts included would consist of:
- Minimum rentals over the lease term.
- Lessee guarantee of the residual value. If the lessee agrees to make up any deficiency below a stated amount, the entire stated amount must be included.
- Penalties for failure to renew; however, if the related renewal period is included in the "lease term," the penalty amount is not included.
- Calculations for the lessor would also include any guarantee of the residual value or rental payments beyond the lease term by a financially capable unrelated party.

Money-Over-Money Transaction: A non-tax lease or conditional sales contract in the guise of a lease in which the title is intended to pass to the lessee at the end of the lease term.

Mortgagee Waiver: A document in which a mortgagee acknowledges that certain property on its mortgagor's premises is owned by a third party (the lessor), and is leased to the mortgagor, and in which the mortgagee agrees to recognize and not interfere with the lessor's rights respecting its property.

Municipal Lease: A lease to a municipality or other state or local government or governmental agency, which may be, but is typically not a true lease, but from which the interest earnings to the lessor are tax-exempt.

NAICS: The North American Industry Classification System (NAICS) is the standard used by federal statistical agencies in classifying business establishments for the purpose of collecting, analyzing, and publishing statistical data related to the U.S. business economy. [source: https://www.census.gov/eos/www/naics/]

Net Lease: A lease in which all costs in connection with the use of property, such as maintenance, insurance, and property taxes, are paid for separately by the lessee and are not included in the rental payment to the lessor.

Net Present Value: The total discounted value of all cash inflows and outflows from a project or investment.

Nominal Option: A purchase option that allows the lessee to purchase the equipment at the end of the lease for $1, or some other minimal payment, such that they are extremely likely to exercise the option and the lessor is unlikely to have a "meaningful residual interest." The fact that the lessor has no residual interest in the asset at the end of the term is enough to "re-characterize" it as a secured sale or financing transaction rather than a true lease. (Other names sometimes used include Nominal Purchase Option, Bargain Purchase Option, $1 Purchase Option, $1 Out, Buck Out, $101 Purchase Option, and more).

Non-Appropriation Clause: A provision in a municipal lease which addresses the contingency that the municipal lessee's governing body may not appropriate funds to pay lease payments in future fiscal years.

Non-Recourse: A type of borrowing in which the borrower (a lessor in the process of funding a lease transaction) is not at-risk for the borrowed funds. The lender expects repayment from the lessee and/or the value of the leased equipment; hence, the lender's credit decision will be based upon the creditworthiness of the lessee, as well as the expected value of the leased equipment. Lessors may be non-recourse from a credit review, but seldom does this relinquish documentation-oriented risks.

Non-Tax Lease: Any lease in which the lessee is, or will automatically become, the owner during or at the end of the lease term of the property and, therefore, is entitled to all the tax benefits of ownership.

Any lease, which in substance, is, in fact, a conditional sales contract, money-over-money transaction, purchase money security agreement, or other lease intended as security.

OEM: Original Equipment Manufacturer

Open-End Lease: A lease in which the lessee guarantees the future residual value of the property to be realized by the lessor at the end of the lease.

Operating Lease: From an accounting perspective, any lease that has the characteristics of a usage agreement, and also fails to meet any of the criteria set forth under ASC 842 for a finance lease. (See Service Lease).

Option to Purchase: A right to purchase a property at a future date; a call.

Orderly Liquidation Value (OLV): The orderly liquidation value (OLV) is typically part of an appraisal of hard tangible assets (i.e., equipment). It is an estimate of the gross amount that the tangible assets would fetch in an auction-style liquidation with the seller needing to sell the assets on an "as-is-where-is" basis. The term orderly implies that the liquidation would allow for a reasonable time to identify all available buyers and the seller would have control of the sale process.

Origination System: A system of record for lease and loan origination data from quoting to a credit application, all the way through documentation and funding. This data enables lessors and lenders to track the progress of origination pipelines across all stages of the origination lifecycle.

Paper Out: A process used for electronic documents to convert the electronic document to a paper document for the purposes of transfer.

Partial Open-End Lease: A lease in which the lessee guarantees the residual value of the property, but (as opposed to an open-end lease) does not share in any appreciation of the property.

Partnership: A business enterprise owned by two or more parties who are jointly and severally liable for all business liabilities and who share management authority.

Payments in Advance: A payment stream in which the lease payment is due at the beginning of each period during the lease.

Payments in Arrears: A payment stream in which each lease payment is due at the end of each period during the lease.

Payoff: A payoff is an amount that will retire a debt or other obligation at any given point in time. The term has commonly been used in reference to both loans and non-cancelable leases.

Personal Property: Tangible personal property as defined by IRS Section 38 and retention of right, title, and interest includes its assignment to another lessor or creditor.

Personal Property Tax: A tax on the ownership of personal property; a type of ad valorem tax imposed by certain states and their political subdivisions.

Placed in Service: In leasing, for income tax purposes, "placed in service" means in use for its intended purpose.

Plaintiff: A party who brings a lawsuit.

Pledge: A bailment of property to a creditor to secure payment of debt or performance of some obligation.

Points: One percent or one percentage point (1.00 percent); a point also represents 100 basis points.

Portfolio Characteristics: Portfolio characteristics are the data elements used in portfolio segmentation and calculation of performance indicators.

Portfolio Management System: A system of record for funded and booked leases and loans. It tracks the transaction, asset, and customer account data for the life of the transaction. This data serves as a key input for portfolio monitoring, billing, collecting, customer service, and asset and end of lease management. Many other terms may be used for this including Accounting and Servicing System, Lease Management System, Lease Accounting System, or Servicing Platform.

Portfolio Performance Indicators: Statistical measurements used to compare historical norms to business goals and identify trends in a portfolio.

Portfolio Segmentation: Segmentation is the division of the portfolio and market data into subsets or groupings consisting of specific characteristics and concentrations for further analysis. Each lessor approaches market and portfolio segmentation in a manner that fits their particular company strategy. There are numerous varieties in approach to segmentation, for example, a company may segment by industry, by company size, by number of employees, by revenue, or by number of assets on lease.

Power of Attorney (POA): This is written authorization to act on behalf of another for specified actions.

Present Value: The discounted value of a payment or stream of payments to be received in the future, taking into consideration a specific interest or discount rate. The present value represents a series of future cash flows expressed in today's dollars.

Principal: The amount borrowed or the superior authority in a relationship.

Probability of Default (PD): The probability of default provides an estimate of the likelihood that a borrower will be unable to repay debt obligations.

Progress Payments: Payments required by an equipment vendor or manufacturer before delivery of equipment to be leased. The progress payments lessen the outlay necessary for the vendor to purchase the equipment or the manufacturer to build the equipment and it adds an economic penalty if an order is canceled mid-stream.

Proprietorship: A business enterprise owned by one person who is directly liable for all business liabilities.

Purchase Money Security Interest (PMSI): A security interest in a property to secure the payment of the purchase price of the property.

Purchase Option: An option in the lease agreement that allows the lessee to purchase the leased equipment at the end of the lease term for either a fixed amount or at the future fair market value of the leased equipment.

Purchase Order: An offer for the purchase of an item of property. The purchase order will normally specify the terms and conditions under which the buyer is willing to make the purchase; when accepted by the seller it becomes the purchase contract.

Purchase Upon Termination (PUT): An agreement between the lessor and lessee wherein the lessee agrees to buy, and the lessor agrees to sell, the leased equipment for a predetermined amount upon termination of the lease.

PUT Agreement: A Purchase Upon Termination agreement is between the lessor and lessee wherein the lessee agrees to buy, and the lessor agrees to sell, the leased equipment for a predetermined amount.

Quick Ratio: The ratio between current assets (less inventory) and current liabilities as shown on a balance sheet. Also referred to as the acid test. This test indicates a party's liquidity.

Recourse: A type of borrowing in which the borrower (a lessor funding a lease) is fully at risk to the lender for repayment of the obligation. The recourse borrower (lessor) is required to make payments to the lender whether or not the lessee fulfills its obligations under the lease agreement. Recourse borrowing arrangements may, or may not, take the underlying lease payment stream into account. It is not unusual where repayment is based on equal principal plus interest.

Relative Value (RV): Relative value is a method of determining an asset's value that takes into account the value of similar assets.

Remarketing: The process of selling or leasing the leased equipment to another party upon termination of the original lease term or default by the lessee. The lessor can remarket the equipment or contract with another party, such as the manufacturer, to remarket the equipment in exchange for lease renewal payments.

Remarketing Agreement: An agreement where the vendor manages or assists in the remarketing of assets upon a lessee's default.

Renewal Option: An option in the lease agreement that allows the lessee to extend the lease term for an additional period beyond the expiration of the initial lease term in exchange for lease renewal payments.

Rental: A periodic lease payment. A lease whose non-cancelable term is less than a year (by the hour, day, month).

Rental Agreement: A short service lease, usually less than 12 months in duration.

Replevin Action: A lawsuit seeking an order from a judge requiring the lessee to surrender the equipment at a certain date, time, and place, or face additional legal action.

Repurchase Agreements: An agreement where the vendor agrees to purchase contracts under specific circumstances.

Reserves: An account established to cover losses on uncollected receivables.

Residual: The value of the leased property at the end of the lease term as estimated at the time the lease is executed; term value. Although the terms "residual value" or "term value" are sometimes used in reference to the actual value of the property at the conclusion of the term, the term "realized value" is the more commonly used and more appropriate term for the actual value of the property at the conclusion of the lease term.

Residual Guarantee: An agreement that the vendor guaranties all or a portion of the residual position priced into the lease structure.

Residual Value: The expected value of leased equipment at the end, or termination, of the lease.

Residual Value Insurance (RVI): A type of insurance that helps companies manage asset value risk by guaranteeing an adequately maintained asset will have a specified residual value at a future date.

Return on Assets (ROA): A common measure of profitability based upon the amount of assets invested; ROA is equal to the ratio of net income to total assets.

Return on Equity (ROE): A measure of profitability related to the amount of invested equity; ROE is equal to the ratio of net income available to common stockholders to common equity.

Revenue Procedure: An official statement published by the IRS that either affects the rights or duties of taxpayers or other members of the public under the Internal Revenue Code and related statutes, treaties, and regulations.

Revenue Ruling: A public administrative ruling by the IRS that applies the law to a particular factual situation. Such ruling can be relied upon as precedent by all taxpayers.

Revolving Line of Credit: A type of credit that does not have a fixed number of payments. An example of consumer revolving credit would be credit cards. Corporate revolving credit facilities are typically used to provide liquidity for a company's day-to-day operations.

Right of First Refusal: Right of First Refusal (also called First Right of Refusal) document which requires that the lessor has the right to review and accept or refuse to accept all new applications from the vendor.

Risk-Based Pricing: Risk-based pricing is a method adopted by many lenders and lessors where the rate on a transaction is determined not only by the time value of money but also by an estimation of the probability of default.

Robotic Process Automation (RPA): Configured software that mimics the actions of humans to carry out repetitive tasks automatically; may, but doesn't always include, cognitive functions of AI.

Running Rate: The rate of return to the lessor, or cost to the lessee, in a lease based solely upon the initial equipment cost and the periodic lease payments, without any reliance on residual value, tax benefit, deposits, or fees. This rate is also referred to as the "stream rate."

Safe-Harbor Lease: A lease created under the Economic Recovery Tax Act of 1981 (ERTA) to transfer federal tax benefits from a party who could not use them to a party who could. A Safe-Harbor Lease was a lease only for federal income tax purposes and not for commercial law purposes. Safe-Harbor Leasing was repealed by The Tax Equity and Fiscal Responsibility Act of 1982 (TEFRA).

Sale-Leaseback: A transaction in which the original user sells an asset to a lessor and leases it back. The seller-lessee records either a current gain or loss, or a deferred gain from the sale, and classifies the leaseback in accordance with proper lease accounting.

Sales-Type Lease: From the lessor's perspective, a lease that meets any of the five criteria presented in ASC 842 is a sales-type lease.

Section 179: A provision of the Internal Revenue Code that allows the taxpayer to elect to deduct certain types of property as a direct expense against income, rather than depreciating the asset over its tax life, as set forth by the IRS.

Securitization: A device of structured financing where an entity seeks to pool together its interest in identifiable cash flows over time, transfer the same to investors either with or without the support of further collaterals, and thereby achieve the purpose of financing. Though the end-result of securitization is financing, it is not "financing" as such, since the entity securitizing its assets is not borrowing money but selling a stream of cash flows that was otherwise to accrue to it.

Security Deposit: A specific amount paid at the inception of the lease by the lessee to ensure full compliance with the lease and to provide the lessor with some protection against defaults, delays, or other failures of performance by the lessee. Occasionally, advance periodic lease payments may serve the purpose of a security deposit, but more frequently, the security deposit is a separately identified obligation.

Service Lease: A lease in which the lessor provides service(s) such as maintenance and care of the leased property. The cost of such service(s) may be built into the lease or it may be paid under a separate maintenance agreement that the lessee was required to purchase. Also, a form of Operating Lease. Other names for this type of lease include Gross Lease, Maintenance Lease, Bundled Lease, and Full-Service Lease.

Severance Agreement: (See Real Estate Waiver.) In agricultural leasing, this document is the acknowledgment by an owner (landlord) or mortgagee of real property that the leased equipment belongs to the lessor and they can remove it (may also be called Easement).

Sinking Fund Rate: A sinking fund rate is the earnings rate applied to the balance of investment during sinking fund (or disinvestment) phases and is an essential element of yields based on after-tax cash flows (such as the Multiple Investment Sinking Fund "MISF").

Split TRAC: A Split TRAC transaction meets the requirements for true lease treatment for tax purposes but may also be classified as an operating lease for GAAP. The Split TRAC provision is structured so that the lessor assumes some of the estimated residual value risk. This may be achieved by the lessor and the lessee taking pro rata portion of the risk or by limiting the risk to the lessee.

Standard Industrial Classification (SIC): Standard Industrial Classification (SIC) codes are four-digit codes used for classifying business by industry. Although replaced by the more flexible six-digit NAICS coding system, the SIC code is still widely used for industry classification in the private sector. The Occupational Safety & Health Administration (OSHA) website, continues to maintain a SIC Manual. [Sources: https://www.osha.gov/pls/imis/sicsearch.html]

Statutory Law: The body of law enacted by legislatures.

Stipulated Termination Values: The value of leased property at given points in time during the lease term as agreed by both lessor and lessee. This is used for purposes of determining liability upon early termination of the lease.

Stream Rate: (See running rate.)

Syndication: Method of selling property whereby the promoter (the syndicator) sells interests or shares in the property to investors in the form of a partnership, limited partnership, or tenancy in common, to raise funds to cover the selling price.

Synthetic Lease: A financing agreement designed to be treated as a loan for tax purposes and a lease for accounting purposes.

System of Record: A core system of record serves as the "Source of Truth" for a particular set of information.

Tax Accounting: The method of accounting used to report a company's financial activity for tax reporting purposes, as prescribed by the IRS.

Tax Lease: (See True Lease.)

Tax Reform Act Of 1986 (TRA '86): The tax law that affected a major overhaul of the U.S. tax system by lowering the MACRS (Modified Accelerated Cost Recovery System), repealing the Investment Tax Credit (ITC); and repealing the transitional finance lease rate.

Tenor: The amount of time left for repayment or until the expiration of a financial contract.

TEFRA: Tax Equity and Fiscal Responsibility Act of 1982

Term Loan: A loan with a fixed maturity date and stipulated periodic payments.

Terminal Rental Adjustment Clause (TRAC): A lessee guaranteed residual value for vehicle leases (automobiles, trucks, or trailers), the inclusion of which will not, in and of itself, disqualify the tax lease status of a tax-oriented vehicle lease.

TRAC Lease (TRAC): A lease on a qualified automobile, truck or trailer, which may be considered a true lease for federal income tax purposes even though it contains a Terminal Rental Adjustment Clause (TRAC), which effectively guarantees the lessor the residual value. Note the mere existence of a TRAC does not, in and of itself, assure true lease status. To qualify as a true lease for federal income tax purposes, the lessor must also: Maintain a minimum at-risk position equal to borrowings used to fund the vehicle (in essence, non-recourse financing); obtain a lessee certification that the lessee will use the vehicle more than 50 percent for business.

True Lease: A lease, which for tax purposes, fails to meet all of the tests for a conditional sales contract under IRS Revenue Ruling 55-540 and therefore entitles the lessor to qualify for the tax benefits of ownership and the lessee to claim the entire amount of the lease rental as a tax deduction.

Trustee: A person, or entity that holds title to, or a security interest in, leased property for the benefit of the parties to a lease.

Ultimate Net Loss (UNL): Pools of shared risk. In a UNL loss pool, funds in the pool are used to cover the ultimate net loss, before repossession, resale, and legal remedies have been exhausted.

Ultimate Net Loss (UNL) Agreement: An agreement where the vendor guaranties a portion of the potential loss, generally in a pooled structure for all contracts in that pool.

Underwriter: One who agrees to purchase any securities of an issue remaining unsold.

Unearned Income: The difference between the gross investment and the asset cost under a capital lease represents the unearned income that will be recognized as income over the term of the lease.

Unguaranteed Residual: The estimated residual value of the leased property exclusive of any portion guaranteed by the lessee or by a third party unrelated to the lessor. If the guarantor is related to the lessor, the residual value is considered unguaranteed.

Uniform Commercial Code (UCC): A code of commercial law enacted by individual states. Certain sections of the UCC govern lien perfection, the effect of perfection or non-perfection, and the priority of security interests and agricultural liens.

Use Tax: A tax imposed on the use of tangible personal property within a taxing jurisdiction.

Vehicle Title: In the U.S., the certificate of title for a vehicle is a legal document, which establishes an individual or business as the legal owner of a vehicle.

Vendor: A purveyor of equipment from whom a lessor purchases equipment at the specific request of a lessee for a lease to that lessee; a supplier.

Vendor Leasing: Lease financing offered to an equipment end-user in conjunction with the sale of equipment. Vendor leases can be provided by the equipment vendor (two-party lease) or a third-party leasing company with a close working relationship with the equipment vendor.

Vendor Program: Vendor programs are a relationship with a manufacturer and seller of equipment.

Venue: The physical location, or specifically the court, which will hear a legal dispute between parties.

Vicarious Liability: Liability imposed upon a person even though they are not a party to the particular occurrence (e.g., the owner of a motor vehicle is vicariously responsible for injuries even though they are not driving the car at the time of the occurrence). In the case of a lease, the lessor is considered the owner of the vehicle.

VIN: Vehicle Identification Number

Waiver: The voluntary relinquishment of a known right.

Warehouse Line: A short-term revolving credit facility extended by a financial institution for the funding of leases before permanent funding is finalized. It allows the leasing company to age and amass its portfolio without compromising lending capacity.

Wet Lease: A gross lease, traditionally for aircraft or marine vessels, in which the lessor provides bundled services such as the payment of property taxes, insurance, maintenance costs, as well as all personnel, fuel, and provisions to operate the craft.

Working Capital: Working capital loans are short-term, unsecured loans for business owners in need of access to funds to run or grow their businesses.

Write-Down: A deliberate reduction in the book value of an asset (as to reflect the effect of obsolescence).

Yield: The rate of return to the lessor in a lease investment

Tables and Figures

Tables

Figures

Made in the USA
Middletown, DE
21 August 2023

37086004R00235